A Journey toward Influential Scholarship

A Journey toward Influential Scholarship

Insights from Leading Management Scholars

Edited by

Xiao-Ping Chen and H. Kevin Steensma

OXFORD
UNIVERSITY PRESS

Oxford University Press is a department of the University of Oxford. It furthers the University's objective of excellence in research, scholarship, and education by publishing worldwide. Oxford is a registered trade mark of Oxford University Press in the UK and certain other countries.

Published in the United States of America by Oxford University Press
198 Madison Avenue, New York, NY 10016, United States of America.

© Oxford University Press 2021

Library of Congress Control Number: 2021939200

ISBN 978-0-19-007072-4 (pbk.)
ISBN 978-0-19-007071-7 (hbk.)

DOI: 10.1093/oso/9780190070717.001.0001

1 3 5 7 9 8 6 4 2

Paperback printed by Marquis, Canada
Hardback printed by Bridgeport National Bindery, Inc., United States of America

Contents

Contributors

Rajshree Agarwal is the Rudolph Lamone Chair in Strategy and Entrepreneurship at the Robert H. Smith School of Business at the University of Maryland. She is also the Director of the Ed Snider Center for Enterprise and Markets. With an initial background in economics, Rajshree now uses an interdisciplinary lens to examine the role of innovation and enterprise in the evolution of individual careers, firms, industries, and economies.

Soon Ang is a Distinguished University Professor at Nanyang Technological University (Singapore) and received her PhD from the University of Minnesota. She is the founder of the Center for Leadership and Cultural Intelligence and the Culture Science Institute. She publishes extensively in many disciplines and is a world authority in cultural intelligence, leadership, and outsourcing. She pioneered cultural intelligence, authored foundational books (Stanford University Press), and created the world's first multimedia situational judgment tests for cultural intelligence. A multiple-award-winning academic with a strong scientific-practitioner ethos, Soon has attracted multiyear, multimillion-dollar research grants from the Defense Science and Technology Agency and the Prime Minister's Office (Singapore). Her honors include the Distinguished Leadership Award for International Alumni (University of Minnesota), the Distinguished Walter F. Ulmer, Jr., Award (Center for Creative Leadership, USA), the first Nanyang Award for Research and Innovation in the Social Sciences, and the Public Administration Medal (Silver) for excellent education and research from the president of the Republic of Singapore.

Blake E. Ashforth is a Regents Professor and Horace Steele Arizona Heritage Chair in the Management and Entrepreneurship Department at the W. P. Carey School of Business at Arizona State University. He received his PhD from the University of Toronto. His research concerns the ongoing dance between individuals and organizations, including socialization and work adjustment, identity and identification, and respect and dignity, as well as the links among individual-, group-, and organization-level phenomena. His recent work has focused on dirty work, ambivalence, and anthropomorphism. Blake is a Fellow of the Academy of Management and a winner of the Lifetime Achievement Award from the Academy's Organizational Behavior Division and the Distinguished Scholar Award from the Academy's Managerial and Organizational Cognition Division.

Sigal Goland Barsade is the Joseph Frank Bernstein Professor at the Wharton School at the University of Pennsylvania and is the area coordinator of the organizational group within the Management Department at Wharton. Her research focuses on emotions in organizations as well as organizational culture, including topics such as models of group emotion, emotional contagion, emotion culture, emotional intelligence, affect and performance, and affective diversity. Her research has been published in journals such as the *Academy of Management Journal*, *Administrative Science Quarterly*, the *Journal of Applied Psychology*, the *Journal of Personality and Social Psychology*, *Organization Science*, and *Organizational Behavior and Human Decision Processes*. She has served on the editorial boards of the *Administrative Science Quarterly*, the *Academy of Management Review, Organizational Behavior and Human Decision Processes, and Organization Science* and is currently serving on the executive committee for the Organizational Behavior Division of the Academy of Management.

Xiao-Ping Chen is the Philip M. Condit Endowed Chair Professor in Business Administration at the Michael G. Foster School of Business, University of Washington. She is a Fellow in the Academy of Management, the American Psychological Association, and the Society for Industrial and Organizational Psychology. Xiao-Ping has served as Editor-in-Chief of *Organizational Behavior and Human Decision Processes* (2010–2016) and President of the International Association for Chinese Management Research (IACMR), and she is currently Editor-in-Chief of *Management Insights*, a bilingual (Chinese and English) magazine for business educators and practitioners. She is a coauthor of *Leadership of Chinese Private Enterprises: Insights and Interviews* and author of more than 10 books in Chinese, including *Empirical Methods in Organization and Management Research* and *Leading across Cultures*. She has received the Scholarly Impact Award of the *Journal of Management* (2019), the Best Paper of Chinese Management Research award of Peking University Press (2018), and the Distinguished Scholarly Contribution Award of IACMR (2016), among others. She received her PhD in social psychology from University of Illiois at Urbana-Champaign.

Jason A. Colquitt is the Franklin D. Schurz Professor of Management and Organization at the University of Notre Dame's Mendoza College of Business. He received his PhD in organizational behavior from Michigan State and his BS in psychology from Indiana University. His research interests include justice, trust, and personality. He has published more than 40 articles on these and other topics in the *Academy of Management Journal*, the *Academy of Management Review*, the *Journal of Applied Psychology*, *Organizational Behavior and Human Decision Processes*, and *Personnel Psychology*. He is a past Editor-in-Chief of the *Academy of Management Journal* and served as an Associate Editor of that journal. He is a recipient of the Society for Industrial and Organizational Psychology's Distinguished Early Career Contributions Award and the Cummings Scholar Award for early to mid-career achievement, sponsored by the Organizational Behavior Division of the Academy of Management.

Henrich R. Greve is the Rudolf and Valeria Maag Chaired Professor of Entrepreneurship at INSEAD. He has a PhD in business from Stanford University. His main work concerns organizational learning, interorganizational diffusion, and social networks, although recent work also has examined community evaluation, misconduct, and decision making in sports. His publications are almost evenly distributed among the four major journals of influential management research—there are slightly more in the *Academy of Management Journal*—and he has published in sociology and economics. He is currently the Editor of *Administrative Science Quarterly*. He was an Associate Editor of *Administrative Science Quarterly* for six years and Senior Editor of *Organization Science* for six years. He is a Fellow of the Academy of Management.

Anita M. McGahan is a University Professor and the George E. Connell Chair in Organizations and Society at the University of Toronto. Her appointments are in management, global affairs and public policy, medicine, and public health. She is a Senior Fellow at Massey College, Senior Associate at the Institute for Strategy and Competitiveness at Harvard University, Chief Economist in the Division of Global Health Innovation at Massachusetts General Hospital, and a past President of the Academy of Management. From 2014 to 2019, she was a faculty member of the MacArthur Foundation Research Network on Opening Governance. Anita earned both her PhD and AM at Harvard University in two years. She holds an MBA as a Baker Scholar from Harvard Business School and a BA from Northwestern University, where she was elected to Phi Beta Kappa. She also spent several years at both McKinsey & Company and Morgan Stanley & Company. Her research program focuses on private entrepreneurship in the public interest.

Hayagreeva Rao is the Atholl McBean Professor of Organizational Behavior at the Graduate School of Business at Stanford University and Professor of Sociology at Stanford University. He studies collective action within organizations and in markets. His research and, by implication, his teaching revolve around scaling up mobilization, innovation, and talent in organizations. He served as an Editor of *Administrative Science Quarterly* and is a Fellow of the Academy of Management and Sociological Research Association as well as a Fellow of the Center for Advanced Study in Behavioral Science. His most recent publication is "Crossing Categorical Boundaries: A Study of Diversification by Social Movement Organizations," along with Dan J. Wang and Sarah A. Soule, in the *American Sociological Review*. His book, coauthored with Bob Sutton of the School of Engineering at Stanford, is *Scaling Up Excellence*. The book is a *Wall Street Journal* bestseller and was included in the best business books to read in 2014 by *Financial Times, Inc. Magazine, Amazon, Forbes*, the *Washington Post*, and *Library Journal*.

Sandra Lynn Robinson is a Professor and Distinguished University Scholar at the University of British Columbia, having received her PhD from Northwestern University. She studies primarily dysfunctional workplace behavior, such as deviance, trust betrayal, territorial behavior, and ostracism. Sandra has published in a wide range of journals, including the *Journal of Applied Psychology, Administrative Science Quarterly*, and the *Harvard Business Review*, and has received numerous research awards, including the Academy of Management Organizational Behavior Division's Cummings Award, the Western Academy of Management Ascendant Scholar award, and the *Journal of Management Inquiries* Distinguished Scholar Award. Sandra also has served in various professional capacities, such as Associate Editor of *Academy of Management Discoveries* and Representative at Large of the Western Academy of Management, as well as serving for five years on the Chair Track of the Organizational Behavior Division. As a Vancouver native, Sandra feels fortunate to live, work, and play where she grew up and especially enjoys spending time at her cabin with her husband.

Olav Sorenson holds the Joseph Jacobs Chair in Entrepreneurial Studies, is a Professor in the Strategy Area, and is the Faculty Research Director of the Price Center for Entrepreneurship & Innovation at the UCLA Anderson Graduate School of Management. Prior to returning to UCLA, he was the Frederick Frank '54 and Mary C. Tanner Professor of Management at the Yale School of Management. He also has held ladder appointments at the University of Chicago, London Business School, and the University of Toronto. Olav received his AB from Harvard College, his MA and PhD from Stanford University, and an honorary doctorate from the University of Aalborg. In 2018, he received the Global Award for Entrepreneurship Research for his lifetime contributions to the study of entrepreneurship and innovation.

H. Kevin Steensma is the Michael G. Foster Professor of Management at the Foster School of Business at the University of Washington. He received his PhD from the Kelly School of Business at Indiana University. His research interests include interfirm collaboration, technology strategy, intellectual property rights, and the flow of knowledge between firms. His work has been published in the *Academy of Management Journal, Organization Science, Strategic Management Journal*, the *Journal of Applied Psychology*, and the *Journal of International Business Studies*, among other journals. In addition to teaching at the University of Washington, he has taught at the Indian School of Business and the Grenoble Ecole de Management in Grenoble, France.

James D. Westphal conducts research in the areas of strategic management and organizational theory, with a focus on social and psychological processes in corporate governance and strategic decision making. His recent work includes *Symbolic Management: Governance, Strategy, and Institutions* (Oxford University Press). Jim has received the Best Paper Award from the Organization and Management Theory Division on five occasions. He received the Parasuraman Outstanding Publication Award and twice received the Researcher of the Year Award (Michigan) and Research Excellence Award (Texas). He has been elected to the Macro-Organizational Behavior Society and the Fellows of the Academy of Management and the Strategic Management Society and has served as Division Chair of the Academy's Strategic Management Division. His work has been referenced in a range of popular outlets, including *Business Week,* CNBC, the *Economist,* the *Financial Times, Fortune, Harper's,* National Public Radio, the *New York Times,* the *New Yorker,* the *Wall Street Journal, and* the *Washington Post.*

Jing Zhou is the Mary Gibbs Jones Professor of Management, PhD Program Director, Director for Asian Management Research and Education, and Organizational Behavior Area Coordinator at Jones Graduate School of Business at Rice University. Her research centers on creativity and innovation, including antecedents of creativity, creativity receiving, and the impact of creativity on organizational innovation and effectiveness. She is a Fellow of the American Psychological Association, the Association for Psychological Sciences, and the Society for Industrial and Organizational Psychology, and Academy of Management. She has served as Associate Editor of the *Journal of Applied Psychology* and on editorial boards of the *Academy of Management Journal*, the *Academy of Management Review,* the *Journal of Applied Psychology*, and the *Journal of Management.* She has coedited the *Handbook of Organizational Creativity* (with Christina Shalley), the *Oxford Handbook of Creativity, Innovation, and Entrepreneurship* (with Christina Shalley and Michael Hitt), and the *Handbook of Research on Creativity and Innovation* (with Bess Rouse). Her courses on leading innovation and negotiation are popular with executive audiences. She has received awards for excellence in research and teaching. Two studies she coauthored have received the *Journal of Management's* Best Paper Award. She holds the honorary appointment of Research Fellow at Cambridge University.

Introduction

What Is Influential Management Research and Why Is It Important?

Xiao-Ping Chen and H. Kevin Steensma

Fifteen years ago, in *Great Minds in Management: The Process of Theory Development*, Professors Kenneth Smith and Michael Hitt (2005) emphasized theory building for a relatively young field of study (i.e., management) and invited a number of prominent management scholars, including Albert Bandura, Henry Mintzberg, Jeffrey Pfeffer, and Karl Weick, to record their accounts of how they developed their important theories. Many of the theories developed by these scholars were groundbreaking at the time, and their influence was sustained over a long period of time.

With the fast advancement in technology and globalization in the past 15 years, however, as many new organizational phenomena have emerged or become salient, they have caught the attention of a new generation of management scholars who have since delved deeply into their study. As a result, new theories, perspectives, frameworks, and insights have been offered to explain these new phenomena. Thus, we feel that it is time to update this book and to let these influential management scholars share their stories and experiences.

Influential management research is often based on sharp observations of organizational phenomena combined with careful investigations and testing of explanations across situations and time. Currently, many studies published in top-tier management journals that are called "theory-driven" make only incremental contributions to our understanding of organizational phenomena, and very few are phenomenon-driven (Barkema, Chen, George, Luo, & Tsui, 2015; Chen, Friedman, & McAllister, 2017). The Covid-19 pandemic, the emerging gig economy, and the rapid advancement in technology, for example artificial intelligence (AI), blockchain, and the internet of things (IOT), pose unprecedented challenges to organizations that beg management scholars' attention. Observing these challenges, studying them, and developing new theoretical accounts will help management research stay current and relevant.

Xiao-Ping Chen and H. Kevin Steensma, *Introduction* In: *A Journey toward Influential Scholarship*. Edited by: Xiao-Ping Chen and H. Kevin Steensma, Oxford University Press © Oxford University Press 2021. DOI: 10.1093/oso/9780190070717.001.0001

Influential management research often entails multiple research studies that build on each other to demonstrate a significant organizational phenomenon, to reveal the reasons and mechanisms that can explain or predict it, and to identify boundary conditions that may amplify or constrain phenomena. Such research is neither niche nor narrow; rather, it has broad appeal and can potentially influence the thinking of scholars who do not directly study the organizational phenomena in question.

Influential management research also falls under the umbrella term responsible research, which refers to credible and useful research that not only contributes to the academic literature but also has meaningful implications for management practices that contribute to the welfare of the larger society (https://rrbm.network). In other words, the influence of such research is not restricted to academia or organizations; it can be extended to include all stakeholders—customers, employees, suppliers, communities, and shareholders.

Most management scholars strive to establish an identity in a particular field of organizational research, but there are very few whose names become synonymous with a specific stream of inquiry. To identify such scholars, we surveyed over 120 early-stage management scholars who are currently at leading institutions and solicited their assistance. We asked them to think about the research streams and theoretical frameworks that most significantly influenced their own research, as well as those scholars who have entered the management field post-1990 (roughly) and have proposed or substantially advanced these research areas. Based on the survey responses, we invited over a dozen of these influential scholars to contribute to this book, chronicling the anecdotes and insights behind their published work that may help others as they chart their own scholarly paths.

To help the authors in retracing their journeys, we posed a few guidelines, asking them to do the following:

- Tell the backstory of how their research ideas came about and were developed, that is, the motivation and impetus for them to select their particular research foci, the challenges they faced, and the mistakes they made and corrected in getting their work published
- Describe the methodological rigor that guided their research, including the different kinds of methods they adopted in triangulating the validity and generalizability of their findings
- Share their experience of how to develop essential collaborative relationships, manage the peer review and publication processes, and disseminate findings

- Reflect on why and how their approach to research contributed to their own career success

What follows is a volume that contains 12 influential scholars' recountings of and reflections on the journeys they have taken. Each is unique and fascinating in its own way, and collectively they uncover the many diverse pathways to achieving influential scholarship. Among the twelve scholars, six are in the strategy/entrepreneurship area, and six are in the field of organizational behavior/human resource management. Six are women, and six are men. Some focus more on their research program and its evolution, some put more emphasis on the lessons learned and on offering their advice, and some tend to weave their academic progress tightly into personal stories and experiences. To make the reading experience interesting and dynamic, we have organized the chapters as follows.

Chapter 1

We start with Blake E. Ashforth's chapter, because of not only its provocative title and fascinating storytelling but also its natural fit to our theme of phenomenon-driven theory development. Ashforth is known for his seminal work on many areas: socialization and work adjustment, identity and identification, respect and dignity, dirty work, ambivalence, and anthropomorphism. It is evident that he has explored and studied different phenomena over the course of his career, instead of focusing on one particular organizational phenomenon; he is truly a trailblazer of several research paths. His chapter is full of energy, fun, humor, and inspiration and in addition offers advice and many practical tools to pursue path-blazing ideas. As he writes, "instead of settling for the doable, how about reaching for the inspirational?"

Chapter 2

Soon Ang's own cross-cultural experience and her observation of many expatriate managers and international students in Singapore inspired her to explore, theorize, and develop the new construct of cultural intelligence and empirically test its potential effects on people's decision making, cross-cultural problem solving, cultural adaptation, and creative performance on international assignments. More important, she paid equal attention to the implementation of her research findings in developing training programs to improve people's cultural intelligence in many high-profile projects. Her metaphor of two bowls—science and practice—expresses harmoniously the influential scholarship we highlight in this book.

Chapter 3

James D. Westphal traces the imperative for his research interests back to the day when he was conducting tedious data analysis for a consulting company. When he looked at the data from the perspective of corporate governance, he identified interesting patterns that intrigued him and led him to dig deeper and more broadly, as well as triggering him to pursue a PhD and launch a type of interdisciplinary inquiry that was not conventional in management research at the time. His continuous effort helped to build the legitimacy of the research that flourished afterward. Westphal has been making significant contributions to the corporate governance literature, publishing more than 20 articles in *Administrative Science Quarterly* alone.

Chapter 4

Likewise, Sigal Goland Barsade has studied emotion and its effects on organizational behavior since her PhD days, when few organizational scholars paid much attention to emotion in the workplace. She recounts the personal experience in her workplace that inspired her to study emotion and the way she blazed this research path, following the principle " 'go big' in both theory and method." Moreover, although all of her studies have focused on emotions, none has made incremental progress over the other; rather, in her "high risk/ high reward" strategy, each of her studies explores a different aspect or level of emotion and its consequences for individual, team, and organizational outcomes. Through these approaches Barsade has become a leader in the study of emotions, primarily collective emotion, including the phenomena of emotional contagion, group affect, affective diversity, and emotional culture, as well as workplace loneliness, companionate love, subconscious affect, and many other phenomena related to the affective side of organizing.

Chapter 5

Henrich R. Greve has adopted a systematic approach to his academic journey. He recounts his contribution to the organizational performance feedback literature, one of multiple research streams he has worked on. To explain how organizational performance relative to the aspiration level on one or more organizational goals influences organizational search and change, Greve first embarked on an empirical test of an old theory and then developed a new theoretical framework that shaped the development of this literature and made it flourish. Greve shares his wisdom, like a friend talking to you over coffee, with intellectually stimulating ideas and insights: "a great theory deserves perfect data," "retesting old theory has two forms of appeal relative to creating new theory," and "a book with deeper theory and many untested ideas can seed the ground for additional research on a research stream" are just a few.

Chapter 6

Olav Sorenson is best known for his work on the importance of social relationships for entrepreneurs, termed "embedded entrepreneurship." Based on his observation that many entrepreneurs start their businesses in the place where they live (rather than a place that has the most efficiency) and have more success by staying in the same place (rather than moving to a new place), Sorenson started his journey to answer the "why" question of such phenomena and, with great focus and persistence, was able to publish a series of important articles to explain the home-court effects. His advice is insightful and practical: to become an influential scholar, you should identify important problems to solve, rather than just filling in a gap; find good coauthors to collaborate with, rather than clutching onto the famous ones; and hone your writing skills nonstop.

Chapter 7

Jason A. Colquitt shows how persistent his research interest has been in justice-related issues. It was like love at first sight when he encountered this topic as an undergraduate working on an honors thesis. After many years of diligent work, he became a main contributor to the justice literature, providing a comprehensive, new measure of justice, the first metaanalysis of the literature, and integrations of justice with three other areas: teams, personality, and trust. With more than 30 studies published on this topic, Colquitt has become a central figure in justice research. In recounting and reflecting on his journey, he adopts the theoretical framework of psychological empowerment (Spritzer, 1995), which encompasses three main components: intrinsic interest, mastery of various methodologies, and valuing the practical implication of justice research in improving the culture of the workplace.

Chapter 8

Hayagreeva Rao takes a different approach to reflecting on his journey. Instead of spelling out the academic contributions he has made to the literature on collective action within organizations and in markets, or listing the more than 50 studies he has published, Rao writes about his seemingly accidental encounters with many great minds in the field—how they work together, drink together, and publish together. The chapter is full of personal stories that include the fun and enjoyment he experiences in fulfilling his intellectual curiosity through the study of social movement and collective action. Meanwhile, the humility and appreciation of friendship/colleagueship intertwined in his writing are remarkable.

Chapter 9

Jing Zhou has devoted her entire career to studying creativity in the workplace, publishing more than 25 studies and four books in the past 25 years. She recounts how her interest in creativity started when she was a doctoral student in the early 1990s, when "creativity" was not even a research topic in the field of organizational behavior. She recounts that once she set her research focus on creativity, she made her research plans and strategically selected her dissertation advisor and collaborators along the way, systematically building her research program by studying antecedents to creativity, the conditions under which negative affect has an impact on creativity, and the receiving side of creativity. She emphasizes that building a systematic program of research is crucial for knowledge creation and true understanding of a given phenomenon in its depth and breadth. Her approach to formulating research questions based on organizational phenomena or through challenging widely held assumptions is laudable.

Chapter 10

Rajshree Agarwal draws on the evolutionary lens to depict her journey as a lifelong learner, passionate about upward mobility in intellectual, psychological, and economic realms. She has published more than 60 studies in these realms, through which we get to witness her professional evolution as a researcher from an economist to a strategic management scholar who integrates economics, psychology, and sociology perspectives to understand the antecedents and consequences of the enterprising individuals, organizations, and economies. As she writes, "ideas don't know what discipline they are in," so we should "eschew" the " 'straitjacket' of hypothesis-deductive frameworks that we often impose upon the way we conduct or present research, in favor of 'question-based' research and truly embracing abduction."

Chapter 11

Sandra Lynn Robinson has focused her career on studying the "dark side" of organizational behavior and is recognized as one of the original authors to bring the field's attention to negative and harmful behavior in the workplace. Her award-winning research has introduced and launched a number of topical areas of study, including psychological contract violation, workplace deviance, and territoriality in organizations. Here, she shares personal stories that capture the highs and lows of her career, from early setbacks to scholarly prominence, and the lessons she's learned along the way. The common theme, throughout the 10 principles of influential scholarship she covers here, is quality over quantity, and her goal is to provide inspiration and hope to those facing their own academic career challenges.

Chapter 12

Anita M. McGahan takes a stand as a senior scholar to reflect on her journey and offers her advice to young scholars about what is important and meaningful to study as a management scholar. McGahan's journey to influential scholarship took a few turns, starting with a conventional approach to studying industry structure and industry change and evolving into today's research on private entrepreneurship in the public interest, an extremely important but understudied area that she is passionate about. While few scholars can pull off a research stream that is truly interdisciplinary in nature, McGahan has been successful in publishing her studies in a wide range of journals, including global public health, human rights, medicine, psychiatry, and so on. McGahan not only views herself as a scholar and educator, but also as a citizen who can help organizations to achieve its great potential in solving the most important challenges of our time—including climate change, global health, immigration, and poverty alleviation.

We conclude with a summary of the uniqueness and commonalities revealed in these scholars' journeys, and we propose a process model of influential scholarship.

We strongly hope that the reflections and insights offered by the contributors to this book will inspire a new generation of management scholars to feel excited about their research and see its implications for helping and guiding organizations to achieve future success.

We would like to thank Giselle Antoine, Elizabeth Campbell, Crystal Farh, Anna Fung, Abhinav Gupta, Andrew Hafenbrack, Ralph Heidl, Michelle Lee, Stephen Lee, Zhi Liu, Jackson Lu, Majid Majzoubi, Jen Rhymer, Kira Schabram, and Joseph Shin for carefully reviewing these chapters and providing constructive, critical, and insightful comments and suggestions.

References

Barkema, H., Chen, X. P., George, G., Luo, Y. D., & Tsui, A. S. (2015). West meets East: New theories and concepts. *Academy of Management Journal*, 58(2), 460–479..

Chen, C. C., Friedman, R., & McAllister, D. (2017). Seeing and studying China: Leveraging phenomenon-based research in china for theory advancement. *Organizational Behavior and Human Decision Processes*, 143, 1–7.

Smith, K. G., & Hitt, M. A. (2005). *Great minds in management: The process of theory development*. Oxford: Oxford University Press.

1

Why the Heck Did *That* Happen?

The Alchemy of Theory-Building

Blake E. Ashforth

Your job description as a management scholar is essentially to indulge your curiosity for the greater good. To that end, two of the most powerful words in scholarship are "Why?" and "How?" Scholarship is largely about figuring out why and how things work in the weird and wonderful ways that they do so that you might nudge our organizations in constructive ways. Scholarship, in short, is largely about *theory* and, therefore, *theory-building*. But as Hillman (2011: 607) noted, "if research methods are science, theory is an art." Put differently, theory-building is that aspect of scholarship that most resembles alchemy, the mysterious process of turning disparate findings and thoughts (lead) into a coherent statement of why and how things work (gold). How the heck do we do this?

Because the successes in my career stem mostly from theory-building, I'll focus much of my attention on the alchemy through which we somehow create theories. In the spirit of this book, I'll use the ups and downs of my own career as a platform for riffing about the process of theory-building, along with some thoughts on research collaborations, the review process, and career considerations if you boldly decide to pursue big ideas (my fervent hope).

A Bit of Background

Skimming my CV, you'd be hard-pressed to discern a common theoretical thread. But my overarching research passion—to use Jane Dutton's apt term from a professional development workshop (PDW)—has always been to better understand how systems affect individuals (and to a lesser extent, vice versa). Being a lifelong comic book fan, I know the value of a catchy origin story. While I was never bitten by a radioactive Procter & Gamble or rocketed to Zappos as a baby, as it happens, one event *was* particularly important.

Blake E. Ashforth, *Why the Heck Did* That *Happen?* In: *A Journey toward Influential Scholarship.* Edited by: Xiao-Ping Chen and H. Kevin Steensma, Oxford University Press. © Oxford University Press 2021. DOI: 10.1093/oso/9780190070717.003.0001

During high school, I was in the library and stumbled across a *New York Times* article ("The mind is a formidable jailer," 1973) on the famous Zimbardo Stanford prison study. I was riveted. How could nice, normal university students be turned into sadistic guards and cowering prisoners in a matter of days? And what does that say about our institutions in general? Nerd that I am, I was so curious that I wrote an embarrassingly long term paper on the effects of prison on inmates. (I even got to visit a prison during a school outing, but I was too cowed to ask any questions! I'd like to think that Zimbardo would have understood.)

This overarching research passion has fueled my ongoing interests in work-based identity/identification (how individuals define themselves through their organizations and work), socialization (how organizations shape newbies), and the dark side of organizations (how our institutions give rise to corruption, petty tyranny, burnout, and so on). The beauty of a passion so unwieldy—what OB topics *don't* touch on "how do systems affect individuals?"—is that there is a never-ending spate of cool questions to ponder. How do people doing "dirty work" (stigmatized jobs), like sewer workers and lobbyists, think about their jobs and themselves? Are they proud? Embarrassed? How does the identity of an organization, group, or individual shape identities at other levels of analysis? How does corruption spread throughout an organization such that, when the initial bad apples eventually leave, the corruption continues? Why do seeming "organizational saints" feel it's OK to do very unsaintly things, such as engage in self-serving behavior and display intolerance of others? How do strong and potentially disruptive emotions, such as the revulsion soldiers feel at the prospect of killing, become normalized in organizations so that individuals and organizations alike can continue to function?

Finding the Right Tools

I was originally trained in survey design and analysis. This training became my prism—and my prison—for judging what research questions could be pursued. If I couldn't measure it with a survey, I wasn't going to pursue it. Like eating our vegetables and looking both ways before crossing the street, we know we're *supposed* to let our choice of research questions drive our choice of methods. But given how difficult it is to become reasonably expert in a method, we invert that logic: we only study what is amenable to the methods with which we're already comfortable. And that can be a *very* limiting dynamic.

As time went on, I became disenchanted with survey methods. Not because they weren't effective—they were—but because I thought, in full arrogance mode, "Why spend all this time trying to prove to others something that I think I've already worked out?" I wanted to ask questions, not prove answers. Also, if I'm being honest with myself, methodology and statistical analysis were never my forte; I was competent, but I sought a higher bar than that. So it wasn't all that difficult to leave a rickety boat for something a bit sturdier.

That was when I tentatively tried qualitative methods, especially interviewing. The singular beauty of qualitative methods is that they are more about learning than verifying. Every interview and every hour of observation told me something new, and the challenge of knitting all these disparate fragments into a meaningful framework was irresistible to me. I've never had the patience for jigsaw puzzles, but making sense of qualitative data is much like solving a puzzle—except (and this is huge) there's no predetermined picture that you're trying to fit the pieces into. (That would make for very good religion but very bad science.)

And, at the end of the day, people love a good story. Interviews invite people to tell *their* story vis-à-vis the issue in question. Once interviewees realize that you really do just want to know how *they* see things and that you're not there to judge them, then the stories flow—often with brutal honesty. Interviewing is the ultimate method for curious scholars because it's a socially acceptable way of being a voyeur. I once interviewed a funeral director and was coding the subsequent transcript with my coauthor, Carol Kulik. She was aghast that I had asked him if he would ever embalm a family member. I shrugged—"Why not?" I had a good rapport with him, and the question was related to our research question about the interface between individuals and service roles. Would I have asked that if I had met him at a neighborhood barbeque? I highly doubt it. But that's my point; interviews can take you to challenging places that polite conversations often can't.

So You Want to Build a Theory?

The notion of storytelling brings me to theory-building, a story of a different sort and the cornerstone of scholarship (Shepherd & Suddaby, 2017). As Fiske (2004: 132) describes it, "good theories posit causal relations, attempt coherence, form a good narrative, aim for parsimony, are testable, prove fertile, and solve problems." Theory is what we use to both guide data collection and make sense of data in order to better understand phenomena and solve important problems—or at least move us toward a better theory.[1] Theory is what we use to discuss what, how, and why, along with the boundary conditions of who, where, and when (Whetten, 1989).

"Too Much of a Good Thing?"

But we seem to have an 800-pound gorilla sitting rudely in our research garden.[2] There's a recurring debate in our field about whether we already have too many theories (e.g., Pfeffer, 2014; Suddaby, 2014). A theory is an equal opportunity *resource* that we can all draw on to help explain how the world of organizations operates; given how complex, dynamic, and equivocal that world has become, it's hard for me to imagine that we suffer from having too many resources. It's like suffering from too much fresh air. The real issue, as others have argued, is that there's a lot of untested and thinly tested theory, and our top journals are unfortunately allergic to publishing the constructive replications that we desperately need (e.g., Hambrick, 2007; McKinley, 2010). This creates the sense that we have a lot of conceptual weeds cluttering our garden.

Fair enough. Yet, even if a theory is as yet untested, the heuristic value of intuitively plausible—and often hard to operationalize—arguments can help shape our thinking about organizations. Personally, I've found the writings of Erving Goffman, John Van Maanen, and Karl Weick, among many others, very helpful in my own work—despite the difficulty of empirically validating some of their arguments—precisely because they thought deeply and incisively beyond the bounds of what data narrowly showed or perhaps *could* show. At the end of the day, a weed is just "a plant in the wrong place" (Wikipedia.org), unwelcome in one spot but perhaps welcome in another. So my view of the how-much-theory issue is to let the plants grow if they can and trust in the gardeners—the scholars and practitioners—to sort out what actually works best for their purposes.

---

[1] I once asked a mentor of mine, Bob House, why he named a chapter "A 1976 theory of charismatic leadership." He said it was because he wanted to signal that every theory is essentially a work in progress, and to encourage future scholars to improve his theory. Now *that's* a scholar's scholar!

[2] The heading of this section is the subtitle of Hambrick (2007: 1346).

What Is a Worthwhile Research Question?

As the earlier thumbnail sketch of my background suggests, I often like to start a theory paper (or a qualitative study in search of a theory) with a thorny but provocative question.[3] The bigger the question and the fewer the concrete leads, the more intrigued I am.

This begs the question of what constitutes a worthwhile research question. Fortunately, there are excellent treatments of this issue elsewhere (e.g., Corley & Gioia, 2011; Davis, 1971; Mathieu, 2016; Shepherd & Suddaby, 2017), so we can keep this brief. You're looking for something intriguing—and, if you're lucky, cool and even wow-ish—in that it represents a theoretical puzzle and a (potentially) important phenomenon or problem. It's a question that *matters*. So promising avenues include meaningful gaps in theory (emphasis on *meaningful*), emergent phenomena, contradictions in the literature, counterintuitive findings and events, troubling trends, and difficulties with which managers and employees are wrestling. One of the best compliments you can hear from a fellow scholar is "Man, I wish *I'd* thought of that!" and from a practitioner, "Wow, that's very helpful for me to know!"

Let me add one more promising avenue for intriguing research questions that I don't see reflected in the treatments in the previous paragraph that I actually use regularly. I like to start a theory paper with a provocative and potentially meaty topic or phenomenon that has likely *always* been part of organizational life but has been underexplored, at least in organizational contexts. Examples my coauthors and I have looked at include anthropomorphism, ambivalence, spirituality and religious concepts, role transitions, emotion, defensive behavior, labeling, and mindlessness. In each case, we wondered how the essential idea might help us better understand organizational dynamics. Take emotion as an example. Reflecting trends in psychology, organizational scholarship was dominated by behaviorist and cognitive perspectives—which made some sense given that organizations are agentic and goal-oriented. But that preoccupation with behavior and cognition bugged the contrarian in me: surely, I thought, there's an important role for emotions as well? The genesis was as simple as that. As often happens, though, with a fundamental topic or phenomenon like emotion, my coauthor

---

[3] When I say "I," please realize that I seldom work alone. I find working with collaborators incredibly enriching in terms of the diversity and quality of the ideas generated and in terms of the rich and rewarding social experience. I've worked with over 60 coauthors, and there's only been a few times that I thought, "Once was plenty." I'd like to claim that I'm an astute judge of character, but I think it's got much more to do with how engaging collaborations tend to be. So by "I," I simply mean my tendencies irrespective of who my coauthors happen to be.

(Ron Humphrey) and I soon realized that we needed to hone in on narrower applications. (More on this process later.) Thus, our general interest in the sprawling topic of emotions was refined into one paper on emotional labor and another on how organizational life is suffused with rich and consequential emotions.

The Danger of Grand Theories

I mentioned that contradictions in the literature are one avenue to intriguing research questions. Perhaps because of my unwieldy interest in how systems affect individuals, I like to unify disparate ideas into an overarching "systemic" framework. So when I hear that one theory conflicts with another, my reflex is not to just pick one over the other so that I can get on with the paper at hand (as I think we tend to do in our scholarly articles) but to try to reconcile them. In fact, a career-long dream of mine was to write a grand theory of organizational dysfunctions that would tie most of them together. But I came to realize there's a reason why middle-range theories rather than grand theories dominate organizational studies: we need abstract thinking that focuses on grounded and diverse phenomena, implying a rough balance between generalizability and accuracy (Pinder & Moore, 1980). Theories that lose sight of the ground in the interests of grand abstraction often become untethered to reality. (More on this as well later.)

So how do you actually distill an overarching research passion and some midrange research interests into worthwhile research questions—and then create theory to address them? I've had the good fortune of doing many visiting speaker gigs and PDWs, and the question I get asked the most is "Where do you get your ideas from?" I wish I had a pithy answer (the *Farmers' Almanac*?), but the best I can offer is this: *trust the process.*

One Process for Building Theory

What process, you ask? Here is the one that works for me, with two addendums. First, there is *no* one best way to theorize, so think of these as tips you may want to consider as you find *your* best way. Second, I aspire to research that represents breakthroughs for the field (admittedly small *b* breakthroughs) rather than incremental contributions (although I think my method can assist with incrementalism as well). To be sure, we need both kinds of research.

Breakthroughs represent what March (1991) calls exploration and Ashford (2013) calls home runs, where the reader is galvanized to think of organizational phenomena in a very different and enlightening way. In contrast, incremental research represents exploitation and hitting singles, where previous breakthroughs are refined into tight, empirically assessed, theoretical statements. If exploration is about blazing paths, then exploitation is about paving them. Exploitation is the necessary spadework of normal science—developing measures, tinkering with the mix of variables (predictors, moderators and mediators, outcomes), relaxing boundary conditions, and so on. Exploitation is where the bulk of research occurs: one significant breakthrough, such as the idea of goal setting (Locke & Latham, 2013), can generate decades of incremental research.

Why am I emphasizing path-blazing rather than path-paving research? First, as Barney (2005: 283) put it, "if one only asks little questions, then one can only develop little answers." I think the pressing challenges of organizational life demand the big answers that only big questions can generate. Second, path-paving, by definition, is more programmatic and therefore better understood. Third, I've cringed through many PDWs where well-meaning speakers provided tips on getting a job and tenure that invariably promoted path-paving (more on that as well later)—as if the paths would just blaze themselves. Instead of settling for the doable, how about reaching for the inspirational?

So how might you blaze a new path?

Getting the Lay of the Land

- Roam broadly in the literature and everyday experience. I love having an excuse to lose myself in reading, doing what I do when travelling in cities for the first time: putting away the map (the dominant models and literature reviews, if they exist) and following my nose, seizing on whatever looks interesting in the moment. Don't be afraid to read outside of management. But be forewarned by Mintzberg's (2005: 365) admonition: "the library is the worst place in the world in which to find a research topic." Journal articles tend to double down on what is already known—and it's a good bet that someone (most likely the author!) is already working on the recommendations that fall under "implications for future research." In contrast, you can put a lot of stock in Sutton's (1997) point that strong ideas can come from weak sources. So don't feel too guilty about reading *People* magazine and watching reality TV.

(Personally, I find novels, investigative reports, first-person accounts, and ethnographies very helpful; I'd include poetry if I had the patience for it.) For that matter, great ideas often come from simply being vigilant in your everyday life and talking to people about their experiences and difficulties. I once had a taxi driver who happened to be a former bounty hunter. Given my interest in dirty work, I grilled the poor guy all the way to the airport. Ashford (2013) adds that questions that are *personally relevant* are more likely to inspire you to seek deeper meanings (see also Amabile & Hall, in press). Uninspiring questions result in uninspired answers. And if you're bored, I guarantee your readers will be, too. The bottom line in all this is that the wider you roam and the more deeply you then engage, the more you'll discover intriguing things that no buttoned-down model or review has considered—or would consider.

- Remember that theories are built from the center out (from a core concept, question, or relationship). Like a growing village, we create these assemblies of thought where the borders are poorly mapped and the links to other theories and disciplines are often not well understood. So in building your village, journey to nearby villages, towns, and cities by thinking of them as "living membranes which allow osmosis of ideas to take place" (Bedeian, 1989: 3). In my experience, most major conceptual breakthroughs come from breadth, not depth. Breadth means you're spanning levels of analysis, theories, disciplines, and settings, juxtaposing disparate things. Depth just means that you're digging a deeper hole, and deep holes do not let in much light: deeper holes are what incremental theory-building is all about. Or, to use a different metaphor, if depth is like the proverbial boy with the hammer to whom everything looks like a nail, then breadth is like the jack-of-all-trades with tools for every occasion. (See Epstein, 2019.) Who would you rather have tackle a novel problem?

Roughing Out a Path: Exploring Ideas

- Because you've put away the map in order to wander, it's very common to feel very lost very soon and to question what the heck you're doing. It's like finding yourself in a deep, dark forest, with no discernible path out. Forgive the Zen moment, but "you need to get lost before you can get found" (Gioia, 2004: 103). The deeper and darker the forest, the greater the potential for discovering something truly original.

- How do you find your way out of the forest? You think about blazing a path. Jot down ideas and interesting findings as you read. (For you qualitative types, this is akin to open coding and memoing.) At this point, you really are just trying to get a handle on where you are and where you might (ultimately) want to go. Don't be too concerned with actually building a path yet because you don't know what direction to take or what obstacles you'll encounter. You are *that* lost.

- In quant research, outliers and anomalies are usually considered enemies because they undermine mathematical elegance. In theory-building, as in qual research, outliers and anomalies are often your best friends because they signal something unusual and unexpected, spurring a quest for why they exist (Gibbert, Nair, Weiss, & Hoegl, 2021; Whetten, 2002). Entire theories can spring from something that doesn't make conventional sense. My early interest in dirty work stemmed in part from the fact that the literature on self-esteem suggests that individuals doing tainted jobs should not like themselves very much, yet ethnographies of actual "dirty workers" suggest the exact opposite. So while doing your broad reading, conversing, and experiencing, be vigilant for the counterintuitive finding, telling anecdote, paradox, and novel event. And push yourself periodically by trying provocative thought experiments and counterfactual thinking (e.g., "what might it take to change that positive relationship into a negative one?"; "could causality flow both ways?"; see Johns, 2021). No less a path-blazer than Albert Einstein often began with a simple cognitive tickle such as "Imagine that . . ." or "What if . . .?" (Isaacson, 2008).

- As the ideas and findings start to accumulate, you'll begin to see linkages, themes, and potential kernels for a paper. (This is akin to axial coding.) The direction(s?) your path might take is becoming clearer. However, I don't actively look for linkages, themes, and ideas; I find they naturally percolate as a happy byproduct of the immersion. Lots of little eurekas. Ultimately, many don't pan out, but each is a prod to further thinking.

- Needless to say, if you're doing all this with coauthors (almost always a good idea), then you want to periodically compare notes and bounce your impressions and emergent thinking off them. I'm often amazed at how even a brief conversation can spark breakthroughs that no amount of alone-time would have accomplished.

Clearing the Path: Working Out Ideas

- As the linkages, themes, and ideas percolate, write them down. They needn't be fully formed or elegantly written; you're really just riffing on promising leads, whether it results in a bullet point or a page of rambling thoughts. As someone once said, writing *is* thinking; writing helps you work through the issues. I believe it's a big mistake to start writing only after you have The Big Idea and a careful game plan. This leads to premature closure and ultimately a shallow paper. To paraphrase Weick (1979), "how can you know what you think until you see what you write?"

- Throughout the process, but especially as ideas percolate, make liberal use of figures and tables (Whetten, 2002). It's said that a picture is worth a thousand words; attempting to distill your free-floating ideas into figures and tables helps you cut to the heart of the matter, think through likely contingencies, and identify gaps and promising directions. These figures and tables—like many of the little eurekas along the way—may not make the final cut, but they are immensely helpful stepping stones. As a doctoral student, I submitted a rambling proposal to my thesis advisor, Hugh Arnold. Exasperated by the hot mess, he said, "give me a diagram." Trying to distill that sea of ink into a single model proved to be *the* turning point in my theorizing. Regarding figures for empirical studies, the sweet spot for parsimony seems to be four to six variables for causal models, encompassing moderated mediation and/or serial mediation (thanks, John Bush, for the background); for theory papers, there is much more latitude because the authors aren't actually testing the model and can therefore be as inclusive as they wish. Regarding tables, the sweet spot for parsimony seems to be 2x2s or 2x3s for mapping out exhaustive typologies with mutually exclusive categories. Check out Miles, Huberman, and Saldaña (2014) for various other ways to play with data.

- It also helps to freely blend deduction, induction, and abduction. Deduction is reasoning from general principles to specific instances. For example, speaking of blazing paths, what would path-goal theory[4] have to say about how a leader might behave in this situation you've heard about? Induction is abstracting from specific instances to more general principles. How might certain leader behaviors you observed

---

[4] This is a heartfelt nod to Martin Evans and the aforementioned Bob House, two of my treasured mentors during my doctoral studies at the University of Toronto.

better inform path-goal theory? And abduction is making an inferential leap (really, a leap of faith) from a data point, area, or level to a seemingly distal or unrelated topic. If this insight is true of path-goal theory, might it also be true of transformational leadership theory? My point is that the ongoing *interplay* among the three processes leads to richer theories: theorizing needs to travel up, down, and across. If you can't think of a plausible example (even if hypothetical), then your general theory may be unmoored from reality—the ultimate arbiter; if you can't think of how your rich findings might generalize to other settings, then you have anecdotes, not a theory; if your thinking is siloed, then so is its likely impact.

- Be mindful that there is an important sweet spot for how truly novel your arguments can be (McKinley, Mone, & Moon, 1999). Readers are looking to assimilate what you have written with what they know and value: arguments that are low on novelty tend to bore readers (including the gatekeepers, your journal reviewers), and arguments that are very high on novelty tend to be difficult for readers to relate to. The sweet spot, then, is novelty that is high enough to excite their interest but not so high as to leave them with few hooks for assimilation. Similarly, there's an important sweet spot for timing: too early in the "life cycle" of ideas and readers can't relate to your thinking, too late and they've moved on to richer thinking.

- As your thoughts begin to gel, begin to focus your reading. As I tell my doctoral students, "start wide but finish narrow" (Ashforth, 2016: 369). You will read far more than can or should ever be reflected in the ultimate paper. You needn't know "everything" about a topic (who does?), but you do need to know the major theories (and their critiques), recent developments and trends, emergent phenomena that bear on the topic, what scholars are suggesting for future research, and so on. In short, you need to become an expert. Take heart, though: while it's impossible to read everything relevant, diminishing returns *will* set in. (Clearly, it's a lot easier to become an expert in a relatively new and lightly researched topic than an old and heavily researched one—but that doesn't mean there isn't juice left in virtually all topics. I can foresee a 2032 journal call for "New Directions in Goal Setting." The final word is never written.)

- Because you're writing as you're reading, each informs the other in a virtuous circle. The result is a mash-up of thought riffs, some well-developed and others not so much. To look at one of my papers at this stage would likely leave you questioning my sanity: "All this reading and writing and you just have these random notes?" Well, yes. But this is where all those riffs start to coalesce into deeper themes and cool arguments (akin to selective coding) as if in a chemical reaction. This is where theorizing with a capital *T* becomes most evident. Themes get refined into core research questions, arguments get fleshed out into coherent theoretical statements, moderators and mediators are posited, outcomes and feedback loops are identified, specific examples are offered to ground and illustrate abstract arguments, and lingering questions (for future research) and practical implications are suggested.

- Let me expand on two oft-neglected aspects of theory papers: boundary conditions and practical implications. *Boundary conditions* refer to the context or constraints within which a theory applies (Busse, Kach, & Wagner, 2017)—typically, as noted, who, where, and when (Whetten, 1989). Put differently, they are the assumptions under which a theory operates. Perhaps your arguments apply mainly to women (who), or Asian countries (where), or during the first year of employment (when). Boundary conditions often emerge as you discover empirical exceptions to your argument and mull over how the argument may apply to diverse contexts. (A moderator, by the way, is essentially a boundary condition that applies to only a limited part of a model.) If the boundary conditions are not made clear early in the paper, then reviewers will start wondering, "but wouldn't this apply differently to men [or whatever]?" Stating your boundary conditions removes that nagging question. In my experience, reviewers seldom question boundary conditions because they appear early—before the reviewers really know where the paper is going—and simply become the water in which your theoretical fish are swimming. In the discussion section, you then either relax the boundary conditions and briefly speculate on how they may affect your arguments or simply punt the entire issue to "implications for future research."

As for practical implications, sadly, they often represent a tale of treacle and the trite, with authors jotting down blindingly generic and obvious takeaways for practitioners (e.g., "managers should be supportive of employees"). Any (midrange) theory worth the name should be capable of generating specific and actionable ideas for practitioners. Rather than treat practical implications as an annoying afterthought, as many of us do, invest real thought in how your theorizing might actually help improve the world of organizations. After all, that question is precisely why our field matters.

Mapping the Path: Writing Up Your Ideas

- A paper should read as if it was written with a single voice, flowing clearly, coherently, and logically through the abstract, introduction, always-selective literature review, core arguments, and discussion. An elegant, linear read that is both systematic and parsimonious. But, oddly enough, *inelegance and nonlinearity are usually the rule—not the exception—as the theory gets articulated.* I freely jump around the paper, playing with a mediator here and a limitation there, a bullet idea for the introduction, and so on until the paper starts to look reasonably coherent. (The last three things I write definitively are the discussion, introduction, and abstract, in that order.) As the paper coheres, gaps get identified (for further focused reading and writing), sections get reordered, material that is proving tangential gets dropped, and rough notes get refined. I'm guessing that scholars who try to write an elegant and linear draft from the outset are especially prone to writer's block: they become intimidated by their own lofty expectations.
- Because theory writing is essentially storytelling, be mindful of what makes for an engaging story: an evocative title ("Camping on seesaws" [Hedberg, Nystrom, & Starbuck, 1976], not "Social and technological change, learning, and organizational structure"), an intriguing plot (research question), interesting characters (previous findings and theorizing, phenomena, variables), a provocative narrative that builds and resolves tension (well-crafted arguments), and a satisfying conclusion (implications for theory, research, and practice). Also, stories are more engaging when they use the active voice and first person ("We argue that . . ." v. "It is argued that . . ."/"The authors argue that . . .").[5] Dane (2011: 335) adds: "my hunch is that articles that have a hint of flair, a dash of deviance, or a pinch of humor may actually fare well in the peer-review process (despite being subject to nitpicky critiques along the way)." Note, though, his all-important qualifiers: a hint, a dash, and a pinch.
- As Tourish (2020: 101; see also Grey & Sinclair, 2006) argues, "it seems that many of us feel compelled to make our theories more complex than

---

[5] Years ago, I wrote a book on role transitions and received the copy editor's changes in one massive batch. He had changed all of my active, first-person prose into numbingly stilted statements (e.g., "I once spoke with . . ." became "The author had occasion to interact with . . ."—*ugh!*). It took me two weeks to undo the damage, and even now I wince at some of the turgid phrasing I missed. Copy editors, in my view, often try to outacademic actual academics. I far prefer copy editors with a light touch who let you retain your preferred voice.

they really are to show off how clever we are." Fight this compulsion. In refining your ideas, continuously strive for clarity, precision, and simplicity in your writing (Ragins, 2012). Convoluted and muddled writing suggests convoluted and muddled thinking; if you can't express your argument in clear prose then you probably don't yet fully understand it. Call this the Mom Test: if she can readily understand your argument, you're on the right track. As Einstein is reputed to have said, "simplicity on this side of complexity is easy; simplicity on the other side takes real thought."

- In my experience, not many theory papers are rejected because the core ideas are wrong; they're rejected because the execution is weak. In short, *the devil is in the details*. This is why—and it will sound like an exaggeration, but it's not—if I'm the first author, you could not change even a comma on a final draft without me noticing it. Why? Because to execute well—to transform a hot mess into an elegant and linear argument—you have to polish and polish and then polish some more. Grant and Pollock (2011: 873) note that 10 is the *Jeopardy*-like answer to the question "On average, how many times do winners of the *AMJ* Best Article Award rewrite the introduction to their work?" Polishing requires many reads through the paper (but usually not the whole paper in a single gulp). Like a carpenter meticulously sanding a rough board, you're constantly striving for a smoother (i.e., clearer and more succinct) way to express your thinking. I'll bet even Shakespeare was embarrassed by his first drafts.[6]

- A major part of the polishing process entails soliciting friendly reviews: "friendly" in the sense that you select them and they aren't your actual journal reviewers, not in the sense that they'll just coo at your paper. If all you want is positive feedback, give it to your mother. But because friendly colleagues also don't want to hurt your feelings, ask them to review it with the critical eye they normally use for a conventional review. And ask specifically about those touchy areas that you're not that confident about. My go-to reviewer was Gary Johns, who would provide the unvarnished truth (mothers wouldn't like him) but then work with you to figure out how to solve the problems. You couldn't ask for a better role model.

---

[6] I recently skimmed my 1986 dissertation. I remember thinking way back then that this was the greatest writing since Hemingway. (OK, I'm exaggerating, but only somewhat.) When I read it with my 2019 eyes, I was mortified. Runaway jargon, turgid sentences, clumsy transitions, the works. My takeaway? There is no shortcut to becoming a good scholarly writer; it takes copious practice mixed with lots of brutally frank feedback.

- Finally, when you're happy with your rigorously buffed draft, let it sit for a week or two. The interlude will cleanse your mental palate so that when you give the paper the final read—preferably along with your coauthors—you will see it through fresh eyes. It's always surprising how many changes (although mostly small) we make to our supposedly "finished" papers at this stage.

It Takes a Village

Scholarship can be a lonely calling. We read, we ponder, and we write—all solitary activities, if we let them be. And the life of a scholar attracts a lot of introverts (and squirrely people, but that's for another day). We all know the stereotype of the wild-haired scholar slaving away in his or her lab or study, puttering and muttering away in splendid isolation.

But that's only one model. The other, of which I'm a huge fan, is active and ongoing collaboration. As organizational life becomes ever more complex, dynamic, and equivocal, and as our theories and methods become ever more elaborate and esoteric, the benefits of collaboration become ever more apparent. As I once wrote about a conference hosted by Dave Whetten and Paul Godfrey that helped kickstart interest in identity in organizations, "I learned more from a weekend together than I could from a month alone" (Ashforth, 1998: 272). It was amazing how a few days with insightful people talking about a particular topic helped to energize us all. More recently, I was working with Kristie Rogers on a paper on respect. We were at different schools by then, so we Skyped and emailed regularly. Kristie wasn't satisfied with our progress and suggested visiting me for a week at Arizona State University. I demurred at first, not seeing the advantage of face time compared to Skype. Boy, was *I* wrong! We accomplished more in that week together than we had in the previous month apart. Something about the face-to-face dynamic kicked us into a higher gear in terms of both productivity *and* quality. The synergies of collaboration can make a paper far better than if one of the coauthors wrote it alone.

I noted earlier that I've been profoundly lucky with my collaborations in that almost all have been richly rewarding. In thinking about with whom to collaborate, I suggest looking for several qualities:

- *Personal rapport.* Yes, we're all professionals and we can work with colleagues with whom we don't really click. However, having a personal rapport injects liking and trust, which greatly facilitate the free exchange of ideas and constructive feedback. And, hey, it's a lot more fun.

- *Complementary and supplementary knowledge, skills, and abilities.* Because we gravitate to people we like, and we tend to like people who are similar to us, we often work with colleagues who replicate our competencies. This can be a big mistake if you're working on a project that requires diverse competencies (and these days, most do). I was really fortunate to work with Ray Lee and Alan Saks earlier in my career, whose quant skills far exceeded mine. That said, there is also a need for at least some supplementarity, where you *share* knowledge, skills, and abilities. Given the complexity alluded to in both organizational life and organizational studies, good things tend to happen when you talk issues out with someone who also knows the literature, methods, settings, and so on. In my experience, one plus one usually equals three.
- *Work styles.* This one isn't nearly as crucial because all collaborations mix together-time with alone-time, allowing some diversity in work styles. Still, it can be rough if one partner is a procrastinator and the other isn't, one has a chaotic way of writing (me!) and the other doesn't, and so on. Unlike the other two qualities, however, this one is difficult to suss out before committing to a collaboration. At a minimum, though, given that academics need to juggle many balls, it's important to agree on a rough timeline for deliverables.

Given the theme "It takes a village," it seems only appropriate to thank all those with whom I have worked over my career—as a mentee, a colleague, a mentor, and, really, when you think about it, all three at once in every relationship! At the end of the day, we are all students, and our fellow students are also our best teachers.

But What About the %&#$ Review Process?

Lifting the Curtain (A Little)

You have now sent your carefully crafted paper to a top journal and are awaiting the reviews. Top journals routinely reject over 90% of their submissions. This makes authors and editors very wary: authors, because they naturally fear the long odds; editors, because they fear a Type I error, accepting flawed papers that will reflect poorly on them and the journal. All this fear makes for strange dynamics. A very promising paper is unlikely to receive a glowing review;

rather, the feedback will be so measured and circumspect that neophyte authors often interpret good news (*I've been invited to revise and resubmit!*) as bad news (*man, they must hate my paper!*). As a reviewer and editor, I'm always dismayed when authors are invited to revise a promising paper but never do: we scared them off.

But believe it or not, reviewers and editors are not sadists—it just seems that way. Reviewers and editors are also not a species apart; they are you and me. And *we*, the collective that plays all three roles, want the same thing: to make very good papers into great papers (despite the abrupt or dismissive tone that some reviewers and editors inexcusably adopt).

Editors have a difficult question: *can you substantially address the concerns of the review team in the next major revision?* The paper may ultimately go through multiple rounds of reviews, but the question never wavers. This is why my mantra of "polish, polish, and polish some more" is so important; you want the review team to think you've spent every waking moment honing your paper.

Rindova (2008) discusses the most common errors that authors make when revising their papers—including dismissing comments as failures of the reviewers/editor to understand their brilliance, cosmetic changes (putting lipstick on a pig), and not prioritizing the editor's comments—but the one I want to elaborate on is "doing everything that's asked." That sounds like an odd error; you've made them happy, haven't you? Well, perhaps not. As the saying goes, "a camel is a horse designed by a committee," meaning that it's important that you retain your vision and voice for the paper. As Rindova (2008: 302) put it, "The reviewers and editor do not want to see a camel; they want to see a better horse."

And, let's face it, not every comment deserves your attention. Let's call this Ashforth's 50/30/20 rule:

- 50% of comments are valid and helpful.
- 30% of comments are idiosyncratic to the particular reviewer, meaning that other reviewers wouldn't raise them and don't view them as central (or perhaps even relevant) to the paper. Perhaps the reviewer sees some tangential avenue to explore, or wants a secondary analysis that adds little value, or wants you to include the brilliant work of "John Smith" (guess who this reviewer is?). Typically, idiosyncratic comments neither really help the paper nor really hurt it.
- 20% of comments are just plain wrong and even stupid. Perhaps the reviewer doesn't understand an extant theory, method, or analysis, or only skimmed your paper, or wrote their review hastily, leaving you—like a

fortune teller reading tea leaves—to divine what they may have meant. And sometimes reviewers want you to write *their* preferred paper and try to hijack *your* paper to do so.[7]

We can quibble about the numbers. My point is that your job as the author is to be selective in what you address. A good editor will help you sort through the comments, emphasizing the first category and glossing over or politely vetoing the others. But often editors don't know an area well, are fearful of upsetting reviewers, or (my pet peeve) write glorified form letters telling you to address the reviewers' concerns.

My advice? Focus mostly on the 50%, using them as the foundation for your changes. Do the 30% as long as they don't hurt the integrity of your paper (a gray area, I realize). To put it crassly, the motto here is "lose the battle, win the war" (i.e., get published). But don't do the 20%. At the end of the day, it's your name on the paper, and if the reviewer's comment strikes you as wrong, have the courage of your convictions. However, never ignore a comment; instead, be gracious and clear in explaining your reasoning.

A Tale of Two Papers

Let me offer contrasting examples where I didn't and did follow my own advice. I'll avoid specifics because I'm not out to offend anyone. We had submitted a theory paper and were invited to revise and resubmit it. *Whoo-hoo!* But, *uh-oh*, the editor wanted us to ditch a major argument and go in a very different direction. We thought this was wrong-headed, but we also wanted to publish in this journal—and, hey, a bird in the hand is supposed to be worth two in the bush. So we swallowed hard and did our best to address not just the letter but the spirit of the editor's recommendation. The result was a service-able draft, but one that was doomed from the start to be inferior. And guess what? The reviewers weren't too happy either. We limped through two more rounds of revisions before the editor pulled the plug. We felt that we had been set up to fail, and we were left kicking ourselves for not having the courage of our convictions.

In the second example, we had again submitted a theory paper and again received a revise and resubmit. In an eerie case of déjà vu, the editor wanted us

---

[7] The most egregious case I've experienced was when we submitted a quant study on the psychology of identification and a reviewer wrote that s/he wanted us to convert it into a *qual* study on the *sociology* of identity! (*Sure, we'll get right on that.*)

to ditch a major argument and go in a very different direction—and yes, one that we thought was wrong-headed. (In this case, we saw the comment as idiosyncratic rather than wrong per se.) And just to turn the screws a bit more, it was the editor's major recommendation. We again swallowed hard, but this time for a very different reason: we had decided to push back. We explained very carefully why we thought our original direction made more sense and, with the guidance from the rest of the review, turned in a second draft we thought was much better than the first. But there was the matter of this ticking time bomb: *we had said no to the editor's major recommendation!—what were we thinking?* But guess what? The editor very graciously accepted our reasoning and the reviewers appeared to be happy as well. After another couple of rounds of review, the paper was accepted. This was easily one of the best experiences I've had with a review and I'm forever grateful to the editor for her open-mindedness.[8]

Path-Blazing or Path-Paving? Career Considerations

As a newly minted professor, I was willfully naïve about promotion and tenure. I was far more interested in path-blazing than path-paving and didn't think about how that might affect my CV come P&T time. I just figured if I did interesting work good things would happen, so I didn't fret much about hitting certain journals with a certain frequency. This relaxed attitude allowed me to pursue diverse topics and questions, despite the obvious cost of having to ramp up anew with each new challenge. It also allowed me to be something of a magpie, pursuing whatever shiny object intrigued me in the moment. (It sounds much better when Alvesson and Sandberg [2014: 978] call it "intellectual nomadism.") Indeed, throughout my career, I've deliberately avoided developing a long-term research agenda. My prior jobs in the Ontario government and a Canadian bank gave me an unhealthy disdain for bureaucracy (I still draw on those experiences as examples of how not to run organizations)—and, to me, a long-term agenda smacked of bureaucratic constraint. I was afraid that my agenda would become my jail and that my research calling would start to feel more like a research job. Research is too hard to do well if you don't really enjoy it. And, more rationally, I was afraid that a long-term agenda would squeeze out the short-term opportunism that allows me to be

---

[8] Just because I know you hate loose ends, the first example ultimately had a happy ending, too. We went back to our original draft, included the revisions we actually liked from the reviews, and had the good fortune to publish the paper in another journal.

very flexible in what I tackle. An unexpected chapter invitation? A chance to collect data? A respected colleague asking if I want to work with them? I wanted the freedom to decide and so I've never had a firm game plan beyond my immediate assortment of commitments. (Mind you, those commitments often tie me up for a couple of years at a time.)

Would I recommend a similar meandering path for today's doctoral students and untenured professors? Yes and no. Let me start with no. The market for positions at research-oriented universities is very competitive, so universities want to see clear evidence of a promising research agenda that will enable you to leverage your expertise to crank out high-quality research. In short, they want to see a focused research identity and at least a medium-term game plan of programmatic research. Unfortunately, this is a sure recipe for path-paving—for exploitation, not exploration (unless you cleverly pair a path-blazing dissertation with a path-paving agenda for your early career). Further, given the high standards for tenure that prevail at many research-oriented universities, you are expected to have cranked out an impressive quantity of high-quality research to attain tenure. This is difficult to do under the best of circumstances, and so individuals are again counseled to leverage their expertise in the interests of meeting the high standards.

One result, alluded to earlier, is that PDWs routinely promote techniques for path-paving. These can be summed up as the "charm bracelet approach" to science. As a teenage boy, I had no idea what to get my younger sister for her birthday and Christmas. My Mom, bless her, solved that problem by giving her an empty charm bracelet; suddenly, I just needed to buy her a new charm twice a year! As with a charm bracelet, path-paving scholars can regularly add or swap out independent variables, moderators, mediators, and dependent variables. They can relax boundary conditions, extend their extant models to new settings, use new and esoteric analytical methods, and so on. I've also heard in these same PDWs that a great way to cement your reputation as a path-paver is to revise a scale or develop a new one, perform a metaanalysis, and publish at least three articles in your paved area so that others will feel compelled to throw you a bone and cite your work.

To be sure, this is generally sound advice—if path-paving is indeed your passion; otherwise, this crassly instrumental view of research with its obsessive box-ticking is a sure soul-killer. Clearly, my restless and meandering approach is the antithesis of path-paving and these techniques and so runs high career risks.[9] It's not surprising, then, that many scholars become risk-averse and opt for path-paving even if their heart lies in path-blazing.

---

[9] I realize that many individuals who are initially denied tenure are able to find a new position elsewhere and go on to have very fulfilling careers. I worry, though, about the personal and social costs we pay for imposing such lofty standards so early in what will hopefully be a very long career.

As to yes, I fear that much is lost when the field implicitly rewards path-paving at the expense of path-blazing. The field itself is deprived of potential breakthroughs—just imagine if Jay Barney, Jane Dutton, Ed Freeman, or Henry Mintzberg had decided to play it safe and sit on their field-changing ideas. And the individual—*if she wants to tackle big issues* (and I suspect that many if not most of us entered the field for this very reason)—has to settle for a paler version of her imagined best self. Who hasn't had a really cool idea that they've talked themselves out of because it just doesn't seem feasible at their career stage? Career constraints make us cowards and run the risk of turning intrinsic motivation into extrinsic motivation. Pursuing an incrementalist agenda when your heart is elsewhere is a good way to court burnout. But what about posttenure, you may ask, when you're suddenly free to pursue whatever research opportunities you fancy? The pernicious thing about burnout is that it often saps the will to try something new, with all those daunting switching costs. So instead you sigh at your romantic fantasy and slog through the next incremental step (Ashforth, 2005). It's appalling how often our research productivity tanks after receiving tenure.[10] What a sad waste.

I also think a meandering path that's more about breadth than depth is a great hedge against escalating commitment and obsolescence. Just as financial advisors caution you to diversify your stock portfolio, having a portfolio of research interests guards against risking your reputation on a single interest. Two more contrasting examples. I once cowrote a tough critique of a certain scholar's theory that was his major claim to fame. He got wind of it and invited us to submit it to a special issue he was editing. We thought, "Wow, he's really open-minded. This is what scholarship is meant to be." Yeah, right. Dr. OneNote then nickle-and-dimed us to death, relentlessly whittling down the parts of our paper that were most critical of his theory. After we had signed off on the paper (while holding our noses), he actually deleted portions of our critique and inserted the following as if *we* had written it: "unfortunately, for a variety of reasons, the authors cannot test [Dr. OneNote's] model here"!! My take on this very sordid catch-and-kill incident? Dr. OneNote had a huge personal investment in his theory and, *by God!*, was not about to let anybody criticize it. Conversely, I once presented a paper at the Academy of Management annual conference and an audience member said that what I was arguing was clearly wrong according to such-and-such an article by . . . Ashforth! I responded along the lines of, "Using me to refute me? Geez, I guess I can't go

---

[10] I recognize this is partly because other professional opportunities arise, such as administration, exec ed, consulting, and case and textbook writing. But I fear that, for many people, the fires that once stoked their research passion have cooled significantly because of the rigors of getting tenure.

wrong no matter what I say!" My point is not to humblebrag (although, gosh, that did sound good); it's that with eclectic interests, there's less reason to feel possessive and defensive about a particular line of thought. Let the scholarly chips fall where they may.

If you *are* a scholar who indeed feels called to tackle big issues, I don't want to sugarcoat the challenge here; pursuing breakthroughs is clearly a high-risk/high-reward proposition. Big-name home run hitters also strike out a lot. But take some inspiration from the findings of Podsakoff, Podsakoff, Mishra, and Escue (2018: 509). Despite the compelling argument for "no,"

> over half (53%) of the authors who have published high-impact articles [at least 1,000 *Web of Science* citations] in the field of management do so within the first 7 (pre-tenure) years of their career, and . . . 14% of all of the authors who published a high-impact article did so while they were still doctoral students. Moreover, about half of these early-career scholars served as either the sole author or the primary author.

A Fertile Middle Ground?

Might there be some middle ground that would enable you to do work with breakthrough potential while not risking your career quite so much? *Yes!* Looking at my own career with 20/20 hindsight (because the foresight was certainly missing!), my meandering approach was not random. As I said, my research interests and questions were informed by an overarching research passion to understand how systems affect individuals. And so my eclectic investigations and thinking about a particular question often inadvertently informed my thinking about other research questions with which I was toying—or cued me to think about disparate questions I might tackle later. (I used to scrawl such thoughts down and stick them in an idea drawer [yes I called it that], which I'd skim through when I was looking for inspiration.) For me, abduction wasn't confined to specific papers; it became a habit of thinking. Take my interest in organizational socialization. While pondering how organizations influence newcomers, it occurred to me that this process would help explain the dynamics associated with another interest of mine, the dark side of organizations. One result was a paper on the normalization of corruption in organizations, with Vikas Anand.

My point is that I think it *is* possible, through the *synergy* of one's research interests, to simultaneously realize the fruits of both breadth and depth. (See

Alvesson & Sandberg, 2014.) This synergy equips you to pursue discrete breakthroughs (breadth) while having enough related questions (depth) to leverage your expertise. And if you are currently mulling over a really cool idea but are fearful of the challenge, rather than dwell on all the reasons why you *shouldn't* go forward, think of all the reasons why you *should*; not the least of which is that you'll feel *inspired* to be the kind of scholar that perhaps you hoped to be when you started your scholarly career. All of those scholars noted earlier—Barney, Dutton, and so on—at some point came to a similar crossroads, and we are all the better for the brave choice they made.

Conclusion

"Theory" often seems to be a dirty word in the popular imagination, suggesting impractical and sterile ideas delivered on embossed paper from smug occupants of an ivory tower. And, in all honesty, theory can be that. But it can also be so much, much more. It is theory, done well, that helps provide answers to the essential six questions of any perplexing mystery: what, why, how, where, who, and when? It is theory that not only identifies issues but explains and predicts, enabling agency in a complex, dynamic, and equivocal world. It is theory, in short, that moves mountains.

And it is you, the proud *theorist*, who makes all this possible. What will be *your* mountain?

Acknowledgments

My deepest thanks to Xiao-Ping Chen, Deb Salac, H. Kevin Steensma, and an anonymous reviewer for their helpful comments on an earlier draft, and to Kristie Rogers and Beth Schinoff, whose interview for the MOC Distinguished Scholar Award prodded my thinking about some of the topics here.

References

Alvesson, M., & Sandberg, J. (2014). Habitat and habitus: Boxed-in versus box-breaking research. *Organization Studies, 35*, 967–987.

Amabile, T. M., & Hall, D. T. In press. The undervalued power of self-relevant research: The case of researching retirement while retiring. *Academy of Management Perspectives.*

Ashford, S. J. (2013). Having scholarly impact: The art of hitting academic home runs. *Academy of Management Learning & Education, 12*, 623–633.

Ashforth, B. E. (1998). Epilogue: What have we learned, and where do we go from here? In D. A. Whetten & P. C. Godfrey (Eds.), *Identity in organizations: Building theory through conversations* (pp. 268–272). Thousand Oaks, CA: Sage.

Ashforth, B. E. (2005). Becoming vanilla pudding: How we undermine our passion for research. *Journal of Management Inquiry, 14*, 400–403.

Ashforth, B. E. (2016). Exploring identity and identification in organizations: Time for some course corrections. *Journal of Leadership & Organizational Studies, 23*, 361–373.

Barney, J. B. (2005). Where does inequality come from? The personal and intellectual roots of resource-based theory. In K. G. Smith & M. A. Hitt (Eds.), *Great minds in management: The process of theory development* (pp. 280–303). Oxford, UK: Oxford University Press.

Bedeian, A. G. (1989). Totems and taboos: Undercurrents in the management discipline. *The Academy of Management News, 19*(4), 2–6.

Busse, C., Kach, A. P., & Wagner, S. M. (2017). Boundary conditions: What are they, how to explore them, why we need them, and when to consider them. *Organizational Research Methods, 20*, 574–609.

Corley, K. G., & Gioia, D. A. (2011). Building theory about theory building: What constitutes a theoretical contribution? *Academy of Management Review, 36*, 12–32.

Dane, E. (2011). Changing the tune of academic writing: Muting cognitive entrenchment. *Journal of Management Inquiry, 20*, 332–336.

Davis, M. S. (1971). That's interesting! Towards a phenomenology of sociology and a sociology of phenomenology. *Philosophy of the Social Sciences, 1*, 309–344.

Epstein, D. J. (2019). *Range: Why generalists triumph in a specialized world.* New York: Riverhead Books.

Fiske, S. T. (2004). Mind the gap: In praise of informal sources of formal theory. *Personality and Social Psychology Review, 8*, 132–137.

Gibbert, M., Nair, L. B., Weiss, M., & Hoegl, M. (2021). Using outliers for theory building. *Organizational Research Methods, 24*, 172–181.

Gioia, D. A. (2004). A renaissance self: Prompting personal and professional revitalization. In R. E. Stablein & P. J. Frost (Eds.), *Renewing research practice* (pp. 97–114). Stanford, CA: Stanford University Press.

Grant, A. M., & Pollock, T. G. (2011). From the editors: Publishing in *AMJ*—Part 3: Setting the hook. *Academy of Management Journal, 54*, 873–879.

Grey, C., & Sinclair, A. (2006). Writing differently. *Organization, 13*, 443–453.

Hambrick, D. C. (2007). The field of management's devotion to theory: Too much of a good thing? *Academy of Management Journal, 50*, 1346–1352.

Hedberg, B. L. T., Nystrom, P. C., & Starbuck, W. H. (1976). Camping on seesaws: Prescriptions for a self-designing organization. *Administrative Science Quarterly, 21*, 41–65.

Hillman, A. (2011). Editor's comments: What is the future of theory? *Academy of Management Review, 36*, 606–608.

House, R. J. (1977). A 1976 theory of charismatic leadership. In J. G. Hunt & L. L. Larson (Eds.), *Leadership: The cutting edge* (pp. 189–207). Carbondale, IL: Southern Illinois University Press.

Isaacson, W. (2008). *Einstein: His life and universe.* New York: Simon & Schuster.

Johns, G. 2021. Departures from conventional wisdom: Where's the next opposite effect? *Academy of Management Discoveries, 7*, 10-14.

Locke, E. A., & Latham, G. P. (Eds.). (2013). *New developments in goal setting and task performance.* New York: Routledge.

March, J. G. (1991). Exploration and exploitation in organizational learning. *Organization Science, 2*, 71–87.

Mathieu, J. E. (2016). The problem with (in) management theory. *Journal of Organizational Behavior, 37*, 1132–1141.

McKinley, W. (2010). Organizational theory development: Displacement of ends? *Organization Studies, 31,* 47–68.

McKinley, W., Mone, M. A., & Moon, G. (1999). Determinants and development of schools in organization theory. *Academy of Management Review, 24,* 634–648.

Miles, M. B., Huberman, A. M., & Saldaña, J. (2014). *Qualitative data analysis: A methods sourcebook,* 3rd ed. Thousand Oaks, CA: Sage.

Mintzberg, H. (2005). Developing theory about the development of theory. In K. G. Smith & M. A. Hitt (Eds.), *Great minds in management: The process of theory development* (pp. 355–372). Oxford, UK: Oxford University Press.

Pfeffer, J. (2014). The management theory morass: Some modest proposals. In J. A. Miles (Ed.), *New directions in management and organization theory* (pp. 457–468). Newcastle upon Tyne, UK: Cambridge Scholars.

Pinder, C. C., & Moore, L. F. (Eds.). (1980). *Middle range theory and the study of organizations.* Boston, MA: Martinus Nijhoff.

Podsakoff, P. M., Podsakoff, N. P., Mishra, P., & Escue, C. (2018). Can early-career scholars conduct impactful research? Playing "small ball" versus "swinging for the fences." *Academy of Management Learning & Education, 17,* 496–531.

Ragins, B. R. (2012). Editor's comments: Reflections on the craft of clear writing. *Academy of Management Review, 37,* 493–501.

Rindova, V. (2008). Editor's comments: Publishing theory when you are new to the game. *Academy of Management Review, 33,* 300–303.

Shepherd, D. A., & Suddaby, R. (2017). Theory building: A review and integration. *Journal of Management, 43,* 59–86.

Suddaby, R. (2014). Editor's comments: Why theory? *Academy of Management Review, 39,* 407–411.

Sutton, R. I. (1997). The virtues of closet qualitative research. *Organization Science, 8,* 97–106.

The mind is a formidable jailer. (1973, April 8). *The New York Times.* https://www.nytimes.com/1973/04/08/archives/a-pirandellian-prison-the-mind-is-a-formidable-jailer.html.

Tourish, D. 2020. The triumph of nonsense in management studies. *Academy of Management Learning & Education, 19,* 99–109.

Weick, K. E. (1979). *The social psychology of organizing,* 2nd ed. Reading, MA: Addison-Wesley.

Whetten, D. A. (1989). What constitutes a theoretical contribution? *Academy of Management Review, 14,* 490–495.

Whetten, D. A. (2002). Modelling-as-theorizing: A systematic methodology for theory development. In D. Partington (Ed.), *Essential skills for management research* (pp. 45–71). London: Sage.

2

Cultural Intelligence

Two Bowls Singing

Soon Ang

Introduction

Cultural intelligence (CQ) refers to an individual's and an organization's capability to function effectively in situations characterized by cultural diversity (Ang & Van Dyne, 2008; Earley & Ang, 2003). Developed at the turn of the century, CQ forges new research directions for scholars, and offers new solutions to organizations. In terms of research, scholars from more than 20 academic disciplines (including management, social sciences, economics and finance, arts and humanities, decision sciences, engineering, and medicine) have cited CQ in journals, proceedings, and book chapters. CQ has spawned doctoral theses across the myriad disciplines.

Beyond academia, CQ, especially its measurement (Ang, Van Dyne, Koh, Ng, Templer, Tay, & Chandrasekar, 2007; Van Dyne, Ang, Ng, Rockstuhl, Tan, & Koh, 2012) also shapes the policies and practices of global human capital across a wide range of industries. These industries include aviation, consulting services, counselling and mental health, education, finance, high tech, food, real estate, oil and gas, etc.; as well as in government and nonprofit sectors (e.g., armed forces, education, judiciary courts, public service, and religious missions). As of now, more than 100,000 people across 161 nations have received their CQ profile via the Cultural Intelligence Survey (CQS; Ang, Van Dyne, Koh, Ng, Templer, Tay, & Chandrasekar, 2007) or the expanded CQS (E-CQS; Van Dyne, Ang, Ng, Rockstuhl, Tan, & Koh, 2012), the first set of validated instruments measuring CQ.

The rigor and impact of my research has resulted in a number of awards. They include four prestigious awards for my scientific leadership and achievements: (1) the Distinguished Leadership Award for International Alumni (University of Minnesota); (2) the Walter F. Ulmer, Jr. Applied Research Award (Center for Creative Leadership, USA); (3) the inaugural Nanyang Award for Research and Innovation in the Social Sciences—the highest recognition given to an outstanding faculty member at the university and the first awarded

Soon Ang, *Cultural Intelligence* In: *A Journey toward Influential Scholarship*. Edited by: Xiao-Ping Chen and H. Kevin Steensma, Oxford University Press. © Oxford University Press 2021. DOI: 10.1093/oso/9780190070717.003.0002

to a social scientist; and (4) in September 2019, installation as Distinguished University Professor at Nanyang Technological University (NTU), an honor conferred to five faculty members to date at NTU for their extraordinary scholarly achievements across multiple research disciplines and global recognition. I have also won awards from the Academy of Management, the American Psychological Association, the Association of Computing Machinery, and others.

"Two bowls singing," the subtitle of this chapter, symbolizes the resonance of CQ research with scientists (bowl 1) and practitioners (bowl 2). A singing bowl vibrates and produces a long-lasting resonant tone when struck by a mallet. In the physical sciences, resonance is a phenomenon that occurs when the frequency at which a force is applied is nearly equal to one of the natural frequencies of the system on which it acts. This causes the system to oscillate with larger amplitude than when the force is applied at other frequencies. In a similar fashion, striking the right chords with both target audience groups—scientists and practitioners—is important. Scientists primarily address the "what" and the "why" of phenomena, whereas practitioners focus on resolving the "how" of solving problems in their environment.

Importantly, the two bowls reinforce and impact each other in "sympathetic resonance", where a vibratory body responds to the external vibrations of another body that shares a harmonic similarity. In this context, the

Figure 2.1 Two Tibetan Singing Bowls.
Source: Standard License from ShutterStock.
Also, watch whiteboard: https://www.youtube.com/watch?v=hm5Fa9x3GaM

"science bowl" excites the "practice bowl" through offering evidence-based practices for developing culturally intelligent individuals and organizations. Conversely, the "practice bowl" energizes the "science bowl" through practice-based evidence, where practice reveals meaningful phenomena and problems that stimulate new scientific inquiry and evidence on CQ (Rousseau & Gunia, 2016). Hence, the metaphor of the two bowls singing and their sympathetic resonance underscores the symbiosis between science and practice.

For the two bowls to "sing," they need to rest on a solid base. The solid base involves institutional building and community building to sustain the research beyond individual researchers. Building institutions, such as the Center for Leadership and Cultural Intelligence (the world's first research center on CQ) and the Culture Science Institute, both at the Nanyang Business School, attract resources such as funding, faculty members, and postdocs with deep expertise on culture science, PhD students interested in culture research, and opportunities for research collaborations with organizations. Growing the community of scientists and practitioners interested in CQ bridges both the scientific and practice realms and enables the two bowls to sing in harmony. Thus, the wooden base signifies the critical enablers (institution and community building) that advance the impact of CQ exponentially beyond what a single or even a few scientists can achieve.

In this chapter, I reflect on my journey and approach to starting and sustaining the resonance of CQ. I've organized the chapter in five parts. First, I describe the genesis of CQ. In the second and third sections, I describe how I strike the "science bowl" and the "practice bowl," respectively. Fourth, I share the importance of institution and community building as a metaphorical "base" for the two bowls. Fifth, I conclude with my future aspirations for the science and practice of CQ.

The Genesis of Cultural Intelligence

Pre-2000: The Y2K Bug

I started out my career in the early 1990s focusing on solving problems faced by the IT profession, which faces unique challenges. With the rapid advances of technology, IT professionals often wrestle with obsolescence of their technical skills. Moreover, the IT profession is not just a technical profession but also a helping profession, since IT professionals work with a variety of stakeholders to solve IT problems in organizations. These factors create substantial performance problems for IT professionals and the organizations that employ them.

The idea of CQ struck me in 1993, when I got involved with a range of organizations in aviation, finance, and other industries, to solve the "Y2K" problem. Many organizations at that time were revamping their IT systems so as to avoid this problem—issues related to the formatting and storage of data involving dates, as many IT systems had represented four-digit years with only the final two digits.

From cognitive ability (IQ) to practical intelligence. I collaborated with these organizations to help them select effective programmers. Instead of focusing only on technical competence and cognitive ability, I examined "practical intelligence," as comprising four capabilities: managing self, task, career, and others (Sternberg, Forsythe, Hedlund, Horvath, Wagner, Williams, Snook, & Grigorenko, 2000). In the context of IT professionals, managing others includes managing six different stakeholders: (1) sponsors, (2) clients, (3) end-users, (4) supervisors, (5) peers, and (6) subordinates.

From practical intelligence to cultural intelligence. While examining practical intelligence, I discovered a new challenge faced by IT professionals. Although the programmers possessed good technical skills, they could not always work with others from different cultures. For instance, one organization I worked with hired many IT programmers from Australia, China, India, Malaysia, the Philippines, Vietnam, and elsewhere to debug the Y2K problem and to update its software applications. Differences in working norms and habits created huge conflicts between the local management and the programmers, as well as among programmers from different cultures. The powerful yet invisible role of culture struck me—how do people with vastly different norms and habits due to their cultural backgrounds work effectively with one another? I realized the need for a different type of intelligence, and began my foray into research on culture and intelligence.

Culture

Culture refers to the shared values, norms, and practices of a group of people. The late Harry Triandis, who was the "father" of cross-cultural psychology, visited NTU several times and played an instrumental role in my grounding in culture research. His research focused on cross-cultural comparisons and laid an important foundation for understanding intercultural challenges. For instance, his treatise on subjective culture (Triandis, 1972) provided a comprehensive model to explain how distal factors (such as physical environment and historical events) influence more proximal macro factors (such as economic activities and labor structure), which in turn shape pancultural psychological processes that create subjective cultures.

Intelligence

The field of intelligence dates back more than a century, beginning with the development of the first IQ test by French psychologists Alfred Binet and Theodore Simon. Since then, scholars have long debated the nature of intelligence. Sternberg (2019: 23) noted that "intelligence has been used for more than a century to refer to a fairly standardized set of cognitive abilities." Contemporary research on intelligence now embraces a much wider view of intelligence that goes beyond a singular general intelligence (g) factor, and extends beyond academic settings. Early examples of contemporary views of intelligence include multiple intelligences (Gardner, 1993), emotional intelligence (Mayer & Salovey, 1993), and practical intelligence (Sternberg et al., 2000).

Despite the diverse views held by intelligence scholars, "almost all definitions of intelligence . . . agree on one thing—that intelligence crucially involves the ability to adapt to the environment" (Sternberg, 2019: 23). In this regard, the different forms of intelligences enable individuals to adapt to the demands of different environments. For instance, IQ focuses on the academic environment; EQ on the emotional environment; and practical intelligence on the real-world context of solving practical problems.

Further, Sternberg's (1986) multiloci framework of intelligence proposed that meeting the demands of any environment requires not only mental capabilities, but behavioral capabilities as well. Mental capabilities include metacognition (processes used to acquire and understand knowledge); cognition (knowledge structures); and motivation (processes to direct and sustain energy on a particular task). Behavioral capabilities refer to outward manifestations or overt actions required to accomplish the task effectively.

Cultural Intelligence—The Birth of a New Construct

My research on cultural intelligence integrates two bodies of research—culture and intelligence; and extends existing faceted models of intelligence (e.g., emotional intelligence, practical intelligence, multiple intelligences) into the intercultural realm.

Cultural Intelligence research addresses the question: *Why are some individuals and organizations more effective in crossing cultures than others? How do they become effective?* This question shifts the dominant focus of cross-cultural psychology and management research in the twentieth century from a comparative approach (i.e., why and how do cultures differ) to a capability approach. Defining what this capability entails to help people and organizations bridge cultural differences marks the major contribution of my research on CQ.

My sabbatical after Y2K offered me a timely space to explore and integrate the two established bodies of research on culture and intelligence. Christopher Earley and I secured a two-book contract with Stanford University Press to explicate this new construct. The two books targeted two different audiences—the first book scientists, and the second practitioners. This challenged me to strike two bowls.

Some people have asked me, "Why did you embark on the research with a book, instead of writing a conceptual piece for a journal?" Writing a book freed me from the constraint of page and word limits required by journals, and allowed me to develop ideas of CQ in greater depth and breadth. I drew from multiple disciplines—intelligence, culture, cultural anthropology, cross-cultural psychology, and cross-cultural communication—to develop the ontology of CQ. Unlike some authors who write what they know, I wrote to discover. The writing process exhilarated and inspired me to dig more deeply into the CQ phenomenon.

Bowl 1: The Science Bowl

Scientists focus on the rigor of scientific inquiry, which centers on the "what" and the "why" questions of a construct or a phenomenon. As with any study of a new construct, I first defined the essential concept of CQ (what is CQ and how it was similar to and different from other constructs) and its nomological network. Next, I developed a valid measure of CQ in order to test theories and advance empirical research.

I articulated three major principles, which I describe as three "strikes" of the science bowl. They are (1) the conceptualization of CQ; (2) the measurement of CQ; and (3) the nomological network of CQ.

Strike 1: The Conceptualization of Cultural Intelligence

The extant research on cross-cultural competencies offers a wide array of frameworks and measures to assess cultural competencies. (See the review by

Leung, Ang, & Tan, 2014.) A challenge to this body of work, however, is the "jingle and jangle" of constructs—where constructs with the same meaning are labeled differently while constructs with different meanings are labeled similarly (Gelfand, Imai, & Fehr, 2008).

Rather than adopting the inductive approach popular in the extant literature (see Matsumoto & Hwang, 2013), I conceptualize CQ using a theoretically deductive approach. First, I define CQ as a set of capabilities of individuals, teams, or organizations that enable them to function effectively in culturally diverse settings. As such, CQ refers to a culture-general construct that is independent of specific cultural settings (see also Ng & Earley, 2006). Moreover, unlike traditional notions of cultural competence that focus on cultural knowledge and skills (i.e., demonstrated behaviors), CQ emphasizes dynamic and motivated processing of information in culturally novel and diverse settings via two additional capabilities: metacognition and motivation (Ang, Ng, & Rockstuhl, 2020a).

Second, drawing from the multiple-loci-of-intelligence framework (Sternberg, 1986), Linn Van Dyne and I (2008) have proposed four distinct dimensions: (1) metacognitive CQ (i.e., a person's capability to acquire and make sense of cultural knowledge); (2) cognitive CQ (i.e., a person's knowledge about how cultures are similar to and different from each other); (3) motivational CQ (i.e., a person's capability to direct attention and sustain energy toward learning to function effectively in intercultural contexts); and (4) behavioral CQ (i.e., a person's capability to exhibit a wide repertoire of verbal and nonverbal behaviors in intercultural interactions; see also, on code-switching, Molinsky, 2007).

Building on this individual-level construct, Andrew Inkpen and I advanced a firm-level conceptualization of CQ (Ang & Inkpen, 2008). We asked this question, "Why are some firms more efficient and effective in their international ventures than others?" Drawing on a resource-based view of the firm, we proposed three components of firm-level CQ: (1) managerial CQ (i.e., the CQ of the top management team); (2) competitive CQ (i.e. the firm's capability to identify, calibrate, and manage international competition); and (3) structural CQ (i.e., the development of routines and norms to govern intra- and interorganizational interfaces).

Strike 2: Measurement

With the conceptualization of CQ, I developed valid measures of CQ to advance empirical research and promote evidence-based practices. Here

I describe the rigorous methodological process we undertook in developing the multiple probes of CQ.

The original 20-item Cultural Intelligence Survey (CQS). Van Dyne and I developed the first psychometric instrument for assessing CQ (Ang et al., 2007) based on a four-factor model. We validated and triangulated our measure following a rigorous scale development and validation process.

First, we developed operational definitions for each of the four factors of CQ based on a thorough review of the relevant literatures and interviews with eight global executives. Second, we generated an initial item pool of 53 items to allow for psychometric refinement. Third, we asked a panel of scientists and executives to rank-order the items in terms of clarity, readability, and fidelity. We retained the 10 best items for each CQ factor, resulting in an initial 40-item version.

We then refined and validated the scale in a series of six studies. In Study 1, with participants from Singapore, we assessed the factor structure of the scale using confirmatory factor analyses (CFA). We deleted items with high residuals, low factor loadings and small standard deviations or extreme means, and low item-to-total correlations. This resulted in a 20-item version that demonstrates discriminant validity of the four factors, and high internal consistencies (ranging from .71 to .85). In Study 2, we replicated the psychometric properties of the 20-item scale with a different sample from Singapore.

In the next three studies, we tested the generalizability of the 20-item scale across time (Study 3), countries (Study 4), and methods (Study 5). In Study 3, we examined the longitudinal measurement invariance of the CQS across a four-month period using CFA. This involved testing for invariance of factor loadings, intercepts, and means. Results showed that the CQS demonstrated factorial and intercept invariance, suggesting that the scale has high test-retest reliability. At the same time, we found that latent means changed over time, supporting our conceptualization of CQ as a malleable construct that can be developed. In Study 4, we assessed the equivalence of the CQS across a Singaporean and US samples using a sequential test of model invariance. Results demonstrate strong support for the four-factor structure in both samples.

In Study 5, we tested the generalizability of the self-report measure of CQS with an observer measure of CQS using multitrait, multimethod (MTMM) and CFA. In a sample of US executives, we obtained self-reports and observer reports of their CQ and interactional adjustment. For the CQS to be generalizable across methods, results from both self-reported and observer-reported measures would need to be similar. The results demonstrated both convergent and discriminant validity of the CQS. For instance, self-ratings and observer-ratings of all the four factors were significantly correlated ($r = .41$ to $r = .54$), suggesting convergent validity. Further, these correlations are higher than correlations of the validity diagonal, suggesting discriminant validity. Results of the CFA MTMM analyses further show that traits explained 43% of the total variance while methods explained only 22%, confirming the generalizability of the scale across self-ratings and observer ratings.

In addition to the reliability and factor structure, we tested the criterion validity of the CQS in Study 5. The results showed that self-rated CQS predicted observer-rated interactional adjustment. Similarly, observer-rated CQS also predicted self-rated interactional adjustment. These results provide strong evidence for the predictive validity of CQS.

In Study 6, we tested the incremental predictive validity of the CQS, controlling for cognitive ability and EQ. We measured three outcomes: cultural judgment and decision-making (CJDM), interactional adjustment, and mental well-being. Our results demonstrated (1) the four factors from the outcomes had discriminant validity; (2) metacognitive CQ and cognitive CQ predicted CJDM; and (3) motivational CQ and behavioral CQ predicted interactional adjustment and well-being, controlling for demographics (age, sex), cognitive ability, and EQ.

The 37-item E-CQS. Following the 20-item CQS, my colleagues and I developed an expanded version to measure subdimensions of the four CQ factors (Van Dyne et al., 2012). The E-CQS comprises 11 subdimensions. Specifically, metacognitive CQ includes planning, awareness, and checking. Cognitive CQ encompasses both cultural-general and culture-specific knowledge. Motivational CQ distinguishes between intrinsic interest, extrinsic interest, and self-efficacy for intercultural encounters. Finally, behavioral CQ includes flexibility in verbal behaviors, nonverbal behaviors, and speech-acts.

Specifying subdimensions of the four broad CQ factors facilitates (1) more nuanced theorizing, especially in terms of explicating underlying processes of CQ effects; (2) more precise matching of cultural intelligence predictors and outcomes; and (3) identification of concrete ways to train cultural intelligence. Importantly, the distinction between culture-general and culture-specific knowledge in cognitive CQ enables a more contextualized application of CQ to different domains. *Culture-general knowledge* refers to understanding of universal (etic) elements of culture, as measured in the original CQS. By contrast, context-specific knowledge refers to understanding of domain-specific (emic) norms and expectations of a specific group of people. Domains could be a country (e.g., how do people decline a request in Japan) or a specific subculture based on professions (e.g., business managers, teachers, diplomats, etc.) or demographic groupings (e.g., age, gender, etc.). Incorporating context-specific knowledge offers a "plugged and played" source for more precise predictions in different contexts.

Using data from 286 individuals from more than 30 countries, we conducted CFA to assess the discriminant validity of the subdimensions within each CQ factor. Results showed that the data fit well to the hypothesized model for each factor. We also conducted CFA to assess the 11-factor vis-à-vis the 4-factor structure. Results showed that the fit of the former, with four correlated second-order factors, was better than the latter, with four correlated first-order factors. This provides support for the 11 subdimensions of the four-factor CQ.

Performance-based measures of CQ. The CQS and E-CQS are report-based measures of CQ. Responding to Gelfand and colleagues' (2008) call for methodological diversity, Rockstuhl, Ng, Lievens, Van Dyne, and I embarked on developing situational judgment tests (SJTs) as a form of performance-based measure of CQ (Rockstuhl, Ang, Ng, Lievens, & Van Dyne, 2015). We chose to develop multimedia SJTs over the more common text-based SJTs so as to achieve greater task stimulus fidelity. Moreover, since "life is not multiple choice," we adopted a constructed-response (i.e., open-ended) format rather than a selected-response (i.e., closed-ended) format for greater response fidelity. That is, participants had to watch short video scenarios of intercultural conflict in the workplace, and then describe what they would do to resolve the conflict.

Our research shows promising predictive validity of the SJT. In three studies involving students and professionals working in multicultural teams, we found that SJT performance predicted peer-rated task performance and citizenship behaviors, controlling for the Big Five personality traits, general cognitive ability, international experience, and demographic characteristics (Rockstuhl et al., 2015).

Another performance-based measure is the assessment center. We developed the CQ assessment center with George Thornton, who visited the center. The assessment center exercise assessed behavioral CQ: the ability of participants to vary their behaviors to suit the cultural context. To do so, participants played the role of a leader who had to give feedback to two subordinates, one from a Western culture with a direct style of communication, the other from an Asian culture with an indirect style of communication. We hired and trained professional Caucasian and Asian actors to enact the roles of the subordinates based on actors' assigned cultural profiles. We then video-recorded participants' interactions with the two subordinates and coded their variations in speech-acts and verbal and nonverbal behaviors across the two episodes of interaction.

Strike 3: A Nomological Network

Understanding how CQ is related to other constructs is key to establishing its construct validity. Linn Van Dyne and I proposed a CQ nomological network in the *Handbook of Cultural Intelligence* (Ang & Van Dyne, 2008). A metaanalysis involving 167 empirical studies and 199 independent samples (N=44,155) reveals that CQ relates meaningfully to a diverse range of constructs (Rockstuhl & Van Dyne, 2018). I will review empirical evidence of the nomological network of CQ briefly here (see also Ang, Ng, & Rockstuhl, 2020b; Van Dyne, Ang, & Tan, 2019).

Antecedents. Studies show that Big Five personality traits and international experience predict CQ (Ang, Van Dyne, & Koh, 2006; Rockstuhl & Van Dyne, 2018) but the strength of these relationships depends on boundary conditions. For example, Li, Mobley, and Kelly (2013) found that learning style moderates the relationship between experience and CQ, such that people with divergent learning styles are more likely to translate their international experiences into higher CQ. Chao, Takeuchi, and Farh (2017) have suggested that implicit culture beliefs affect how individuals develop their CQ during international assignments via cultural adjustment.

Correlates. Studies demonstrate that CQ is distinct from, and related to, other forms of intelligence such as IQ and EQ (e.g., Ang et al., 2007; Rockstuhl & Van Dyne, 2018). Other correlates of CQ include global identity (Erez, Lisak, Harush, Glikson, Nouri, & Shokef, 2013)—the sense of belongingness to a global versus a local community; and context dependence (Adair, Buchan, Chen, & Liu, 2016)—an individual's attentiveness to contextual cues during communication.

Outcomes. Research demonstrates that CQ predicts many outcomes. Examples include (1) sociocultural adjustment (e.g., Ang et al., 2007; Chen, Kirkman, Kim, Farh, & Tangirala, 2010; Firth, Chen, Kirkman, & Kim, 2014; Volpone, Marquardt, Casper, & Avery, 2018); (2) cultural judgment and decision-making (Ang et al., 2007); (3) job performance, including task (e.g., Chen, Liu, & Portnoy, 2012) and contextual (Ng, Van Dyne, & Ang, 2019) performance; (4) leadership performance (e.g., Groves & Feyerherm, 2011; Rockstuhl, Seiler, Ang, Van Dyne, & Annen, 2011); (5) negotiation effectiveness (e.g., Imai & Gelfand, 2010); (6) creativity (Chua & Ng, 2017; Xu & Chen, 2017); and (7) cultural learning (e.g., Morris, Savani, & Fincher, 2019).

Metaanalytic structural equation modeling by Rockstuhl and Van Dyne (2018) showed that both a four-factor CQ model and a general latent CQ model predicted observer-rated task performance via two mediators: sociocultural adjustment and cultural judgment and decision-making. The results of the metaanalysis suggest a bifactor model of CQ, where the CQ factors provide both holistic and unique information.

The Resonance of the Science Bowl

Here I will discuss how the three "strikes" of the science bowl—the conceptualization, measurement, and nomological network of CQ— resonated with and contributed to the scientific community.

Conceptualization. In a review of 100 years of culture research in the *Journal of Applied Psychology,* Gelfand, Aycan, Erez, and Leung (2017: 523) called for the focus of research to shift from cross-cultural differences to cross-cultural interactions, and for researchers to be "in closer contact with the cultural intelligence and diversity management literatures to develop theories capturing processes and outcomes of cross-cultural interactions." Hence, CQ's paradigmatic shift from cross-cultural difference to cross-cultural interactions two decades ago continues to resonate with scientists today.

Gelfand et al. (2008) also highlighted three notable contributions of CQ. First, CQ "breaks new ground" by integrating culture and intelligence. In doing so, CQ broadens the extant intelligence literature by addressing the demands of a culturally diverse environment. Second, the CQ construct offers theoretical parsimony, synthesis, and coherence as it captures the different bases of capabilities (cognitive, metacognitive, motivational, and behavioral) that many other cultural competency frameworks do not. Third, CQ also offers theoretical precision and cleans up the "jingle and jangle" of the extant cultural competence literature.

Measurement. This stream of research on CQ measurement offers three contributions to the field. First, the 20-item CQS ignited an exponential growth of empirical research on CQ by offering scientists a validated measure of CQ. Publishing the full scale in an article (Ang et al., 2007) allowed other researchers to incorporate CQ into their research questions and design their studies more readily, thus allowing us to accumulate and advance our knowledge of CQ. Indeed, Rockstuhl and Van Dyne's (2018) metaanalysis showed that in a relatively short span of 10 years, the field has accumulated a significant number of studies examining the predictive validity of CQ using the CQS (199 independent samples; N=44,155).

Second, the CQS provided researchers with a valid measure to assess CQ. Kraimer, Bolino, and Mead (2016: 90) remarked that the CQ framework and the CQS "prompted recent, highly cited empirical research" in expatriation. In a comprehensive review of existing cultural competence measures,

Matsumoto and Hwang (2013) concluded that the CQS is one of the three measures in the field that holds the most promising evidence for measuring cultural competence. This review shows that, consistently across studies conducted in different countries, results confirm the four-factor structure of CQ, and demonstrate high internal consistencies for the factors in the scale (above .70).

Third, the different probes of CQ (the report- and performance-based measures) allow for triangulation of findings, as well as offering choices for researchers depending on the outcomes of interest. I recommend that researchers choose the type of CQ measure they will use depending on their research question and design and the feasibility of the assessment.

The nomological network. Establishing the nomological network of CQ, especially in how CQ predicts outcomes, offers important construct validity evidence for the scale. Matsumoto and Hwang (2013: 856) remarked in their comparison of 10 cultural competence scales that "there is considerable evidence for the concurrent and predictive ecological validity of CQ with samples from multiple cultures." The explication of the CQ nomological network has also contributed to the advance of science by "connecting research across disciplinary borders," and—even within the field of management—"helps to integrate a broad number of topics" (Gelfand et al., 2008: 377). This is made possible by offering to researchers across different disciplines a common intellectual framework and validated measures of CQ.

Challenges

Striking the "scientist bowl" is not without its challenges. The construct of CQ, as a "new kid on the scientific block," has raised many questions from reviewers concerning its nature. Here I share two significant ones we have encountered.

The nomenclature of intelligence. The influential economist John Maynard Keynes famously said, "The difficulty lies not so much in developing new ideas as in escaping from old ones" (cited in Shtulman, 2017: 252). I have experienced how old ideas could constrain the appreciation of new ideas. Reviewers and editors, reflecting the broader debate among psychologists about the meaning of the term "intelligence," raised concerns about our use of the "intelligence" label. This debate stems from the established tradition of research on IQ tests focusing on intelligence as a general cognitive ability (Sternberg, 2019). Proponents of this narrow view of intelligence questioned whether noncognitive capabilities such as CQ constitute a form of intelligence. Sternberg (2019: 24) noted how, "despite the definition of intelligence as adaptation, the usual use of the term has little to do with adaptation.... 'Intelligence' has been used for more than a century to refer to a fairly standardized set of cognitive abilities."

Addressing reviewers' concerns on the nature of CQ requires a deep understanding of the huge body of research on intelligence. This includes understanding the historical context of research on intelligence and how researchers from diverse disciplines have defined and measured it. Recent reviews and integration of the diverse views of intelligence provided a strong theoretical basis for the conceptualization of CQ, in two ways (Sternberg, 2019). First, our definition of CQ as a capability to function effectively in culturally diverse settings (Earley & Ang, 2003) aligns with contemporary conceptualizations of intelligence as a person's adaptability to a specific environment (Sternberg, 2019). Sternberg has argued that "intelligence crucially involves the ability to adapt to the environment" and that "intelligence . . . always occurs in, and hence is mediated by, a cultural context" (2019: 23, 24).

Second, Sternberg's (1986) multiloci framework of intelligence at the molar (including metacognitive, cognitive, and motivational capabilities) and behavioral levels within a person offers the theoretical basis for conceptualizing the four factors of CQ (metacognitive, cognitive, motivational, and behavioral capabilities).

The discriminant validity of a new construct. A second common review point concerns the discriminant validity of CQ. Reviewers have often asked how CQ is distinct from related constructs such as other forms of intelligence, personality, and existing cultural competences. This reflects a common "growing pain" associated with "young" constructs like CQ.

To respond to reviewers' requests, we dug through the large and unsystematic body of literature on intercultural competencies and compared CQ with other intercultural competency models and instruments (Ang et al., 2007; Ang et al., 2020a; Leung et al., 2014). We also designed research studies to measure as many related constructs (e.g., IQ, EQ, personality, other cross-cultural competencies, etc.) as possible to demonstrate discriminant validity and incremental predictive validity.

I credit the eventual breakthrough in the CQ research journey to our having the persistence and tenacity to respond to reviewers' questions and requests. As an editor and reviewer myself, I know that reviewers put in great effort to help authors strengthen their studies. Therefore, as an author, I treat every reviewer's points and suggestions seriously and with respect. Even if a reviewer's suggestion does not work, I find alternative ways to address the underlying concern. I ensure that the revised manuscript addresses the weaknesses of the previous manuscript and emerges as a stronger study.

Bowl 2: The Practice Bowl

Practitioners focus primarily on how CQ can solve their problems. To help it resonate with practitioners, I have adopted two major approaches: (1) conducting sustained inquiry and observations in organizations, and (2) designing evidence-based interventions.

Strike 1: Sustained Inquiry and Observations in Organizations

Engaged scholarship involves close collaboration with organizations to understand a complex phenomenon and uses scientific inquiry to help them solve complex problems (Van de Ven, 2007). Here I discuss two strategies for working with organizations: conducting translational research and choosing collaborative relationships carefully.

Conducting translational research. Reaching out to organizations requires a different language. One significant difference between the practice audience and the science audience lies with the preference for in-depth case studies versus experiments. Practitioners often prefer case studies because they are richer in contextual details, which allows them to decide for themselves whether the case situation is like their own, and thus whether the findings— the "how"—truly apply to them.

In writing the second book in our two-book contract with Stanford University Press (Earley, Ang, & Tan, 2006), we relied more on vignettes and case studies of real intercultural challenges to bring out our points, rather than statistical results. Instead of expounding on the conceptual basis of CQ, the second book focuses on applying CQ in solving management problems, including how to succeed in global work assignments, how to build high-performing multicultural teams, and how to lead people from different cultures. Subsequently, I moved from writing practice-oriented materials myself to finding collaborators who can translate CQ research into accessible trade books. David Livermore is a key partner who successfully translated CQ research into accessible trade books to reach the practice community (e.g., Livermore, 2015).

We also disseminated our research to the practice community through conferences. Kok-Yee Ng and I organized our first CQ conference targeted at practitioners in Shanghai. As China was growing exponentially in its global trade, demand for CQ was also growing. Organizing this CQ conference was a cross-cultural adventure in itself, as it was conducted in Mandarin (which required us to use a translator). The conference succeeded in disseminating our work to a practice audience, as it attracted more than 400 practitioners and gained attention in the local press. Shortly after the conference, we received many requests for a Chinese version of our CQ scale. Not having completed our extensive validation of the scale, we scaled back on our outreach to practice. We were simply not ready.

Choosing collaborative relationships with care. Cultural intelligence caught the attention of many large multinational organizations once Stanford University Press released the first book. I received numerous requests from organizations expressing interest in applying CQ to their work. Many asked me to give a talk or conduct workshops for executives. Responding to all these requests was neither feasible nor effective. Instead, I prioritized my collaborations with industry. I worked with early adopters who seriously intended to nurture a long-term research and development partnership rather than organizations who wanted a one-shot intervention, such as giving a talk or conducting a workshop. Giving priority to long-term partnerships enables me to probe more deeply the problems and phenomena the organizations face, to design interventions and collect data to assess their impact, and to offer contextualized solutions to solve the organizations' real challenges.

Over the years, I have collaborated with a number of local and global organizations. Local organizations include the Singapore Armed Forces and the Public Service Division of the Prime Minister's Office. With these large organizations, Ng and I developed systematic and evidence-based leadership development interventions that were contextualized to the organizations' culture and leadership demands. Outside Singapore, we collaborated and worked with SAP Labs China (Shanghai) on working in global teams; with the International Air Transport Association (Switzerland) on designing its global leadership development and performance management systems; with the International Organization for Standardization (Switzerland) on global standards setting; and with Nippon Telephone and Telegraph (Japan) on developing an online e-learning module on CQ.

I have also extended my collaborations to work with educators, since the Ministry of Education in Singapore has designated cultural intelligence (global awareness and cross-cultural skills) as a key twenty-first-century competency for students. I partnered with principals and teachers of elementary and middle schools to infuse CQ into their curriculum. This has required that we first develop capabilities in teachers to teach CQ. It has also required that we translate our research into age-appropriate concepts and materials so as to resonate with elementary and middle school students. Students now learn about CQ in different subject areas (e.g., second language, literature, social studies), inbound and outbound exchange programs, and service-learning journeys.

Strike 2: Designing Evidence-Based Interventions

Organizations and schools believe that CQ is important for the challenges of the twenty-first century. What they lack are systematic interventions to help develop CQ in their employees and students. Many have assumed that they could develop CQ in their leaders or students by merely exposing them to intercultural experiences, whether through an overseas assignment or working in multicultural teams.

To debunk this myth, Ng, Van Dyne, and I published a study in *Academy of Management Learning and Education* explaining why experience is not equal to experiential learning (Ng, Van Dyne, & Ang, 2009). We argued that CQ enhances leaders' ability to engage in the full cycle of experiential learning of concrete experiences, reflective observations, abstract conceptualization, and active experimentation. Further, we suggested how organizations can translate leaders' experiences into experiential learning through their policies and practices for global work assignments.

Two related research paradigms have influenced our thinking regarding the design of interventions for CQ development (see also Ng, Tan, & Ang, 2011; Ng et al., 2009): situated learning (Lave & Wenger, 1991) and experiential learning theory (Kolb, 2015). Both emphasize the importance of actual experiences for the development of complex capabilities such as CQ. Situated learning theory posits that "knowing" cannot be separated from "doing" and that working on authentic or realistic tasks facilitates learning (Lave & Wenger, 1991). Experiential learning theory provides an account of how individuals might develop their CQ from intercultural experiences. In particular, this theory suggests that learning occurs in a cycle of (1) engaging in concrete experiences, (2) reflecting critically on the experiences, (3) abstracting these reflections into general theories to guide future behavior, and (4) experimenting actively with the new behaviors to assess their effectiveness.

Based on these theories, our interventions emphasize a combination of knowledge, powerful experiences, and feedback. For instance, in our long-term collaboration with the International Air Transport Association, the trade association that represents and leads the global aviation industry, we infused CQ into their Intercultural Leadership Engagement and Development Program—an intensive leadership program targeted at grooming high-potential leaders. Ng and I developed a multimedia case study that described the context, process, and outcomes of the association's transformation into a culturally intelligent organization (Ng & Ang, 2012), based on our theory on how firms' global culture capital (i.e., organizational mindset and routines) shapes their cosmopolitan human capital (i.e., CQ and intercultural experience) (Ng et al., 2011).

Evaluating the effectiveness of evidence-based interventions is essential in our collaborative partnerships with organizations. We have adopted quasi-experimental designs, such as the recurrent institutional cycle design (Campbell & Stanley, 1963), for interventions that are conducted on a cyclical basis (e.g., annual programs). We have collected self and observer CQ ratings before and after an intervention with different cohorts of participants. We have then assessed the different cohorts of data for measurement equivalence, before comparing the postintervention scores of a cohort with the preintervention scores of the next cohort (as a comparison, baseline measure) to assess the impact of the intervention. In addition to quasi-experimental designs, we have also adopted person-based analyses to identify distinct clusters of participants with differentiated growth. This approach not only offers more fine-grained insights into how different subgroups of participants benefit from the CQ intervention but also offers insights into factors that contribute to the different patterns of growth.

Our interventions extend beyond training and development to include selection. In one instance, we worked with a global organization that was going through a worldwide restructuring, where a number of local offices had to cease operations. The restructuring resulted in the redeployment of a group of employees to regional offices. Given that regional offices are more culturally diverse than local offices, the organization wanted to know whether CQ could predict who would perform better in regional offices. To address this question, we designed a study with the organization to assess employees' CQ using the multimedia SJT. Three months after employees were redeployed to the regional offices, we collected performance data from their new supervisors. Our results showed that employees who performed better in the multimedia SJT received higher performance ratings after three months into their jobs in the regional offices, thus demonstrating the value of the CQ multimedia SJT for selection.

The Resonance of the Practice Bowl

The overwhelmingly positive response from industry early in my CQ journey demonstrated the resonance of the CQ concept with practice. Cultural intelligence shapes the global human capital policies and practices of multinational corporations in different ways. For instance, the International Air Transport Association adopted CQ as a key performance metric in their performance appraisal system. Through the Center for Cultural Intelligence in Michigan, organizations such as Coca-Cola, Google, IBM, MacDonald's, and Unilever have incorporated CQ into their talent management programs; and more than 100,000 individuals from over 161 nations have received their CQ profiles by completing the CQS or E-CQS. In addition, as many as 400 universities teach CQ in various programs, including study-abroad and MBA programs.

Challenges

As we did with the science bowl, we faced challenges with striking the practice bowl. Practitioners value speed, while scientists value rigor. Organizations often want quick solutions to their problems, which poses a challenge to scientists' need for rigorous and evidence-based solutions. As a scientist-practitioner, I need to respect the timelines of organizations yet not succumb to their pressure by pushing out instruments or interventions prematurely. It is also important that I educate my practice-collaborators about the importance of designing interventions based on scientific principles of inquiry.

Another challenge arises from top leadership transitions in long-term projects. Typically CEOs stay for three to five years, while some of my projects span a decade. When the original sponsor of the project leaves the organization, the research team needs to socialize the new leader in the project. I have learned that developing a rigorous measurement system to demonstrate the "returns on investment" enables us to offer critical evidence to win over new management and gain their buy-in.

The Wooden Base: Institutional and Community Building

Providing a stable base to support the two bowls is critical. Institution and community building draws valuable resources and opportunities and, more importantly, creates a larger ecosystem for disseminating, advancing, and sustaining the research on CQ. In 2004, Ng and I started the Center for Leadership and Cultural Intelligence at the Nanyang Business School. In operating a research center in a business school, it is imperative that we strike the science bowl and the practice bowl concurrently. The center's mission—to lead in the knowledge, assessments, and programs for growing culturally intelligent leaders and organizations—reflects this scientist-practitioner identity and focus on applied research.

Shortly after we founded the center, Professor Guan Ning Su, then president of NTU, recognized the potential impact of CQ research and unequivocally funded the center for our research. The grant enabled me to build a community of scientists through CQ conferences and competitive grants. For instance, we organized CQ conferences to gather culture scientists to push the boundaries of research on CQ. We awarded competitive grants to promote research on CQ, and we shortlisted candidates to present their research proposals. This strategy resulted in rigorous and creative research proposals on CQ. For example, Chen, Kirkman, and Kim's winning proposal on CQ in expatriate employees won the Best Paper Award at the 2009 Academy of Management conference and was subsequently published in the *Academy of Management Journal* (Chen et al., 2010).

Developing and sustaining any programmatic research requires close collaborative relationships with scientists and practitioners. Two criteria guide my choice of close collaborators—people who "sojourn" with me in this pilgrim's journey with CQ. First, I look for complementary fit—those who bring a fresh research perspective or question, a new discipline, or new content into existing research on CQ. Second, I look for people who are highly motivated in their pursuit of excellence (in science or in practice) as well as competent. Over the years, I have developed close collaborations with scientists and practitioners from more than 20 nations in North America, Europe, Asia, Australia/New Zealand, the Middle East, and elsewhere.

In 2009, I started another center, the Culture Science Institute, with former colleagues C. Y. Chiu and Ying-Yi Hong, which was funded by the NTU President at that time, Bertil Andersson. While the Center for Leadership and Cultural Intelligence focuses on applied research, the Culture Science Institute focuses on basic research on culture, at four levels of analysis—(1) culture and the brain (neuroscience), (2) culture and the mind (cognition), (3) culture and behavior, and (4) culture and society. These two centers complement each other in terms of the research questions addressed. Extending the spectrum of research on culture, the two centers work jointly to attract more culture scientists to the Nanyang Business School, and so the school supports a vanguard of culture science experts, including cognitive scientists (e.g., Krishna Savani, Zou Xi) and neuroscientists (e.g., George Christopoulos).

The two centers also attract a number of postdocs and doctoral students from different parts of the world. To date, postdocs and PhD students from China, France, Germany, India, Japan, the Philippines, Portugal, South Korea, and the United States have come through the two centers. They bring diverse perspectives and extend my capacity to push new boundaries in our CQ research.

The Future of Cultural Intelligence

As I enter the third decade of my journey, two ideas to create new resonance for the science and practice bowls excite me. I share these two ideas here.

The Science Bowl: Cultural Intelligence 2.0

To date, CQ research examines intercultural interactions primarily through a horizontal differentiation lens. That is, they tend to focus on cross-cultural differences in the way people think, feel, and act as a result of socialization in different cultural environments. The horizontal differential lens emphasizes anxiety reduction and uncertainty due to unfamiliarity during intercultural interactions (Gudykunst, 1993).

The vertical differentiation lens offers a different and increasingly important perspective based on social injustice and status and power disparities (Bunderson & Van der Vegt, 2018). Status characteristics theory and status organizing process suggest that evaluations people make of others often result in unequal social interactions. Attributes such as nationality, ethnicity, and gender evoke inequality and power imbalance due to sociohistorical events such as colonialization, oppression, and marginalization. Vertically differentiated interactions create different concerns for members of the dominant group versus the minority groups. Building on this stream of research, I intend to broaden the conceptualization of CQ to embrace dynamics of vertical differentiation, from the point of view of both the dominant and minority groups.

The Practice Bowl: Culturally Intelligent Virtual Humans

Advances in information and communication technology create exciting opportunities to revolutionize CQ training. For instance, we can leverage artificial intelligence and immersive technologies such as virtual reality to develop culturally adaptive agents—interactive digital agents who can adapt their verbal and nonverbal behaviors according to different cultural norms.

Using culturally intelligent virtual humans to train and develop CQ in actual humans could offer several advantages. First, it would reduce the need for human trainers, making what is currently labor-intensive training more scalable and cost-efficient. Second, by offering an immersive experience, this kind of high-fidelity training would elicit trainees' reactions as though they were *in* the situation, as opposed to eliciting trainees' reactions *to* a low fidelity simulation. Third, the virtual humans could record and store interaction data, including the tracing of attentional and emotional processes of the trainee. This would allow for online real-time feedback to trainees to enhance their self-awareness and learning.

Conclusion

I started the research on CQ in 2000. Twenty years later, I look back at this journey with satisfaction about three key contributions of my efforts. First, by integrating the science on culture and intelligence, I have catalyzed a paradigmatic shift from studying cross-cultural differences to studying intercultural capabilities. By anchoring the research in the multiloci theory of intelligence, I have offered a comprehensive yet parsimonious construct to define the cognitive, metacognitive, motivational, and behavioral bases of CQ. The widespread adoption of this paradigmatic shift in diverse academic disciplines demonstrates the resonance of the CQ construct with scientists.

Second, I have developed multiple instruments to measure CQ, including report-based measures (i.e., the 20-item CQS and 37-item E-CQS) and performance-based measures (i.e., multimedia intercultural SJT, the assessment center, and sociometer to assess honest signals). These complementary measures allow for triangulation of findings and enable researchers to choose the appropriate measures based on the purpose and context of their research.

Third, CQ also exerts important influence in the private and public sectors, as well as in education at all levels, ranging from universities to elementary and grade schools. Through deep, engaged scholarship with organizations, my work shapes policies and practices directly and indirectly, and helps leaders become more effective.

In describing my journey, I chose the metaphor of "two bowls singing" to symbolize the resonance of CQ with science and practice. The sympathetic resonance of the two bowls also highlights the virtuous circle between science and practice. Good science makes the practice bowl sing. Important questions and insightful observations from practice make the science bowl sing. When the two bowls "sing" together, they create a deep humming resonance that will last longer and create a deeper impact on the listener. .

Acknowledgments

Supporting the two bowls and sustaining their resonance requires an intentional effort to build institutions and the community of scientists and practitioners. I am grateful to NTU for support and recognition of my work. I also thank my collaborators, specifically Kok-Yee Ng, Linn Van Dyne, Thomas Rockstuhl, David Livermore, Mei-Ling Tan, Vanessa Barros, and Yih-Tin Lee for their blessed friendship and for being my partners-in-crime in my journey.

In addition, I thank Kok Yee Ng, Cynthia Beath, Thomas Rockstuhl, Xiao-Ping Chen, and the two anonymous reviewers for their constructive and insightful comments on earlier drafts of this chapter.

References

Adair, W. L., Buchan, N. R., Chen, X. P., & Liu, D. (2016). A model of communication context and measure of context dependence. *Academy of Management Discoveries, 2*, 198–217.

Adair, W. L., Hideg, I., & Spence, J. R. (2013). The culturally intelligent team: The impact of team cultural intelligence and cultural heterogeneity on team shared values. *Journal of Cross-cultural Psychology, 44*, 941–962.

Ang, S., & Inkpen, A. C. (2008). Cultural intelligence and offshore outsourcing success: A framework of firm-level intercultural capability. *Decision Sciences, 39*, 337–358.

Ang, S., Ng, K. Y., & Rockstuhl, T. (2020a) (forthcoming). Cultural competence. In *The Oxford research encyclopedia of psychology*. New York: Oxford University Press.

Ang, S., Ng, K. Y., & Rockstuhl, T. (2020b) (forthcoming). Cultural intelligence. In R. J. Sternberg & S. B. Kaufman (Eds.), *The Cambridge handbook of intelligence* (2nd ed.). New York: Cambridge University Press.

Ang, S., & Van Dyne, L. (Eds.). (2008). *Handbook of cultural intelligence*. New York: M. E. Sharpe.

Ang, S., Van Dyne, L., & Koh, C. (2006). Personality correlates of the four-factor model of cultural intelligence. *Group & Organization Management, 31*, 100–123.

Ang, S., Van Dyne, L., Koh, C., Ng, K. Y., Templer, K. J., Tay, C., & Chandrasekar, N. A. (2007). Cultural intelligence: Its measurement and effects on cultural judgment and decision making, cultural adaptation and task performance. *Management and Organization Review, 3*, 335–371.

Bunderson, J. S., & Van der Vegt, G. S. (2018). Diversity and inequality in management teams: A review and integration of research on vertical and horizontal member differences. *Annual Review of Organizational Psychology and Organizational Behavior, 5*, 47–73.

Campbell, D. T., & Stanley, J. C. (1963). *Experimental and quasi-experimental designs for research*. Palo Alto, CA: Houghton Mifflin.

Chao, M. M., Takeuchi, R., & Farh, J. L. (2017). Enhancing cultural intelligence: The roles of implicit culture beliefs and adjustment. *Personnel Psychology, 70*, 257–292.

Chen, G., Kirkman, B. L., Kim, K., Farh, C. I., & Tangirala, S. (2010). When does intercultural motivation enhance expatriate effectiveness? A multilevel investigation of the moderating roles of subsidiary support and cultural distance. *Academy of Management Journal, 53*, 1110–1130.

Chen, M. L., & Lin, C. P. (2013). Assessing the effects of cultural intelligence on team knowledge sharing from a socio-cognitive perspective. *Human Resource Management, 52*, 675–695.

Chen, X. P., Liu, D., & Portnoy, R. (2012). A multilevel investigation of motivational cultural intelligence, organizational diversity climate, and cultural sales: Evidence from U.S. real estate firms. *Journal of Applied Psychology, 97*, 93–106.

Chua, R. Y. J., Morris, M. W., & Mor, S. (2012). Collaborating across cultures: Cultural metacognition and affect-based trust in creative collaboration. *Organizational Behavior and Human Decision Processes, 118*, 116–131.

Chua, R. Y., & Ng, K. Y. (2017). Not just how much you know: Interactional effect of cultural knowledge and metacognition on creativity in a global context. *Management and Organization Review, 13*, 281–300.

Crotty, S. K., & Brett, J. M. (2012). Fusing creativity: Cultural metacognition and teamwork in multicultural teams. *Negotiation and Conflict Management Research, 5*, 210–234.

Earley, P. C., & Ang, S. (2003). *Cultural intelligence: Individual interactions across cultures*. Palo Alto, CA: Stanford University Press.

Earley, P. C., Ang, S., & Tan, J. S. (2006). *CQ: Developing cultural intelligence at work*. Palo Alto, CA: Stanford University Press.

Erez, M., Lisak, A., Harush, R., Glikson, E., Nouri, R., & Shokef, E. (2013). Going global: Developing management students' cultural intelligence and global identity in culturally diverse virtual teams. *Academy of Management Learning & Education, 12*, 330–355.

Firth, B. M., Chen, G., Kirkman, B. L., & Kim, K. (2014). Newcomers abroad: Expatriate adaptation during early phases of international assignments. *Academy of Management Journal, 57*, 280–300.

Gardner, H. (1993). *Multiple intelligences: The theory into practice*. New York: Basic Books.

Gelfand, M. J., Aycan, Z., Erez, M., & Leung, K. (2017). Cross-cultural industrial organizational psychology and organizational behavior: A hundred-year journey. *Journal of Applied Psychology, 102*, 514–529.

Gelfand, M. J., Imai, L., & Fehr, R. (2008). Thinking intelligently about cultural intelligence. In S. Ang, & L. Van Dyne (Eds.), *Handbook of cultural intelligence* (pp. 375–388). New York: M. E. Sharpe.

Groves, K. S., & Feyerherm, A. E. (2011). Leader cultural intelligence in context: Testing the moderating effects of team cultural diversity on leader and team performance. *Group & Organization Management, 36*, 535–566.

Gudykunst, W. B. (1993). Toward a theory of effective interpersonal and intergroup communication: An anxiety/uncertainty management (AUM) perspective. In R. L. Wiseman & J. Koester (Eds.), *International and intercultural communication annual, Vol. 17, Intercultural communication competence* (pp. 33–71). Thousand Oaks, CA: Sage Publications.

Imai, L., & Gelfand, M. J. (2010). The culturally intelligent negotiator: The impact of cultural intelligence (CQ) on negotiation sequences and outcomes. *Organizational Behavior and Human Decision Processes, 112*, 83–98.

Kolb, D. A. (2015). *Experiential learning: Experience as the source of learning and development* (2nd ed.). New Jersey: Pearson Education.

Korzilius, H., Bücker, J. J., & Beerlage, S. (2017). Multiculturalism and innovative work behavior: The mediating role of cultural intelligence. *International Journal of Intercultural Relations, 56*, 13–24.

Kraimer, M., Bolino, M., & Mead, B. (2016). Themes in expatriate and repatriate research over four decades: What do we know and what do we still need to learn? *Annual Review of Organizational Psychology and Organizational Behavior, 3*: 83–109.

Lave, J., & Wenger, E. (1991). *Situated learning: Legitimate peripheral participation.* Cambridge, UK: Cambridge University Press.

Leung, K., Ang, S., & Tan, M. L. (2014). Intercultural competence. *Annual Review of Organizational Psychology and Organizational Behavior, 1*, 489–519.

Li, M., Mobley, W. H., & Kelly, A. (2013). When do global leaders learn best to develop cultural intelligence? An investigation of the moderating role of experiential learning style. *Academy of Management Learning & Education, 12*, 32–50.

Livermore, D. A. (2015). *Leading with cultural intelligence: The real secret to success.* New York: AMACOM.

Matsumoto, D., & Hwang, H. C. (2013). Assessing cross-cultural competence: A review of available tests. *Journal of Cross-Cultural Psychology, 44*, 849–873.

Mayer, J. D., & Salovey, P. (1993). The intelligence of emotional intelligence. *Intelligence, 17*, 433–442.

Molinsky, A. (2007). Cross-cultural code-switching: The psychological challenges of adapting behavior in foreign cultural interactions. *Academy of Management Review, 32*, 622–640.

Morris, M. W., Savani, K., & Fincher, K. (2019). Metacognition fosters cultural learning: Evidence from individual differences and situational prompts. *Journal of Personality and Social Psychology, 116*, 46–68.

Ng, K. Y., & Ang, S. (2012). *Leading change globally with cultural intelligence.* Singapore: Center for Innovation Research in Cultural Intelligence and Leadership.

Ng, K. Y., & Earley, P. C. (2006). Culture + intelligence: Old constructs, new frontiers. *Group and Organization Management, 31*, 4–19.

Ng, K. Y., Tan, M. L., & Ang, S. (2011). Global culture capital and cosmopolitan human capital: The effects of global mindset and organizational routines on cultural intelligence and international experience. In A. Burton, & J. C. Spender (Eds.), *The Oxford handbook of human capital* (pp. 96–119). New York: Oxford University Press.

Ng, K. Y., Van Dyne, L., & Ang, S. (2009). From experience to experiential learning: Cultural intelligence as a learning capability for global leader development. *Academy of Management Learning & Education, 8*, 511–526.

Ng, K. Y., Van Dyne, A., & Ang, S. (2019). Speaking out and speaking up in multicultural settings: A two-study examination of cultural intelligence and voice behaviors. *Organizational Behavior and Human Decision Processes, 151*, 150–159.

Rockstuhl, T., Ang, S., Ng, K. Y., Lievens, F., & Van Dyne, L. (2015). Putting judging situations into situational judgment tests: Evidence from intercultural multimedia SJTs. *Journal of Applied Psychology, 100*, 464–480.

Rockstuhl, T., Seiler, S., Ang, S., Van Dyne, L., & Annen, H. (2011). Beyond general intelligence (IQ) and emotional intelligence (EQ): The role of cultural intelligence (CQ) on cross-border leadership effectiveness in a globalized world. *Journal of Social Issues, 67*, 825–840.

Rockstuhl, T., & Van Dyne, L. (2018). A bi-factor theory of the four-factor model of cultural intelligence: Meta-analysis and theoretical extensions. *Organizational Behavior and Human Decision Processes, 148*, 124–144.

Rousseau, D. M., & Gunia, B. C. (2016). Evidence-based practice: The psychology of EBP implementation. *Annual Review of Psychology, 67*, 667–692.

Shtulman, A. (2017). *Scienceblind: Why our intuitive theories about the world are so often wrong.* New York: Basic Books.

Sternberg, R. J. (1986). A framework for understanding conceptions of intelligence. In R. J. Sternberg & D. K. Detterman (Eds.), *What is intelligence? Contemporary viewpoints on its nature and definition* (pp. 3–15). Norwood, NJ: Ablex.

Sternberg, R. J. (2019). A theory of adaptive intelligence and its relation to general intelligence. *Journal of Intelligence, 7*, 23–39.

Sternberg, R. J., Forsythe, G. B., Hedlund, J., Horvath, J. A., Wagner, R. K., Williams, W. M., Snook, S. A., & Grigorenko, E. L. (2000). *Practical intelligence in everyday life.* Cambridge, UK: Cambridge University Press.

Triandis, H. C. (1972). *The analysis of subjective culture.* New York: Wiley.

Van de Ven, A. H. (2007). *Engaged scholarship: A guide for organizational and social research.* Oxford, UK: Oxford University Press.

Van Dyne, L., Ang, S., Ng, K. Y., Rockstuhl, T., Tan, M. L., & Koh, C. (2012). Sub-dimensions of the four factor model of cultural intelligence: Expanding the conceptualization and measurement of cultural intelligence. *Social and Personality Psychology Compass, 6*, 295–313.

Van Dyne, L., Ang, S., & Tan, M. L. (2019). Cultural intelligence. In R. Griffin (Ed.), *Oxford bibliographies in management.* New York: Oxford University Press.

Volpone, S. D., Marquardt, D. J., Casper, W. J., & Avery, D. R. (2018). Minimizing cross-cultural maladaptation: How minority status facilitates change in international acculturation. *Journal of Applied Psychology, 103*, 249–269.

Xu, X.-J., & Chen, X.-P. (2017). Unlocking expatriates' job creativity: The role of cultural learning, and metacognitive and motivational cultural intelligence. *Management and Organization Review, 13*, 767–794.

3

Making Sense of a Seemingly Random Walk

A Path toward Interdisciplinary Scholarship, and How to Avoid the Pitfalls along the Way

James D. Westphal

In this chapter I trace the origins of my research on corporate governance and describe the wide range of pitfalls and challenges I encountered early in my career. My research is fundamentally interdisciplinary, integrating social psychological, political, sociological, and economic processes to explain the determinants and consequences of corporate governance. It spans levels of analysis, from the cognitions of individual directors to firm-level corporate governance policies and to the influence of cultural norms at the societal level. The premise of the chapter is that many of the challenges I faced in developing this program of research are symptomatic of conducting cross-level, interdisciplinary research on virtually any topic in organizational theory and strategic management, and thus any lessons learned should be broadly applicable beyond the domain of corporate leadership and governance.

My program of research on behavioral governance had its origins in the boredom and disappointment of my early professional experience. After graduating with a degree in economics, I joined the executive compensation practice of a large management consulting firm in San Francisco. Rather than developing innovative compensation policies that promoted the strategic goals of high-technology companies in Silicon Valley, as I was led to expect, I found myself spending hour after hour reading proxy statements and annual reports of Fortune 500 companies, coding data on executive compensation plans. What could be more tedious than carefully recording information about the incentive plans of large industrial companies? Answer: conducting *historical* analysis of the incentive plans at each of those companies over the previous 10 years. The tedium of this work prompted several questions: why did I not listen to my undergraduate adviser and pursue a PhD in economics,

James D. Westphal, *Making Sense of a Seemingly Random Walk* In: *A Journey toward Influential Scholarship.*
Edited by: Xiao-Ping Chen and H. Kevin Steensma, Oxford University Press. © Oxford University Press 2021.
DOI: 10.1093/oso/9780190070717.003.0003

rather than listening to my roommate, who thoughtfully advised me to "get smart and make a lot of money"? Why did firms feel compelled to prolong my tedium by providing even more information about executive compensation than was legally required, including verbal descriptions of incentive plans? Prolonged boredom is the mother of invention, and tedium prompts a desperate search for variation. So as the weeks and months of proxy analysis dragged on, I wondered: what explains the variation in these plans, how have they changed over time, and why?

My attempts to answer these questions, along with a great deal of help, mentoring, support, and luck, ultimately led to a program of research on behavioral governance. I noticed that long-term incentive plans were often justified in proxy statements as a means of aligning executive pay with shareholder performance. Later I recognized such communications as a kind of impression management, framed in terms of agency theory. I also noticed that firms sometimes adopted long-term incentive plans without actually implementing them (i.e., without making grants under the plan), a practice I later recognized as a kind of symbolic decoupling.

In addition, I began to question the value of my work as a compensation analyst. In "pricing" an executive position, I was encouraged to use surveys that were known to price relatively high. Our proprietary survey included a disproportionate number of clients, most of whom elected to pay at the 75th percentile of the market (with our blessing, of course). The focal client would dutifully follow the same policy, thus ratcheting up the market rate for the benefit of our other clients. In pricing lower-level positions, by contrast, consultants seemed content to use surveys that priced surprisingly low. I would later recognize this as another kind of decoupling: consultants enhanced the legitimacy of the pay-setting process, by ostensibly applying their specialized expertise in compensation and scientific survey design to develop compensation plans that promoted shareholder interests, when in fact they served a coordinating function among the leaders of public companies that increased executive compensation and perquisites, reduced compensation risk, and promoted organizational inequality.

At the time I only knew that nothing I was doing or learning in management consulting could be explained by the economic theories of compensation and labor markets that I had learned as an undergraduate student. It also seemed unlikely that the econometric methods that were taking over empirical research in economics in the 1980s would be sufficient to examine the behavioral processes I was observing. I looked into the research of faculty at surrounding business schools and discovered the field of organization studies, including the work of Jeff Pfeffer, Barry Staw, Charles O'Reilly, Richard Scott, and others. Although I wouldn't put it together for several years, I knew the theory and evidence described in these studies could help explain some of the corporate governance practices I had observed. When I described the field of organizational studies to my undergraduate adviser, who had invested considerable time mentoring me over four years, and then announced my intention to enter a PhD program in business, his reaction was memorable: "uh oh," he sighed, "this sounds like sociology, and in a *business school*. So you want to be a pseudo social scientist and a sellout. Who will write you a letter?"

He had failed to recognize the warning signs. Although an economics major, I had taken coursework in psychology, political science, and anthropology that provided opportunities for interdisciplinary "research" and writing (e.g., an economics paper on how the Bay Area Rapid Transit system failed initially because it ignored cultural heterogeneity in the Bay Area, and a paper on the microeconomics of ritual for a cultural anthropology class; the rather tepid comments I received on these papers were my first exposure to the challenges of interdisciplinary theorizing). My admission to the PhD program at Kellogg was the best (and luckiest) thing to happen in my professional life. The program was interdisciplinary but, better than that, maintained a productive dialectic between interdisciplinary creativity and discipline-based rigor (along with a healthy dose of motivation by fear). Although I was one of the few macro students in the Department, I had a superstar mentor in Ed Zajac, who was deeply respected by the micro faculty. I was safely on the outside looking in, my preferred social structural position. I witnessed lively exchanges between cognitive and social psychologists, economic sociologists, and strategic management scholars. The ethos of the department challenged me to synthesize neoinstitutional theory, intergroup relations, research on power and politics, social network theory, and economics to explain governance phenomena. It's a career-long project, but over time I've come to appreciate the complementarities between these perspectives. Intergroup relations theory complements (some versions of) neoinstitutional theory in explaining deviations from economic efficiency at different levels of analysis, whether in-group/out-group biases in decision making, decoupling of organizational policies, or allocative inefficiency in financial markets. Prevailing economic theories such as agency theory can be reconceived as institutional logics that are leveraged by powerful actors in their impression management activities, a kind of "symbolic management" that legitimizes their activities and perpetuates their power. And social networks serve to amplify and enable many of these processes.

Passing the comprehensive exam at Kellogg required a good understanding of contemporary research in cognitive and social psychology, and a working knowledge of experimental methods. As a macro student without firsthand experience in experimental research, I felt compelled to read everything published in the top psychology journals over the previous five years, while also regularly attending psychology and organizational behavior seminars. By the time I reached the dissertation stage, I had developed a taste for specifying the micromechanisms that underlie hypothesized relationships. Since the comprehensive exam questions required original hypotheses, I developed the compulsive habit of considering how any psychological theory or mechanism I encountered might connect to my research interests in corporate governance and strategy. The result was an "idea file" with hundreds of meso- and cross-level hypotheses, most worthless, but a few providing the raw material for studies.

The particular brand of interdisciplinary research emerging at Kellogg, together with a background in economics, turned out to be a good fit with strategic management. Cognitive psychology is one step removed from microeconomics, both theoretically and methodologically. Psychological biases are measured as deviations from rationality, and the standard of evidence in laboratory research is aligned with the methodological priorities of contemporary economics. Some versions of neoinstitutional theory help explain deviations from rational decision making *and* organizational efficiency. In short, this interdisciplinary approach to theory development and testing provided the foundations for a cross-level, behavioral theory of strategy, and conversely suggested a more strategic or agentic organizational theory. "Behavioral strategy" could be distinguished from traditional organizational theory by its attention to social mechanisms that explained deviations from efficiency. Symbolic management, for example, is a key mechanism of behavioral strategy because it provides a comprehensive, cross-level explanation for how and when the strategic behavior of firm managers leads to persistent deviations from organizational efficiency. The external economic and institutional environment, the political behavior of managers (as individuals and groups), and organizational policy and structure are all integral to symbolic management (see Westphal & Park, 2020).

At the same time, while behavioral strategy is consonant with economics to the extent that organizational behavior is measured against the "benchmark" of economic efficiency, it also subverts economics. In symbolic management theory, the rhetoric of economics is integral to the impression management of firm leaders that sustains decoupling between external appearances and internal practices on the one hand and organizational reputation and efficiency on the other. For those of us who believe economic efficiency and performance is important but find economic theory and methodology limiting (and somewhat tyrannical), this approach to strategic management and organization theory is particularly satisfying. It was less satisfying to my undergraduate adviser, who described the experience of reading my articles as "patricide by a thousand cuts. Other than that, it's great."

While deeply appealing to me on an intellectual level, this cross-level, interdisciplinary approach presented a range of practical challenges and pitfalls as the foundation for an academic career. In the remainder of the chapter I describe a number of these challenges, along with partial solutions I have discovered (or stumbled across) along the way.

The Challenges and Pitfalls of Interdisciplinary Research in Strategy and Organization Theory (and Some Partial Solutions)

Baiting the economists. Early in my career I tended to position behavioral theory *against* economic theory. A number of my early papers, or initial versions of them, began with an implicit or explicit critique of economic perspectives on governance such as agency theory and then introduced behavioral theory as a superior alternative. This had a number of undesirable consequences. First, editors were more likely to invite economists to review the article. Second, those economists would become skeptical and annoyed, if not angry, three pages into reading it, and thus (1) more likely to review it for the wrong reasons (i.e., to defend their discipline and identity, and perhaps to edify their lessers), (2) less likely to view the theory and results with an open mind, and (3) more likely to dig in their heels and remain intransigent throughout the review process. An economist reviewer on one early paper, for example, argued that symbolic decoupling (e.g., adopting a long-term incentive plan with the stated purpose of aligning executive pay with shareholder performance but not actually implementing the plan) was economically efficient and fully consistent with agency theory. Why? Because once the plan was announced and investors reacted positively, there was no longer any need to follow through with implementation. Firm leaders have successfully signaled their intent to govern efficiently and protect shareholder interests; making grants under the plan would be an unnecessary cost to shareholders and thus inefficient. Never mind that our theory and analysis demonstrated that firms with powerful CEOs and weak boards were more likely to engage in decoupling, and that symbolic management reduced the likelihood of governance reforms and other strategic changes believed to promote shareholder interests. The reviewer never backed down. Due to our initial framing of the study, my coauthor and I had stacked the deck against ourselves. The best we could hope for was a two-to-one vote in favor of acceptance.

Rather than positioning behavioral theory against economics, a more fruitful approach is to acknowledge how our theories leverage economic constructs, and how our studies leverage economic methods. Behavioral strategy leverages the constructs of organizational and market efficiency in assessing the consequences of firm governance and strategic decision making and relies heavily on econometrics for theory testing. The most successful theories coopt or subvert constructs from competing disciplines. The resource-based view coopted constructs from organizational theory in describing the sources of sustainable competitive advantage. Barney (1991) sought to absorb organizational theory rather than attack it directly. Sociological constructs such as charismatic leadership, imprinting, and social cohesion were absorbed into a model of economic rents. As mentioned above, behavioral governance likewise absorbs economic constructs such as agency costs, incentive alignment, monitoring, and organizational efficiency. The same principle applies to dealing with disciplinary differences in virtually any professional conversation, whether the topic is recruiting, school strategy, or scholarship. A strategy of inclusion is almost always preferable to opposition. In distinguishing between "behavioral" and "economic" candidates for a faculty position, I was justifiably reminded by my colleagues that economists are interested in behavior too.

What's your category? As we know from the multidisciplinary literature on categories, while self-identities are normally multidimensional, social evaluation resists categorical complexity: most people have difficulty assessing individuals or organizations that belong to a variety of seemingly disparate categories (Brewer & Brown, 1998; Negro, Koçak, & Hsu, 2010). By its very nature, interdisciplinary research resists easy categorization. In organizational theory and strategy, the problem is compounded by a proliferation of "horizontal" categories and different levels of analysis (i.e., "vertical" categories). Are you organization theory, strategy, entrepreneurship, organizational economics, economic sociology, management, corporate social responsibility, technology, international? And are you micro, macro, or meso? Researchers who have trouble answering these questions, or whose work crosses several of these categories, are disadvantaged early in their careers.

Categorical complexity is less of a problem among close colleagues. At Kellogg, my fellow students and most of the faculty knew my research and intellectual orientation fairly well; there was no need for social categorization. But it became a constraint as I approached the job market. At the Doctoral Consortium of the Organization and Management Theory Division of the

Academy of Management, a "faculty mentor" asked me whether I was organization theory or strategy. "Both," I confidently replied. "Hmm, that's a challenge," she said. When I described my dissertation research at a round-table discussion, a debate ensued as to whether my topic was micro or macro. "Maybe it's meso," someone suggested. Others looked uncertain, and the question was left hanging. In truth, these questions have been left hanging for twenty-five years. Research that examines institutionalization, decoupling, individual and group-level social psychological biases, social influence through network ties, strategic decision making, and firm performance is inherently hard to classify; it is organization theory, strategy, psychology, sociology, micro, macro, and meso, among other things. My failure to confront the problems of categorical complexity, and to address the career risks of conducting interdisciplinary research more generally, reflected a combination of hubris, naïve faith in meritocracy, and introversion. I viewed the classification of research into broad categories as simpleminded and biased, much as I viewed the classification of people, policies, art, and other social, cultural, or intellectual products. But of course this ignored the reality of organizational and market processes, an ironic blind spot for an organization theorist (or a strategy scholar). Jobs must have designated categories, and a candidate for a strategy position who crosses over from strategy into other (sub)disciplines is usually disadvantaged relative to "pure" strategy candidates at each stage of the recruiting process. I was less likely to make short lists, less likely to get interviews, and less likely to get the attention of faculty where I did interview. I was surprised to find that when I interviewed for a strategy position, organizational faculty often did not attend my talk, and when I interviewed for organization theory positions, strategy faculty were often absent.

The cross-category disadvantage extends to other career opportunities. Journal editors frequently look for board members who fit certain categories. Professional groups and societies look for potential members, leaders, and organizers whose research can be unambiguously categorized. These disadvantages tend to diminish significantly over time, as one's research becomes better known in the field. Eventually, research that occupies a unique position at the intersection of different subfields is more likely to be recognized as novel and innovative, providing a compensating advantage at the promotion stage. The challenge for interdisciplinary scholars is to avoid falling through the cracks in the meantime.

In order to compensate for these disadvantages early in their careers, it is especially important for interdisciplinary scholars to have a concise and compelling capsule description of their research program that can be easily understood and appreciated by scholars in different disciplines. If you can't rely on categories to succinctly describe what you do, then you need an especially pithy and memorable "elevator pitch" to get your foot in the door. The best approach is usually to focus on a particular hypothesis or finding. Young scholars are often tempted to focus on theory and/or data in describing their research, because they have been trained to frame their ideas in terms of theory, and they are often immersed in the data and excited about it. But theory and data only become meaningful when anchored to specific arguments, predictions, and findings. In conversation, theoretical framing serves only to categorize the research. As a doctoral student, I tended to introduce my research in conversation by referring to symbolic management, power, and governance, which failed to convey what was interesting or unique about my work and left people uncertain how to categorize it. The reaction was likely "I think he's an institutional theorist and/or a corporate governance person." Over time I've learned to keep the theoretical framing to a sentence or less, go straight to hypotheses and findings, and then finish by abstracting to theory, for example:

> "I do research on symbolic management and governance. For example, we've found that firms in which CEOs have power over their boards are more likely to formally adopt incentive plans that appear to make CEO pay contingent on firm performance, but they are less likely to actually implement the plans. We also find that firms get a positive stock market reaction from adopting these plans, even when the plans are decoupled, or not implemented. We think the findings suggest . . . a political perspective on symbolic action."

By starting with a specific finding, I give the audience a better understanding of the kind of research I do and how it connects to broader categories like symbolic action or governance. I also leave them with something interesting, concrete, and memorable. The content can be adapted to different audiences, both in terms of the finding(s) I choose to highlight and the contributions I mention toward the end. I may also briefly describe the data, depending again on the orientation of the audience, the uniqueness of the data, and its importance to the contribution.

It is critical for students and junior faculty to have a variety of capsule descriptions of their research at the tips of their tongues when they go to conferences, interviews, or otherwise have the chance to meet with faculty outside their group, and they should be practiced at matching the description to their interlocutor. In addition to giving practice presentations, students need to role-play informal conversations about their research with faculty, beginning as early as possible in the doctoral program. This exercise has a variety of side benefits, including the ability to develop more focused and compelling research presentations, as students learn how to frame their work to different audiences. It is also especially important for the introverted among us to build such conversations into our schedules. As a doctoral student, I could follow my natural proclivity for social procrastination. I had the luxury of substituting independent, hard work that I was passionate about for professional interactions that carried the risk of negative social evaluations. Suddenly four years had gone by, and I had given only a few research presentations. I rationalized this neglect with a kind of scholarly arrogance. ("If you want to know about my research, read the papers," I told myself.) On the other hand it seems unrealistic to expect introverted doctoral students, of whom there are many, to transition quickly from doctoral seminars to giving PowerPoint presentations in front of a room of senior faculty. Informal role plays, or other forms of structured conversation, can be a kind of stepping stone to giving more formal research presentations.

What's the contribution? Interdisciplinary research has the potential to make a broad contribution that crosses disciplines and literatures, but it can also fall through the cracks and have little impact. The outcome depends heavily on whether the research is framed appropriately. The first step in properly framing a study is to recognize its primary contribution. In organization theory and strategy, a study may contribute to research on a phenomenon or context while also making a broader theoretical contribution. The audiences for each type of contribution may be very different, though in some cases partially overlapping. Thus, it is very important for interdisciplinary scholars to appreciate the relative value of their contributions to different literatures and audiences. In my own research, I frequently struggle with the question of whether an individual study makes a more important contribution to research on a phenomenon or context (e.g., boards, strategic decision making, top management) or to the literature on a broader theoretical mechanism (e.g., institutionalization, symbolic decoupling, social discrimination). To resolve this dilemma, it is critical for interdisciplinary scholars that they solicit input from a diverse set of colleagues and be willing to substantially revise their framing in response. Many of us learn this lesson the hard way, and I still sometimes fail to revise the framing of my papers appropriately in response to feedback from colleagues or reviewers.

The first article from my dissertation is a good example. In this study, I examined how increases in board independence from management prompted CEOs to engage in interpersonal influence behavior toward outside directors, such as ingratiation and persuasion, which more than compensated for the effect of greater independence on CEO compensation and other policy outcomes (Westphal, 1998). The study contributed to research on boards,

by explaining why board independence from management may have counterproductive effects on corporate governance policy that harm shareholder
interests. But it also contributed to research on power, by explaining why and
how the loss of structural power can prompt social influence processes that
more than offset the structural disadvantage. I was enamored with the latter
contribution, in part because I thought that framing the article in terms of a
broad literature, such as the literature on power and influence, would appeal
to a diverse array of scholars on the job market. I ignored verbal and nonverbal
feedback in my practice talk (I only had one, because I didn't really want feedback), as well as pointed comments from committee members suggesting that
the contribution to boards and governance was more compelling. I only revised the framing slightly from the initial draft to the final, published version,
despite a rather poor showing on the job market. As a result, the article fell
well short of its potential impact.

The second study from my dissertation was a different story. It also contributed to research on governance, by showing that friendship ties between
CEO and board improved board effectiveness and performance by increasing
timely advice and counsel from outside directors on strategic issues. And it
made broader theoretical contributions, in this case to the literatures on social
networks and incentives. But this time I listened to my colleagues and focused
the framing on boards and governance. The result: this article has been cited
more than three times as much as the first study from my dissertation, even
though they made similarly important contributions to research on behavioral governance.

Strong articles often have more than one important contribution, and it
can be difficult to choose between them in framing a study. Early in my career I sometimes convinced myself that I didn't need to choose; I could give
them all equal weight. This approach rarely survives the review process. The
initial submission of my article "Collaboration in the Boardroom" (Westphal,
1999) proudly listed contributions to theory and research on boards (effectiveness, independence, CEO-board relationships, and board involvement
in strategy), executive incentives, executive social networks, and feedback
seeking behavior. The reviewers were frustrated and annoyed with this
framing, describing it as "incoherent," "lack[ing] in focus," "overreaching,"
and "weakly supported." At first I was indignant: each of the contributions was
legitimate and defensible, and contributing to a variety of disparate literatures
should be a strength, not a weakness. But my senior colleagues at Texas set
me straight. My article lacked an identity; what was it primarily about, and
who was it mainly for? I had failed to resolve the classification problem again,
while also failing to recognize that contributions to literatures as disparate

as economic incentives, boards, and social networks require disproportionately more support than contributions to one literature or closely interrelated
literatures. After receiving stern warnings from my colleagues, indignation
gave way to fear, and I refocused the framing narrowly on the safest contribution (CEO-board relationships). In the next round, one reviewer and the
editor suggested that I had overreacted and "thrown the baby out with the
bathwater." In the final round I settled on a compromise approach that included a primary contribution (i.e., a new perspective on board independence
from management and CEO-board relationships) and several secondary
contributions, including a better understanding of how and when managerial
incentives can improve strategic decision making and firm performance.

This general approach to framing the contributions of a study, in which a
primary contribution is fully described and supported in the introduction,
and one or more secondary contributions are briefly introduced up front
and supported more fully in the discussion section, has become my default
starting point in writing the introduction and discussion sections of an article. It lends structure and coherence to the framing without oversimplifying
the contribution, and it can be adapted to input from the review process. If
reviewers are particularly enthusiastic about a secondary contribution, it
can be given more weight in the introduction and/or discussion sections
and perhaps even elevated from a secondary to a primary contribution. Such
flexibility is especially important in the review process for interdisciplinary
research, as the reviewer base is typically diverse, making it especially difficult
to predict how reviewers will react to contribution claims. Mentioning secondary contributions in the introduction also increases the long-term impact
of a study, at least on average. While the immediate audience is normally determined by the primary contribution, signaling further contributions early
in the paper and then elaborating on them in the discussion section will help
broaden the audience over time.

Building and articulating a coherent theoretical framework. Because interdisciplinary theories of strategy and organization are often complex and
multidimensional, they may come across as fragmented and lacking in coherence. Among the most common criticisms of my early articles were that the
hypotheses did not "hang together well enough" or "tried to do too much" and
should perhaps be divided into two or three papers. Sometimes this concern
can be addressed by articulating the underlying, metalevel mechanism that
links the various hypotheses. However, interdisciplinary theories are often
hard to summarize in terms of a single mechanism or construct, except at a
very high level (e.g., social psychological bias, power, or institutions). A more
practical solution is often to explicitly articulate the structure that underlies

the theoretical arguments and hypotheses. In my early articles I often characterized the theory as "a framework," without articulating its structure. As one reviewer admonished me, "a bunch of hypotheses is not a framework." In most strong papers there is a latent structure to the hypotheses, but authors often fail to recognize or describe it. A useful heuristic in diagnosing the structure of a framework is to look for symmetry, complementarities, and/or a natural progression in the hypotheses. Analyzing the structure of a theory can also help identify ways to tighten the framework further.

Sometimes the structure of a framework is intrinsic to the theory, and sometimes it becomes apparent only in the context of prior research. An example of the first type is my study with Ed Zajac on the decoupling of stock repurchase plans (Westphal & Zajac, 2001). This study examined very different determinants of institutional decoupling, including CEO power over the board, board interlock ties to other decoupling firms, and prior instances of decoupling at the focal firm. Adding to the complexity, we also examined prior experience with decoupling of a different policy (CEO long-term incentive plans). The original title of the paper simply listed the determinants: "Decoupling Policy from Practice: CEO Power, Board Interlock Ties, and Prior Experience with Decoupling." Unsurprisingly, friendly reviewers found the article fragmented and disjointed. Our solution was to identify latent structure in the theory and make it explicit. CEO power over the board amplified the effect of (1) prior *internal* experience with decoupling, and (2) prior *external* experience with decoupling from board appointments, and both kinds of experience generalized across policy domains. (That is, experience with decoupling one kind of policy increased the likelihood of decoupling a different kind of policy.) Although the micromechanisms underlying the effect of each independent variable were quite different, they formed a kind of hierarchical, symmetrical structure (see fig. 3.1).

There was also a logical progression to the framework. Each determinant raised the level of analysis, from the most micro (CEO power over the board) to the firm level (prior experience with decoupling at the focal firm) and to the most macro (the ego-network level). The theory also progressed from policy-specific hypotheses to cross-policy predictions. By identifying the latent symmetry and logical progression of the hypotheses, we were able to craft a coherent narrative description of the theory based on its *structure*, even though the *content* of our theoretical arguments invoked mechanisms as disparate as social influence, vicarious learning, and routines.

Analyzing the structure of a theory can also help identify opportunities to enhance the contribution without sacrificing coherence, and may even reinforce it. We initially worried that adding hypotheses about cross-policy effects

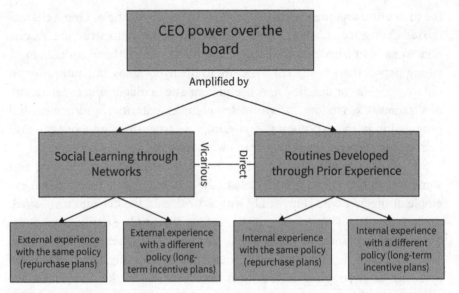

Figure 3.1 Articulating the structure of a theoretical framework: Hierarchical symmetry (Westphal & Zajac, 2001)

(e.g., prior decoupling of one policy predicts subsequent decoupling of another policy) would overcomplicate the paper, leading to the familiar reaction that we were "trying to do too much." Once we appreciated the latent structure in our framework, however, we recognized that cross-policy hypotheses reinforced the coherence of our theory, because they fit within its symmetrical structure and logical progression.

In some cases the latent structure of a framework is best appreciated in the context of prior research. In our recent study on the negative psychological and reputational effects of ingratiation (Keeves, Westphal, & McDonald, 2017), we examined how ingratiatory behavior by executives toward the CEO can elicit emotions and behaviors that ultimately damage the CEO's reputation. We theorized that ingratiation triggers feelings of resentment toward the CEO, both in the executive who engages in ingratiation and among others who witness it, and that resentment can motivate social undermining of the CEO in communication with journalists. We also hypothesized that the effect of ingratiation on resentment would be especially strong when the CEO was a racial minority or a woman. Here was another interdisciplinary theory constituted of a diverse set of constructs and mechanisms, including social influence, resentment, attribution error, intergroup bias, and social undermining. Simply listing the hypotheses and findings would not be well received by reviewers; why examine this particular behavior (social undermining in communication with journalists), and why this particular moderator (minority race and gender)?

For this study, the latent structure of our framework became apparent when the hypotheses were juxtaposed with extant theory. Prior research had shown that ingratiation can lead to recommendations and endorsements that enhance external reputation. For example, flattery and opinion conformity by top executives toward the CEO increased one's likelihood of receiving the CEO's recommendation for a board appointment at another firm (Westphal & Stern, 2006). Moreover, these benefits were mediated by the CEO's positive affect or increased liking of the ingratiator. When our theoretical framework is considered in light of this prior research, a kind of inverse or "mirror" symmetry becomes apparent. As shown in figure 3.2, while extant theory suggests how ingratiation leads to endorsements that enhance external reputation by increasing the influence target's positive affect for the ingratiator, our study explains how ingratiation leads to social undermining that *damages* external reputation by triggering *negative* affect (i.e., resentment) *on the part of* the ingratiator *toward* the influence target.

And while prior research has shown that intergroup biases reduce the benefits that women and racial minorities derive from engaging in ingratiation, our study showed that similar biases *augment* the reputational *costs* to women and racial minorities of being the *targets* of ingratiation. As in Westphal and Zajac (2001), moreover, the hypotheses traversed a logical progression

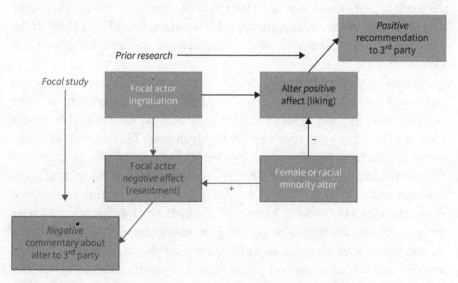

Figure 3.2 Articulating the structure of a theoretical framework: Symmetry in the context of prior research (Keeves, Westphal, & McDonald, 2017)

from the very micro (intrapsychic biases that triggered resentment) to the social psychological (intergroup biases that amplified resentment) to external, social factors (social undermining that damages reputation). Thus, we were able to craft a coherent narrative to describe our theory by highlighting the symmetry and logical progression of its structure, even though the constructs and micromechanisms that made it up were highly diverse.

At the same time, this narrative depiction of our theory reinforced the primary contribution of the study, which was to the literature on power and influence, while supporting secondary contributions to very different literatures, including research on social networks, women and minorities in corporate leadership, and the social psychology of leadership. In identifying the symmetrical structure in our theoretical framework, we also uncovered a novel contribution of the findings. In particular, we noted that little research in the social network literature had examined the causes and consequences of asymmetric network ties composed of opposing emotions or behavior. Our findings had revealed a social and psychological mechanism that explains the formation of asymmetric ties characterized by positive affect and social support in one direction and resentment and social undermining in the other.

Articulating the structure of a theoretical framework is an effective solution to a fundamental challenge in interdisciplinary theorizing, namely, how to resolve the trade-off between coherence and completeness of explanation. It is not merely a compromise between the two but a way to increase one without sacrificing the other. And while greater complexity can reduce the aesthetic appeal of a theory, complex forms of symmetry, such as inverse or nested symmetry, can enhance its appeal (Eisenman, 1967; Weyl, 1980). If the structure can be presented as a logical progression, the appeal is greater still (White, 1987).

Negotiating the peer review process. The peer review process presents special challenges for organizational theorists and behavioral strategy scholars. The reviewer base in these fields is extremely broad, and the evaluative criteria employed by editors and reviewers are highly diverse. The reviewers assigned to my articles have included social psychologists, economic sociologists, and financial economists, as well as scholars from very different subfields of management and strategy. As a result, my paper submissions routinely have three reviewers who (1) define a "theoretical contribution" differently; (2) refer to very different literatures in assessing the contribution; (3) have different assumptions about what should be measured and validated empirically (e.g., whether microlevel social and psychological processes need to be directly assessed); and (4) use different criteria to evaluate methodological rigor (e.g., generalizability, precision of measurement, controlling for endogeneity, and so on). In light of such heterogeneity, it is normally impossible to fully satisfy all three reviewers.

My default approach to addressing this dilemma has evolved over time. Early in my career I would decide which reviewer I agreed with (if any) and then attempt to persuade the others to accept this point of view. I was treating the review process as a kind of debate, akin to the back-and-forth in a doctoral seminar. But unlike my fellow students, reviewers were not particularly interested in my point of view. Their comments reflected strongly held, implicit assumptions that were unlikely to change through the course of a review process. Through trial and error and the patient mentoring of colleagues, I came to realize that, rather than engaging reviewers in a debate, a better approach is to find common ground. Even when I disagree with a reviewer's comment, I can usually find something in the comment to build on. But finding common ground with reviewers is often a lengthy process that requires considerable theoretical and/or empirical investigation, as well as the assistance of coauthors and colleagues. Our initial response to negative reviewer comments is typically defensive and dismissive, as authors seize on any weakness in the reviewer's arguments and look for differences in the reactions of other reviewers. The first step toward finding common ground is to move past this initial defensiveness, and gain a deeper understanding of the reviewer's perspective on our study. If the reviewer appears to be from another (sub) field, which is often the case in interdisciplinary research, as I've noted, then it can be helpful to seek advice from a colleague in that area. If possible, solicit their input at two points in the process: first in understanding the reviewer's concerns and the assumptions that may underlie them, and second in anticipating the reviewer's likely reaction to your response.

The outcome of this process is usually a more nuanced assessment of the reviewer's comment and the identification of a viable way to address the reviewer's concern and improve the article. In most cases, the reviewer has identified a legitimate problem, or their comment suggests that some element of the paper needs clarification or further development. I may not fully agree with the reviewer's characterization of the problem, assessment of its severity, or recommended solution, but in most cases their concern reveals a weakness in the paper, and this provides the basis for common ground. The default structure of my response has three components: (1) acknowledge that the reviewer's comment raises a legitimate issue; (2) describe in detail how I have addressed the issue; and (3) give the reviewer due credit for the improvement. I may explicitly disagree with the reviewer, but more often I simply note any differences in passing. Even if the review is very negative, the spirit of my response is collaborative: the focus is on describing and explaining valuable revisions to the paper that were spurred by the reviewer's comments. A positive and constructive response tends to elicit a more positive and constructive review in the next round.

At the same time, it is also important to highlight strengths of the article in a way that points to discipline-based differences in assumptions that may be influencing reviewers' concerns, in responding to both the reviewers and the editor. For example, if a reviewer's methodological comments are focused on econometric approaches to addressing endogeneity that are difficult to implement in a study based on survey questionnaires, then I highlight the measurement and generalizability benefits of using large-sample survey data. If a reviewer discounts the contribution of the study in a way that seems to question whether novel explanations of corporate governance practices can be considered a "theoretical" contribution, then I reference prior corporate governance studies that are widely acknowledged to have made such contributions. The spirit of these assertions is not to discredit the reviewer but to surface the assumptions that underlie their critique, while highlighting the trade-offs inherent in different methodologies and approaches to theory development. The implicit or explicit message is that these different approaches are complementary, not (merely) competing.

Balancing competing objectives: The portfolio approach. Early in their careers, interdisciplinary scholars face an array of competing objectives: maximizing rigor versus increasing relevance; extending a research stream versus experimenting with a new one; and leveraging one's specialized training and expertise versus learning new theories and methods, to name a few. An effective approach to managing these tensions is to conceive your research as a loose portfolio of projects, united by an evolving set of two to three common themes, ideally of a conceptual rather than a purely methodological nature. The portfolio may have a core-periphery structure, where the core is bounded by your specialized training and expertise and represents your primary area of contribution and the periphery includes experimental, long-term projects that carry substantial risk of failure—at least in medium term—but also present significant learning opportunities. Embracing a portfolio strategy of this kind early in my career was critical to inducing a kind of disciplined risk taking that paid off over the long term. Several of the high-risk, long-term projects I began as a doctoral student or assistant professor ultimately failed, or have yet to succeed, but a few have become some of my best (or at least favorite) studies posttenure.

A successful research stream on the periphery of the portfolio may eventually become part of the core, to be replaced by a new set of uncertain, long-term projects. The portfolio approach encourages experimentation, because failed projects are accepted as inevitable, and in fact necessary to the evolution of the larger portfolio. But the experimentation is also disciplined, because it must have some connection to the core, and scholars must continue to invest in their core research streams. Research collaborations can help mitigate the risks of experimentation and accelerate the learning process that often goes along with starting a new research stream, though collaborations are only effective learning mechanisms if each member of the team is fully engaged in the research project.

Bridging to practice: Timing is everything. The impact of research on management practice and policy is increasingly important to students, donors, and university leaders, and it often becomes increasingly important to faculty on a personal level as they progress in their careers. However, I've learned that the impact of research on practice and policy depends as much on timing as on the inherent importance of the work. My paper on the influence of demographic minorities on boards, coauthored with Laurie Milton (Westphal & Milton, 2000), should have been a bombshell. It provided systematic evidence of social discrimination against female and racial minority directors and revealed the social conditions that reduced discrimination. When the study was published, we sent out a provocatively worded press release to a variety of reporters, and we sat by the phone and waited . . . and waited. In the year 2000 there was very little interest in board diversity among corporate governance experts, top managers, or directors. Our study was only referenced in the press more than 10 years later, when diversity was finally recognized as a critical issue in corporate leadership. The notion that research lags practice is misleading; research often leads practice, but only gains attention when practitioners are interested in the topic and ready to address it.

Impact on scholarship and practice both take time, and is difficult to control. Impact on scholarship typically accumulates gradually over a long period of time and often persists as research exerts an indirect influence on later generations of scholars. Impact on practice tends to arise suddenly and often dissipates nearly as fast. In either case, success requires patience and perseverance, important qualities for any researcher, but perhaps especially for the interdisciplinary scholar.

References

Barney, J. (1991). Firm resources and sustained competitive advantage. *Journal of Management,* *17,* 99–120.

Brewer, M. B., & Brown, R. J. (1998). Intergroup relations. In D. T. Gilbert, S. T. Fiske, & G. Lindzey (Eds.), *The handbook of social psychology* (4th ed., pp. 554–594). New York: McGraw-Hill.

Eisenman, R. (1967). Complexity-simplicity: I. Preference for symmetry and rejection of complexity. *Psychonomic Science, 8,* 169–170.

Keeves, G., Westphal, J. D., & McDonald, M. (2017). Those closest wield the sharpest knife? How ingratiation leads to resentment and social undermining of the CEO. *Administrative Science Quarterly, 62,* 484–523.

Negro, G., Koçak, Ö., & Hsu, G. (2010). Research on categories in the sociology of organizations. *Research in the Sociology of Organizations, 31,* 3–35.

Westphal, J. D. (1998). Board games: How CEOs adapt to increases in structural board independence from management. *Administrative Science Quarterly, 43,* 511–537.

Westphal, J. D. (1999). Collaboration in the boardroom: The consequences of social ties in the CEO/board relationship. *Academy of Management Journal, 42,* 7–24.

Westphal, J. D., & Milton, L. P. (2000). How experience and network ties affect the influence of demographic minorities on corporate boards. *Administrative Science Quarterly, 45,* 366–398.

Westphal, J. D., & Park, S-H. (2020). *Symbolic management: Governance, strategy, and institutions.* Oxford, UK: Oxford University Press.

Westphal, J. D., & Stern, I. (2006). The other pathway to the boardroom: How interpersonal influence behavior can substitute for elite credentials and demographic majority status in gaining access to board appointments. *Administrative Science Quarterly, 51,* 169–204.

Westphal, J. D., & Zajac, E. J. (2001). Explaining institutional decoupling: The case of stock repurchase programs. *Administrative Science Quarterly, 46,* 202–228.

Weyl, H. (1980). *Symmetry.* Princeton, NJ: Princeton University Press.

White, H. (1987). *The content of the form: Narrative discourse and historical representation.* Baltimore, MD: Johns Hopkins University Press.

4

What I Have Learned . . . in My Journey as a Scholar

Sigal Goland Barsade

My entry into the field of organizational behavior began at the family dinner table, when my parents would come home and talk about their workdays. My father recounted particularly vivid stories about the human dimensions of events at work and his approach to leadership and managerial problem solving. I was fascinated by these stories, which is probably why, despite originally choosing economics as my undergraduate major (viewed by my parents as the most useful degree if you were not going to be an engineer), I very quickly changed to psychology. In my senior year at UCLA, two things happened that pointed me to my career as an academic in the field of organizational behavior. I conducted a senior honors thesis in psychology examining the bases of power in a health care context under the supervision of Dr. Bert Raven, and I concurrently took an elective course in industrial/organizational psychology (a field that until that point I did not know existed). These two events sparked my love for research and led me to a domain I find very meaningful—people's behavior at work. I had originally considered becoming a clinical psychologist, but ultimately decided that while not everyone needed or could afford to go to a therapist, most people spend much of their lives working. Thus, if I could help make people's work lives better, I could have a broader impact in making people's lives better.

I worked in a series of jobs prior to applying to a doctoral program, doing so for several reasons. Importantly, one was to observe as many different types of organizations as possible before I began studying them. When searching for my first position, I quickly realized that no one was going to put me in the position of CEO or VP of HR, so I began instead with a first-row view of senior leadership. For almost two years, I worked as an executive assistant at several companies, including working (abroad) for the CEO of an international concrete company and for the VP of merchandising at a Los Angeles start-up. What was tremendously valuable in all of these positions was that I was able to

Sigal Goland Barsade, *What I Have Learned . . . in My Journey as a Scholar* In: *A Journey toward Influential Scholarship.* Edited by: Xiao-Ping Chen and H. Kevin Steensma, Oxford University Press. © Oxford University Press 2021. DOI: 10.1093/oso/9780190070717.003.0004

observe firsthand my colleagues and bosses, without really being seen. Most important, the experience made me even more curious and knowledgeable about what happens in organizations. Seeing them in action and carefully listening to the people who work within them became the impetus for my best research ideas and interests.

Indeed, I have learned that, ideally, anyone thinking of entering a doctoral program should spend some time working in a nonresearch setting for at least a year or two. This allows ideas to come not only from filling gaps in the research literature but also from observing and understanding people at work. My UC Berkeley doctoral mentor, Barry Staw, reinforced this view for me. He is one of the smartest, most innovative, and rigorous scholars I know, and I was supremely lucky to have been trained by him through both his words and his examples. One of the things I learned from Barry was to actively *not* look at the research literature when you are first thinking about your ideas but to go by what interests you in the real world. It is also important to regularly reach into the working world once you are a faculty member. You can do so through field studies, listening carefully to your students discuss their work experiences, including in executive education programs, or consulting to organizations. In line with this, posttenure/senior faculty may find it useful to take a sabbatical and spend some time actually working in an organization to refresh their ideas and perspectives—I have been considering doing so. Paying active attention to what is happening more broadly and societally within the work domain is helpful as well.

Real-world experiences have driven or influenced almost all of my studies, and this early work experience led to one of my most influential and highly cited articles to date, "The Ripple Effect: Emotional Contagion and Its Influence on Group Behavior" (Barsade, 2002), which examined the construct of emotional contagion in groups and its psychological and behavioral outcomes. My interest in emotional contagion in groups, a process through which moods or emotions are transferred from person to person in a group, both automatically and consciously, began at the LA start-up where I worked prior to graduate school. I came to the idea of emotional contagion from my experience of interacting with Melissa (a pseudonym), a coworker. Melissa worked on the same floor as I did at the start-up. I did not report to her, or even work much directly with her, but her desk was fairly close to mine, so I was exposed to her and everyone else working with her. The problem was that Melissa was chronically crabby and irritable (what I was later able to label *high negative affectivity*; see Watson, Clark & Tellegen, 1988). I knew that I found Melissa unpleasant to be around but did not think much more about it until—one day—she left for a vacation. Once Melissa was no longer in the office, I noticed something fascinating: our office environment completely changed, and me with it. I felt happier, lighter, as if my shoulders were lifting from a position of clenched anxiety, and even more interesting, I saw the same in everyone else. There were no Hollywood musical scores, but there was a palpable, positive emotional shift. Then, when Melissa returned from her vacation, everything went back to the way it had been before. While this naturally occurring field experiment consisted of only an N of 1, I was deeply struck by how one person could have such a strong effect on a whole group, particularly since we did not even report to her. What really struck me was that it was mainly about her mood and nonverbal cues. This experience really stayed with me, and when it was time to choose my dissertation topic, I returned to it. I wanted to understand whether what I had seen at work was in fact real, that is, do employees actually catch emotions from each other without even needing to speak to one another or realizing it is happening? As an organizational scholar, I was also interested in whether catching these emotions subsequently influenced performance or other workplace outcomes.

While I did "forget the literature" when initially thinking about what whether group-level emotional contagion could exist and whether it could influence group processes and outcomes, I then followed another addendum I learned from Barry Staw, which was that once you have thought of your idea, it is absolutely critical to go back to the research literature and read everything you can find about it. This is to make certain that the exact idea has not already been tested, that you have investigated the literature exhaustively to build your underlying theory, and that you have considered all possible relevant variables. I have learned to read everything I can find about a topic (and my reference sections are often very, sometimes overly, long), and I know I am finished reading when all the articles begin to cite each other.[1] In my theorizing, I have learned to build at least two, if not three, types of arguments for each hypothesis. I often find it helpful to draw from a variety of fields—primarily from within management theory, of course, but also from psychological theory, and other social science domains, such as sociology and anthropology.-

In sum, I have learned that interesting organizational behavior research arises from problems or phenomena you see occurring in organizational life

---

[1] A quick note about citations. I have also learned that it is important to cite appropriately, or it can influence the perceived reliability of your entire article. For example, I have noticed that authors sometimes indicate that there is a relationship between A and B but then provide a citation that only confirms the existence of A or B rather than the relationship between them. Sometimes, authors also cite work incorrectly or cherry-pick rather than offering a balanced argument. This not only makes their theorizing inaccurate but also reduces the reliability of the entire article.

(either directly or by description), and prior theory is then crucial for helping to build the theory to answer these questions.

What I Have Learned . . . about High Risk/High Reward Research

When I began my studies of emotional contagion in groups, no research I knew of had yet been conducted on the topic.[2] This made it exciting but also arguably very risky because the phenomenon might not really exist or might be too difficult to measure, in which cases I could be left with a nonpublishable dissertation. I (perhaps naively) did not care. Something else I had learned to do was to pursue what truly interests you theoretically, even if it is risky, and this attitude was encouraged by both Barry Staw and my other wonderful mentor at UC Berkeley, Charles O'Reilly. The concept of emotional contagion met those criteria: it was of great interest to me; I had seen it in action in an organization; and I thought it could have tremendous ramifications for how group emotions form and cohere, and ultimately for how groups perform. However, the experimentation to examine this phenomenon was elaborate, time-consuming, and intricate. There was a good chance that even if the phenomenon existed, I might not be able to capture it in the micro way in which I was testing it. However, my view was that at worst I would have attempted something ambitious and then moved on—not ideal, but recoverable. In short, it was the beginning of a high risk/high reward strategy that I would continue to pursue throughout my career.

Having said this, perhaps with the caution of seniority and some hindsight on the importance of luck, I can understand why someone might see this approach as a dangerous one, particularly given our field's overly short tenure clocks: conducting research this way takes longer for each article, with a higher cost if the article fails. On the other hand having a smaller number of very strong articles can compensate for not having a large number of more midrange or more iterative articles. I was very fortunate that my first position

---

[2] At the time I was planning my dissertation topic and design, Elaine Hatfield, a pioneer in modern-day emotional contagion research had not yet published about the topic. Only when I was deep in the dissertation process, having already conducted my data gathering, did I discover that she had just begun publishing a body of work about emotional contagion. While her research focused exclusively on dyadic contagion and I was exclusively examining the emotional contagion in groups and its organizational outcomes, it was disconcerting at best to discover that my dissertation topic (which I thought I was the only one investigating) was actually being actively researched and already published by someone else. I immediately contacted Elaine Hatfield to hear more about her work. She likely heard the panic in my doctoral student voice, and she assured me there was space for both of our research questions. She then graciously sent me the galleys of her excellent book *Emotional Contagion*. Luckily, she was right. Another lesson learned.

at Yale had a long promotion clock, which give me the opportunity to pursue this type of strategy with less timeline concerns. (Some faculty have been de facto replicating this timeline by switching universities after their first few years and restarting their tenure clocks.)

A downside of "going big" theoretically is that it is also a riskier strategy because very often you are examining something new that the field may not yet be quite ready for or even interested in. I saw this happen to one of my favorite articles, "Implicit Affect in Organizations," coauthored with Lakshmi Ramarajan and Drew Westen, a theory article about subconscious affect in organizations (Barsade, Ramarajan, & Westen, 2009). In this article we built a new and detailed model of the three types of implicit affect and their ramifications for organizational life. Not very much research had yet been done in this domain, and while I view it as one of my best articles, its impact through citation counts has not yet reflected this. In addition, when you go big theoretically, there are sometimes risks in not being able to really clarify the concept initially to the satisfaction of reviewers, which makes it harder to publish, or you may accidentally find yourself threatening the turf of a different group of scholars, which can then put your article in political jeopardy, making it harder to publish. Even so, I have found it is unquestionably worth it.

It is worth noting, though, that while I speak of "high risk/high reward" as a conscious strategy, I did not actually choose it consciously. Rather, it was a natural outcome of how I was trained to do research (a very similar point to that made by Sue Ashford (2013) about early imprinting of research style in her excellent article about scholarly impact and academic home runs). All the projects I observed or took part in as a doctoral student—with my two Berkeley mentors and Jennifer Chatman, a junior faculty coauthor at Northwestern at the time (and Berkeley doctoral student alumna)—involved either big ideas or very elaborate and rigorous multimethod/measure studies, and usually both. I learned from these teachers that the way to do research is to "go big," both theoretically and methodologically.

What I Have Learned . . . about "Going Big" Theoretically and Methodologically

I have learned that going big methodologically means putting as much evidence as is reasonable in one article. I never "slice thin" to create more articles, and only once so far in my career have I used a data set in two studies—and that was a huge data set that took over three years to design and gather. In most of the studies I have conducted, I have learned that it is important to adopt a multimethod, multimeasure (often including behavioral coding, video ratings, text analysis, and objective outcomes), and/or multirater research approach. These elements do not all have to be in each article, but the more you have, the richer and more convincing the argument. Taking this approach very much helped with the successful publication of my emotional contagion article. For example, I measured emotional contagion via participants' emotions through facial expression and body language, coded every 30 seconds by three trained video-coders; via participants' ratings of their own pre- and post-emotions; and via participants' ratings of each other's pre- and post-emotions. All three measures triangulated and made for a much more convincing argument than any one of them would have alone. When the reviewers asked for more evidence in the revision process, I reran the entire study, video coding and all, but without a confederate, even though I was not sure whether these analyses would ultimately be included in the article. (They weren't.)

Particularly when investigating new constructs, I have learned it is important to measure and test them in as many ways as possible to be sure you have what you think you have and that it is a reliable finding. In another example of this, my coauthor Mandy O'Neill and I used multiple methods and raters in a longitudinal field study (Time 2 outcomes were collected 16 months after Time 1 predictor variables) that introduced the construct of emotional culture, and specifically the construct of a culture of companionate love (affection, caring, compassion, and tenderness) ("What's Love Got to Do with It?: The Influence of a Culture of Companionate Love and Employee and Client Outcomes in a Long-Term Care Setting," Barsade & O'Neill, 2014). The study took place in a long-term care facility, and we measured the construct in three ways: (1) research assistant observer ratings of the emotional culture of companionate love on the unit; (2) the emotional culture of companionate love artifacts rated by the administration of the units; and (3) survey self-reports of employees as "informants" describing the culture through measuring the degree of companionate love expressed by their fellow staff on the unit. As in my emotional contagion study, all three measures triangulated and made the argument stronger. Importantly, it also allowed for more confidence in the future use of only one of these measures (for example, the employee survey), when researchers might find themselves in a setting that did not practically allow for all of these to be measured. We measured the influence of the culture of companionate love on myriad employee outcomes, and then looked to see how the culture could also influence patient outcomes, and even further out to family outcomes—expanding the range and implications of the study. Conducting this study took a tremendous amount of effort and time. Not only that, but so that we could make the point that the culture of companionate love was not just relevant in healthcare and primarily to female employees, the beauty of *Administrative Science Quarterly* is that it allows you to enter more data in the discussion section, and using an additional sample of primarily men in 3,201 employees spanning seven different industries (bio-pharmaceutical, engineering, financial services, higher education, real estate, travel, and utilities). Using the same employee culture of companionate love scale we used in this study, we found that employees' ratings of the culture of companionate love were significantly positively correlated with measures of job satisfaction, commitment to the organization ($r = 0.21$, $p < 0.001$), and accountability for work performance ($r = 0.07$, $p < 0.01$) – and that there were significant differences both across and within industries. Indeed a more recent study (Adler, Bleise, Barsade & Snowden), examined both a culture of companionate love and hope and showed that they had significant effects in different ways (including cohesion and resilience separately) in gunnery units within the army setting.

Another example of "going big" in methods was a field study with my coauthors Teresa Amabile, Jen Mueller, and Barry Staw ("Affect and Creativity at Work," Amabile, Barsade, Mueller & Staw, 2005) examining the longitudinal influence of higher positive affect on greater workplace creativity. In this study we had 222 participants in 26 project teams across three companies complete daily diaries and surveys through the entire project, varying from 9 to 38 weeks (with a mean of 19 weeks), and with an amazing mean response rate of 75%. This data yielded 11,471 open-ended daily diaries, which were coded in multiple ways by three or more research assistants at a time. This type of research takes a tremendous amount of time for both data collection and coding but really pays off in terms of the rigor of the study and confidence in the findings. The amount of work that Professor Amabile and her team put in to get this much reliable, longitudinal data, was extraordinary. This research study was an example of me saying yes after the data itself was gathered, but then working to create the affect data from the 11,471 daily dairies, and working together with an amazing team to predict the longitudinal effect of affect on creativity and visa-versa.

I have also learned that it is important to have as much realism as possible in organizational studies—either by going out into the field or, if staying in the physical or online lab, by trying as much as possible to bring the workplace into that setting through realistic workplace tasks or simulations. This makes a significant difference to confidence in the results and the impact of the article. I first learned this type of methodological rigor in the multirater, multimethod assessment center studies at the Institute of Personality Assessment and Research (IPAR, now called the Institute of Personality and Social Research) at UC Berkeley during my doctoral studies (which resulted in my first published article, "Affect and Managerial Performance: A Test of the Sadder-but-Wiser vs. Happier-and-Smarter Hypotheses," Staw & Barsade, 1992). This approach was also used in an elaborate laboratory simulation study with Jenny Chatman, which was begun during my doctoral studies ("Personality, Organizational Culture and Cooperation: Evidence from a Business Simulation," Chatman & Barsade, 1995). I used what I had learned about joint realism and rigor in those studies in the first independent research work I did on group emotional contagion, as I've mentioned. In this emotional contagion study, I intentionally chose a managerial decision-making task in which participants conducted a salary bonus negotiation on behalf of a subordinate. The participants were given a collectivistic goal (do the best for the company) and a competitive goal (do the best for your particular subordinate). The study design and operationalization were intricate. It was a two (Valence: Positive/Negative) by two (Energy: High/Low) between subjects design, where the confederate not only had to pretend to be part of the group and infect others with emotion but also leave the room without being seen after completing the postquestionnaire so he could be a "new" participant just 15 minutes later in the next experimental session. I spent hours working with this confederate and doing pretests to be sure he stuck to the "cognitive script" across the conditions while successfully enacting one of the four emotional roles to which he was randomly assigned. I checked regularly throughout the process to be sure he was being empirically perceived as sticking to his affective character (a very important part of any confederate manipulation). The confederate was an undergraduate acting major, and I told him later he was likely the only actor in the world who had had his success in acting empirically validated. In addition to the participants' self-reports, I used multiple video cameras to achieve (1) a view of the confederate alone for a manipulation check (as I knew I would not want the coders to see the other group members), (2) a view of each group member without the confederate, and (3) an overall view of the group as a whole. This allowed me to ensure that both separate individual participant coding and overall group process and outcome coding could be conducted. All of this needed to be considered in advance so that valuable participant time resources would not be wasted.[3]

---

[3] Indeed, I have learned that doing a careful, contextual laboratory study can take as much time as the most comprehensive field study.

With regard to realism in the lab, I have learned that the best laboratory studies (both physical and virtual) are those in which I have created a context as close as possible to that of an actual organizational environment (e.g., Barsade, 2002; Chatman & Barsade, 1995; Filipowicz, Barsade & Melwani, 2011; Melwani & Barsade, 2011). For example, in an article I published with Tori Huang and Vangelis Souitaris (Huang, Souitaris & Barsade, 2019) about how group hope and group fear competed with each other in explaining the escalation of commitment to a losing course of action among entrepreneurial teams, it took our first author, Tori Huang, an hour just to train the participants about the complexities of the simulation for each of the 66 groups in the sample. We succeeded in creating a much deeper approximation of real entrepreneurial team processes by having a sophisticated, in-depth "start-up organization" simulation in which the participants thought they were risking their own (real) money (after using up the initial money given to them by the experimenter) for the chance to win a large cash prize. We designed the experiment to be longitudinal, with an average of 8.7 "year" rounds (SD = 3.5 rounds) (with a minimum of 3 and a maximum of 21 rounds), and we measured participants' ratings of team-level hope and fear for each "year" round. We also rated participants' behavioral engagement throughout the experiment (which served as our mediator) through videotapes of the entire process. The setting was elaborate and immersive, with multiple time periods, and allowed us to better recreate real-world processes in a laboratory setting in a way that had not yet been done in the escalation of commitment literature.

With regard to the real world, here are a few notes on what I have learned about doing field studies. Such studies are critical to our discipline's ability to get closer to what is actually happening "on the ground" in organizations, allowing organizational behavior scholars to see if findings occur across contexts and how they differ between contexts. They are also very difficult and time-consuming to execute successfully. The difficulty comes mainly from the administration of the study. This includes not only executing it but also getting the organization excited and committed to it (*never* go forward with a field study without a committed champion who has the power to implement it) and ensuring you have a sufficiently large, representative sample and the organization will not be bought out and cease data collection midstudy. That happened to me once after I had gathered a tremendous amount of data for one of the first studies in the field examining the influence of emotional intelligence on workplace performance. I had collected all the predata, including a 45-minute emotional intelligence ability test for over 500 applicants. I was waiting three months to receive the first quarter's employee performance data, everything was ready to go—and then the company was bought out, with my study a casualty of the acquisition.

There are so many different contextual factors in the field and so much complexity in the execution of a field study, particularly when looking at behavioral or financial measures, that an effect needs to be strong to show itself consistently. However, field studies are critical to reaching the next step of knowledge in our field, and the very nature of the field setting can make an article highly interesting due to the sample and context. For example, from a methodological perspective, my article with Ward, Turner, and Sonnenfeld (2000) ("To Your Heart's Content: A Model of Affective Diversity in Top Management Teams") stood out due to our ability to gain access to the self-report personality data of major CEOS (including CEOs drawn from some of the largest companies listed on the NASDAQ Stock Exchange) and their senior management teams. That is, rather than try to estimate personality and group dynamics from outside the organization, thanks to Jeff Sonnenfeld and his CEO Academy, we had the unique ability to gain direct access to self-reports of these CEOS and their senior management teams. Not only did this article "go big" in introducing a new theoretical construct of affective diversity, we were also able to "go big" methodologically by testing the construct in the field, with the self-reports of the predictor and team dynamics from a very compelling and relevant sample, as well as predicting objective financial performance – a very difficult metric to achieve.

In addition, there are some constructs that cannot be effectively cultivated in the lab. In emotions research, for example, it can be very difficult to meaningfully generate some emotions. It is also very difficult to cultivate in the lab the long-term relationships that are more representative of actual ongoing organizational teams and relationships. This is not to say that the lab is not helpful. Beyond the obvious causal inferences and control, the laboratory setting is very useful for enabling the analysis of micro-processes that need more involved measures and methods—including physiological, video, or other coding methods that would be very difficult, if not impossible, in the field. However, as organizational scholars, if we are to understand organizations, we cannot assume that our laboratory results will automatically generalize to field settings, and over time it is important to have our constructs tested across various field settings.

This leads to a thought about the meaning of lack of replication: if a result does not replicate from lab to field, or from field to field, or even from lab to lab, it does not mean that we necessarily have a "replication crisis" or that researchers are unethical, p-hacking, incompetent fools. It more likely means we are engaging in the proper, iterative process of science (Kuhn, 2012) in a particularly complex domain—the human psyche and behavior. Results may or may not replicate, and it is in learning about when they do and do not that we learn more about our phenomenon of interest.

All of this relates to a broader point about generating interesting and relevant research—the importance of methodological versatility. This allows for testing phenomena in the most appropriate and comprehensive way possible and not being limited in one's questions by being limited in one's methods. One of the things I so appreciated about my doctoral training, and that I actively encourage when training doctoral students, is learning the importance of being able to do the study that best fits the question, using the most appropriate method. This could include, for example, field studies, lab and field experimentation, archival research, video-coding techniques, network methodologies, qualitative studies, physiological measures, and simulations. While it is impossible to be proficient across all methods, being proficient in at least two or three is very helpful to fully understanding and testing one's ideas.

I do want to offer a strong caveat, however. When I say I learned about putting as much as possible into one study, I definitely do not at all mean that every study must, for example, have two different types of methods (e.g., a lab and field study together). Very often, a single method (with multiple raters or measures) is absolutely sufficient and actually most appropriate. For example, if an elaborate, immersive study (or studies) has taken place in a laboratory, with multiple raters, video ratings, behavioral outcomes, and so forth, it is not necessary or fair to require an additional field study to try to show generalizability. That should be left to future field studies. In this vein, a disturbing trend has begun whereby reviewers and editors ask scholars who have very rich field data (but the data did not allow the collection of mediators, for example) to supplement their study with a laboratory study. While, of course, as organizational behavior scholars we ultimately want to understand what drives results, this can also be more appropriately the province of future research. Furthermore, these "tacked on" laboratory or online M-turk/Qualtrics studies may not be the most appropriate way to determine these mediators and moderators. While there should be as much triangulation and sophistication in the data collection as is reasonable, reviewers and editors should also exercise judgment about when more data might be needed rather than turning it into a rote request.

Overall, with regard to method, one of the most important things I have learned is to pay intense attention to every detail in your study. Take the time at the beginning to plan extensively what you are going to study. In terms of methodology, ensure you spend as much time creating your materials, such as designing your survey questions, training your confederates, creating your manipulations, and coding videos, texts, and archival data, as you do on your theorizing and writing. This is important in both lab and field, but if you have easier access to laboratory participants (either in person or online), this becomes even more critical in the field. This is because field researchers are accessing a very scarce resource—a set of employees who are busy, and who, along with their organizations, are giving you their time. Gathering as much information as possible (without inducing participant fatigue, of course) is the essence of engaging in responsible field research. However, given the contextual nature of such research, you may not have thought of everything, and you must be aware that it will be very difficult, if not impossible, to go back after you have gathered your data. Consequently, make sure you have asked as broad a set of questions as possible and have achieved as high a response rate as you can. In addition, always make sure, in both the laboratory and field, to run an in-depth pretest. Ultimately, the excellence of your method—be it lab or field or archival or simulation—will carry the day as much as your theorizing. As I have learned, you need to "go big" in both theory and method.

What I Have Learned about . . . Coauthors

I have always loved coauthoring and have only published one sole-authored study in my career—my dissertation. Coauthors do many things to improve the research and final article. They further ideas, help with accessing data and improving designs, share in the workload, increase motivation, enhance the writing, and often become lifelong friends. In fact, on a metalevel, coauthors have been a major source of learning for me from the very beginning, from coauthoring with my mentors to coauthoring with my contemporaries and to coauthoring with my students. This does not mean that coauthoring does not come without costs. From a career perspective, particularly earlier on, there is always a question about what part of the work comes from you or the coauthor. As a way to deal with this, particularly early on in your career, while you do not need to publish alone, you do need to be first author with some frequency, particularly in the domains that define your research identity.

Though it's disappointing, I have also learned that until you have achieved tenure, you should ideally not continue to publish with your advisors/mentors from graduate school(beyond any projects that already exist from your graduate school days—clearly do not drop those). One of my few regrets is that I was not able to conduct more studies with my doctoral advisors, as it was so much fun and gratifying to work with them. However, there is a danger that you will not receive enough credit in the beginning to make it worthwhile.

After tenure—do whatever you would like (with the mild cautionary note that similar questions may be asked at the full professor promotion level—but not as much). Definitely—after becoming full professor—you can absolutely do what you would like!

All this is not to say there are no cautionary tales about coauthoring. I have been very fortunate that most of my coauthoring experiences have been good, but the very few that have not been successful have been somewhat painful, even when involving well-meaning coauthors. Usually, problems are related to misaligned expectations. As a result, I have learned to be very honest about expectations regarding all aspects of how I work and the roles everyone will play in the project. For example, regarding timing, people have different needs and availability throughout their careers, and being upfront about your time frame and availability leads to much clearer expectations. I have also learned to be very clear about how processes will unfold. I, for example, like to write and rewrite. I see writing as a collaborative and iterative process, and if that is not what your coauthor expects or wants, it can be a problem. At the beginning of a project, I have learned, it is important to candidly discuss the maximum number of authors and the authorship order. This does not mean that there will not be changes, but it gives a good sense of who is responsible for what, at least initially, and allows people to gracefully bow out (myself included) if the coauthorship does not make sense. Most important, I have learned that my relationships with my colleagues are more important to me than any one article.

What I Have Learned ... about How Things outside Academia Lead to Better Research

I have learned that living a full and balanced life leads to better research creativity, motivation, and emotional stability. I was supremely fortunate to marry my husband, Jonathan Barsade, who has been my greatest friend, supporter, and cheerleader. He has been emotionally and practically supportive (for example, pulling an "all-nighter" to recover my corrupted dissertation document the day before it was due—after I had given up at 1 a.m., gone to bed, and resigned myself to graduating the next semester; or when he would take our children to visit family during a few – or many - key crunch times). Regarding children, we knew we wanted them and liked the idea of being younger parents (thinking the stamina would be helpful—and it was!). Thus, we decided to have our first child just before the last year of my doctoral program. She was born in June, the summer prior to my fourth and last year of my doctoral program, and then I went on the job market in December/late January—which was the timing of the job market at that time.[4] This timeline worked well, and I recommend that doctoral students interested in and considering having a child feel comfortable doing so any time after their comprehensive exams, as there is rarely as much relative free time again, particularly once you are a junior faculty member. Two years into my first job at the Yale School of Management, we had our second child. While there was no maternity policy yet, and I did not receive any teaching reduction, I was allowed to front-load my teaching into one semester before his birth in May, which gave me flexibility. Our third child was born 10 years after our first (still no teaching reduction but again the ability to front-load my teaching, which was very helpful). She was born in my last year at Yale, before I joined the faculty at Wharton.

Throughout my career, our children and family have been an integral part of my life, which is to say an integral and productive part of my work life as well. This is not to say that all has been easy. When faced with challenges we got creative. For example, my husband commuted from New Haven to his job in Dallas for two years, and then from New Haven to Los Angeles for three years after that, when our two eldest children were young. While he came back every weekend without fail, it meant I was home alone with the two children during the week. In looking for help, we had the good fortune to be able to send our children to Creating Kids, an amazing childcare center directly across the street from our house. We also had fantastic au pairs (many of whom we are still in touch with today). While the stint of long-distance family life was of course difficult, it was worth it. After I left Yale and moved to Wharton, we finally all lived in the same place again (in fact, it was a nonnegotiable criterion for us all at that point). The process of going full speed ahead with both work and family was not always easy, but it was incredibly fulfilling and put everything that was happening at work, both good and bad, into perspective. I found that I was living something my Wharton colleague Nancy Rothbard has found evidence for, that integrating work life into family life

---

[4] This relates to an issue I have as yet tried unsuccessfully to help with in my role as Organizational Behavior Division chair regarding the moving up of the OB job market to early in the fall—and sometimes even late summer. I am concerned about the possible harm our field is doing to our doctoral students as they do not have the full fall to prepare for the job market, so the earlier job market keeps them in programs for longer than needed, with the commensurate loss of income. This process given an (apparent) advantage to a subset of first-mover schools trying to obtain faculty members by pressuring them into early decisions who they may not have otherwise said yes to but unfortunately has forced most schools to move up their hiring dates. This process is not useful for the doctoral students, or likely even the first-mover universitiees (as hires may be more likely to leave if they have been pressured out of fear to accept an offer that otherwise they would have taken the time to consider more carefully and realize that it was not a good fit), nor to our doctoral education system as a whole (particularly as it adds fiscal pressure on doctoral programs to support students for a longer time, and thus reduce the number of new students admitted into the field)

enriches work life (Rothbard, 2001). I was more grounded, and had a better perspective and greater empathy, and it helped my psychological resilience in the inevitably difficult times we all have in our daily work lives. In the other direction, my work also helped to give perspective and relevance when things were more challenging related to family matters.

I would like to stress that the benefits of work–life balance are not only about family. The balance can come from volunteering, hobbies, callings, sports, exercise, music—whatever one does outside work that helps keep perspective, stamina, and creative energy. Indeed, one of my proudest accomplishments was, while a junior faculty member, helping to cofound the Connecticut Children's Museum with Sandra Malmquist, its executive director. I think I spent at least two top-level articles' worth of time on this when one might have reasonably argued that they would have been better for my career. However, the creative outlet, satisfaction of community outreach, and partnership with an amazing group of people fed directly into my research and helped me stay motivated, energetic, and optimistic, even when dealing with the usual setbacks of our field. I would argue that it actually helped the overall quality of my work. Nevertheless, this is not an exhortation that one need not work hard and focus to succeed. It would be disingenuous to say I was able to do all this and not work very hard. I did, and still do, frequently. I spend a tremendous amount of time on work, and usually enjoy it, although occasionally it was not balanced; there are certainly times in one's career when one needs to hunker down—sometimes for relatively long stretches of time—and just get the work done. However, overall, I have learned that it would have been a major disservice to both family, work and other aspects of my life if I had put everything else on a long-term hold until a particular "tenure" or "full professorship" or other important work milestone was met. For me work is a textured part of the rest of life, not something life waits for.

What I Have Learned . . . Not to Do

I have discussed above all the things that I have learned "to do"—but equally of help are all the things I have learned not to do, which I describe here.

I have learned not to hold onto projects that are not worth holding onto, even after significant effort has been invested in them—and to drop them relatively quickly. Projects should be dropped for a variety of reasons; clearly, if hypotheses prove to be incorrect or if the data collection efforts will not come to fruition, or even if my coauthors and I let a project lag and just can't seem to complete it (sometimes serving as behavioral evidence that the project is "meh" and should likely be dropped). There have been many incredibly time-intensive field and lab studies that my colleagues and I executed well but had no significant results. I have long considered it a shame that there is no "Journal of Null Results" in which authors' methods and theory would be reviewed as rigorously as in other journals but without the requirement of significance. Some journals are now heading in this direction, and I think it bodes well for our field. However, I have learned that if you think your study is not viable, either due to results or an unintended fatal flaw that can't be remedied (particularly in field settings, where it can be harder to go back), let the study go, preferably quickly. Otherwise, it can be both a time sink and, worse, a psychological albatross.

I definitely do not think this is the case if you have determined that you have a well-done, well-argued article and have entered the review process. In that case, persistence, and grit are not only worthwhile but absolutely necessary. Stay true to the good research you know you did. You may have had an unlucky draw in reviewers or associate editors, or your rejection could be the result of academic politics or turf wars. If you believe in your study, it is important to persist. This persistence is particularly important when the primary thing that is holding you back is your own fear of having the article rejected.

I have learned that one should not be a disagreeable reviewer. Having been on many editorial boards, a special edition associate editor, a reviewer of countless articles, and a receiver of reviews, I am taken aback by how condescending, mean-spirited, and arrogant some reviewers can be. Reviews are not meant to be punching bag sessions or opportunities to "enlighten" the ignorant or less scholarly pure among us. I assume that anyone who has sent in an article has done so in good faith, and in general, I adopt the principle of "MRI," the most respectful interpretation. I grant you that some articles can be infuriating, annoying, or just poorly done. However, when authors submit articles they do not do so with negative intentions but with hope and sincerity. Knowledge in our field will grow, and feedback will be better accepted, if it is offered constructively and positively. There is a way to write the same review more positively—your points are still communicated and will be received better than if you are being mean-spirited.

Having said that, I have also learned that it is a good idea as an author to be responsive to your reviewers, whether they are mean-spirited or not. Most of the articles my colleagues and I have written have been improved through the review process. Reviewers often dedicate significant time and thought to reviews, and adopting the MRI toward them, as well, is helpful in the review process. It is also more likely to lead to one's article being published. I was recently a reviewer on an article in which the authors sent back a revision containing one-line responses to the reviewers' comments, more or less saying that they disagreed, and that was it. While that was certainly their right as authors, it was not helpful for moving their article forward in the review process. This is not to say you cannot respectfully disagree with reviewers and editors and still prevail. There have been situations where I absolutely disagreed with both, but in such cases I put forth a respectful and very thorough argument, and I have not seen this impede article acceptance.

I have learned *not* to make a habit of saying no. Rather I have learned that it is generally better to say yes"(judiciously) as often as possible. I realize this goes against the current ethos of learning how to better say no and "saying no" support groups. However, many of the most successful and unique opportunities I have had during my career came out of saying yes to an unexpected and unsolicited request to join a phone call, meeting, conference, speaking opportunity, or study opportunity with wonderful coauthors whom I did not initially know. Even joining committees or doing volunteer work for the field have had great benefits. For example, my *Administrative Science Quarterly* article about affective diversity with Andrew Ward, Jean Turner, and Jeff Sonnenfeld (2000) came from a dinner I had with an acquaintance at the Academy Meetings, when he said he had a colleague, Andrew Ward, who was doing a study with Jeff Sonnenfeld and he thought it could be a good collaboration. If I had said no to dinner, or no to meeting Andrew Ward, or no to the collaboration, this research study would not have happened. I have many stories like this in which an invitation to meet with someone, or give a talk, that would have been easier to say no to led to unique data gathering opportunities, even including the largest research grant I have ever received. I realize that we all become inundated, but my orientation has always been to stay open to opportunities, as they have led to some of the best research I have done and experiences I have had, enhancing the conditions for creativity and productivity. Yes, it is unquestionably a challenge to maintain balance (and that could be an entire chapter in its own right), but I have learned that saying yes more often than no is worth it.

I have learned that we must not be cruel to ourselves. I cannot tell you how many academics, at all stages, berate themselves for a variety of things: for example, they haven't produced enough articles; they have produced too many articles that are not significant enough; they haven't published in journals where they thought they should; publishing takes them too long; they were passed over for an award they should have received, or a professional society or conference to which they should have been invited; and of course the big ones—they didn't receive the job they wanted, or tenure (the first time), or full professorship promotions. I have seen successful scholars (to the outside world) still displaying their sensitivity and insecurity many years later about formative negative experiences they have had in the field, or ruminate about ways they have not been successful or were not respected in the way they thought they should have been. I understand the feelings of hurt and anger, but one thing I have learned is that we are often our own harshest career judges. No one else is looking at, or giving thought, to our publication records and career progression as much as we are. That is not to say that one should not be realistic or take in negative feedback. For example, if there is something specific that I have done that has gone poorly, I allow myself to feel it first, and then I analyze the experience, and genuinely try to take away a learning from it, and promise myself I will apply these lessons in the future. If I do that, I find it brings me rewards in terms of being less likely to repeat the mistake, as well as greater peace of mind. Overall, I have learned that we should be kinder to ourselves, give ourselves a break, and appreciate what we have accomplished.

Conclusion

I have learned that everyone's journey is different when creating a rigorous and interesting research career. Thus, one could legitimately ask what the reader has to gain from what I have learned . . . My hope is that this chapter will inspire scholars who see themselves in it, or who could see themselves in it, and help them to realize that they are not alone. My hope is that some of my views will spark ideas or debates in the minds of readers and future scholars, leading to greater insights. My greatest hope is that what I have learned will help other scholars learn, succeed, and thrive in one of the most interesting and important careers out there.

References

Amabile, T. M., Barsade, S. G., Mueller, J. S., & Staw, B. M. (2005). Affect and creativity at work. *Administrative Science Quarterly, 50*, 367–403.

Ashford, S. J. (2013). Having scholarly impact: The art of hitting academic home runs. *Academy of Management Learning & Education, 12*, 4, 623–633.

Barsade, S. G. (2002). The ripple effect: Emotional contagion and its influence on group behavior. *Administrative Science Quarterly, 47*, 644–675.

Barsade, S. G., & O'Neill, O. A. (2014). What's love got to do with It? The influence of a culture of companionate love and employee and client outcomes in a long-term care setting. *Administrative Science Quarterly, 59*, 551–598.

Barsade, S. G., Ramarajan, L., & Westen, D. (2009). Implicit affect in organizations. In B. Staw and A. Brief (Eds.), *Research in Organizational Behavior, 29*, 135–162.

Barsade, S. G., Ward, A. J., Turner, J. D. F., & Sonnenfeld, J. A. (2000). To your heart's content: A model of affective diversity in top management teams. *Administrative Science Quarterly, 45,* 802–836.

Chatman, J. A., & Barsade, S. G. (1995). Personality, organizational culture and cooperation: Evidence from a business simulation. *Administrative Science Quarterly, 40,* 423–443.

Filipowicz, A., Barsade, S. G., & Melwani, S. (2011). emotional transitions in social interactions: beyond Steady state emotion. *Journal of Personality and Social Psychology, 101,* 541–556.

Huang, T. Y. Souitaris, V, & Barsade, S. G. (2019). Which matters more? Group fear versus group hope in entrepreneurial escalation of commitment to a losing venture. *Strategic Management Journal, 40*(11), 1852–1881.

Kuhn, T. S. (2012). *The structure of scientific revolutions.* University of Chicago Press.

Melwani, S., & Barsade, S. G. (2011). Held in contempt: The psychological, interpersonal, and performance outcomes of contempt in a work setting. *Journal of Personality & Social Psychology, 101,* 503–520.

Rothbard, N. P. (2001). Enriching or depleting? The dynamics of engagement in work and family roles. *Administrative Science Quarterly, 46*(4), 655–684.

Staw, B. M., & Barsade, S. G. (1993). Affect and managerial performance: A test of the sadder-but-wiser vs. happier-and-smarter hypotheses. *Administrative Science Quarterly, 38,* 304–331.

Watson, D., Clark, L. A., & Tellegen, A. (1988). Development and validation of brief measures of positive and negative affect: The PANAS scales. *Journal of Personality and Social Psychology, 54*(6), 1063.

5

From One Empirical Study to 150

Performance Feedback Research

Henrich R. Greve

Let me start with a personal note. I was surprised to be asked to contribute to a book on influential management research streams because the subject runs counter to some features of my research agenda. I typically like to start new forms of research, or question existing forms, and there are so many interesting theories and research topics in the field that I have never stayed focused on a single one for long. Still, I understood why I was asked to contribute to this book. Performance feedback is a rapidly growing research stream, I have had a role in starting and promoting it, and it is exactly the kind of organizational research that is popular among management scholars because it involves organizational responses to environmental pressures. Performance feedback research is about organizational responses to adversity. When does the organization start searching for solutions to the problem (or even, threat) of low performance on one or more goals and what kind of solutions does it find? When will it make changes in response to the low performance? Answering these questions is of interest both as a basic social science question and as a highly practical question with managerial implications. Many jobs depend on managers getting this answer right. Many unscientific forms of advice to managers, provided by advisors unaware of the conclusions of performance feedback research, are therefore harmful.[1]

My research on performance feedback started in 1994, in a very typical way. It is a fundamental problem facing organizations, and as with all fundamental problems, theory and some evidence were already in place. Specifically, the famous pages 120–127 in Cyert and March (1963) provided an excellent statement of the theory, and there was direct precursor research on organizational change (Manns & March, 1978) and slightly less direct precursors

---

[1] My favorite example is the Balanced Scorecard, which would be a wonderful tool if managers were more rational than our research suggests they are. If our findings on the use of this tool in the real world hold true (Audia, Brion, and Greve, 2015), its use will prevent timely solutions of organizational problems by letting managers indulge in self-enhancing goal selection.

Henrich R. Greve, *From One Empirical Study to 150* In: *A Journey toward Influential Scholarship*. Edited by: Xiao-Ping Chen and H. Kevin Steensma, Oxford University Press. © Oxford University Press 2021. DOI: 10.1093/oso/9780190070717.003.0005

in a research stream on risk taking (e.g., Bromiley, 1991; Fiegenbaum, 1990; Fiegenbaum & Thomas, 1986), that was mostly dormant at the time. I was a doctoral student and had just discovered excellent data for testing the theory using market share data and format (strategic position) changes in radio stations. The only problem was that my dissertation was on another topic (Greve, 1995, 1996), and I was in a hurry to graduate, so I just coded the data and promised myself not to analyze it until I had a job. In fact, following the sage advice of my dissertation chair, Jim March,[2] I did not tell the other dissertation committee members that I had the data. He was confident that they would order me to analyze it before leaving Stanford University, which would delay my work on my dissertation studies.

The theory and findings of performance feedback should be familiar enough now that I don't need to repeat them, but it is worthwhile examining how my research started. The theory of problemistic search is that low performance triggers search for solutions. However, "low" is not defined on an absolute scale; instead it means lower than an aspiration level for a given goal. The aspiration level is gradually updated based on what the same organization and its peers experience. For my research, this meant that I needed a sample of organizations that cared about the same goal; that I could follow over a long enough time that I could update their aspiration levels; and that made some changes as a result of search. The main extensions of the theory that I made were to (1) clarify that search resulted in change, so a theory of search could predict change; (2) note that risk considerations would influence the relationship from performance to change; and (3) distinguish between social (peer) and historical (own) sources of aspiration levels. The radio broadcasting data were perfect for the study. The findings were so clearly in support that it proved easy to publish (Greve, 1998), and a follow-up study using the same data was also straightforward (Greve, 2002).

Note on starting research streams: a great theory deserves perfect data. I know there are arguments in the literature that there should be a trade-off between the theoretical progress and the data quality needed to publish a study, and I agree that journals can make that trade-off (Sutton & Staw, 1995). I don't think scholars should. If you want your theory to get attention, give it a strong start. I was lucky to have data come so easily for this test, but for most theoretical tests spending more time to collect better data is worth the extra effort. For some reason, untested theory can remain untested for a long time, even when it is written in a famous book or cited by everyone, so there is no

---

[2] Yes, James G. March, author of the behavioral theory of the firm.

reason for urgency. There is a very good reason for patience: better tests get more attention.

Given how old the theory was, it is interesting to consider why it had not been examined before in the way I did, and what novelty my study had to offer. I think the answer to the first question is that this theory, in 1963, was ahead of its time. Cyert and March (1963) gave a complete and well-specified theory that to a modern reader translates directly to an empirical test, but at that time empirical methods were less developed, and the theory was read as more of a metaphor than an empirical hypothesis. That's understandable; but it has always been harder for me to understand why modern readers didn't see the empirical test clearly enough. The empirical test literally jumped off the pages of their book, so the only remaining problem was to find data that fit.

What I had to offer was very little, and mostly on the empirical side. I added some alternative theoretical suggestions on how to interpret the original statement on the performance to search relation (Figure 1 in Greve, 1998) and settled on one of them as being the most plausible. I made the simple assumption that search translated directly into a probability of making changes, so I could use a search theory to study likelihood of change. This transition from search to change made me worry enough about risk considerations that I ended up writing much more theory about risk than later researchers have needed to. (But see Kacperczyk, Beckman, & Moliterno, 2015.)[3] The rest of my additions were empirical. It did not seem plausible to me that the performance to change relation would have the same slope above and below the aspiration level, so I used the old technique of spline variables to capture the difference.[4] Updating the historical aspiration level requires a parameter that is unknown to the researcher and complicates the estimation very much if we try to estimate directly, so I used a simple optimization approach that compares log likelihood levels at different parameter values. The spline variables and parameter estimation approaches quickly became part of the normal methodology for performance feedback research. Different ways of creating and using aspiration levels have been proposed and compared empirically in later studies (Blettner, He, Hu, & Bettis, 2015; Bromiley & Harris, 2014; Hu, Blettner, & Bettis, 2011; Labianca, Fairbank, Andrevski, & Parzen, 2009; Moliterno, Beck, Beckman, & Meyer, 2014; Washburn & Bromiley, 2012) and seems likely to become an active branch of this theory.

---

[3] Although this simplifying assumption has worked very well in empirical research so far, I have always thought that it left room for more research on how search translates into change.

[4] I know that management researchers prefer statistical techniques to have fancy names, so I asked colleagues doing econometrics and statistics for an accepted and better-sounding term than *spline*. There isn't any.

Note on old theory: I have found that retesting old theory has two forms of appeal relative to creating new theory. The first is that the age of the theory is typically a good indicator of its importance, or at least the importance of the question it seeks to answer. The second is that older theory that is yet untested is often very easy to turn into an empirical study because the methodological limitations faced by researchers then were so much greater than they are now.

After the first study on performance feedback, one problem stuck to my mind. Remember that this was a period with much research on population ecology and much consideration of how organizational inertia prevents change (e.g., Hannan, 1997; Ruef, 1997). Organizational inertia is greater in large and old organizations (Hannan & Freeman, 1984), so there would be good reason to suspect that the small and (often) young radio stations I studied would be a particularly easy test of the theory. None of the reviewers examining my first study thought of it, but once the study was published it would only be a matter of time until someone made that critique. My test may have been too easy and not generalizable across different types of organizations. I definitely did not want this research to end up as theory and evidence of how only radio stations (and maybe restaurants) made changes.

Clearly, for the next empirical test I needed data on large and preferably also old organizations with significant assets and history that committed them to the past. In fact, whether the findings still held for such organizations was an interesting question for me. So I collected data on performance and changes in the shipbuilding industry. This was a very extensive and time-consuming data collection project, but I knew it would give two studies, one on R&D intensity and innovations and one on production assets. Both are important for shipbuilders because the assets (shipyards and equipment) are what builds ships, and innovations add value to them. By the way, I knew that the innovation study would be an easy sell and the asset study would be harder to publish because management journals love innovations but rarely think that production assets are important. I was right, though fortunately the asset study could be published the same year as the innovation study, and in a good journal (Greve, 2003a, b).[5] The data collection proved worthwhile because the theory held also for these firms and outcomes. The addition of these two studies gave the theory a much firmer empirical foundation and drew attention to it as well. With the predictions found to hold for radio stations and shipbuilders, it seemed plausible that the many organizations with assets, employees, and age in between would also follow its predictions.

---

[5] *Industrial and Corporate Change* was perfect for the asset study because economists read it too, and they think assets are important.

At the same time, I wrote a book to give a longer treatment of the theory and to bring in precursor work and work from related disciplines, and to discuss more freely ideas that were not easy to test right away. Articles are typically stripped of theoretical statements beyond those needed for the specific empirical test, so they often give insufficient suggestions for future research. The aim of the book was to provide a resource to others wanting to do this research (Greve, 2003c), so that they could easily use theory that I had identified as untested, or write their own theoretical additions, and follow up with empirical tests and study writing. A book with deeper theory and many untested ideas can seed the ground for additional research on a research stream. Indeed, the acceleration in research on performance feedback can be dated to the publication of the book and these two studies in the same year.

Note on follow-up studies: even if reviewers overlook a problem with the generalizability of findings, that does not mean that I forget it. Any weakness of an early published study in a research stream is a good reason to conduct follow-up research. The data to do so may be hard to get, but again, patience is a virtue.

Note on authorship: so far, four studies and a book were all single authored. This was not entirely planned,[6] but it is something I have done when trying to start other research streams too. For writing a study that may start a research stream, it is valuable to fully control the data collection, analysis, and study writing. This is unlike studies in established research streams, because these are often done more easily with coauthors. The single-author model gives the opportunity to be very exacting in the empirical procedures, to formulate the theory just as I want it, and to be patient. I have only deviated from this rule when another scholar was absolutely necessary to formulate a study that started a research stream (e.g., Greve & Rao, 2012).

After the three publications in 2003, I took a break from this research stream. I wanted to see whether others started working on it and how they reacted to it, because that would indicate what the best next step would be for me to take. In addition, I did not want to look like I wanted to monopolize the theory and try to publish a lot before others got a chance to work on it. In the meantime, I was working on the causes and effects of interorganizational networks, an entirely different research stream that had existed long before I got my PhD, but with enough unsolved problems related to how networks change over time that I could work on some interesting studies with

---

[6] I asked Jim March to coauthor the first study on performance feedback, and he declined. He said that I already had the idea clearly formulated and had the training necessary to do it, so there was no need for him. I always knew him to be gracious, but I wish he had been willing to take more of the credit.

coauthors (e.g., Mitsuhashi & Greve, 2009; Rowley, Greve, Rao, Baum, & Shipilov, 2005) and coedit a special issue (Brass, Galaskiewicz, Greve, & Tsai, 2004). I had enough to do and wanted to see if the studies and book I had put out inspired others.

Note on building streams: a research stream is something much bigger than one author or a set of authors; it is a set of ideas that inspire researchers. Research that cannot inspire should be looked at critically. Is it uninteresting or poorly done, or does it overlap with better work? Or might it be ahead of its time? *Inspire* means that others do research that replicates, extends, and criticizes it. It is not enough to count citations, because they can be ceremonial or just acknowledgments of an idea. *Inspire* means that others are using your work as a template for their own.

Note on stepping back: once a research stream is taking shape, the need for control is no longer important. It is actually more important to help others get started, both theoretically and empirically. Their independent work will give significant insights.

I started the research again once I realized that interest in performance feedback research had grown, and people were reusing their current data or collecting new data to test performance feedback theory (e.g., Audia & Brion, 2007; Baum, Rowley, Shipilov, & Chuang, 2005; Haleblian, Kim, & Rajagopalan, 2006; Miller & Chen, 2004; Moliterno & Wiersema, 2007; Park, 2007; Schwab, 2007). It was also clear that this research stream reproduced well. Articles contained replications and extensions, and most articles had extensions because the fundamental research ideas in this stream easily extend in many directions. The data collection and methodology held high quality across author teams, indicating that the initial publications had given enough information to establish a "recipe" for what a performance feedback study should look like, and authors did not try to do cheaper kinds of research with less secure conclusions. They did make sensible variations in the research design to fit the context and to obtain types of evidence that were different from what earlier studies had provided.

Note on quality: when starting a research stream, the data collection and methodology of the first studies are important both because they set a standard that follow-up studies need to meet and because the quality of the methods documentation determines how well the methods are understood. Too difficult and too easy methods are both problematic because future research should happen, and it should give correct answers.

After seeing that this research stream had become established, I entered it again. Nearly all the new work I have done since has been coauthored, with my data or others' data, with my ideas or others' ideas. All of it has solved problems or made extensions. With data on innovative organizational forms obtained by Silvia Massini we could examine whether organizations with different performance levels chose their reference groups differently (Massini, Lewin, & Greve, 2005). With the shipbuilding data it proved possible to look more closely at the effect of size on reactions to performance feedback (Audia & Greve, 2006). Data on the insurance industry that I originally collected for a different research idea proved helpful in examining how organizations react to performance feedback on multiple goals (Greve, 2008). Data on Indian business groups collected by Balagopal Vissa proved useful for examining how performance feedback has different effects depending on the organizational structure (Vissa, Greve, & Chen, 2010). Data on Canadian investment banks collected by Andrew Shipilov helped discover how performance and network position goals influence the partner selection of organizations (Shipilov, Li, & Greve, 2011). Data on Canadian firms' changes in governance collected by Andrew Shipilov and Tim Rowley gave findings on how performance acts along with interorganizational imitation to influence behaviors (Shipilov, Greve, & Rowley, 2010) and how media coverage can serve as a goal (Shipilov, Greve, & Rowley, 2019). Data on the airline industry collected by Vibha Gaba and myself gave more information on multiple goals, especially when failure on each goal can potentially lead to the organization failing (Gaba & Greve, 2019). An experimental study let us examine how problemistic search was influenced by self-enhancement (Audia, Brion, & Greve, 2015) A study using survey data collected by Chanan Ben-Oz gave more direct access to performance and aspiration level assessments than the earlier studies using archival data had done (Ben-Oz & Greve, 2015).

The ideas for the work mentioned in the previous paragraph came from different sources, and the most important source was conversations with colleagues. Once performance feedback research started accumulating, scholars looked at it carefully and started having doubts or questions about elements of the research, and I often ended up hearing about them. Often the questions came with suggestions of potential answers, or ideas for data that would be suitable for answering them. The study with Pino Audia came out of a discussion we had at an Academy of Management Association meetings. Colleagues at INSEAD are interested in how interorganizational governance or partnership ties affect behaviors, and were a valuable source of ideas on how these influences work along with performance feedback. The start of this research from archival data has led to questions of whether the findings would still hold when doing experiments or surveys. Many scholars have asked the question "Does the goal X predict change Y," where either the goal X or the type of change Y or both have not been examined yet. I have ended up doing joint research studies with many scholars who have raised a question that we could think of a way to solve. Most research studies in this stream have been done by others than me because it is easy to use the theory to formulate new hypotheses and design studies to test them, so there is no need for my involvement.

Thanks to the work of many others, there was significant growth in the evidence on performance feedback, as well as in related areas of learning theory and the behavioral theory of the firm. To make it easier for newcomers to enter these fields of research, I have collaborated on some reviews of the research. (Argote & Greve, 2007; Gavetti, Greve, Levinthal, & Ocasio, 2012; Greve & Gaba, 2017; Greve & Teh, 2018). I am also pleased to see that not all reviews have involved me or my close collaborators (Posen, Keil, Kim, & Meissner, 2018; Shinkle, 2012; Verver, van Zelst, Lucas, & Meeus, 2019).

Note on taking stock: once a research stream has become large, review studies can serve two complementary roles. One is to summarize the research done so far, showing which empirical questions are answered best and which have missing or unclear answers. The other is to focus on the structure of the theory and its mechanisms and relations to other parts of organization theory, and through that point to especially important areas of research.

This research stream has now reached the stage at which some reorientation could be very valuable. I am not sure it will happen, but I can see a fundamental reason and some recent movement indicating that it is a possibility. The fundamental reason is that the original theory addressed the relation from performance feedback to search and onward to change. I made an empirical simplification of studying the relation from performance feedback to change, but this empirical simplification does not mean that the theory of search can be ignored. The theory of search, in turn, has as one of its main statements that search is myopic. It is originally guided by proximity to the problem (the performance shortfall), or to solutions that are readily at hand, but can become less myopic after the initial myopic search has failed.

My first studies of performance feedback were guided by search theory. I had done an interview study of how radio stations were managed (without publishing the findings) and knew that their preferred performance measure of market share was tightly coupled with the format, so low performance would directly lead to a search for a new format, just as in my empirical test (Greve, 1998). I was familiar with the shipbuilding industry from a year of working for a customer of that industry and through interviewing managers of shipping companies, and I knew that production assets and innovations were among the few tools available for competing in that industry—except for price cuts, of course, which was always their least preferred option. My studies followed the assumption that shipbuilders would direct their search and change efforts to those areas (Greve, 2003a, b). I thought that following search theory carefully in selecting performance and change variables was helpful for showing effects.

Later research showed that I was wrong. A wide range of studies examined performance in the form of return on assets (ROA), which is an important but very generic type of performance, and the studies have linked ROA to a broad range of organizational changes. The conventional search theory that I followed could not have predicted such a wide range of effects. A fair reading would suggest that ROA is a kind of master switch that starts all kinds of search, something I had mentioned as a possibility in my book but never quite believed was possible. Based on the evidence so far, the "master switch" hypothesis is very much a possibility now. This means that the theory is more important than I thought because it predicts more kinds of behaviors. So instead of search being directed mostly at solutions near the problem, it seems to spread out quite widely. This also means that the theory is less precise than I thought because the mechanism of myopic search is unexpectedly weak.

Or is it? This is where the reorientation of the research stream becomes a possibility. Current research predicts *when* organizations will change based on performance feedback. Suppose we change the focus to *what* changes organizations will make based on performance feedback. What theory should we use, and what findings can we expect?

Some recent movements in the field suggest possible routes. One option is to look at how ROA may suggest a direction of search. Because low ROA leads to fewer resources in the organization (returns are lower), it is better to conserve resources when ROA is below aspirations (Kuusela, Keil, & Maula, 2016). Similarly, reconfiguring resources for exploration is better when low ROA indicates strategic problems, whereas exploitation of the current advantage is better when ROA is above aspiration levels (Dothan & Lavie, 2016). These studies revisit the fundamental idea of myopic search and take advantage of the one way in which ROA is specific enough to trigger myopia: it is directly linked to available resources.

A second option is to look at non-ROA goals, often in combination with ROA, to examine which goal most affects the changes, and whether the non-ROA goal can be linked to myopic search. This is usually easier to do with reference to search theory because ROA is the least specific of the major goals that organizations hold. For most other goals, it should be possible to pin down the types of changes that would be myopic responses. I did an early study with growth as a goal, based on the old idea that executives prefer their organizations to be large (Berle & Means, 1932), finding that organizations pursued growth as long as they were not engaged in trying to solve a problem of low ROA (Greve, 2008). Later, I and coauthors looked at other goals with more specific search than ROA, in each case finding clear evidence of myopic search directed by the more specific goal, which was either safety or governance (Gaba & Greve, 2019; Shipilov et al., 2019; Shipilov et al., 2011). This approach of studying myopic search works because most goals are more specific than ROA, and has the added advantage of allowing us some progress in understanding how goal conflicts affect organizations.

A third option is to consider the possibility that search results in more than one option, and to examine how decision-makers choose among them. Here, it is natural to connect the theory to organizational politics and coalition building, which was also part of the behavioral theory of the firm (Cyert & March, 1963). Cyndi Man Zhang and I have looked at how firms make choices on what other firms to acquire as a function of coalition building in their boards of directors (Greve & Zhang, 2017; Zhang & Greve, 2019). This research has not been easy to publish because we reformulated the question to be specifically about how firms choose among alternatives given that the decision to change has been made, which means that the research looks very different from the usual performance feedback study. Instead of examining rates of change with performance relative to the aspiration level as the predictor, we examine choices of actions with performance relative to the aspiration level as a context and the potential for coalitions as the main variable. There are indications in the field that interest in coalition building is increasing, however, so this could be a good time to match performance feedback and coalition theory.

Note on reorientation: research streams that don't expand or reorient run out of steam and die, so reorientation is good as long as it is meaningful. Here, the reorientation is a return to a fundamental question, which is often needed because research streams tend to accumulate in topical peaks, causing some of the broad original issues to be overlooked.

Note on reorientation participation: research streams that are large enough to reorient don't need any founder to direct the reorientation, and there is no ownership of the stream that gives the founders specific rights to control when reorientation happens. I participate and contribute to reorientations that interest me and I have suitable data for. I ignore the others.

Among these three options that are currently being investigated, it seems likely that examination of multiple goals will be the one that will see most research in the beginning. It is very closely related to earlier work, and it gives potential to build new theory in two directions. One is how the goal conflict is resolved, and the other is how myopic search is done. Multiple goals research has been done by many research teams already and has given very productive findings (e.g., Baum et al., 2005; Gaba & Bhattacharya, 2012; Gaba & Greve, 2019; Gaba & Joseph, 2013; Joseph & Gaba, 2015; Kacperczyk et al., 2015; Kotlar, Fang, De Massis, & Frattini, 2014b; Nielsen, 2014; Stevens, Moray, Bruneel, & Clarysse, 2015). Indeed, the long list of citations I just gave is incomplete. Vibha Gaba and I sought to mark this as an important topic in our outline of research opportunities for performance feedback at the organization and group levels (Greve & Gaba, 2017). Indeed, how organizations handle multiple goals by selecting one of them depending on circumstances, or weighting both, or some other way, is part of the inspiration for a book that Pino Audia and I just finished (Audia & Greve, 2021).

It is likely that the work on coalitions will also become a large branch of this research stream. It connects many issues that interest management scholars because it sees the organizational leadership as grappling with problems of responding to poor performance, but also having internal struggles because individuals have different ideas of what solutions are best, or simply have different preferences because of their power base. These are classic issues in organizational theory (e.g., Fligstein, 1990; Hambrick & Mason, 1984; Pfeffer & Salancik, 1978), and they continue to get significant research attention. This branch of research could be particularly influential because it connects the research stream on performance feedback with related research streams on top management team and CEO discretion and choice of action (e.g., Hambrick, 2007; Mishina, Dykes, Block, & Pollock, 2010; Tuggle, Sirmon, Reutzel, & Bierman, 2010) and especially with the research connected with intraorganizational politics (Desai, 2016; McDonald & Westphal, 2003; Stern & Westphal, 2010).

This interaction with related streams is related to a broader process that has started: an expansion of performance feedback research into related fields. Within the broader field of management, there has been a recent increase in studies on performance feedback in family firms (Chrisman & Patel, 2012; Kotlar, De Massis, Fang, & Frattini, 2014a; Kotlar et al., 2014b; Kotlar, Massis, Wright, & Frattini, 2018). Outside the field of management, there is now work on performance feedback in public administration (Ma, 2016; Nielsen, 2014). Performance feedback has also seen work in economics, including experimental work led by Nobel laureate Reinhard Selten (Rosenfeld & Kraus, 2011; Selten, 2008; Selten, Pittnauer, & Hohnisch, 2012). I don't know the dynamics of any of these fields well enough to estimate how far this research will expand, but I will be following its growth to see how well the theory performs when moved out of its original context of business organizations.

Note on related research: research streams can grow either in isolation or in dialogue with related research streams. Both approaches are productive, but it seems that the healthiest approach is to start in isolation in order to develop a clear set of findings, and then to initiate dialogue in order to incorporate effects that initially were overlooked.

I now have my own database of publications, which reached 131 studies at last count, and I know of a metaanalysis reporting findings from 156 studies (Verver et al., 2019). This research stream has become so big that I can no longer keep track of it, which I find both rewarding and frustrating. It has come so far that it does not need me anymore, and I find it very rewarding to see that I am now unnecessary.

It is often said that it is hard to predict what research will become influential, and that there is a certain random component to it. I believe both of those statements are true. I also believe that once a research study has become influential, what follows is less random and much easier to predict. This is important to know, because starting research streams is important but growing and directing them is even more important. Anything that starts but does not grow will fall short of its potential. Scholars who want to contribute to the healthy growth of a research stream they have been involved in starting can help nudge it forward, make it attractive for others to join, suggest changes in direction, and help summarize its conclusions. The notes given in this chapter are my suggestions for how this can be done. I am sure there are other approaches that also work, but at least I can attest to the effectiveness of these.

References

Argote, L., & Greve, H. R. (2007). A behavioral theory of the firm—40 years and counting: Introduction and impact. *Organization Science, 18*(3), 337–349.

Audia, P. G., & Brion, S. (2007). Reluctant to change: Self-enhancing responses to diverging performance measures. *Organizational Behavior & Human Decision Processes, 102*(2), 255–269.

Audia, P. G., Brion, S., & Greve, H. R. (2015). Self-assessment, self-enhancement, and the choice of comparison organizations for evaluating organizational performance. *Advances in Strategic Management: Cognition and Strategy, 32*, 89–118.

Audia, P. G., & Greve, H. R. (2006). Less likely to fail: Low performance, firm size, and factory expansion in the shipbuilding industry. *Management Science, 52*(1), 83–94.

Audia, P. G., & Greve H. R. (2021). *Organizational Learning from Performance Feedback: A Behavioral Perspective on Multiple Goals.* Cambridge University Press: Cambridge.

Baum, J. A. C., Rowley, T. J., Shipilov, A. V., & Chuang, Y.-T. (2005). Dancing with strangers: Aspiration performance and the search for underwriting syndicate partners. *Administrative Science Quarterly, 50*(4), 536–575.

Ben-Oz, C., & Greve, H. R. (2015). Short- and long-term performance feedback and absorptive capacity. *Journal of Management, 41*(7), 1827–1853.

Berle, A. A., & Means, G. C. (1932). *The Modern corporation and private property.* New York: New York: Harcourt, Brace and World.

Blettner, D. P., He, Z.-L., Hu, S., & Bettis, R. A. (2015). Adaptive aspirations and performance heterogeneity: Attention allocation among multiple reference points. *Strategic Management Journal, 36*(7), 987–1005.

Brass, D. J., Galaskiewicz, J., Greve, H. R., & Tsai, W. (2004). Taking stock of networks and organizations: A multi-level perspective. *Academy of Management Journal, 47*(6), 795–814.

Bromiley, P. (1991). Testing a causal model of corporate risk taking and performance. *Academy of Management Journal, 34*(1), 37–59.

Bromiley, P., & Harris, J. D. (2014). A comparison of alternative measures of organizational aspirations. *Strategic Management Journal, 35*(3), 338–357.

Chrisman, J. J., & Patel, P. C. (2012). Variations in R&D investments of family and nonfamily firms: Behavioral agency and myopic loss aversion perspectives. *Academy of Management Journal, 55*(4), 976–997.

Cyert, R. M., & March, J. G. (1963). *A behavioral theory of the firm.* Englewood Cliffs, NJ: Prentice-Hall.

Desai, V. M. (2016). The behavioral theory of the (governed) firm: Corporate board influences on organizations' responses to performance shortfalls. *Academy of Management Journal, 59*(3), 860–879.

Dothan, A., & Lavie, D. (2016). Resource reconfiguration: Learning from performance feedback. Silverman, B. S. (ed), *Resource Redeployment and Corporate Strategy*, 319–369: Emerald.

Fiegenbaum, A. (1990). Prospect theory and the risk-return association. *Journal of Economic Behavior and Organization, 14*, 184–203.

Fiegenbaum, A., & Thomas, H. (1986). Dynamic and risk measurement perspectives on Bowman's risk-return paradox for strategic management: An empirical study. *Strategic Management Journal, 7*, 395–407.

Fligstein, N. (1990). *The transformation of corporate control.* Cambridge, MA: Harvard University Press.

Gaba, V., & Bhattacharya, S. (2012). Aspirations, innovation, and corporate venture capital: A behavioral perspective. *Strategic Entrepreneurship Journal, 6*(2), 178–199.

Gaba, V., & Greve, H. R. (2019). Safe or profitable? The pursuit of conflicting goals. *Organization Science, 30*(4): 647–667.

Gaba, V., & Joseph, J. (2013). Corporate structure and performance feedback: Aspirations and adaptation in M-form firms. *Organization Science, 24*(4), 1102–1119.

Gavetti, G., Greve, H. R., Levinthal, D. A., & Ocasio, W. (2012). The behavioral theory of the firm: Assessment and prospects. *Academy of Management Annals, 6*, 1–40.

Greve, H. R. (1995). Jumping ship: The diffusion of strategy abandonment. *Administrative Science Quarterly, 40* (September), 444–473.

Greve, H. R. (1996). Patterns of competition: The diffusion of a market position in radio broadcasting. *Administrative Science Quarterly, 41*(March), 29–60.

Greve, H. R. (1998). Performance, aspirations, and risky organizational change. *Administrative Science Quarterly, 44* (March), 58–86.

Greve, H. R. (2002). Sticky aspirations: Organizational time perspective and competitiveness. *Organization Science, 13*(1), 1–17.

Greve, H. R. (2003a). A behavioral theory of R&D expenditures and innovation: Evidence from shipbuilding. *Academy of Management Journal, 46*(6), 685–702.

Greve, H. R. (2003b). Investment and the behavioral theory of the firm: Evidence from shipbuilding. *Industrial and Corporate Change, 12*(5), 1051–1076.

Greve, H. R. (2003c). *Organizational learning from performance feedback: A behavioral perspective on innovation and change.* Cambridge, UK: Cambridge University Press.

Greve, H. R. (2008). A behavioral theory of firm growth: Sequential attention to size and performance goals. *Academy of Management Journal*, *51*(3), 476–494.

Greve, H. R., & Gaba, V. (2017). Performance feedback in organizations and groups: Common themes. In L. Argote & J. Levine (Eds.), *Handbook of group and organizational learning*: forthcoming. Oxford: Oxford University Press.

Greve, H. R., & Rao, H. (2012). Echoes of the Past: Organizational foundings as sources of an institutional legacy of mutualism. *American Journal of Sociology*, *118*(3), 635–675.

Greve, H. R., & Teh, D. (2018). Goal selection internally and externally: A behavioral theory of institutionalization. *International Journal of Management Reviews*, *20*, S19–S38.

Greve, H. R., & Zhang, C. M. (2017). Institutional logics and power sources: Merger and acquisition decisions. *Academy of Management Journal*, *60*(2), 671–694.

Haleblian, J., Kim, J.-Y. J., & Rajagopalan, N. (2006). The influence of acquisition experience and performance on acquisition behavior: Evidence from the U.S. commercial banking industry. *Academy of Management Journal*, *49*(2), 357–370.

Hambrick, D. C. (2007). Upper echelons theory: An update. *Academy of Management Review*, *32*(2), 334–343.

Hambrick, D. C., & Mason, P. A. (1984). Upper echelons: The organization as a reflection of its top managers. *Academy of Management Review*, *9*(2), 193–206.

Hannan, M. T. (1997). Inertia, density, and the structure of organizational populations: Entries in European automobile industries, 1886–1981. *Organization Studies*, *18*(2), 193–228.

Hannan, M. T., & Freeman, J. (1984). Structural inertia and organizational change. *American Sociological Review*, *49*, 149–164.

Hu, S., Blettner, D., & Bettis, R. A. (2011). Adaptive aspirations: performance consequences of risk preferences at extremes and alternative reference groups. *Strategic Management Journal*, *32*(13), 1426–1436.

Joseph, J., & Gaba, V. (2015). The fog of feedback: Ambiguity and firm responses to multiple aspiration levels. *Strategic Management Journal*, *36*(13), 1960–1978.

Kacperczyk, A., Beckman, C. M., & Moliterno, T. P. (2015). Disentangling risk and change: Internal and external social comparison in the mutual fund industry. *Administrative Science Quarterly*, *60*(2), 228–262.

Kotlar, J., De Massis, A., Fang, H., & Frattini, F. (2014a). Strategic reference points in family firms. *Small Business Economics*, *43*(3), 597–619.

Kotlar, J., Fang, H., De Massis, A., & Frattini, F. (2014b). Profitability goals, control goals, and the R&D investment decisions of family and nonfamily firms. *Journal of Product Innovation Management*, *31*(6), 1128–1145.

Kotlar, J., Massis, A., Wright, M., & Frattini, F. (2018). Organizational goals: Antecedents, formation processes and implications for firm behavior and performance. *International Journal of Management Reviews*, *20*(S1): 3--18.

Kuusela, P., Keil, T., & Maula, M. (2016). Driven by aspirations, but in what direction? Performance shortfalls, slack resources, and resource-consuming vs. resource-freeing organizational change. *Strategic Management Journal*, 1101–1120.

Labianca, G., Fairbank, J. F., Andrevski, G., & Parzen, M. (2009). Striving toward the future: Aspiration-performance discrepancies and planned organizational change. *Strategic Organization*, *7*(4), 433–466.

Ma, L. (2016). Performance feedback, government goal-setting and aspiration level adaptation: Evidence from Chinese provinces. *Public Administration*, *94*(2), 452–471.

Manns, C. L., & March, J. G. (1978). Financial adversity, internal competition, and curriculum change in a university. *Administrative Science Quarterly*, *23*, 541–552.

Massini, S., Lewin, A. Y., & Greve, H. R. (2005). Innovators and imitators: Organizational reference groups and adoption of organizational routines. *Research Policy*, *34*(10), 1550–1569.

McDonald, M. L., & Westphal, J. D. (2003). Getting by with the advice of their friends: CEOs' advice networks and firms' strategic responses to poor performance. *Administrative Science Quarterly, 48* (1), 1–32.

Miller, K. D., & Chen, W.-R. (2004). Variable organizational risk preferences: Tests of the March-Shapira model. *Academy of Management Journal, 47*(1), 105–115.

Mishina, Y., Dykes, B. J., Block, E. S., & Pollock, T. G. (2010). Why "good" firms do bad things: The effects of high aspirations, high expectations, and prominence on the incidence of corporate illegality. *Academy of Management Journal, 53*(4), 701–722.

Mitsuhashi, H., & Greve, H. R. (2009). A matching theory of alliance formation and organizational success: Complementarity and compatibility. *Academy of Management Journal, 52*(5), 975–995.

Moliterno, T. P., Beck, N., Beckman, C. M., & Meyer, M. (2014). Knowing your place: Social performance feedback in good times and bad times. *Organization Science, 25*(6), 1684–1702.

Moliterno, T. P., & Wiersema, M. F. (2007). Firm performance, rent appropriation, and the strategic resource divestment capability. *Strategic Management Journal, 28*(11), 1065–1087.

Nielsen, P. A. (2014). Learning from performance feedback: Performance information, aspiration levels, and managerial priorities. *Public Administration, 92*(1), 142–160.

Park, K. M. (2007). Antecedents of convergence and divergence in strategic positioning: The effects of performance and aspiration on the direction of strategic change. *Organization Science, 18*(3), 386–402.

Pfeffer, J., & Salancik, G. R. (1978). *The external control of organizations.* New York: Harper and Row.

Posen, H. E., Keil, T., Kim, S., & Meissner, F. D. (2018). Renewing research on problemistic search—A review and research agenda. *Academy of Management Annals, 12*(1), 208–251.

Rosenfeld, A., & Kraus, S. (2011). *Using aspiration adaptation theory to improve learning.* AAMAS, 423–430.

Rowley, T. J., Greve, H. R., Rao, H., Baum, J. A. C., & Shipilov, A. V. (2005). Time to break up: The social and instrumental antecedents of exit from interfirm exchange cliques. *Academy of Management Journal, 48* (3), 499–520.

Ruef, M. (1997). Assessing organizational fit on a dynamic landscape: An empirical test of the relative inertia thesis. *Strategic Management Journal, 18*(11) (December), 837–853.

Schwab, A. (2007). Incremental organizational learning from multilevel information sources: Evidence for cross-level interactions. *Organization Science, 18*(2), 233–251.

Selten, R. (2008). Experimental results on the process of goal formation and aspiration adaptation. *International Symposium on Algorithmic Game Theory*, Berlin, Heidelberg.

Selten, R., Pittnauer, S., & Hohnisch, M. (2012). Dealing with dynamic decision problems when knowledge of the environment is limited: An approach based on goal systems. *Journal of Behavioral Decision Making, 25*(5), 443–457.

Shinkle, G. A. (2012). Organizational aspirations, reference points, and goals. *Journal of Management, 38*(1), 415–455.

Shipilov, A. V., Greve, H. R., & Rowley, T. J. (2019). Is all publicity good publicity? The effect of media pressure on the adoption of governance practices. *Strategic Management Journal, 40*(9), 1368–1393.

Shipilov, A. V., Li, S. X., & Greve, H. R. (2011). The prince and the pauper: Search and brokerage in the initiation of status-heterophilous ties. *Organization Science, 22*(6), 1418–1434.

Stern, I., & Westphal, J. D. (2010). Stealthy footsteps to the boardroom: Executives' backgrounds, sophisticated interpersonal influence behavior, and board appointments. *Administrative Science Quarterly, 55*(2), 278–319.

Stevens, R., Moray, N., Bruneel, J., & Clarysse, B. (2015). Attention allocation to multiple goals: The case of for-profit social enterprises. *Strategic Management Journal, 36*(7), 1006–1016.

Sutton, R. I., & Staw, B. M. (1995). What theory is not. *Administrative Science Quarterly*, *40*(3), 371–384.

Tuggle, C. S., Sirmon, D. G., Reutzel, C. R., & Bierman, L. (2010). Commanding board of director attention: Investigating how organizational performance and CEO duality affect board members' attention to monitoring. *Strategic Management Journal*, *31*(9), 946–968.

Verver, H., van Zelst, M., Lucas, G. J. M., & Meeus, M. T. T. (2019). Understanding heterogeneity in the performance feedback—organizational responsiveness relationship: A meta-analysis. *OSF Preprints*, https://doi.org/10.31219/osf.io/hq4uw.

Vissa, B., Greve, H. R., & Chen, W. R. (2010). Business group affiliation and firm search behavior in India: Responsiveness and focus of attention. *Organization Science*, *21*(3), 696–712.

Washburn, M., & Bromiley, P. (2012). Comparing aspiration models: The role of selective attention. *Journal of Management Studies*, *49*(5), 896–917.

Zhang, C. M., & Greve, H. R. (2019). Dominant coalitions directing acquisitions: Different decision makers, different decisions. *Academy of Management Journal*, *62*(1), 44–65.

6

Embedded Entrepreneurship

Olav Sorenson

Caveat Emptor

In the 1980s and 1990s, Jim March taught a legendary course on leadership at Stanford.[1] Two elements of the course made it remarkable. First, he taught the course entirely from great pieces of literature. In the year that I took it, these included *Don Quixote, Othello,* and *War and Peace.* But legend has it that in many years, he simply asked students on the first day of class what they wanted to read and then taught the course from those literary works.

Second, he brought his own unique lens to the lessons of leadership. The lesson that comes to mind here came from George Bernard Shaw's *Saint Joan.* Jim would use the story of Joan of Arc to explore the distinction between geniuses and heretics. Both innovate. Both challenge the status quo. But while history smiles on some, those proven right, celebrating them as geniuses, it frowns on others, those who turn out to have been wrong, denigrating them as heretics.

But are geniuses and heretics really any different? In betting on a horse race, the stock market, or an idea, someone will always win. Did they win because they had some special insight—seeing a truth that no one else saw—or did they simply get lucky?

The pages of this book are filled with the words and wisdom of geniuses. But any attempt to learn only from success stories deserves a word of warning. These success stories have been chosen in hindsight. In methodological terms, listening only to these accounts amounts to selection on the dependent variable. Many others may have followed similar paths only to find themselves at dead ends—and perhaps defamed as heretics.

The reader should also exercise caution in reading these retrospections for another reason. Despite their best intentions not to revise history, people have

---

[1] Although no record can fully capture the experience of this class, those interested in learning more about the lessons Jim taught in this course can read his book *On Leadership* (March & Weil, 2005). Some aspects of his lecturing style, moreover, have been captured in the film *Passion and Discipline: Don Quixote's Lessons for Leadership.*

Olav Sorenson, *Embedded Entrepreneurship* In: *A Journey toward Influential Scholarship.* Edited by: Xiao-Ping Chen and H. Kevin Steensma, Oxford University Press. © Oxford University Press 2021. DOI: 10.1093/oso/9780190070717.003.0006

a tendency to recall their actions as being the product of calculation and intention. In retrospection, accidents become experiments. Chance events become fated. Meanderings become plans and strategies.

The editors have done their best to guard against this revisionism. They have encouraged all of us to tell the true story behind our research paths, to discuss the missteps that have been made along the way. In my own attempts to recall the random and the regrettable, I have revisited many of the early drafts of these studies, published and unpublished, and a plethora of emails and notes related to them. Despite these attempts to avoid retrospection, however, I would hardly consider myself immune from either hubris or vanity.

Readers should therefore digest this story with a grain of salt. The history I describe here almost certainly has more coherence than an account of the evolution of my ideas would have had if I had written one at the time. The lessons learned have often been inferred without a counterfactual. They detail patterns of behavior, but these patterns may as easily reflect superstition as wisdom.

Embedded Entrepreneurs

Although I have written on a wide range of topics, from corporate strategy to the sociology of science, the research for which I have received the most attention has been on the importance of social relationships to entrepreneurs (Rickne et al., 2018). Many others have pointed to the same phenomenon (e.g., Aldrich & Zimmer, 1986; Larson, 1992). What has been distinctive of my approach to this topic has been to connect it to space and place.

Most social relationships connect people to those who live and work in the same places they do. Overlapping in physical space provides opportunities for people to meet—whether at a school, a church, a club, or a workplace (Feld, 1981). Being close also reduces the cost of developing and maintaining the relationship (Stouffer, 1940). People from the same place have more common interests and acquaintances. Meeting for coffee or dinner requires less travel time if someone is nearby. The odds of unplanned meetings—happening to see a person at a store or on the street—also decline exponentially with distance. These planned and unplanned interactions both strengthen the relationship and provide opportunities for exchanging ideas and information. People therefore end up socially embedded in particular industries (social spaces) and places.

Social relationships influence entrepreneurial outcomes in at least three ways. The first, the demonstration effect, helps to determine who becomes an entrepreneur. The second, the mobilization effect, contributes to the ability of entrepreneurs to build organizations—to raise capital, to hire employees, to secure suppliers, and to attract customers. The third, the anchor effect, roots them to the places in which they have become embedded.

Consider first the demonstration effect. Deciding to found a firm often depends on seeing someone else, a peer, doing it. Although this effect could stem in part from being able to call on that peer, perhaps a friend or a colleague, for insight into the pros and cons of entrepreneurship, much of this effect probably occurs even without interaction. Seeing similar others becoming entrepreneurs, particularly successful entrepreneurs, gives people confidence that they too could do it (Bosma et al., 2012; Sorenson & Audia, 2000). It also sends signals of the economic attractiveness of founding a firm and of the legitimacy of entrepreneurship as a career path (Stuart & Ding, 2006; Sørensen & Sorenson, 2003).

When individuals decide to become entrepreneurs, social relationships have a second, mobilization effect. Entrepreneurs must raise capital, recruit employees, and secure suppliers. Social relationships facilitate this resource mobilization phase. Most early financial capital, for example, comes either from friends and family (Ruef, 2010) or from professional investors with whom the entrepreneur has a prior relationship or at least where the entrepreneur has someone who can introduce her to the investors (Sorenson & Stuart, 2001). Early employees also frequently have prior relationships to the entrepreneur (Ruef, 2010).

Relationships help to facilitate the raising of capital and the recruiting of employees, buyers, and suppliers in three ways. Most start-ups fail. Prospective investors, employees, and partners therefore rightfully approach these commitments with caution. When they have connections to the entrepreneurs, they may have better information about the start-up and better insight into its odds of success. Or they may simply overestimate the entrepreneur, believing the person more able and the ideas more promising than would an objective outsider (Sorenson & Waguespack, 2006). Family and friends might even fund or collaborate with an entrepreneur simply for the satisfaction of supporting the person.

Finally, social relationships create an anchoring effect. Part of this anchoring comes from the resource mobilization effect. Entrepreneurs have the highest odds of success when they start their businesses in places where they have deep roots (Dahl & Sorenson, 2012). But the anchoring effect goes beyond this simple profit calculation. People also value spending time with friends and family. Entrepreneurs therefore prefer to locate their firms in places where they have loved ones (Dahl & Sorenson, 2009; Figueiredo et al., 2002).

In fact, people sometimes even become entrepreneurs because they want to live in a particular place but cannot find a job there.

This perspective and these ideas have informed a stream of studies and projects. I will not discuss every one in detail, but I will try to provide the backstory on a few of them.

First, a Failure

In 1995, when Netscape went public and the entire world became enamored with the internet and its commercial potential, I had been studying at Stanford. Silicon Valley, much of it located on land adjacent to Stanford and owned by the university, sat at the epicenter of that boom (or bubble). It seemed as though everyone wanted to become an entrepreneur or to join a start-up. Magazines, meanwhile, celebrated Silicon Valley as the future of the economy. Being in the midst of the phenomenon undoubtedly spurred my interest in both clusters and entrepreneurship.

Soong Moon Kang, a fellow graduate student (in the Engineering Economic Systems program), shared these interests. We spent hours discussing the ideas. Much of the classic literature on economic geography had argued that location choice stemmed from the need to access physical inputs, such as coal or iron ore (Weber, 1928). But as production moved from being physical to digital, we felt that location choice should shift to depending on proximity to social inputs, such as the availability of specialized suppliers.

We embarked on a research project to explore this idea, focusing on multimedia manufacturers. In 1995, the machines used to press CD-ROMs cost tens of thousands of dollars. Hundreds of firms began to enter the business of publishing CD-ROM titles—copying, selling, and distributing discs. Many of the early titles essentially substituted for physical books. You could, for example, purchase a dictionary, an encyclopedia, or an industry directory on one of these CD-ROMs.

Multimedia production never became an industry. Technological advances soon allowed anyone with a personal computer to produce their own CD-ROMs. But at the time, the population seemed perfect to us. It had emerged recently, meaning that we could observe the entry locations of even the very first entrants. It also had a small enough number of firms that it seemed feasible to find all of the founders.

We developed a survey to find out what places founders had considered as potential locations for their firms. We conjectured that entrepreneurs would focus on places where they had lived and places with large concentrations of multimedia manufacturers. We further speculated that those entrepreneurs who chose the places where they had the deepest connections would do best. With financial support from the Alfred P. Sloan Foundation (through a grant to Bill Miller), we mailed our survey to more than 500 entrepreneurs.

Despite receiving responses from more than 100 of them, we ran into an unexpected problem: we had been planning to use whether or not the entrepreneur moved to found their firm as our independent variable of interest, but we had no variation on that variable. Almost no one had moved; 94% founded their firms in the places where they had already been living.

Reflections. We had to abandon the project. But we felt it important to understand better why it had failed. Did we write our questions poorly? Did respondents misunderstand them? Did we ask the wrong questions?

We decided to debrief a few of the respondents. I vividly recall one conversation in Sunnyvale, California. We arrived and found the entrepreneur seated in a stand-alone garage that had been converted into an office. He sat at a desk piled high with colorful 3 1/2-inch floppy discs. Behind him sat stacks of hardware in rack-mounted columns.

A few minutes into the interview, we asked him why he had started his firm where he did. He responded: my wife did not want the mess in the kitchen. In other words, he thought our question had been about why he had his office in the garage instead of in the house, not why he had chosen Sunnyvale instead of some other city.

In fact, as the conversation continued, it became clear that he had never even considered another location. He just founded his firm where he had been living. We heard similar stories from our other interviewees.

Those interviews changed my thinking. Although I had already expected social relationships to have a (resource) mobilization effect, I had not been thinking that they would have an anchoring effect as well. That insight also highlighted a problem with both the classic and contemporary literatures on economic geography. Both considered the question of location choice from the perspective of an omniscient and unconstrained social planner. But entrepreneurs face constraints, have interests beyond their businesses, and often do not even engage in active choice.

Sometimes the value of a project comes more from how it influences one's own thinking than from where it gets published or how it influences others.

The Persistence of Clusters

The immobility of entrepreneurs has an interesting implication: if founders begin businesses in the places where they live and in the industries in which they have worked, or in closely related ones, then industry clusters could persist for long periods of time even if they do not represent the most efficient geographic distribution for an industry. In clustered industries, the opportunities to gain industry experience occur primarily in places with existing concentrations of firms. So the places with these clusters have the largest pools of would-be entrepreneurs in the industry.

Clusters themselves, moreover, might emerge from simple self-reinforcing stochastic arrival processes. By chance, one location could have a few more early entrants. That location then has a larger pool of able entrepreneurs in the industry, meaning that more future entry occurs in the same location. More entry again leads to more potential entrepreneurs, creating a loop of positive feedback.

That idea represented a major departure from the literature. Both the classic and the recent literatures on economic geography had argued that the geographic distribution of firms stemmed from economic efficiency. In other words, industry clusters have emerged because firms have benefited from being located near large numbers of rivals (agglomeration externalities), perhaps because they have shared information, specialized suppliers, or an unusually high-quality pool of employees.

But the idea that industry clusters reflect economic efficiency depends on two implicit assumptions: (1) entrepreneurs choose the places that maximize their expected profits, and (2) the places that maximize these profits do not vary from one entrepreneur to the next.

Although I had the intuition that these assumptions seemed wrong, I did not have the data to test my ideas. Soon, however, I had the good fortune to meet someone who did. In August 1995, I decided at the last minute to drive up from Stanford to attend my first Academy of Management meeting in Vancouver. There I met Pino Audia, when I visited his poster session. We stayed in touch after the conference, and I discovered that he had assembled an amazing data set, one with information on every plant in the shoe industry in the United States, from 1940 to 1989, including where each plant had been located. We agreed to collaborate.

The analyses took a long time. To test the effects of concentration, we introduced a novel type of measure, a distance-weighted density measure (i.e., a distance-weighted count of other plants in the industry). Because this measure required pair-wise calculations for each plant in the industry, for each year, it took my 1997 vintage computer nearly two days to compute each version of the variable.

Pino and I found that footwear plants located in dense concentrations of footwear manufacturers failed at higher rates than those in more remote regions. But, because entrepreneurs in the industry entered these crowded places at even higher relative rates, the industry remained geographically concentrated (Sorenson & Audia, 2000). Clusters persisted in the shoe industry because of where entrepreneurs entered rather than because clustering provided any performance benefits for firms.

In the course of presenting the study, seminar participants at Berkeley, London Business School, UCLA, and the University of Chicago offered an abundance of alternative interpretations of the analyses, ones that could preserve the idea that industry clusters have stemmed from positive agglomeration externalities. As we revised the study again and again, we tried to address each possible explanation—bringing additional analyses to the data or providing more details about the context that would allow us to dismiss them. I view this extensive consideration of alternative explanations as one of the strengths of the study and a probable factor in its success.

In the end, however, this study also benefited from encountering a strong editor. Even in the third round of review at the *American Journal of Sociology*, one of the reviewers continued to complain about not believing our interpretation of the results—agglomerations, the reviewer argued, are efficient. The editor, Roger Gould, recognized that we could not do much more with the data and that the vociferousness with which the reviewer had been arguing signaled that the study might garner a great deal of interest. He therefore accepted the study even though one reviewer remained unsatisfied.

This study led quickly to another on the same subject. When I presented the study with Pino at the University of Chicago, Toby Stuart suggested that we could investigate the same processes using his data on the biotech industry. Although that study began as a replication, Toby and I ended up building out the theory around the mobilization effect and testing it more directly by creating measures for each region of the distance-weighted availability of human, financial, and intellectual resources (Stuart & Sorenson, 2003). That study also struggled a little in the review process before finding a home at *Research Policy*.

Reflections. Despite academia's professed interest in novel ideas, ideas that go against the dominant beliefs are hard to publish. Studies that provide empirical evidence for something that most people already believe or that offer minor modifications of mainstream ideas seem to get the most attention.

Even though the studies I've described here have been highly cited, the articles that cite them often extract only part of the message. They rarely engage the idea that firms fail to benefit from locating in clusters. Instead these studies usually get cited for (1) the idea that spin-off processes play an important role in the creation of clusters, (2) the idea that entrepreneurs rely on their social relationships to mobilize resources to build their firms, and (3) the idea that regions rich in financial and human capital spawn more start-ups.

Relationships and Resources

My most cited study began as a footnote.[2] In the process of writing the article on the geography of the biotech industry (Stuart & Sorenson, 2003), Toby felt that we could not simply show that biotech firms entered in the places that had the largest concentrations of resources. We needed some direct evidence that resource mobilization depended on distance.

Through a grant from the Ewing Marion Kauffman Foundation (through Steve Kaplan's Center for Entrepreneurial Leadership at the University of Chicago), we purchased data on venture capital investments. Those data revealed that venture capitalists did indeed invest disproportionately in start-ups located near their offices. But through the course of analyzing the data, we decided that the idea could support an article in its own right.

In this article, we argued that venture capitalists would invest in companies located near them for two reasons (Sorenson & Stuart, 2001). First, they relied on their social relationships to identify and evaluate promising start-ups. Second, postinvestment, proximity facilitated the process of advising and monitoring their portfolio companies. Although a number of factors could explain the home bias in investing, our social-relationship-based account had one further implication: venture capitalists with more expansive social networks could invest at greater distances.

This article therefore treated the fact that venture capitalists invest locally as a baseline. The analyses focused on demonstrating that social networks, not size or experience, explained which venture capital firms invested in more distant start-ups. In essence, the study focused on interaction effects rather than on the main effects of distance.

One of the methodological innovations of this study involved using a case-control design. The dominant approach to analyzing relationship formation up to that point had been to create a list of all the possible dyads that could exist and to treat each as an observation. In a population with N actors, that would mean $N^2/(N - 1)$ observations. That approach had been feasible in the small, cross-sectional samples that had typically been studied. But with

---

[2] However, the footnote that began it all never made it into the final article. Because the offshoot article got published before the original from which it emerged, we simply cited our published article instead of describing the analysis in a footnote.

more than 6,000 unique investors across many years, for us, it would have meant creating a data set with more than 6 million rows. Variable construction alone would have required weeks with the computing power available to us at the time.

We therefore created our sample by choosing all of the realized relationships—coinvestment relationships that had actually formed—and matching them one-to-one with relationships that had not occurred. That approach meant that we would have 80,000 rows of data instead of 6 million, saving an enormous amount of time without a large loss of information.[3]

The case-control design also had a second benefit: it limited the degree of spatial autocorrelation in the data. Most relationship formation studies have ended up with hundreds of repeated observations of each actor and have included many dyads that undoubtedly have correlated errors due to their similarity or even due to contagion through third-party connections. By sampling the matrix sparsely, the degree of autocorrelation between any two cases included in the estimation remains small.

Reflections.   All of the claims in this study revolved around the interactions between distance and other variables. That approach to theory construction and testing has some advantages. Most notably, people find it far more difficult to come up with alternative explanations for interaction effects. Most endogeneity stories explain a single effect, selection into a treatment. They have a harder time accounting for heterogeneity in the treatment effects.

Studies can provide contributions in many ways: they may offer a truly novel theory, giving readers a new perspective on the world. They may present and analyze data that have unusual features and thus have value even at a descriptive level. Or they may offer a novel approach to analyzing data, whether in terms of measurement or estimation. Great studies seem to offer innovations on at least two or perhaps all of these dimensions.

This study did not necessarily offer a new theory, but it did revive a literature that had been dormant for decades. It also used fairly novel data. Although studies on venture capital now number in the hundreds, at the time ours came out, few had analyzed venture capital data, and no one had connected it to geography. The case-control approach to estimating relationship formation, moreover, had been a methodological innovation.

---

[3] With rare events, most of the information for estimation comes from the few cases with events rather than from the many without them (King & Zeng, 2001).

Home Sweet Home

The final pair of studies I will discuss here represented a return to my first failed attempt at research in this area. Recall that Soong and I had expected entrepreneurs to found firms in places they had lived. We also anticipated that entrepreneurs who opened firms in places where they had deep connections would enjoy more success.

Although I did not have the data to investigate these ideas in 1995, a decade later I found it. Jesper Sørensen introduced me to Danish employer-employee data (see Sørensen & Sorenson, 2007) that had the information one would need. But he did not seem interested in the project, and I did not have direct access to the data. Fate again intervened. When discussing some other research ideas with Michael Dahl, I discovered that he, too, had access. Thus another productive collaboration began.

We originally wrote one article. It first demonstrated that entrepreneurs tended to found their firms in the places where they lived (and that if they did move, they did not move far). It then showed that entrepreneurs who stayed in the regions where they had been living performed better than those who moved.

We submitted that study to the *Journal of Economic Geography* in October 2007. Although the journal offered us the opportunity to revise and resubmit our study, the revision appeared difficult, and we never resubmitted it. During the time it was under review, Michelacci and Silva (2007) came out in the *Review of Economics and Statistics*. That study demonstrated the same fact as the first half of ours—that entrepreneurs move less than employees. The reviewers therefore felt that our study merely replicated Michelacci and Silva's results.

We decided to split the study into two. The first half, on which we had been scooped, became Dahl and Sorenson (2009). Splitting this half off gave us space to do something more than just showing geographic inertia. We estimated entrepreneurs' revealed preferences for locations, characterizing places not just in terms of where they lived but also in terms of industry conditions and proximity to friends and family.

We found some interesting patterns. First, entrepreneurs in choosing locations appeared to be far, far more sensitive to where their friends and family lived than to industry conditions. Second, to the extent that they did weigh the local industry characteristics in their calculations, they seemed systematically attracted to places with more intense competition (see also, Sørensen & Sorenson, 2003).

Splitting off the second half, the more novel part of the study, also allowed us to extend that analysis. We demonstrated that the beneficial effects of having deep roots in a region held not only for firm failure rates but also for firm profits and for the total amount the entrepreneur earned. These results, moreover, held even when using an instrumental variable to account for potential endogeneity in the choice of locations. That study landed in *Management Science* (Dahl & Sorenson, 2012).

Although both halves ended up becoming studies that could stand on their own, the splitting of the original study had a casualty. The original one had demonstrated the negative effects of being in regions with large numbers of competing firms—extending the results from the footwear and biotech studies to the entire range of industries in the Danish economy. But those results ended up being absorbed into industry-region fixed effects in the *Management Science* study in the interest of focusing on the home court advantage for entrepreneurs.

Reflections. Nearly all of my articles have been written with coauthors. Those partners have played different roles. Sometimes they have had the data; sometimes they have done the analysis; sometimes they have had the idea. Regardless of the role played, my collaborations have almost always produced better studies than I could have written on my own.

Over the years, I have adopted a couple of rules for choosing collaborators. First, I need to enjoy interacting with the person. Coauthorships involve a lot of interaction. If you do not get along, it will become draining.

Second, I will only commit to doing one study with a person until we have completed at least one project together. I have been fortunate. Although my collaborations have been more and less productive, I have not had any truly bad coauthors. Bad coauthors can cause misery in many ways: they might disappear for long periods of time. They might do sloppy work on their sections of the project. Or they might insist on first authorship despite having done little of the work. If you have a bad coauthor, you want to stop the bleeding as quickly as possible.

I also have one rule for writing with coauthors: if someone edits a sentence or a passage, another coauthor cannot just revert to the original text. The person who changed the text did it for a reason. Perhaps the person found it unclear or misleading. It might remain unclear or misleading. Anyone should feel free to rewrite it again. But simply reverting to the original text signals either a disrespect for the person who edited it in the first place or that the original author has become too attached to a phrase or sentence.

Additional Thoughts

The reflection sections here have included many thoughts on the research process. But they have not necessarily engaged the central question of this book: What leads to influential scholarship?

The notes that follow reflect my thoughts on this question. I have not done systematic research on any of them. But I feel that they all relate to the production of influential scholarship.

Choosing Projects

Studies that address important topics with novel theory and/or high-quality data get the most attention. They influence both other researchers and often inform the public policy debate. But what counts as important? What qualifies as high-quality data?

Pick important problems.   Theories and theoretical perspectives come and go. Although scholars continue to build on the central insights that theories offer, history forgets most of their nuances and the internal debates about those nuances. Most studies motivated by the need to elaborate a particular theory therefore end up limited and short-lived in their influence.

But important problems persist. Although importance may seem subjective, some problems still enjoy greater consensus in being perceived as important. Global warming. World peace. That's aiming higher than most of us do. But important problems usually affect a lot of people. They often stem from fundamental aspects of human behavior.

In choosing projects, one should therefore ask: How many people does this problem affect? How large an effect does it have on them? Does it shape their health, their wealth, or their well-being?

Important problems often attract a lot of attention, but influential scholarship usually brings a different perspective to understanding these problems. That's the theoretical lens.

The most satisfying research on important problems, moreover, has implications for policy. By implications for policy, I do not mean policy evaluation—research oriented toward assessing the efficacy of a particular intervention. Rather, I have in mind research where the theory and results could inform a wide range of potential policies or interventions.

In choosing projects, one might therefore ask: Who, if anyone, would change their behaviors if they had awareness of the research? Would bureaucrats and legislatures pursue different policies? Would executives or entrepreneurs choose different strategies? Would employees manage their careers differently?

Choose quality over quantity. Most research in management involves the analysis of data. Of late, academics have become enamored with big data. What *big* means varies. Data sets with tens of thousands of cases used to seem large. Many large data sets today include information on millions of something—people, patents, or transactions. As sensor data become more widely available, millions will give way to billions.

But the value of data stems more from their quality than their quantity. High-quality data have high fidelity; the information corresponds to reality. They offer valid measures, connecting closely to theoretical constructs rather than relying on distant proxies. They accurately represent some population, allowing generalization from the sample to the population.

Digital technologies and platforms have dramatically reduced the cost of acquiring data. But the ease of collecting data can become a trap. One could, for example, conceivably email a survey to millions of people, meaning that even a 1% response rate would yield tens of thousands of cases. With a 1% response rate, however, the survey has limited value since one has no idea how well it might represent the sampling frame, the population.[4]

Mechanical Turk and other platforms allow for cheap experiments. Usefully, these platforms often allow for including large numbers of participants in each treatment, hundreds instead of dozens. But, again, one has limited information on who participates in the experiments. In some cases, experiments on these platforms may simply assess the behavior of bots.

Screen scraping has similarly enabled the construction of large data sets at low cost. Often, these data allow researchers to study novel phenomena. But in too many cases, researchers scrape the data and then search for a problem that it could address. As a result, the connections between the variables and the theoretical constructs end up being distant at best.

People also pay too little attention to the provenance of scraped data. Who collected the information originally? What effort has been put into verifying the accuracy of the data?

Do not fear the identification police. Identification concerns whether variance driving the estimates might allow for a causal interpretation of the coefficients. Strategies that support a causal interpretation under

---

[4] With low response rates, selection effects become such a large concern that one should probably just treat a survey as a convenience sample even if the original sampling frame might have been representative of a population.

certain assumptions would include estimation with instrumental variables and differences-in-differences designs.[5] Although management came to the identification revolution later than economics, these concerns have now become central to editors, reviewers, and readers.

But the concerns regarding identification often go too far. All else equal, I too would prefer a study that allows for causal inference. But all else is rarely equal. In the search for causal inference, researchers often sacrifice the picking of important problems. Perhaps the worst form of this malady involves choosing problems on the basis of finding a plausible source of exogenous variation. Many studies that rely on natural experiments are brilliant. But others feel like a solution in search of a problem.

People also forget that providing evidence in favor of a theory, even in support of a causal effect, does not necessarily require a source of exogenous variation. Another effective and compelling strategy involves triangulation: Being explicit about what alternative interpretations might threaten the researcher's preferred account for the results, and then using those alternative theories to develop critical tests that could distinguish between the competing accounts.

Writing Articles

Given the way that most graduate programs train their students, the writing of articles appears to be almost an afterthought. Students take multiple courses on research methods, on econometrics, and on the relevant past research. But few, if any, PhD programs include formal training in writing. Instead they rely on students learning on their own or from informal mentoring.

But what becomes influential and what does not may depend more on how the article describing the research has been written than on anything else. Writing determines who will read the article, whether they will read the whole thing or simply skim the introduction and the tables, and what they will take away from it.

Frame around the phenomenon. Framing helps to determine the audience for the article. Who will find it interesting? Framing also tells readers why they should pay attention to the article. How will it change their thinking?

Authors usually have choices about how to frame articles. I tend to frame mine around the phenomenon, the empirical puzzle. My articles on the persistence of clusters, for example, begin by noting that many industries cluster but that the traditional explanations for clustering fail to fit many of the cases

---

[5] For an excellent yet practical guide to these methodological issues, see Angrist and Pischke (2009).

where we see it. "Home Sweet Home" opens by noting that entrepreneurs remain rooted in place even when other regions appear to offer more favorable environments.

Framing around the phenomenon will usually attract a larger audience. Only those interested in a particular theoretical perspective will read on when a study has been framed in terms of its theoretical contribution. But people from many different perspective often care about the same phenomena, particularly if an important problem has been chosen.

Mind the gap. Among the various ways that authors may open an article, I find the gap approach to framing the least compelling. This framing usually comes in one of two forms. Either the author claims that theories X and Y have been studied independently but never together. Or the author argues that theory X has never been applied to the particular setting and then proceeds to apply theory X to that setting.

This approach to framing has at least two problems. First, as I've noted, this approach limits the audience to those who care about theory X. Second, it does not set up a puzzle, a question to be answered. Who cares? Or perhaps more accurately, why should anyone care? Why would we not simply expect theory X to have the same effects in another setting, or why would theories X and Y not simply have additive effects?

Write well. It often surprises me how poorly many academics write. But then again, despite the fact that we probably spend more time writing than on any other activity, most of us have never had any explicit training in it.

I, too, have had no formal training, but I have tried to train myself. During my first four months as an assistant professor, I spent a large share of my time reading articles carefully, not for what they said but for how they said it. I chose about a dozen articles that I liked and proceeded to read them first at the level of the paragraph and then at the level of the sentence. What did the author hope to achieve with this paragraph or sentence? Why did it appear here instead of earlier or later in the article? At a structural level, writing well means telling the story effectively.[6]

I have also read many a book on writing. One of my favorites is *On Writing Well*, by William Zinsser. These guides include a great deal of advice on how to improve one's writing. They often provide exercises for practicing these principles. At the sentence level, writing well means writing sentences that readers can easily consume. The prose need not be stylish. Few can emulate a Jim March or a Steve Barley. But it should be clear. I will not elaborate

---

[6] The Heath brothers have written an excellent book, *Made to Stick*, on the elements of effective storytelling (Heath & Heath, 2007).

further other than to say that I consider learning to write better to be time well spent.

Writing means revising. My articles often go through 20 or more drafts. Sometimes I will do an entire round of revision focusing simply on eliminating sentences in passive voice or unnecessary adverbs or on trying to ensure that the lengths of my sentences vary. This process takes time. But, as with anything, the more you do it, the better you get at it.

Building an Agenda

Influential scholars are never one-hit wonders. They rarely have portfolios of one-off articles on a wide variety of subjects. Instead, they write a sequence of articles that connect to one another. These studies add up to more than the sum of their individual contributions.

In other words, influential scholars build research programs. That's not to say that they have a series of research studies and projects mapped out from the start. Influential scholars typically develop these programs in two main ways, dynamically responding to the attention and criticism their studies receive.

Replicate.   First, they replicate their successful studies. They do not replicate them in the literal sense of simply rerunning their code. Rather, they engage in conceptual replications, demonstrating that the results do not depend sensitively on a particular setting or a specific way of measuring one of the core constructs.

In studying the persistence of clusters, for example, after first examining the patterns in the footwear industry, I then studied them in the biotech industry. I also wrote a book chapter that extended my dissertation data to study the persistence of clusters in the computer workstation industry. Each of these replications also offered an opportunity for building the theory out in more detail. Toby and I, for example, fleshed out the resource mobilization effect when examining these processes in the biotech industry.

Extend.   Second, those who are building research programs look for the next logical question. Each set of studies I've described here—except of course the first one—emerged to some extent as a series of studies each of which took up a question that had been left open or become salient in an earlier study. The failed multimedia project led me to the idea of cluster persistence. Examining cluster persistence pushed me to examine the resource mobilization effect directly. The "home sweet home" articles (Dahl & Sorenson, 2009, 2012) examine the assumptions underlying the cluster persistence studies. Most research programs have this sense of moving in a series of logical steps.

Enjoy. To close the circle, let me end with another lesson from Jim March. Jim often discussed the importance of deriving pleasure from the process—of leadership, of research, of writing.

Attempting to measure success in terms of having influenced others seems a losing game. We have little control over the ends, whether or not we achieve fame and fortune. Research is consumption. Most of us became academics because we enjoy doing research. Above all, then, it's important to study topics that we find interesting, where we win even if no one else pays attention.

References

Aldrich, Howard E., & Catherine Zimmer. (1986). Entrepreneurship through social networks. *California Management Review 33*, 3–23.

Angrist, Joshua D., & Jorn-Steffen Pischke. (2009). *Mostly harmless econometrics.* Princeton, NJ: Princeton University Press.

Bosma, Niels, Jolanda Hessels, Veronique Schutjens, Mirjam Van Praag, & Ingrid Verheul. (2012). Entrepreneurship and role models. *Journal of Economic Psychology 33*, 410–424.

Dahl, Michael S., & Olav Sorenson. (2009). The embedded entrepreneur. *European Management Review 6*, 172–181.

Dahl, Michael S., & Olav Sorenson. (2012). Home sweet home? Entrepreneurs' location choices and the performance of their ventures. *Management Science 58*, 1059–1071.

Feld, Scott L. (1981). The focused organization of social ties. *American Journal of Sociology 86*, 1015–1035.

Figueiredo, Octavio, Paolo Guimaraes, & Douglas Woodward. (2002). Home-field advantage: Location decisions of Portuguese entrepreneurs. *Journal of Urban Economics 52*, 341–361.

Heath, Chip, & Dan Heath. (2007). *Made to Stick: Why Some Ideas Survive and Others Die.* New York: Random House.

King, Gary, & Langche Zeng. (2001). Logistic regression in rare events data. *Political Analysis 9*, 137–163.

Larson, Andrea. (1992). Network dyads in entrepreneurial settings: A study of the governance of exchange relationships. *Administrative Science Quarterly 37*, 76–104.

March, James G., & Thierry Weil. (2005). *On leadership.* Malden, MA: Blackwell.

Michelacci, Claudio, & Olmo Silva. (2007). Why so many local entrepreneurs? *Review of Economics and Statistics 89*, 615–633.

Rickne, Annika, Martin Ruef, & Karl Wennberg. (2018). The socially and spatially bounded relationships of entrepreneurial activity: Olav Sorenson—recipient of the 2018 Global Award for Entrepreneurship Research. *Small Business Economics 51*, 515–525.

Ruef, Martin. (2010). *The entrepreneurial group.* Princeton, NJ: Princeton University Press.

Sørensen, Jesper B., & Olav Sorenson. (2003). From conception to birth: Opportunity perception and resource mobilization in entrepreneurship. *Advances in Strategic Management 20*, 89–117.

Sørensen, Jesper B., & Olav Sorenson. (2007). Corporate demography and income inequality. *American Sociological Review 72*, 766–783.

Sorenson, Olav, & Pino G. Audia. (2000). The social structure of entrepreneurial activity: Geographic concentration of footwear production in the United States, 1940–1989. *American Journal of Sociology 106*, 424–462.

Sorenson, Olav, & Toby E. Stuart. (2001). Syndication networks and the spatial distribution of venture capital investments. *American Journal of Sociology 106*, 1546–1588.

Sorenson, Olav, & David M. Waguespack. (2006). Social structure and exchange: Self-confirming dynamics in Hollywood. *Administrative Science Quarterly 51*, 560–589.

Stouffer, Samuel A. (1940). Intervening opportunities: A theory relating mobility and distance. *American Sociological Review 5*, 845–867.

Stuart, Toby E., & Waverly W. Ding. (2006). When do scientists become entrepreneurs? *American Journal of Sociology 112*, 97–144.

Stuart, Toby E., & Olav Sorenson. (2003). The geography of opportunity: Spatial heterogeneity in founding rates and the performance of biotechnology firms. *Research Policy 32*, 229–253.

Weber, Alfred. (1928). *Theory of the location of industries*. Chicago: University of Chicago Press.

Zinsser, William. (2006). *On writing well*. New York: HarperCollins.

7

My Journey with Justice

Brainstorming about Scholarly Influence and Longevity

Jason A. Colquitt

My journey toward influential scholarship in justice began in a sea of abstracts on brainstorming. As an undergraduate psychology major at Indiana University, it was time for me to come up with a topic for my honors thesis. My plan was to apply to PhD programs in organizational behavior, so it made sense to focus on OB topics for my thesis. The psychology department at Indiana did not include industrial/organizational faculty or courses, however, so my only exposure to such topics was a summer OB class I'd taken from a part-time instructor. Ironically, few topics stuck out in my memory as especially interesting from that class. The topic that kept getting stuck in my head—for whatever reason—was brainstorming. So the idea generation for my honors thesis began by reading hundreds of abstracts on brainstorming at the library.

Unfortunately, none of the abstracts were sparking an idea that could form the foundation for an honors thesis. My struggles *with* brainstorming had led me *to* brainstorming, but the struggles were continuing. A few weeks later, however, a light bulb mercifully lit up. Now armed with an idea, I set off to find a sponsor for my honors thesis. As best I could tell, the Indiana psychology professor who made the most sense for a study on brainstorming was Jerome Chertkoff. His research focused on a number of small group phenomena, including coalition formation, reward distribution, leader emergence, risk taking, and exiting behavior. I had never had a class with Professor Chertkoff, however, and had never even met him. Still, in a decision I reflect on to this day, he chose to meet with a random undergraduate to listen to an honors thesis idea. Here's the idea I pitched to him: "What if, after all that time spent in a room brainstorming about some problem, the group offered their solution to the boss. But the boss said 'eh . . . we're not doing that.' How would the group react?"

Professor Chertkoff stared ahead, thoughtfully, as he mulled the idea. Back then, I didn't know the specific wheels turning in his head. Now, I realize that

Jason A. Colquitt, *My Journey with Justice* In: *A Journey toward Influential Scholarship.* Edited by: Xiao-Ping Chen and H. Kevin Steensma, Oxford University Press. © Oxford University Press 2021. DOI: 10.1093/oso/9780190070717.003.0007

he was trying to connect the words in my sentence to constructs—and to relationships among constructs. Then came the conclusion that would alter the course of my academic career before it had begun. "I like that idea," he said. "But it's not a brainstorming idea . . . it's a justice idea." He proceeded to open one drawer after another in his filing cabinet until he produced two articles. "Read these, then let's talk." The two articles were Greenberg and Folger (1983) and Folger and Greenberg (1985). Among other things, the articles described how having a voice in decisions can make individuals feel more fairly treated in the context of those decisions. I devoured both articles on my couch that evening. I now had an honors thesis topic, an honors thesis advisor, and a preoccupation for the next few decades.

The purpose of this chapter is to reflect on my particular scholarly journey in the justice literature, from that fateful day at Indiana University, through my PhD program at Michigan State University, to professional stops at the University of Florida and the University of Georgia. As with other chapters in this book, I will summarize my primary contributions to the justice literature while giving some "backstory" to those ideas and projects. I will also reflect on how my approach to scholarly research contributed to some of my career success. Hopefully these reflections will serve their intended purpose of helping other scholars in their own scientific journeys.

One of the points I'll make later in this chapter is to start with theory—have a sense of the conceptual lens that can help explain some phenomenon, and use that lens to shape the project. It therefore makes metatextual sense to do the same with this article. But I won't be starting with a justice theory. As I reflected on my CV in preparation for writing this chapter, I asked myself why I studied the things I did, and why I *kept studying* the things I did. Especially in light of promotions, changes in academic affiliations, and transitions into other academic roles. My answer is intrinsic motivation, broadly defined as existing when tasks are performed because they're interesting and enjoyable—not because they're a means for obtaining some incentive (Kanfer, Frese, & Johnson, 2017). Four decades of research have shown that intrinsic motivation is positively related to both the quantity of work and the quality of work. Put in the context of academia, an intrinsic interest in one's subject matter can foster both research productivity—the number of articles generated—and research quality—the novelty, interestingness, importance, and rigor found in those articles.

There are a number of theories and models that identify some of the conditions that can cultivate intrinsic motivation (e.g., Deci & Ryan, 2000; Hackman & Oldham, 1976; Kahn, 1990; Spreitzer, 1995). Although all could be applied to the structuring of this chapter, I will focus on Spreitzer's (1995) model, for a few reasons. First, it is appropriate in scope for the particular points I wish to make. Second, because it came out early in my graduate school career, I am more aware of my first exposure to it and the impression it made upon me. Third, it has always been a big part of my teaching career and plays a salient role in my OB textbook (Colquitt, LePine, & Wesson, 2019). Put simply, it has always had significant "mindshare" for me, and has been a lens through which I've reflected on my career in the past. Drawing on earlier perspectives (Conger & Kanungo, 1988; Thomas & Velthouse, 1990), Spreitzer (1995) argued that intrinsic motivation—termed *psychological empowerment* in her model—was a function of four cognitions: self-determination, competence, meaning, and impact. I will apply each of those constructs to my particular scholarly journey. But first I'll review what I see as my major contributions along that journey.

Contributions to the Justice Literature

My initial meeting with Professor Chertkoff kicked off an honors thesis that examined group members' reactions when their voice was not followed. Building off of earlier work by Folger and colleagues (Folger, Rosenfield, Grove, & Corkran, 1979), group members were told that they would be performing a brainstorming task, and that they could choose an outside member's brainstorming output to add to their own. The use of a brainstorming task was included as a nod to the original topic that had serendipitously led me to the justice literature. Group members were given background, personality, and academic information on two outside members and were able to pick the one they presumed would be the better brainstormer. The experiment varied whether they got the person they picked and whether an explanation was provided for that decision. Those manipulations then interacted in their effects on fairness perceptions and motivation on the brainstorming task.

Although the results of my thesis seemed promising at the time, I back-burnered the project as I entered graduate school. At the suggestion of Tim Baldwin, a management professor at Indiana, I applied to (and accepted a spot in) Michigan State's PhD program. I had been working with Tim on a study of collaborative learning and—as a Spartan alum—he was certain that Michigan State would be a great fit for me. I later became incredibly fortunate to have John Hollenbeck as my advisor while doing research on team decision-making effectiveness (e.g., Hollenbeck, Colquitt, Ilgen, LePine, & Hedlund, 1998; Hollenbeck, Ilgen, LePine, Colquitt, & Hedlund, 1998). I also did work with Ray Noe on both teams and learning motivation (Colquitt, LePine, &

Noe, 2000; Janz, Colquitt, & Noe, 1997). I continued to read and follow the justice literature, however, focusing many of my class papers on justice ideas. Then, in a stroke of luck, Don Conlon joined the Michigan State faculty as I entered my fifth year in the PhD program. It was during this period that I worked on my first two published articles in the justice literature—which remain my most influential articles to this day.

A Construct Validation of a Measure

As I studied the justice literature during my years at Michigan State, I was struck by the wide variety of measures used in field studies. This observation was first crystallized for me when reading (or rereading) Lind and Tyler (1988)—a landmark review of the literature that was foundational to my understanding of the area. Lind and Tyler (1988) included an appendix that listed many of the measures used at the time. Some measures were "direct"—literally asking participants how fair their boss was, or how fairly their organization treated them. Other measures were "indirect"—asking instead about rules and criteria that were thought to elicit a sense of fairness. I was personally drawn to the indirect measures. There was a clarity and tangibility to words like "impartial," "unbiased," "consistent," and "accurate," relative to a word like "fair." With the indirect measures, I felt like I knew what was living behind construct labels like "procedural justice" and "distributive justice." But there were so many indirect measures—most of them ad hoc scales that would be used once in a single study.

Speaking of construct labels, the mid- to late 1990s was a period of growth in—and debate about—such labels. Greenberg and Folger (1983) and Folger and Greenberg (1985) had built on earlier work by Adams (1965) and Leventhal (1976, 1980) to establish procedural justice—the fairness of decision-making processes—as a construct separate from distributive justice—the fairness of decision outcomes. Such work helped establish that procedural rules like voice, bias suppression, consistency, accuracy, and correctability were conceptually distinct from distributive rules like equity, equality, and need (Adams, 1965; Folger, 1977; Greenberg, 1986; Leventhal, 1976, 1980). Bies and Moag (1986) then added to that landscape with their articulation of interactional justice—the fairness of the communication offered during decisions. Drawing on qualitative insights, they introduced four additional rules: respect, propriety, truthfulness, and justification. I was particularly drawn to the last two, as the provision of an explanation had been a key manipulation in my honors thesis.

A number of chapters debated whether the interactional rules were conceptually distinct from the procedural rules or should instead be viewed as additional concepts under the procedural justice umbrella (Folger & Bies, 1989; Greenberg, Bies, & Eskew, 1991; Tyler & Bies, 1990). One of the only widely used indirect justice measures—Moorman's (1991) scale—came out during this time period. Reflecting that conceptual flux, the measure included justification concepts within its procedural justice dimension and voice and bias suppression concepts within its interactional justice dimension. Around the same time, Greenberg (1993b) introduced a conceptualization that separated the interactional rules into two subfacets: interpersonal justice (reflecting respect and propriety) and informational justice (reflecting truthfulness and justification). That separation was consistent with work in the explanations literature, where the tone of an account was typically viewed as separate from its content (e.g., Gilliland & Beckstein, 1996; Greenberg, 1993c).

It was against this backdrop that I submitted a construct validation piece to *Journal of Applied Psychology* near the end of my fifth year at Michigan State. I had written indirect measure items that hewed closely to the rules introduced in the literature (Bies & Moag, 1986; Greenberg, 1993b; Leventhal, 1976, 1980; Thibaut & Walker, 1975). I then tested the psychometric properties and dimensionality of the items in two samples: an undergraduate class at Michigan State and a nearby automotive parts manufacturer. The results revealed strong factor loadings and reliabilities and support for a structure that separated procedural, distributive, interpersonal, and informational justice into separate dimensions. Colquitt (2001) became the first article I published in the justice realm. Though, as I'll describe a bit later, it was only 25 pages ahead of the second article.

Looking back, I should have viewed it as somewhat precocious to write a measurement article for a literature I had never published in. Fortunately, I was inexperienced enough with the field that such thoughts didn't enter my mind. Then, while the article was still "in press," the measure earned a "shout-out" from Jerry Greenberg during a large conference symposium. Jerry had served as discussant for the symposium and was running a question-and-answer segment. Someone asked him for his advice on measuring justice, given the wide variety of scales that could be used. In a moment that somehow seemed to be playing out in slow motion, Jerry looked around the room and asked, "Is . . . Jason Colquitt here?" I sheepishly stood up from the back of the room as much of the audience craned their necks in my direction. "I was Reviewer 1 on his forthcoming *JAP*," Jerry began. "Use his measure." After collecting a hundred business cards from people who wanted a copy of my article, I walked over to Jerry to introduce myself and thank him for his kind words about my work. He introduced me to a number of other justice scholars and expressed a desire to work together. Meanwhile, the Colquitt (2001) measure cemented itself as the mostly widely used indirect measure in the literature.

In the years since, I have revisited the measurement of justice on a number of occasions. The first occurred in the context of a collaboration with Jerry—the inaugural *Handbook of Organizational Justice* (Greenberg & Colquitt, 2005). Among other things, Colquitt and Shaw (2005) performed a metaanalytic factor analysis based on 16 samples where the Colquitt (2001) measure was used. The results again revealed strong factor loadings and reliabilities and further support for the procedural, distributive, interpersonal, and informational structure. Colquitt, Long, Rodell, and Halvorsen-Ganepola (2015) later observed that—like many other measures in the literature—the Colquitt (2001) items emphasized the degree of adherence to justice rules more than the violation of those rules (see also Colquitt & Rodell, 2015). For example, one interpersonal justice item asks about the degree of politeness in communication without allowing for the possibility that communication is downright rude. We therefore introduced reverse-worded items to the measure, creating what we termed a "full-range" version of it. We further showed that the "full-range" version was a more powerful predictor of negatively valenced outcomes like hostility and counterproductive behavior.

A Metaanalytic Review of the Literature

Around the same time that I began crafting my measure, I began thinking about doing a metaanalysis of the justice literature. Don Conlon and I had wanted to work on something during our one year together at Michigan State, and the metaanalysis seemed like a good choice for that project. Unlike me, Don had actually conducted a number of primary studies that would be included in such a synthesis (e.g., Conlon, 1993; Conlon & Murray, 1996). He had also been trained by Allan Lind, giving him a complementary "mental model" of the literature. And a metaanalysis seemed like something the literature really needed. It had always been blessed with exceptional narrative reviews (e.g., Brockner & Wiesenfeld, 1996; Greenberg, 1987, 1990; Lind & Tyler, 1988), but there's a certain clarity that only a quantitative synthesis can provide. Indeed, Greenberg (1993a) had argued that the justice literature was in its "intellectual adolescence" and that further maturation would require more consensus about definitions, antecedents, and consequences. We felt a metaanalysis could inform the consensus surrounding many of those issues.

As Don and I went about the coding of articles alongside three of my fellow PhD students, we focused intently on nuance in justice measurement. For example, we coded whether a procedural justice variable used a direct measure of fairness perceptions or an indirect measure. If it used the latter, we coded whether it emphasized voice (Folger, 1977; Thibaut & Walker, 1975) or emphasized allocation rules like bias suppression, consistency, accuracy, and correctability (Greenberg, 1986; Leventhal, 1980). Our coding also separated interpersonal justice concepts from informational justice concepts (Greenberg, 1993b). Finally, we also noted cases where measures used some combination of those ingredients. Given the time frame, those "indirect combination measures" wound up being especially common.

We also cast a wide net in terms of the consequences of justice. Those included attitudinal consequences like organizational commitment, trust, and evaluation of authority. They also included behavioral consequences like citizenship behavior, task performance, and counterproductive behavior—termed "negative reactions" at the time. At their most general level, our findings reaffirmed that the fairness of the decision-making process was as impactful—and sometimes more impactful—than the fairness of decision outcomes. Put simply, the concepts that justice scholars had introduced and/or built upon in the 1980s and 1990s (Bies & Moag, 1986; Brockner & Wiesenfeld, 1986; Folger & Greenberg, 1985; Greenberg & Folger, 1983; Lind & Tyler, 1988) did indeed have incremental value beyond the earlier focus on distributive justice (Adams, 1965; Leventhal, 1976). That was true for procedural justice—whether narrowly or broadly conceptualized. And it was also true for interpersonal and informational justice. When it came out in print, Colquitt, Conlon, Wesson, Porter, and Ng (2001) became the second article I published in the justice realm—appearing 25 pages later than Colquitt (2001) in the same issue of the *Journal of Applied Psychology*. Having what would turn out to be my two most highly cited papers in the same issue helped "put me on the map" as a justice scholar. That was particularly so for colleagues who still thought of me as a teams person or a learning motivation person.

Many of the contributions of the Colquitt et al. (2001) metaanalysis can be hinted at by comparing it to its successor: Colquitt, Scott, Rodell, Long, Zapata, Conlon, and Wesson (2013). Aside from providing a framework for the various relationships present in the literature, and illustrating the typical effect sizes for those relationships, Colquitt et al. (2001) did something else. It showed scholars what was missing from the literature. For example, we called for more comprehensive inclusion of justice dimensions within studies while also referencing those dimensions to both supervisor sources and organizational sources. At the time, it was common to—for example—reference procedural justice to an organization but interpersonal justice to a supervisor. That practice confounded content (e.g., bias suppression and consistency versus respect and propriety) with source (e.g., an intangible company versus a tangible person). As another example, we called for more studies linking justice to trust, citizenship behavior, and task performance, as the number of studies with those outcomes had been limited.

Colquitt et al.'s (2013) metaanalysis wound up covering 493 independent samples, versus only 183 for Colquitt et al. (2001). That explosion was fueled by a number of sources. One source was an influx of new theories, as fairness heuristic theory (Lind, 2001), uncertainty management theory (Lind & Van den Bos, 2002), fairness theory (Folger & Cropanzano, 2001), the deontic model (Folger, 2001), and the group engagement model (Tyler & Blader, 2003) brought several lenses to a literature that had possessed few. Another source was an increased emphasis on applying theories from outside the justice literature, such as Blau's (1964) social exchange theory and Weiss and Cropanzano's (1996) affective events theory (e.g., Cropanzano, Rupp, Mohler, & Schminke, 2001; Weiss, Suckow, & Cropanzano, 1999). But another source, in my view, was the increased accessibility of the literature. Colquitt et al. (2001) had given scholars a structure for thinking about the literature, with Colquitt (2001) providing a measure for the constructs in that literature. The resulting decrease in "barriers to entry" likely opened up the justice literature to many new scholars.

Integrating Justice with Other Corners of Organizational Behavior

Shortly after the publication of Colquitt (2001) and Colquitt et al. (2001), I coauthored a narrative review with Jerry Greenberg that pointed to the need to better integrate justice with other corners of OB (Colquitt & Greenberg, 2003). That sort of integration would characterize much of my work for the next decade. Some of those studies would take advantage of the other areas of expertise I'd developed at Michigan State. Others would require me to learn a new literature in much the same way I'd learned the justice literature. My integration efforts focused on three different areas during this time period: teams, personality, and trust.

Justice in Teams
My interest in integrating justice and teams was natural, going back to my first year at Michigan State. On the one hand most of my current research

was in the context of team decision-making effectiveness. On the other hand my fledgling research identity was in the realm of justice. Thus, most of my class papers and discretionary projects had intertwined the two. One example was Colquitt, Noe, and Jackson (2002), which was an empirical test of a paper I'd written for Steve Kozlowski's levels of analysis course. The article was one of the first to aggregate justice to the team level of analysis. Our findings showed that the "justice climates" within manufacturing teams predicted team performance and absenteeism. We also used climate strength as a moderator—which was novel for the time—showing that the effects of justice climate level were especially strong when members exhibited more agreement.

Subsequent theoretical work shed more insights into how and when justice might emerge at the team level of analysis—and how and why it might impact team effectiveness. Quinetta Roberson and I had met several times at conferences, as we were both the same year in grad school, both interested in justice, and both uniquely interested in justice and teams. As she transitioned from Maryland's PhD program to Cornell University and I transitioned from Michigan State's PhD program to the University of Florida, we decided to combine the conceptual portions of our dissertations into an *Academy of Management Review* submission. That article received a "reject-and-resubmit," with the feedback essentially being to deemphasize my dissertation while prioritizing Quinetta's. The end result was an article that used team network characteristics to explain why some teams develop a justice climate whereas others experience "nonconvergence" (Roberson & Colquitt, 2005). We also explored how one could model nonconvergence in a way that could still be linked to team effectiveness.

Although Colquitt et al. (2002) and Roberson and Colquitt (2005) examined justice at the team level of analysis, other work cast teams as a context for examining individual members' justice experiences. For example, the empirical portion of my dissertation examined whether individual members might compare the justice they received with the justice received by their teammates (Colquitt, 2004). Using both classroom teams and teams performing a decision-making task, my results showed that inconsistencies in justice within teams harmed members' attitudes and behaviors—especially when teams were particularly interdependent. Thus, team contexts can "up the ante" for managers when it comes to justice. It's not enough to treat any given member fairly; attention must also be paid to the pattern of treatment within the team. That takeaway was echoed in Colquitt and Jackson (2006), which examined the perceived importance of the various justice rules across individual and team contexts. Although the importance of many rules did not vary, equality, consistency, and voice were viewed as more important in team contexts than individual contexts.

Justice and Personality

My work integrating justice and personality was born, in part, from the results of the Colquitt et al. (2001) metaanalysis. That review yielded an unusual amount of variation in effect sizes for the justice-to-performance linkage. When might justice have stronger versus weaker effects on that critical criterion? I was drawn to personality as one answer, as some of my work in Michigan State's team decision-making laboratory had focused on personality (LePine, Colquitt, & Erez, 2000; Colquitt, Hollenbeck, Ilgen, LePine, & Sheppard, 2002). The question then became how best to approach personality-based moderation of justice effects.

Colquitt, Scott, Judge, and Shaw (2006) drew on the justice theories introduced at the start of the millennium to identify traits that could capture people who were sensitive to justice issues, who ruminated on justice information, and who reacted behaviorally to justice levels. Fairness heuristic theory's focus on trust dynamics (Lind, 2001) resulted in the choice of trust propensity as a trait. Uncertainty management theory's focus on security (Lind & Van den Bos, 2002) resulted in the choice of risk aversion as a trait. Fairness theory's focus on ethics (Folger, 2001; Folger & Cropanzano, 2001) resulted in the choice of morality as a trait. Our results showed that those traits had more significant moderating effects on the justice-performance linkage than did the Big Five dimensions of personality. A follow-up study took a different approach, focusing instead on traits relevant to the employee-employer relationship (Scott & Colquitt, 2007). Those traits included equity sensitivity (Huseman, Hatfield, & Miles, 1987) and exchange ideology (Eisenberger, Huntington, Hutchison, & Sowa, 1986). As in Colquitt et al. (2006), the results showed that the traits—particularly exchange ideology—were more powerful moderators of justice effects than were the Big Five (Scott & Colquitt, 2007).

Justice and Trust

Unlike my work with teams and personality, my integration of justice and trust was not born out of any graduate school experiences. Instead, it grew—at first—out of passing references to trust throughout the justice literature. For example, the relational model suggested that trustworthiness was one criterion used to gauge justice (Tyler & Lind, 1992). As another example, fairness heuristic theory suggested that justice was one means of gathering data relative to trustworthiness (Lind, 2001). As still another example, social exchange theory argued that trust was a key aspect of the exchange dynamic (Blau,

1964)—with that dynamic often being used to explain why justice predicted citizenship behavior (Konovsky & Pugh, 1994). Of course, trust was also one of the outcomes included in the Colquitt et al. (2001) metaanalysis.

Despite those exposures, trust had never quite "clicked" for me as an interest area. All that changed at an annual meeting of the Academy of Management, when I attended an early morning symposium on trust on the last day of the conference. The session contained an in-depth and candid comparison of the various approaches for conceptualizing trust and trustworthiness, including Mayer, Davis, and Schoorman's (1995), McAllister's (1995), and Lewicki and Bunker's (1995). That session gave me a deeper appreciation for the trust literature and made me excited to begin contributing to it. In time, trust would grow to be my secondary area—pushing teams and personality further down my "identity queue." More relevant to this chapter, that session also clarified how to reconcile the different treatments of trust within the various justice theories.

Those reconciliations are best seen in two studies. Colquitt and Rodell (2011) integrated justice theories with Mayer et al.'s (1995) trust conceptualization. We used longitudinal panel data to test whether (1) justice predicted trustworthiness, or (2) trustworthiness predicted justice. We also examined how justice and trustworthiness acted in concert when predicting trust. Importantly, we also tackled how to utilize justice, trustworthiness, and trust measures together, given some of their content overlap. For example, Mayer and Davis's (1999) integrity scale has one item that references a "sense of justice" and another that mentions "trying hard to be fair." Our results showed that informational justice was uniquely potent in predicting trust, with justice and trustworthiness possessing several reciprocal relationships. A subsequent study by Colquitt, LePine, Piccolo, Zapata, and Rich (2012) drew on McAllister's (1995) trust conceptualization. Our results showed that his affect-based trust facet was pivotal to the obligation dynamic that underlies social exchange theory (Blau, 1964). In contrast, his cognition-based trust facet was pivotal to the uncertainty dynamic that underlies uncertainty management theory (Lind & Van den Bos, 2002). Taken together, the two facets provided distinct mechanisms for explaining why justice relates to performance.

An Intrinsic Motivation-Based Model of Scholarly Influence

Having described what I see as my contributions to the justice literature, I turn to a discussion of influential scholarship in general. All of the scholars in this book have been influential in different ways. Some essentially founded their literatures of interest. Others—like me—picked up a baton put in motion by an earlier set of founders. (See Byrne & Cropanzano, 2001, for a spotlight on the founders of the justice literature.) Regardless, what the scholars in this book do share is high levels of research productivity and research quality over an extended period of time. That uniting thread is why intrinsic motivation is a useful construct to consider for career reflections. As noted at the outset, intrinsic motivation is positively related to both the quantity and the quality of work (Kanfer et al., 2017). Why did I continue to work in the justice literature when I could have worked on other topics—or not worked at all? And why were the ideas in my work good enough that they were published in top-tier journals and utilized in research by other scholars? The answer is that I wanted to do the work—and I enjoyed doing the work.

Spreitzer's (1995) model argues that intrinsic enjoyment is rooted in cognitions regarding self-determination, competence, meaning, and impact. In samples of both insurance employees and industrial employees, Spreitzer (1995) linked measures of those four cognitions to other-reports of effectiveness and innovation. The more intrinsically motivated employees felt, the more their colleagues viewed them as proficient and creative. As shown in figure 7.1, I argue that Spreitzer's (1995) model can be applied to understanding

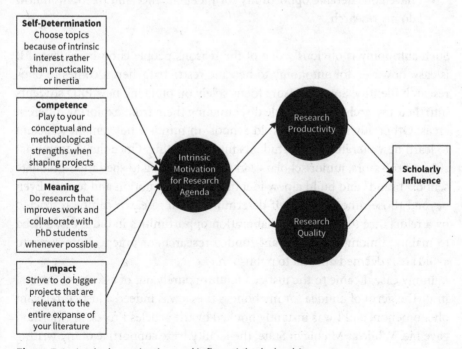

Figure 7.1. Intrinsic motivation and influential scholarship.

how scholarly influence can emerge over time—with the cognitions creating a consistent record of generating articles and a steady stream of novel, interesting, important, and rigorous ideas in them. Notably, Spreitzer (1995) also introduced scales to measure the four cognitions. As I apply each cognition to my own scholarly journey, I'll include adaptations of those scales to illustrate my points.

Self-Determination

Spreitzer (1995) defined *self-determination* as a sense of choice surrounding the initiation and regulation of action. If adapted to the research enterprise, here is how self-determination might be measured (1 = Strongly Disagree; 2 = Disagree; 3 = Slightly Disagree; 4 = Neutral; 5 = Slightly Agree; 6 = Agree; 7 = Strongly Agree). If you want some context for your own ratings of the items, the mean for the original version of Spreitzer's (1995) scale—when aggregated across sources and times—was 16.47.

- I have significant autonomy in determining how I do my research.
- I can decide on my own how to go about doing my research.
- I have considerable opportunity for independence and freedom in how I do my research.

Such autonomy is obviously one of the reasons people choose academia. It is easy, however, for autonomy to become restricted when it comes to one's research identity. Some advisors focus solely on plugging new PhD students into their research streams while discouraging them from exploring different areas. Other advisors are less "old school" in mindset but remain reluctant to learn new literatures that students find interesting. Once they become assistant professors, junior scholars can find it daunting to shed their graduate school "brand" and build a new identity before promotion and tenure. Even beyond those time frames, self-determination in research can be restricted by a reluctance to say no to collaboration opportunities in old areas, a need to maintain momentum in grant-funded research, or practical pressures to avoid areas deemed difficult to publish in.

In my case, I came to the justice literature purely out of a sense of interest in it. The germ of an idea for my honors thesis was indeed a justice-relevant phenomenon, and I was instantly hooked by the articles Professor Chertkoff gave me. While at Michigan State, the faculty were supportive of my writing class papers in the justice area and professing an interest in justice when introducing myself to campus visitors. During this time period, I alternated between viewing my honors thesis as a hobby and as Indiana University-based moonlighting. Regardless, it became the project I would apply concepts to as soon as I'd learned them—whether in methods classes or content classes. Just as important, my honors thesis kept me tethered to the justice domain even as I published in the teams and learning motivation literatures. Of course, the Michigan State faculty also provided support later in my program, as I planned a justice-based dissertation and began doing lead-authored work in justice.

That sense of self-determination extended into my early years at the University of Florida. Once the measurement and metaanalysis projects were published (Colquitt, 2001; Colquitt et al., 2001), I turned to my dissertation (Colquitt, 2004) and to other studies in the "justice in teams" space (Colquitt & Jackson, 2006; Colquitt et al., 2002; Roberson & Colquitt, 2005). From there, however, I went purely on the topics that interested me. I realize, of course, that I was incredibly fortunate to publish enough articles during graduate school that my tenure pressures were lessened. It is easier to use intrinsic motivation as one's compass when extrinsic pressures are not salient. Nonetheless, the question "Am I studying this because I want to, or because I have to?" has remained a key criterion I use to judge any new project.

Competence

Spreitzer (1995) defined competence as a belief in one's capability to perform activities with skill. If adapted to the research enterprise, here is how competence might be measured (1 = Strongly Disagree; 2 = Disagree; 3 = Slightly Disagree; 4 = Neutral; 5 = Slightly Agree; 6 = Agree; 7 = Strongly Agree). To again provide some context, the mean for the original version of Spreitzer's (1995) scale—when aggregated across sources and times—was 17.83.

- I am confident about my ability to do my research.
- I am self-assured about my capabilities to perform my research activities.
- I have mastered the skills necessary for my research.

When I teach topics like intrinsic motivation and self-efficacy to master's and undergraduate students, I discuss the popular business book *Now, Discover Your Strengths* (Buckingham & Clifton, 2001). The book makes the case that performance and engagement are maximized when employees "play to their strengths" rather than focusing on improving their weaknesses. The book also includes a self-assessment that provides the reader's top five strengths. Mine are *achiever, learner, analytical, self-assurance,* and *individualization*—seemingly pretty good for an academic! When I show a video that spotlights the book, I often find myself reflecting on my own career.

Many of my contributions to the justice literature represent playing to my strengths. My earliest classes at Michigan State—including John Hollenbeck's methods class and Neal Schmitt's psychometrics class—gave me an appreciation of measurement. I was also aware that one of my advisor's most influential early works was a measure of goal commitment (Hollenbeck, Klein, O'Leary, & Wright, 1989). Thus, introducing a new measure of justice was "in my wheelhouse," so to speak—even as someone who had not previously published in the literature. Similarly, Jack Hunter's metaanalysis class was a helpful foundation for the Colquitt et al. (2001) metaanalysis, just as Steve Kozlowksi's levels of analysis class was beneficial to my work on justice in teams (Colquitt et al., 2002; Roberson & Colquitt, 2005). I should note that I took Jack Hunter's class as a fifth-year student—a time when most students no longer think about taking methods courses.

Similarly, my formative experiences at Michigan State gave me an appreciation for the application of theory. One of the quotes I remember from John Hollenbeck's methods class was "theory allows you to predict the future—before it happens." And one of my very first publications was a test of John's multilevel theory of team decision-making, which he developed alongside Dan Ilgen (Hollenbeck, Ilgen, et al., 1998). That appreciation for theory was further cultivated by my experiences contributing to—and later editing—the *Academy of Management Journal* (Colquitt, 2013; Colquitt & Ireland, 2009; Colquitt & Zapata-Phelan, 2007). Thus, many of my justice studies used an existing theoretical lens to inspire the choice of variables and to provide the underlying logic for connecting them (e.g., Colquitt et al., 2012; Colquitt & Rodell, 2011). Other work combined theory application with theory extension by doing something intellectually unique with a given lens. For example, Colquitt et al. (2006) uses justice theories to identify relevant trait-based moderators, even though none of those theories focus on personality.

Despite my strengths with theory application and extension, I have never been a particularly gifted builder of new theory. Leaving aside the aforementioned Roberson and Colquitt (2005) article in the *Academy of Management Review,* I have—at the time of this writing—only published one other conceptual theory-building article (Scott, Colquitt, & Paddock, 2009). To put that number in perspective, I have six publications that introduce a new measure and four publications that use metaanalysis. Of course, I could spend a few years really working on the intellectual skill of theory building. I could study past exemplars, read books on creativity, practice more imaginative writing, and so forth. But I would likely never be as good at that skill as others in this book, nor would that skill approach what I bring to empirical studies. Besides, it's simply more fun to do what you're good at. And that counts for a lot when working on an article early on a Saturday morning or late on a Tuesday evening.

Meaning

Spreitzer (1995) defined *meaning* as the value of one's work goal or purpose when judged against one's ideals and standards. If adapted to the research enterprise, here is how meaning might be measured (1 = Strongly Disagree; 2 = Disagree; 3 = Slightly Disagree; 4 = Neutral; 5 = Slightly Agree; 6 = Agree; 7 = Strongly Agree). To again provide some context, the mean for the original version of Spreitzer's (1995) scale—when aggregated across sources and times—was 17.96.

- The research I do is very important to me.
- My research activities are personally meaningful to me.
- The research I do is meaningful to me.

One way of thinking about the meaning of my work is "has my research contributed to making the workplace better for employees?" I personally believe it has, and that's one reason I've remained connected to the justice literature over time. I've heard executives use construct labels like "procedural justice" in conversations with me, showing they've been exposed either to my work or the work of the literature's founders. My research has also been featured in organizational behavior textbooks (Aguinis, Ramani, Alabduljader, Bailey, & Lee, 2019). The students of today grow up to be the bosses of tomorrow, so sensitizing them to issues of justice is vital. Of course, I also talk about my work in my own teaching and in my own executive education experiences.

There is a second way to conceptualize meaning in an academic career, however. Working with PhD students brings intrinsic rewards that working with other sorts of coauthors does not. Teaching PhD students the craft of research combines a scholar's educational and research missions. Parts of the research enterprise that have become "old hat" for scholars can seem new again when seeing those tasks through students' eyes. The enthusiasm of students can also be contagious—injecting positive affect during data collection milestones, data analysis insights, first submissions, revise-and-resubmits, and acceptances. And those acceptances themselves become more meaningful in a number of respects. They become events that help students get jobs, that help them provide for their families, and that help open up future opportunities for them.

Of course, students also provide meaning to work by improving its quality. Kuhn's (1963) description of the essential tension in scholarly work notes the need for both convergent thinking—to learn the work that's been done—and divergent thinking: to see the new places that work needs to go. Collaborations with talented PhD students allows for both sides of that tension. My introducing PhD students to the justice literature acquaints them with the orthodoxy; their unique interests and experiences help me see ideas I would not have. Those "injections of divergence" have taken my work in different directions since the work I've reviewed here. Those directions include additional influences on fairness perceptions beyond justice rules (Rodell & Colquitt, 2009; Rodell, Colquitt, & Baer, 2017) and what causes managers to adhere to justice rules in the first place (Scott, Colquitt, & Zapata-Phelan, 2007; Scott et al., 2009). More recently, those directions also include the effects of venting about unfairness (Baer, Rodell, Dhensa-Kahlon, Colquitt, Zipay, Burgess, & Outlaw, 2018) and the effects of being both fair and timely (Outlaw, Colquitt, Baer, & Sessions, 2019).

Impact

Spreitzer (1995) defined *impact* as influence over strategic, administrative, and operating outcomes within one's department. If adapted to the research enterprise, here is how impact might be measured (1 = Strongly Disagree; 2 = Disagree; 3 = Slightly Disagree; 4 = Neutral; 5 = Slightly Agree; 6 = Agree; 7 = Strongly Agree). To again provide some context, the mean for the original version of Spreitzer's (1995) scale—when aggregated across sources and times—was 13.92.

- My impact on what happens in my literature is large.
- I have a great deal of control over what happens in my literature.
- I have significant influence over what happens in my literature.

Of course, the potential overlap between meaning and impact is apparent. If impact is viewed as changing organizational life for the better, then it has much in common with the my foregoing discussion of meaning. Spreitzer (1995) emphasized impact on the department specifically, however, and the department is the original referent of her items. Indeed, Thomas and Velthouse (1990) argued that the analog for impact in Hackman and Oldham's (1976) formulation is knowledge of results—not significance. Thus, *impact* in the current discussion means "is your work changing your literature of interest?" That question brings to mind Huff's (2009) metaphor of publishing as conversation. An article makes little contribution when it merely *adds to* the conversation; it makes a larger contribution when it *changes* the conversation.

As I reflect on my articles that have had a more sizable impact, two things stand out. First, I've often emphasized having one big article rather than multiple smaller ones. For example, both the Colquitt et al. (2001) metaanalysis and the Colquitt et al. (2013) follow-up could have been split into multiple submissions. Maybe one metaanalysis would focus on attitudes with another focusing on behaviors. Or maybe one submission would emphasize social exchange relationships with another focusing on affective linkages. As another example, the 1,747 employees working in 88 teams in Colquitt et al. (2002) could have been split into two articles, with one examining antecedents of justice climate and another examining consequences. In both cases, however, my focus was on making the work—and the contribution—as complete as possible.

Second, my most impactful articles are relevant to the entire expanse of the justice literature—not merely specific corners focused on a particular linkage or theory. For example, the Colquitt (2001) and Colquitt et al. (2015) measurement studies are relevant to any justice scholar who seeks to measure the construct in the field. As another example, Colquitt et al. (2006) and Colquitt and Rodell (2011) are both relevant to the majority of theoretical perspectives at play in the literature. That's not to say that articles can never be targeted at more niche questions or more focused contributions. I've produced many such articles in my career. Rather, my point is that the projects that most "renew the fire" over time are those that change the literature as a whole the most. After all, it is those articles that other scholars wind up incorporating into their own theorizing or their own research approaches.

Conclusion

Hopefully this chapter has explained how I've influenced the justice literature and why I remain motivated to contribute to it. And hopefully an intrinsic motivation-based lens becomes useful as a perspective for examining the arc of one's academic career. Of course, the reader may remain curious about one additional detail—did I ever publish my honors thesis? Yes, as a matter of fact. Colquitt and Chertkoff (2002) came out three years after I graduated from Michigan State and one year after my first two justice publications (Colquitt, 2001; Colquitt et al., 2001). It was not my first justice publication, nor is it my most highly cited one. It is, however, the project that introduced me to the work of many scholars I've come to know in the years since. And it served as the "on ramp" for the scholarly journey I hope to continue for many years to come.

References

Adams, J. S. (1965). Inequity in social exchange. In L. Berkowitz (Ed.), *Advances in experimental social psychology* (Vol. 2, pp. 267–299). New York: Academic Press.

Aguinis, H., Ramani, R. S., Alabduljader, N., Bailey, J. R., & Lee, J. (2019). A pluralistic conceptualization of scholarly impact in management education: Students as stakeholders. *Academy of Management Learning & Education, 18*, 11–42.

Baer, M. D., Rodell, J. B., Dhensa-Kahlon, R., Colquitt, J. A., Zipay, K. P., Burgess, R., & Outlaw, R. (2018). Pacification or aggravation? The effects of talking about supervisor unfairness. *Academy of Management Journal, 61*, 1764–1788.

Bies, R. J., & Moag, J. F. (1986). Interactional justice: Communication criteria of fairness. In R. J. Lewicki, B. H. Sheppard, & M. H. Bazerman (Eds.), *Research on negotiations in organizations* (Vol. 1, pp. 43–55). Greenwich, CT: JAI Press.

Blau, P. (1964). *Exchange and power in social life.* New York: Wiley.

Brockner, J., & Wiesenfeld, B. M. (1996). An integrative framework for explaining reactions to decisions: Interactive effects of outcomes and procedures. *Psychological Bulletin, 120*, 189–208.

Buckingham, M., & Clifton, D. O. (2001). *Now, discover your strengths.* New York: Free Press.

Byrne, Z. S., & Cropanzano, R. (2001). History of organizational justice: The founders speak. In R. Cropanzano (Ed.), *Justice in the workplace: From theory to practice* (pp. 3–21). Mahwah, NJ: Lawrence Erlbaum.

Colquitt, J. A. (2001). On the dimensionality of organizational justice: A construct validation of a measure. *Journal of Applied Psychology, 86*, 386–400.

Colquitt, J. A. (2004). Does the justice of the one interact with the justice of the many? Reactions to procedural justice in teams. *Journal of Applied Psychology, 89*, 633–646.

Colquitt, J. A. (2013). The last three years at AMJ: Celebrating the big purple tent. *Academy of Management Journal, 56*, 1511–1515.

Colquitt, J. A., & Chertkoff, J. M. (2002). Explaining injustice: The interactive effects of explanation and outcome on fairness perceptions and task motivation. *Journal of Management, 28*, 591–610.

Colquitt, J. A., Conlon, D. E., Wesson, M. J., Porter, C. O. L. H., & Ng, K. Y. (2001). Justice at the millennium: A meta-analytic review of 25 years of organizational justice research. *Journal of Applied Psychology, 86*, 425–445.

Colquitt, J. A., & Greenberg, J. (2003). Organizational justice: A fair assessment of the state of the literature. In J. Greenberg (Ed.), *Organizational behavior: The state of the science* (pp. 165–210). Mahwah, NJ: Erlbaum.

Colquitt, J. A., Hollenbeck, J. R., Ilgen, D. R., LePine, J. A., & Sheppard, L. (2002). Computer-assisted communication and team decision-making performance: The moderating effect of openness to experience. *Journal of Applied Psychology, 87*, 402–410.

Colquitt, J. A., & Ireland, R. D. (2009). Taking the mystery out of AMJ's reviewer evaluation form. *Academy of Management Journal, 52*, 224–228.

Colquitt, J. A., & Jackson, C. L. (2006). Justice in teams: The context-sensitivity of justice rules across individual and team contexts. *Journal of Applied Social Psychology, 36*, 870–901.

Colquitt, J. A., LePine, J. A., & Noe, R. A. (2000). Toward an integrative theory of training motivation: A meta-analytic path analysis of 20 years of research. *Journal of Applied Psychology, 85*, 678–707.

Colquitt, J. A., LePine, J. A., Piccolo, R. F., Zapata, C. P., & Rich, B. L. (2012). Explaining the justice-performance relationship: Trust as exchange deepener or trust as uncertainty reducer? *Journal of Applied Psychology, 97*, 1–15.

Colquitt, J. A., LePine, J. A., & Wesson, M. J. (2019). *Organizational behavior: Improving performance and commitment in the workplace*, (6th ed). Burr Ridge, IL: McGraw-Hill Irwin.

Colquitt, J. A., Long, D. M., Rodell, J. B., & Halvorsen-Ganepola, M. D. K. (2015). Adding the "in" to justice: A qualitative and quantitative investigation of the differential effects of justice rule adherence and violation. *Journal of Applied Psychology, 100*, 278–297.

Colquitt, J. A., Noe, R. A., & Jackson, C. L. (2002). Justice in teams: Antecedents and consequences of procedural justice climate. *Personnel Psychology, 55*, 83–109.

Colquitt, J. A., & Rodell, J. B. (2011). Justice, trust, and trustworthiness: A longitudinal analysis integrating three theoretical perspectives. *Academy of Management Journal, 54*, 1183–1206.

Colquitt, J. A., & Rodell, J. B. (2015). Measuring justice and fairness. In R. Cropanzano & M. L. Ambrose (Eds.), *The Oxford handbook of justice in the workplace* (Vol. 1, pp. 187–202). New York: Oxford University Press.

Colquitt, J. A., Scott, B. A., Judge, T. A., & Shaw, J. C. (2006). Justice and personality: Using integrative theories to derive moderators of justice effects. *Organizational Behavior and Human Decision Processes, 100*, 110–127.

Colquitt, J. A., Scott, B. A., Rodell, J. B., Long, D. M., Zapata, C. P., Conlon, D. E., & Wesson, M. J. (2013). Justice at the millennium, a decade later: A meta-analytic test of social exchange and affect-based perspectives. *Journal of Applied Psychology, 98*, 199–236.

Colquitt, J. A., & Shaw, J. C. (2005). How should organizational justice be measured? In J. Greenberg & J. A. Colquitt (Eds.), *The handbook of organizational justice* (113–152). Mahwah, NJ: Erlbaum.

Colquitt, J. A., & Zapata-Phelan, C. P. (2007). Trends in theory building and theory testing: A five-decade study of *Academy of Management Journal*. *Academy of Management Journal, 50*, 1281–1303.

Conger, J. A., & Kanungo, R. N. (1988). The empowerment process: Integrating theory and practice. *Academy of Management Review, 13*, 471–482.

Conlon, D. E. (1993). Some tests of the self-interest and group value models of procedural justice: Evidence from an organizational appeal procedure. *Academy of Management Journal, 36*, 1109–1124.

Conlon, D. E., & Murray, N. M. (1996). Customer perceptions of corporate responses to product complaints: The role of explanations. *Academy of Management Journal, 39*, 1040–1056.

Cropanzano, R., Rupp, D. E., Mohler, C. J., & Schminke, M. (2001). Three roads to organizational justice. In G. R. Ferris (Ed.), *Research in personnel and human resources management* (Vol. 20, pp. 1–123). New York: Elsevier Science.

Deci, E. L., & Ryan, R. M. (2000). The "what" and "why" of goal pursuits: Human needs and the self-determination of behavior. *Psychological Inquiry, 11*, 227–268.

Eisenberger, R., Huntington, R., Hutchison, S., & Sowa, D. (1986). Perceived organizational support. *Journal of Applied Psychology, 71*, 500–507.

Folger, R. (1977). Distributive and procedural justice: Combined impact of "voice" and improvement on experienced inequity. *Journal of Personality and Social Psychology, 35,* 108–119.

Folger, R. (2001). Fairness as deonance. In S. W. Gilliland, D. D. Steiner, & D. P. Skarlicki (Eds.), *Theoretical and cultural perspectives on organizational justice* (pp. 3–34). Greenwich, CT: Information Age.

Folger, R., & Bies, R. J. (1989). Managerial responsibilities and procedural justice. *Employee Responsibilities and Rights Journal, 2,* 79–89.

Folger, R., & Cropanzano, R. (2001). Fairness theory: Justice as accountability. In J. Greenberg & R. Cropanzano (Eds.), *Advances in organizational justice* (pp. 89–118). Stanford, CA: Stanford University Press.

Folger, R., & Greenberg, J. (1985). Procedural justice: An interpretive analysis of personnel systems. In K. Rowland & G. Ferris (Eds.), *Research in personnel and human resources management* (Vol. 3, pp. 141–183). Greenwich, CT: JAI Press.

Folger, R., Rosenfield, D., Grove, J., & Corkran, L. (1979). Effects of "voice" and peer opinions on responses to inequity. *Journal of Personality and Social Psychology, 37,* 2253–2261.

Gilliland, S. W., & Beckstein, B. A. (1996). Procedural and distributive justice in the editorial review process. *Personnel Psychology, 49,* 669–691.

Greenberg, J. (1986). Determinants of perceived fairness of performance evaluations. *Journal of Applied Psychology, 71,* 340–342.

Greenberg, J. (1987). A taxonomy of organizational justice theories. *Academy of Management Review, 12,* 9–22.

Greenberg, J. (1990). Organizational justice: Yesterday, today, and tomorrow. *Journal of Management, 16,* 399–432.

Greenberg, J. (1993a). The intellectual adolescence of organizational justice: You've come a long way, maybe. *Social Justice Research, 6,* 135–148.

Greenberg, J. (1993b). The social side of fairness: Interpersonal and informational classes of organizational justice. In R. Cropanzano (Ed.), *Justice in the workplace: Approaching fairness in human resource management* (pp. 79–103). Hillsdale, NJ: Erlbaum.

Greenberg, J. (1993c). Stealing in the name of justice: Informational and interpersonal moderators of theft reactions to underpayment inequity. *Organizational Behavior and Human Decision Processes, 54,* 81–103.

Greenberg, J. Bies, R. J., & Eskew, D. E. (1991). Establishing fairness in the eye of the beholder: Managing impressions of organizational justice. In R. A. Giacalone & P. Rosenbield (Eds.), *Applied impression management: How image-making affects managerial decisions* (pp. 111–132). Thousand Oaks, CA: Sage.

Greenberg, J., & Colquitt, J. A. (2005). *The handbook of organizational justice.* Mahwah, NJ: Erlbaum.

Greenberg, J., & Folger, R. (1983). Procedural justice, participation, and the fair process effect in groups and organizations. In P. B. Paulus (Ed.), *Basic group processes* (pp. 235–256). New York: Springer-Verlag.

Hackman, J. R., & Oldham, G. R. (1976). Motivation through the design of work: Test of a theory. *Organizational Behavior and Human Performance, 16,* 250–279.

Hollenbeck, J. R., Colquitt, J. A., Ilgen, D. R., LePine, J. A., & Hedlund, J. (1998). Accuracy decomposition and team decision making: Testing theoretical boundary conditions. *Journal of Applied Psychology, 83,* 494–500.

Hollenbeck, J. R., Ilgen, D. R., LePine, J. A., Colquitt, J. A., & Hedlund, J. (1998). Extending the Multilevel Theory of team decision making: Effects of feedback and experience in hierarchical teams. *Academy of Management Journal, 41,* 269–282.

Hollenbeck, J. R., Klein, H. J., O'Leary, A. M., & Wright, P. M. (1989). Investigation of the construct validity of a self-report measure of goal commitment. *Journal of Applied Psychology, 74,* 951–956.

Huff, A. S. (2009). *Designing research for publication*. Thousand Oaks, CA: Sage.

Huseman, R. C., Hatfield, J. D., & Miles, E. W. (1987). A new perspective on equity theory: The equity sensitivity construct. *Academy of Management Review, 12*, 222–234.

Janz, B. D., Colquitt, J. A., & Noe, R. A. (1997). Knowledge worker team effectiveness: The role of autonomy, interdependence, team development, and contextual support variables. *Personnel Psychology, 50*, 877–904.

Kahn, W. A. (1990). Psychological conditions of personal engagement and disengagement at work. *Academy of Management Journal, 33*, 692–724.

Kanfer, R., Frese, M., & Johnson, R. E. (2017). Motivation related to work: A century of progress. *Journal of Applied Psychology, 102*, 338–355.

Konovsky, M. A., & Pugh, S. D. (1994). Citizenship behavior and social exchange. *Academy of Management Journal, 37*, 656–669.

Kuhn, T. S. (1963). The essential tension: Tradition and innovation in scientific research. In C. W. Taylor & F. Barron (Eds.), *Scientific creativity: Its recognition and development* (pp. 341–354). New York: Wiley.

LePine, J. A., Colquitt, J. A., & Erez, A. (2000). Adaptability to changing task contexts: Effects of general cognitive ability, conscientiousness, and openness to experience. *Personnel Psychology, 53*, 563–594.

Leventhal, G. S. (1976). The distribution of rewards and resources in groups and organizations. In L. Berkowitz & W. Walster (Eds.), *Advances in experimental social psychology* (Vol. 9, pp. 91–131). New York: Academic Press.

Leventhal, G. S. (1980). What should be done with equity theory? New approaches to the study of fairness in social relationships. In K. Gergen, M. Greenberg, and R. Willis (Eds.), *Social exchange: Advances in theory and research* (pp. 27–55). New York: Plenum Press.

Lewicki, R. J., & Bunker, B. B. (1995). Trust in relationships: A model of development and decline. In B. B. Banker & J. Z. Rubin (Eds.), *Conflict, cooperation, and justice* (pp. 133–173). San Francisco: Jossey-Bass.

Lind, E. A. (2001). Fairness heuristic theory: Justice judgments as pivotal cognitions in organizational relations. In J. Greenberg & R. Cropanzano (Eds.), *Advances in organizational justice* (pp. 56–88). Stanford, CA: Stanford University Press.

Lind, E. A., & Tyler, T. R. (1988). *The social psychology of procedural justice*. New York: Plenum Press.

Lind, E. A., & Van den Bos, K. (2002). When fairness works: Toward a general theory of uncertainty management. In B. M. Staw & R. M. Kramer (Eds.), *Research in organizational behavior* (Vol. 24, pp. 181–223). Boston, MA: Elsevier.

Mayer, R. C., & Davis, J. H. (1999). The effect of the performance appraisal system on trust for management: A field quasi-experiment. *Journal of Applied Psychology, 84*, 123–136.

Mayer, R. C., Davis, J. H., & Schoorman, F. D. (1995). An integrative model of organizational trust. *Academy of Management Review, 20*, 709–734.

McAllister, D. J. (1995). Affect- and cognition-based trust as foundations for interpersonal cooperation in organizations. *Academy of Management Journal, 38*, 24–59.

Moorman, R. H. (1991). Relationship between organizational justice and organizational citizenship behaviors: Do fairness perceptions influence employee citizenship? *Journal of Applied Psychology, 76*, 845–855.

Outlaw, R., Colquitt, J. A., Baer, M. D., & Sessions, H. (2019). How fair versus how long: An integrative theory-based examination of procedural justice versus procedural timeliness. *Personnel Psychology, 72*, 361–391.

Roberson, Q. M., & Colquitt, J. A. (2005). Shared and configural justice: A social network model of justice in teams. *Academy of Management Review, 30*, 595–607.

Rodell, J. B., & Colquitt, J. A. (2009). Looking ahead in times of uncertainty: The role of anticipatory justice in an organizational change context. *Journal of Applied Psychology, 94*, 989–1002.

Rodell, J. B., Colquitt, J. A., & Baer, M. D. (2017). Is adhering to justice rules enough? The role of charismatic qualities in perceptions of supervisors' overall fairness. *Organizational Behavior and Human Decision Processes, 140*, 14–28.

Scott, B. A., & Colquitt, J. A. (2007). Are organizational justice effects bounded by individual differences? An examination of equity sensitivity, exchange ideology, and the Big Five. *Group and Organization Management, 32*, 290–325.

Scott, B. A., Colquitt, J. A., & Paddock, E. L. (2009). An actor-focused model of justice rule adherence and violation: The role of managerial motives and discretion. *Journal of Applied Psychology, 94*, 756–769.

Scott, B. A., Colquitt, J. A., & Zapata-Phelan, C. P. (2007). Organizational justice as a dependent variable: Subordinate charisma as a predictor of interpersonal and informational justice perceptions. *Journal of Applied Psychology, 92*, 1597–1609.

Spreitzer, G. M. (1995). Psychological empowerment in the workplace: Dimensions, measurement, and validation. *Academy of Management Journal, 38*, 1442–1465.

Thibaut, J., & Walker, L. (1975). *Procedural justice: A psychological analysis*. Hillsdale, NJ: Erlbaum.

Thomas, K. W., & Velthouse, B. A. (1990). Cognitive elements of empowerment: An "interpretive" model of intrinsic task motivation. *Academy of Management Review, 15*, 666–681.

Tyler, T. R., & Bies, R. J. (1990). Beyond formal procedures: The interpersonal context of procedural justice. In J. Carroll (Ed.), *Applied social psychology and organizational settings* (pp. 77–98). Hillsdale, NJ: Erlbaum.

Tyler, T. R., & Blader, S. L. (2003). The group engagement model: Procedural justice, social identity, and cooperative behavior. *Personality and Social Psychology Review, 7*, 349–361.

Tyler, T. R., & Lind, E. A. (1992). A relational model of authority in groups. In M. P. Zanna (Ed.), *Advances in experimental social psychology* (Vol. 25, pp. 115–191). San Diego: Academic Press.

Weiss, H. M., & Cropanzano, R. (1996). Affective events theory: A theoretical discussion of the structure, causes and consequences of affective experiences at work. In B. M. Staw & L. L. Cummings (Eds.), *Research in organizational behavior* (Vol. 18, pp. 1–74). Greenwich, CT: JAI Press.

Weiss, H. M., Suckow, K., & Cropanzano, R. (1999). Effects of justice conditions on discrete emotions. *Journal of Applied Psychology, 84*, 786–794.

8
Careers as Stochastic Excursions

A Personal Confession

Hayagreeva Rao

On the one hand a person's career may be seen as the outcome of foresight, resolute choices, and purposeful action. On the other hand careers can be seen as stochastic outcomes; Jim March along with his brother wrote a brilliant study on careers as "almost random walks." Much as I'd like to describe *my* career as an outcome of foresight, it was the outcome of stochastic excursions, wherein unexpected peers and events led to conversations that blossomed into research projects and eventually, studies in journal articles and books. My goal is not to offer an exhaustive and exhausting recounting of my career as much as to demonstrate how the arrival of stochastic opportunities unfolded as excursion—that is, adventures with people. For the sake of simplicity, I will organize my account of my career chronologically.

Chance encounters and entry into academia. To begin with, after an undergraduate training in economics in 1978, I went to business school in India at Xavier Labor Relations Institute (XLRI), arguably one of India's finest private business schools. I was a boy from a small town and lacked exposure. XLRI was a magical place; the small class of 80 students, who had been selected after a rigorous test, was full of students from different backgrounds; engineering, science, economics, history, and literature. I went to XLRI hoping to become an executive, and instead, 65 out of my 80 classmates told me that I was a better fit for academia than industry! I must confess that I found the electives in the MBA program boring, and eventually I persuaded the dean to allow me to undertake independent studies with Jittu Singh, a newly minted Wharton PhD who had joined XLRI. His arrival was a chance event that had a profound effect on my trajectory. Jittu was an amazingly generous person and put me through reading James Thompson and listening to Beethoven. I was entranced by both. Thompson's propositions were like Sanskrit verses, and Beethoven's symphonies, conducted by Herbert von Karajan, were captivating. Jittu had also prescribed Jeff Pfeffer's "External Control of Organizations" (Pfeffer &

Hayagreeva Rao, *Careers as Stochastic Excursions* In: *A Journey toward Influential Scholarship.* Edited by: Xiao-Ping Chen and H. Kevin Steensma, Oxford University Press. © Oxford University Press 2021. DOI: 10.1093/oso/9780190070717.003.0008

Salancik, 1978) as our text for the organization design course; little did I know that Jeff was going to be my colleague at Stanford 25 years later!

After XLRI, I decided to sample as many organizations as possible and so joined the Tata Group as an internal management consultant of sorts for three years. The arrival of two senior colleagues who had returned from Case Western Reserve University, Subramaniam Ramnaryan and Venkatraman Nilakant, also played a pivotal role in my evolution. Their arrival at the Tata Group was another chance set of events; they were generous mentors, and they persuaded me that Case Western Reserve University was the best place to go if I sought to change organizations. Eventually I went to Case in 1984 for my doctorate. The pedagogy of the department relied on T-group or training group methods, and I must confess I did feel like a misfit. There was one course in the first quarter, Social Analysis, taught by Eric Neilsen, a former student of Robert Bales at Harvard University, that I found the most stimulating. We were exposed to Durkheim, Marx, and Weber, and our class essay, if I recall rightly, was to write an account of an evening spent with the three giants in a restaurant while I was the waiter and eavesdropped on their conversation about current events. The whole experience really made me look at the external social surround of organizations as a driver of organizational action.

Chance stimuli and my dissertation. My dissertation was on the rise and fall of thrifts. As a foreign student, I did not even know what a thrift was until my warm and wonderful friends in the program made me watch the film "It's a Wonderful Life" a number of times during the Christmas holiday season. The movie showed me that organizational structures such as thrifts relied on the community for the monitoring of managers. I began by interviewing people in a mutual thrift anchored in the Polish community in Cleveland—it was high-performing because community members monitored managers. I was connected to this mutual thrift by Eric and a member of the school's alumni board, and this work eventually led me to wonder whether mutual thrifts failed in the West and South because of poor monitoring by the community. This became the subject of my dissertation, where I used hazard rate models to understand the decline of the mutual form of thrifts and the ascendancy of the stock model of thrifts.

At Case, the Organizational Behavior department was physically located next to the Operations Research department. When I was befuddled by hazard rates and the like, one of the operations research students, an Indian Institute of Technology alum named Shekhar Khot, asked me what I was reading, and when I told him, he mentioned that he could teach me how to do hazard rate analyses on his data set of 5,000 buses and model the failure pattern of gearboxes! The person who taught me the nitty-gritty of it was another

IIT alum there, Sunil Dhamhankar. These chance connections led me to study the rise and fall of thrifts using event history methods.

My job search as a stochastic excursion. In 1988–1989, I was on the job market. I had invested in an expensive suit (it cost $400 in 1988, a fortune for me). My friend and sartorial mentor, Mike Sokoloff, told me not to worry. He was right, in retrospect, but worry I did! I had by then had studies published in the *Academy of Management Review* and *Organisation Studies* (Neilsen & Rao, 1987, 1989)—they were conceptual studies. Yet I realized that pedigree might get in the way: Case was not well known—I recall being interviewed by someone from Rutgers who told me: "you are smart, but you are not from a top 10 school. It is nothing personal, pedigree matters." Years later, the provost of Rutgers asked me to review the school, and I chuckled as I recounted the story to him and declined.

I was interviewed by the Kellogg School, Emory University, Pennsylvania State University, and perhaps one more, whose name escapes me. The visit to Kellogg was inspiring; it was a cold day, and I met Ed Zajac on the macro side and micro colleagues such as Maggie Neale (who later became my colleague at Stanford). I also met Art Stinchcombe and was amazed by his incisive questions. Kellogg did not hire me—that year there were amazing students such as Nitin Nohria (now dean of Harvard Business School), Bill Barnett (now my colleague at Stanford), and Gary Pisano (now at Harvard Business School). They selected no one! (I must admit that I was probably not in the running at all.) Years later, in 2002, I joined Kellogg as a chair professor, and Ed Zajac warmly and graciously told me that they were atoning for their earlier mistake! He was being very generous!

I interviewed at Emory University and felt that my invitation was in large part due to the championing of Karen Golden-Biddle, who had joined Emory a year earlier from Case—she was an ethnographer with a keen eye and remarkable discipline. Emory had Bob Miles as the leader of the Organizations Group, which also included Bob Drazin (who had joined Emory from Columbia) and Rob Kazanjian (who had arrived from Michigan a couple of years before I did). I still recall my first visit to Atlanta—the sheer scale of the airport and traffic was unnerving. Even more disorienting was that when I arrived at the Ritz Carlton, Buckhead, with my one suit in a battered garment bag, the greeter asked me if it was my first visit to the Ritz. I thought to myself: "how could they know?"!

Emory as an incubator. Emory made me a generous offer, and I arrived there with a beat-up car (gifted by a friend), a garment bag, a suitcase, a computer, and boxes of books. I became fast friends with other junior professors who had joined the school in other departments. My first teaching task was a course on strategy—I had never taught that course to MBAs, and Rob Kazanjian would meet me every Friday and spend 90 minutes or so walking me through the teaching plan for the next week. I even memorized his jokes in a desperate bid to survive in the classroom, and to my surprise, I found myself thriving due to his generosity. Bob Drazin , at the time of my hiring, had told me that I was a diamond in the rough—and he patiently read through all of my studies and wielded his red ink pen like a scalpel as he sliced into my argument sprawled out on 30–35 pages. His patient and generous guidance was very critical to me in my research career.

My dissertation, "An Ecology of Agency Arrangements," was eventually published in *American Science Quarterly* (*ASQ*) (Rao & Neilsen, 1992). My only goal in life at that stage was to publish one study in *ASQ*! John Freeman was the editor, and I recall going to a conference at NYU, organized by Joel Baum, where John asked me if I had read his decision letter (this was in the snail mail era). I told him I had not, and he told me "Congratulations, I just accepted your paper." I was in a daze—I don't recall anything about that conference. All I knew was that I had published my study in *ASQ* and my life was complete! Little did I know that I would have more do to with *ASQ* over the years.

In the early years at Emory, a chance event was the arrival of Jay Barney as a speaker. Jay is provocative, curious, and convivial, and we were having an animated conversation about path dependence in the development of new capabilities as an alternative to the prevalent view of capabilities as the outcomes of deliberate managerial actions. In this conversation, I recounted to Jay how I had stumbled across a magazine called *Horseless Age* and discovered that carmakers at the dawn of the automobile industry competed in reliability races to demonstrate the roadworthiness of their cars. If the public thought such "tests tell," carmakers were driven by the motto "Win on Sunday and Sell on Monday." I mentioned to Jay that I was thinking of reputation as the outcome of path dependent wins in reliability races and was building a data set to test these ideas. Soon, an invitation arrived from Ed Zajac saying that he and Jay were organizing a conference for *Strategic Management Journal* and urging me to present the results of this study there. The conference morphed into a special issue, and Ed Zajac, as the deft editor, shepherded my study "The Social Construction of Reputation" to publication (Rao, 1994).

During my early years at Emory, I met Heather Haveman at the Academy of Management meetings, and Heather told me that she had been a reviewer of my *ASQ* study. She had already published two remarkable studies the year before on thrifts. Soon our common interests in thrifts and their social surround led us to begin a study of how selection rather than adaptation underlay the replacement of the self-liquidating thrift by the permanent guaranteed stock form of thrifts—one where there was a difference between stockholders and members. Heather had the remarkable gift of visualizing a table of results before the study was written, and I was impressed by her acuity, curiosity, generosity, and infectious energy. We had great fun rereading Adam Smith's tract on moral sentiments because we saw the organizational structure of thrifts reflecting moral sentiments, and we eventually published our study "Structuring a Theory of Moral Sentiments" in the *American Journal of Sociology (AJS)* in (Haveman & Rao, 1997. She was not just a coauthor but a teacher and a friend, and years later, we published another study on how the Progressive movement underlay the transformation of California thrifts in the American Sociological Review *(ASR)* in 2007.

Another serendipitous occurrence at Emory was a conference organized by Jeff Sonnenfeld, my senior colleague there. Jeff had an incredible Rolodex and invited very interesting people to conferences; he was gracious enough to invite me to a conclave in Sea Island, Georgia, where a number of CEOs listed on NASDAQ and a number of NASDAQ staff as well were present. I learned at this conference that NASDAQ staff were concerned about firms defecting to the NYSE and realized that they saw the process as a social process than one driven by market microstructure considerations. It became clear to me in those two days that whether a firm would leave NASDAQ and join NYSE hinged on the structure of board interlocks; irrespective of whether a firm had directors who were on the boards of NASDAQ firms, NYSE firms, or firms that had defected from NASDAQ to NYSE. After the conference, the irrepressible Jerry Davis arrived for a talk at Emory and not only agreed to share his interlock data but to join me in an excursion into this territory. Jerry was the Usain Bolt of putting together data on board interlocks. We needed to model defection to NASDAQ as a diffusion process—with heterogeneity. Jerry introduced me to Henrich Greve, who knew a lot about how to estimate a heterogeneous diffusion model using the RATE package developed by Nancy Tuma and had already published a study in *ASQ* using a data set of radio stations. Henrich patiently answered my questions, and eventually "Embeddedness, Social Identity and Mobility" was completed and found its way into ASQ (Rao, Davis, & Ward, 2000).

After the study was accepted for publication, Jerry and I met with Henrich at the Academy to thank him for his help, and our dinner conversation (over plenty of wine) led to another study idea. Henrich was a student of Jim March, and soon we were chatting about postdecision regret. We realized that while it had been studied in the context of purchases (buyer's remorse), it had not been studied as the outcome of making a decision based on social proof. We realized that financial analysts decide to cover firms if they are hot, and we argued that when they do so they are likely to make mistakes in their earnings per share forecasts and decide to drop coverage and then continue to follow the stock. "Fool's Gold" appeared in *ASQ* (2001) and was the product of that animated dinner conversation. Henrich soon became a steadfast research collaborator and friend; he knew theory, methods, and programming, unlike me, who knew the first two! He has remained a generous friend since.

Michigan as an accelerator. Around 1996, I had spent seven years or so at Emory and felt the need for a sabbatical to recharge myself. I had met Jane Dutton and Lance Sandelands earlier on a visit to Michigan with Bob Drazin for a conference on the grammar of organizing, and Jane graciously arranged for me to visit Michigan. It was a life-changing experience for me to see Jane developing her work on positive organizing, and Lance contemplating the role of religion, and to partake in the Interdisciplinary Group on Organizing (ICOS). I met Mayer Zald there, who was a man with an erudite mind and a big heart in a small physical frame; we developed a fast friendship, and we would often have lunch. He introduced me to the world of social movements, and our lunches were a game: he would ask me whether I had read this or that piece, and it was a great way to get reconnected with sociology. I taught a doctoral course there for the first time, and an MBA course in the school's demanding teaching environment, and I learned a lot there. Michigan with its rich social science heritage and vast network of scholars opened both doors and windows for me and set me on a path to understand the role of social movements in the world of organizations. Mayer would leave cold Michigan in winter and migrate to Arizona as a visitor to the Sociology Department there, and he taught a course there with Cal Morrill, an ethnographer. Soon Mayer, Cal, and I were writing studies on social movements. The first was "Power Plays," which described how social movements reshape industries and appeared in *Research in Organizational Behavior* (Rao, Morill, & Zald, 2000). Above all, I learned from watching the generativity of Mayer and Jane, and other scholars such as Wayne Baker, Lance Sandelands, Jim Walsh and Sue Ashford.

The nouvelle cuisine studies. I returned to Emory in 1997, recharged and reaffirmed, and began a welter of projects. Rudy Durand had arrived as a visitor and was teaching an undergrad strategy course; he hailed from the *École des hautes études commerciales de Paris* Ecole des Hautes (HEC Paris). He was disappointed that he was moving to EM Lyon Business School in Lyon, France, where he bemoaned the lack of biotechnology, aerospace, and other high-tech industries. Being a foodie, I asked him about haute cuisine in Lyon, and he was not interested. When I suggested that people spent more time deciding which restaurant to go to than which stock to buy, he was more open and looped in Philippe Monin from EM Lyon. I had always been drawn to elite French chefs and found them more interesting than mutual fund managers. If mutual fund managers were under the thrall of regression to the mean, elite French chefs were concerned about the stars awarded by the Guide Michelin. One of them, Bernard Loiseau, had committed suicide when his restaurant was downgraded from three Michelin stars to two.

Rudy, Phillipe, and I felt that we needed to interview chefs and critics to understand how the nouvelle cuisine movement had taken root in France. We sampled elite restaurants and their plebeian counterparts—the bouchons in Lyon—and it was an incredible learning experience for us. Soon we collected data on the signature dishes of each restaurant, classified them as classical or nouvelle cuisine, and modeled the impact of the nouvelle cuisine movement. "Institutional Change in Toque Ville" appeared in *AJS* (Rao, Monin, & Durand, 2003). The play on Tocqueville's name was a reference to chefs' tall hats.

The move to Northwestern.   In 2001, the Management and Organizations Department at Kellogg invited me to move to Northwestern University. The prime movers were Ranjay Gulati, Paul Hirsch, Willie Occasion, and Ed Zajac—all amazing scholars. Paul had an exceptionally keen eye for discerning anomalies; Ranjay was incredibly productive and impactful as he brought in network ideas to reimage the study of alliances; Willie and Ed were in the thick of extending institutional models of organizations. I had visited Kellogg for an interview and been rebuffed in 1989, but all of them persuaded me that the time was ripe. I was already in conversation with Willie and Ed about a textbook on organizations to understand attention, entrainment, mobilization, and engagement processes. I went for a talk, soon was extended an offer, and joined Kellogg in the fall of 2002. Kellogg was also notable because there I met Phil Kotler—whose text on marketing had been my textbook in 1978 at business school in India; never had I thought he'd be a colleague!

Right before the move to Northwestern, Don Palmer called me at home in Atlanta one afternoon, and I was under the impression that he wanted to discuss a study of mine that he had just rejected. Instead, he told me he was calling to invite me to be an associate editor! I was floored—and thought this must be the first time a rejected author had been asked to be an associate editor. I soon learned that rejection was more common than I thought.

At Kellogg, I was learning more about my micro colleagues and understanding how such a top-ranked department in a prominent business school institution functioned. For example, evaluations of teaching were available to students and colleagues alike! One had to improve teaching quality as well as excel in research. In conjunction with the nouvelle cuisine studies, my interest in social movements now pertained to anti and pro chain store movements, and I was fortunate to have Paul Ingram as a collaborator, friend, and coauthor. Paul was a scholar who loved history, institutions, and methods. As we devoured historical accounts and gathered data, we decided to title the study "Store Wars." Paul wrote many a memorable email titled "The Empire Strikes Back" with ideas about how to respond to reviewers. Our study of how the chain store form was buffeted by the anti-chain-store movement that led to the promulgation of hostile laws, and our study of how chain stores responded with the pro-chain-store movement and sought allies and court intervention appeared in *AJS* (Ingram & Rao, 2004).

I went to Kellogg expecting to do research with doctoral students and colleagues, but the surprise was that I learned how to teach executives! Soon after my arrival, Dipak Jain, then dean of the school, asked me to teach in a program on mergers, and Bob Dewar asked me to teach in a program on the market focused organization. Bob took me under his wing and really taught me a lot about executives, and what needed to be done to get research into the executive classroom, in an engaging way with actionable tips. It was both disorienting and challenging, as I had to cope with research challenges and teaching demands. I loved the teaching but could not find a way to say no to teaching in executive programs, since I was a newbie in the school, and soon found myself getting overwhelmed. My colleagues, Ranjay and Ed, in particular urged me to be selective and say no.

I thought I was going to be at Kellogg for the rest of my life, until one day, in 2004, Chip Heath called from Stanford, told me that Stanford was seeking a senior hire, and asked me to recommend people. I listed three people (my coauthors); he said that they had talked to all of them, and the sense was that perhaps I was the person. I was surprised, and initially demurred, but my wiser partner, Sadhna Diwan, suggested to me that the weather was better in California. She was willing to give up a job at the University of Chicago and take one at San Jose State University. So off we went to Stanford—it was all the more surprising because three of my textbooks at business school in India at XLRI had been by Stanford professors: Jeff Pfeffer's *External Control*, Chuck Horngren's *Cost Accounting*, and Jim van Horne's *Fundamentals of Financial Management*. Dipak Jain, the Kellogg dean, said that he would keep my chair at Kellogg vacant until I decided to come back at the end of the year or chose to stay at Stanford.

Stanford as Disneyland. I was apprehensive whether I could be successful at Stanford. I spoke to assistant professors there who had not succeeded there and those who had, full professors who had left the OB area and those who had declined an offer not just in OB but in other areas. It became clear to me that Stanford gave you autonomy and resources, but appreciation was scarce because everybody was expected to excel. I had also attended a class taught by Jim Baron and realized that I could not import what I had done at Kellogg—the students' interests were different. (Stanford students sought to be entrepreneurs, and Kellogg students aspired to be management consultants or brand builders.) The OB group had prominent scholars ranging from Jeff Pfeffer to Mike Hannan.

I recall asking Mike Tushman from Columbia for advice—and he urged me to negotiate my role among such stars. I asked Jeff Pfeffer "What is my role?" and remember him saying: "Your job is to be you—can you do that?" I replied: "I have a comparative advantage—I can be me more easily than others." This was the best gift I received: to be me! Remarkably, Jerry Davis, a Stanford alum and student of Pfeffer, urged me to explore. "Stanford is like Disneyland. There are lots of rides. Don't take the same ride each day!" Both insights influenced the way life unfolded for me at Stanford.

When I had been at Kellogg, I had been selected as a fellow of the Center for Advanced Study in the Behavioral Sciences (CASBS), which is located at Stanford. I had not even known I was under consideration until I received a missive from Doug McAdam, prominent scholar of social movements, and the then director of the center, informing me of my selection. In those days, the review process, I was told, was akin to a tenure process. I negotiated with David Kreps at Stanford that I would spend my first year at Stanford but would be located the center. Based on advice from Woody Powell, I chose an office with a great view and far away from the bathroom! The center was like a monastery. You wrote from 8 to 12, had lunch with a diverse array of scholars, worked some more, played basketball or attended a seminar by the fellows, and ended the day with a glass of wine. The CASBS environment allowed me to complete projects I had started at Kellogg.

The very first study, on French chefs mixing categories and hybridizing their identities, made its way into the pages of *American Sociological Review* (Rao, Monin, & Durand, 2005); it was a corrective to the monochromatic view of identity espoused by organization sociologists. A second study that saw the light of day at CASBS was on social movements, coauthored with Henrich Greve and Jo-Ellen Pozner—then a Kellogg doctoral student. We felt that, for example, the work of Glenn Carroll and Anand Swaminathan looked at the "demand side": how a new segment and category of consumers opened up. We were interested in the supply side: how a social movement drew in more entrepreneurs. We also wanted to understand whether such entrepreneurial behavior materially changed an industry. Soon we were studying the microradio movement as a response to the domination of radio waves by media chains, and we looked at applicants for new spectrum to be allotted to micro radio stations. We looked at the micro radio stations who sought to apply for new spectrum, whether they were given licenses, and whether their entry changed listening shares in radio markets. "Vox Populi" appeared in *AJS* (Greeve, Pozner, & Rao, 2006). Some years later, *AJS* informed us that they had accepted a critique of our study, titled "Vox Regni," that claimed that we had ignored regulatory influences, and gave us a few weeks to respond. We were surprised that we had not known this until the critique was accepted and that *AJS* had not given us more time to respond. Feeling a surge of aggressive energy, we wrapped by our responses, titled our response "Vox Veritatis," and refuted the critiques with empirical analyses. We learned that it was essential to be calm, to recognize the value of dialogue, and to refute critiques through empirical rebuttals rather than assertions and aspersions.

While the next few years were productive, I also became the editor of *ASQ* in 2008, and this meant more work. My goal was to lure in people better than me. Soon Jerry Davis joined as an associate editor, as did Frank Flynn, my Stanford colleague, and Henrich Greve. Even as I was busy with the editor role, new research projects emerged unexpectedly.

As editor at *ASQ*, I felt that we were ignoring consequential organizations such as Walmart, and board members urged me to write an editorial inviting such research. I demurred. I felt it was lame to issue calls for other people to do research, and the best thing for me to do was to start a research project. I duly called Paul Ingram, and we agreed to extend our chain study to the study of Walmart's entry into markets. Paul saw the possibilities better than I did. Before we knew it, along with Lori Yue, his graduate student at Columbia, we were starting out with a study on Walmart's entry: our starting point was that if Walmart and protesters were rational, each would focus on places where they were strong, so Walmart would not encounter protests. Yet the empirical record showed that entry was met with protest, and the first study of our three-part series appeared in *AJS* (Ingram, Yue, & Rao, 2010); two more studies appeared in *American Sociological Review* (Rao, Yue, & Ingram, 2011) and *ASQ* (Yue, Rao, & Ingram, 2013).

The arrival of graduate students is a stochastic shock—and when Sunasir Dutta from India arrived at Stanford, I felt that at long last I could do a study of the Indian army's mutiny against the British in 1857. Sunasir was bright, interested in history and numismatics, and soon gathered data. We presented some initial results at Stanford's Political Science Department, and one of the audience members, a historian of Islam, asked us about the timing of muti-nies. Instantly, we realized that we ought to address the question of what made mutinies possible, and we realized that major religious festivals created "free spaces" for mutiny organizers to recruit and mobilize people; a religious procession often turned into a riot. "Free Spaces" appeared in *ASQ* (Rao & Dutta, 2012). We had conducted many robustness tests that did not feature in the study or the appendix. One such test was to look at what had made soldiers believe the rumor that the British had doctored cartridges with cow fat and pig fat, thereby angering both the Hindu and Moslem communities. Sunasir and I wondered whether there had been an exogenous shock that activated the schema of contamination before the spread of the rumor, and we discovered that in 1857, in a bid to insulate themselves from cholera, villagers would send food (a chapati) to the next village in a chain letter format. Sunasir detected that the propensity to send the chapati was uncorrelated with the actual deaths from cholera in 1856. We quickly showed that sending the chapati had activated a schema of contamination and laid the epistemic ground for the consumption of the cartridge rumor. This study came out in a special issue of *Organizational Behavior and Human Decision Processes*, thanks to the imaginative guest editor, Michael Morris of Columbia. Michael also helped us design an MTurk experiment to show that our account was more general, and it was a wonderful experience.

Stanford was also remarkable because John Meyer, Woody Powell, Dick Scott, Steve Barley, and Bob Sutton were also there. Lunches with John and Dick were illuminating, as were sake-laden evenings with Steve and wine bar visits with Woody. During my fourteen years at Stanford, I have always met Woody at his favorite wine store/tasting room: Vin, Vino in Palo Alto.

Turn to practice: scaling up excellence in firms. Never in my wildest dreams did I ever think I would write a book for managers. It all happened because of the intellectual and personal proximity of Bob Sutton. He lived two streets away from me in Menlo Park, and we soon became wine-drinking buddies, and then organized an executive program on innovation that the participants loved. When they asked us "How can we scale this" both of us gave lame answers, and we realized that we knew next to nothing about scaling. This led us to create more occasions for wine drinking—writing cases, teaching a course, and eventually developing a proposal to write our book for managers, *Scaling Up Excellence* (Rao, 2014). In view of this possibility, I relinquished my position as editor of *ASQ*—since I did not want the journal to be affected by my stochastic explorations.

I had never written a proposal to a commercial publisher such as Random House (who became our publisher), and I learned how to write for a popular audience from Bob, who was both a consummate and a successful writer. Jeff Pfeffer's encouragement me to be me and Jerry's original advice to "try other rides" led me to embark on this adventure. The book upended many assumptions for me. I thought one wrote a book and then sold it. I found out that you wrote a proposal and then got an agent who could organize an auction for the book (given Bob's success), that you had to build a community first, and that the book was a totem for the community. All of these activities were engrossing, and I was pleasantly surprised when the book quickly became a Wall Street bestseller. Although the book sold well, it was bought by firms who gave them to employees, and the *New York Times* disallowed such purchases. Ours was not a diet book or a self-help book bought by individuals.

Near misses and dead-ends. Any recounting of one's career as a series of stochastic excursions must acknowledge failure. However, failure and success are retrospective judgments that occur after an event; instead, the event itself comes as a near miss or a dead-end, or feels like a plain mistake. Instead of listing many of my failures (I have had many!), I thought I'd present a few salient ones in the hope that they will help the reader or at least convey the flavor of what transpired.

Let me begin with a near miss. Last year, Henrich Greve, my friend and co-author, was visiting Stanford. Since he is a student of Jim March, one idea that arose was for both of us to give a gift to Jim in the form of a study that showed skeptics that the garbage can was a model and not a metaphor, and that it need not be deterministic. When I had first read the garbage can study in 1984 at Case, since I was sitting next to operations researchers, I had wondered why Jim and Michael Cohen had not invoked arguments from the theory of queues in production management. Years later, as Henrich and I were revisiting the garbage can study, the notion of queues arose, but we had no idea of how to develop a model that drew on stochastic matching across the queues of people, problems, and solutions. Fortunately, Peter Glynn, from management science, was a leading contributor to the literature of queues, and he joined in the project. We did finish the study, but it was a near-miss because we were only able to get it done after Jim passed away. Jim, of course, knew the rhythms of scholarly work, and he asked us: "will I see the paper before I die"? An enduring regret is that we were unable to do that.

Dead-ends arise in projects, and the danger is escalation of commitment to a failing course of action. One has to give up the idea of a study. One such example was my inability to use the automobile data—that had been collected for the study on reputation—to understand technological change. The initial idea was to demarcate eras of ferment and dominant design. Try as I might, we could never get around issues of endogeneity, and eventually I had to give up the study. It was hard but also freeing at the same time, and allowed me to focus on other projects.

Closing thoughts. Let me turn to the implications of my account of my career as a series of stochastic excursions. I recognize that my career trajectory is unusual; very few people start at Case and end up at Stanford, and so chance played a central role. While chance was prominent, what I did to respond to the chances mattered too. Great scholars like the ones I had allocate their time carefully; you have to show them that you are curious, capable, hard-working, and above all excited. I offer some closing thoughts, based on a sample of one—my own career, and an edge case at that—about how one's attitude toward chance matters. So here goes:

1. *Every place gives you an unexpected gift—embrace it.* We go to places of work with expectations that may be unmet or undermet, but every place confers an unexpected gift. I thought XLRI would equip me to be a business executive, but it allowed me to embark on an academic career. Case faculty supported me but also gave me the opportunity to learn how to teach myself and learn from other students, such as operations researchers. Similarly, I went to Kellogg hoping to do more research but learned how to teach. I thought Stanford would also add to research, but it opened the doors to influencing practice by writing evidence-based books such as *Scaling Up Excellence*. Embrace the gift every place gives you—don't spend time fighting it!

2. *Coauthors are teachers.* I was fortunate to have coauthors and collaborators who were teachers who opened new windows of thought for me. Each coauthor taught me something specific; if Heather could visualize a table of results very quickly, Jerry could write up great introductions and motivations for a study, Paul could develop counterfactuals, and Henrich was able to get me to read and understand Norwegian history when we wrote our study on cultural legacies and organization building in Norway.

3. *Honesty is a network outcome.* We consider honesty to be an individual predisposition. While that may be the case, our networks of coauthors to whom we commit projects are the ones who keep us honest. Let's face it, business school professors can not only have research careers but also make money through consulting and other activities. What enables you to keep your commitment to research alive? It is your coauthors to whom you have to deliver results—be it an analysis, a written document, or a Skype call. All these ensure that the flame of research is kept alive instead of being snuffed by the lure of consulting.

4. *Your life partner matters.* Among all the stochastic excursions in life, the choice of a life partner matters. If you can, choose someone who is

more generous than you—she or he will bring out the best in you—and someone who makes you laugh at your stupidity. I am fortunate to have Sadhna Diwan, my partner, who does both. She is also my best critic. When I give her a draft of a study to read, and she falls asleep, I know it is dead in the water!

5. *Be you.* Above all, as Jeff Pfeffer told me, be you! When your job description is to be you, you devote time to things you love and avoid things you don't. When some of my senior colleagues at Stanford urged me to develop a research program, this gift of Jeff allowed me to tell myself and them: nope—I'd rather do other things.

References

Dutta, S., & H. Rao. (2015). Infectious diseases, contamination rumors, and ethnic violence: Regimental mutinies in the Bengal Native Army in 1857. *Organizational Behavior and Human Decision Processes, 127*, 36–47.

Greve, H., J. Posner, & H. Rao. (2006). Vox populi: Resource partitioning, organizational proliferation and the cultural impact of the insurgent micro-radio movement. *American Journal of Sociology, 112*, 802–837.

Ingram, P., & H. Rao. (2004). Store wars: The enactment and repeal of anti–chain store legislation in America. *American Journal of Sociology, 110*(2), 446–487.

Ingram, P., L. Yue, & H. Rao. (2010). Troubled store: Probes, protests and store openings by Wal-Mart; 1998–2005. *American Journal of Sociology, 116*, 53–92.

Haveman, H., H. Rao, & S. Parachuri. (2007). The winds of change: Political culture and the diversity of organizational forms in the early California thrift industry. *American Sociological Review, 72*(1), 114–172.

Haveman, H., & H. Rao. (1997). Structuring a theory of moral sentiments: Institutional and organizational co-evolution in the early California Thrift industry. *American Journal of Sociology, 102*, 1606–1651.

Neilsen, E., & H. Rao. (1987). The strategy-legitimacy nexus: A thick description. *Academy of Management Review, 12*(3), 523–533.

Pfeffer, J., & G. R. Salancik. (1978). *The external control of organizations: A resource dependence perspective.* Stanford, CA: Stanford University Press.

Rao, H. (2014). *Scaling up excellence: How to get to more without settling for less.* New York: Crown.

Rao, H. The social construction of reputation: Contests, credentialing and legitimation in the American automobile industry; 1895–1912. (1994). *Strategic Management Journal, 15*, 29–44.

Rao, H., G. M. Davis, & A. Ward. (2000). Embeddedness and social identity: Why organizations leave NASDAQ and join NYSE. *Administrative Science Quarterly, 45*, 268–292.

Rao, H., H. Greve and G.M. Davis (2001) Fool's Gold: Social Proof in the Initiation and abandonment of Coverage by Wqall Street Analysts. *Administrative Science Quarterly, 46*, 502–526.

Rao, H., & S. Dutta. (2012). Free spaces as organizational weapons of the weak: Religious festivals and regimental mutinies in the Bengal Native Army, 1857. *Administrative Science Quarterly*, 57, 627–668.

Rao, H., P. Monin, & R. Durand. (2003). Institutional change in Toque Ville: Nouvelle cuisine as an identity movement in French gastronomy, *American Journal of Sociology*, 108(4), 795–843.

Rao, H., P. Monin, & R. Durand. (2005). Border crossing: Bricolage and the erosion of culinary categories in French gastronomy. *American Sociological Review*, 70, 9868–9991.

Rao, H., & E. Neilsen. (1992). An ecology of collectivized agency: Dissolutions of savings and loan associations; 1960–1987. *Administrative Science Quarterly*, 37, 448–470.

Rao, H., & W. Pasmore. (1989). Knowledge and interests in organization studies: A conflict of interpretations. *Organization Studies*, 10(2), 225–239.

Rao, H., L. Yue, & P. Ingram. (2011). Laws of attraction: Regulatory arbitrage in the face of activism in right-to-work states. *American Sociological Review*, 76(3), 365–385.

Yue, L., H. Rao, & P. Ingram. (2013). Informational spillovers from protests against corporations: A tale of Walmart and Target. *Administrative Science Quarterly*, 58(4), 669–701.

9
Building a Systematic Program of Research into Employee Creativity and Innovation

Jing Zhou

Having been fascinated by how people come up with creative ideas, I started building a systematic program of research in the mid-1990s when I was a PhD student. It was an exciting time to start, because the interest in employee creativity was burgeoning in organizations and in management research. Earlier, Amabile's (1996) emphasis on creativity in context was frame-breaking and changed the conversation about the focus of creativity research in the field of social psychology; it also substantially influenced the emergent research into employee creativity in the field of management. Prior to the emphasis on context, much psychological research focused on studying genius or searching for a stable set of traits that could reliably distinguish creative people from non-creative ones. This focus on genius and traits does not speak directly about how to foster employee creativity in the workplace, because it does not take into consideration the influences of major forces in organizations, such as organizational culture, structure, processes, managerial practices, task characteristics, and the social environments in which employees are embedded. Though many employees are not geniuses, under the right conditions, they may be able to come up with new and useful ideas concerning products, services, and processes, which is the definition of workplace creativity (Amabile, 1996). On the other hand if the work context is restrictive, even employees who have strong potential or natural inclination to be creative may not have the opportunity to express their creative potential. Thus, supportive context can nurture and promote employee creativity, whereas unsupportive context may discourage and diminish it.

This premise led me to endeavor to advance the understanding of workplace creativity. I felt that the research field concerning employee creativity was akin to an oil field with rich reserves. When I first stepped foot into this field, I did

Jing Zhou, *Building a Systematic Program of Research into Employee Creativity and Innovation* In: *A Journey toward Influential Scholarship*. Edited by: Xiao-Ping Chen and H. Kevin Steensma, Oxford University Press. © Oxford University Press 2021.
DOI: 10.1093/oso/9780190070717.003.0009

not have a clear roadmap of where to drill oil wells. I was just excited and kept drilling. Over time, three "oil wells"—three lines of inquiry—showed great promise, so I focused on drilling those three "wells." Eventually, this focused effort led to a systematic program of research, revealing a full range of contextual factors or management practices relevant to employee creativity. This research program includes three aspects. In the next four sections, I will first present an overview of this research program, summarizing its key findings and contributions. Then, in three separate sections, I will provide more detail about each of the three aspects of the research program, focusing on revealing the backstories regarding the researcher's thinking or decision-making processes. Finally, I will conclude the chapter by sharing thoughts about research impact and lessons learned in this journey of exploration and discovery of the wealth of knowledge.

Overview of a Systematic Program of Research on Creativity and Innovation

The first aspect of the systematic nature of my program of research is that I use an interactional approach to reveal how the interplay between the actor (e.g., a person or a team) and the context affects creativity. Working either independently or in collaboration with coauthors, I have conducted empirical studies in the behavioral laboratory and at work organizations in different industries to investigate interactional effects of a broad array of personal attributes and contextual factors. The personal attributes investigated include creative personality characteristics (Gough, 1979); creativity-relevant factors of the "Big Five" personality model (Costa & McCrae, 1992)—openness to experience, conscientiousness, and introversion; goal orientation; regulatory foci; and values (e.g., conformity, uncertainty avoidance) (e.g., George & Zhou, 2001; Zhang & Zhou, 2014). The contextual factors investigated include various types of feedback (e.g., feedback valence and feedback style, supervisory developmental feedback, coworker useful feedback), leadership behavior and leader attributes (e.g., transformational leadership, empowering leadership, supervisory close monitoring, emotional intelligence, and trustworthiness), the employee-manager relationship (e.g., guanxi management), influences from customers, the presence of creative coworkers, task characteristics (e.g., task autonomy, task complexity, heuristic tasks), team contexts, social networks, and human resource management systems (e.g., Dong, Liao, Chuang, Zhou, & Campbell-Bush, 2015; Hirst, van Knippenberg, & Zhou, 2009; Hirst, van Knippenberg, Zhou, Quintane, & Zhu, 2015; Liu, Gong,

Zhou, & Huang, 2017; Shin & Zhou, 2003, 2007; Zhou, 1998a, 2003; Zhou & George, 2003). This programmatic research effort has broadened and deepened our understanding of the complex interplay between the actor and the context in predicting creativity. In particular, the systematic nature of this research program facilitated the development of a typology regarding how various configurations of actor-context interactions enhance or restrict creativity (Zhou & Hoever, 2014). For example, a remedial type of interaction depicts the situation in which employees who have fewer creativity attributes benefit more from a certain context condition by exhibiting greater creativity in that context than employees who have more creativity attributes. As another example, a synergistic type of interaction depicts the situation in which employees who have greater natural inclinations to be creative exhibit greater creativity in a context that is specifically suited for triggering and reinforcing such natural inclinations. This typology provides a novel and comprehensive conceptual lens for understanding and predicting how high versus low creativity-relevant attributes interact with positive or negative contexts to boost or reduce employee creativity.

The second aspect of the systematic nature of my research program is investigating conditions under which dissatisfaction and negative affect facilitate creativity, collaborating with Jennifer George. This line of inquiry first revealed how job dissatisfaction, and then showed how negative mood, served to trigger creative endeavor and sustained creative effort (George & Zhou, 2002; Zhou & George, 2001). Prior research regarding affect and creativity had focused on the positive relation between positive affect and divergent thinking. We theorize that the generation of creative ideas in organizations involves a process that goes beyond divergent thinking. The process includes problem detection, divergent thinking, and idea refinement. Our findings highlighted the positive role of dissatisfaction or negative mood in the creative process in terms of detecting a problem and sustaining effort so that at the idea refinement stage the focal employee perseveres until an idea that is truly new and useful has been produced. The series of studies that George and I conducted eventually resulted in a dual-tuning theoretical account. It posits that negative and positive mood facilitate different aspects of the creative idea generation process; in a supportive context, the two mood states work in concert to enhance the overall creative output (George & Zhou, 2007).

The third aspect of the systematic nature of my research program is investigating the receiving side of creativity. This programmatic line of inquiry started with the development of a social-cognitive account of managers' recognition of employees' creative ideas (Zhou & Woodman, 2003), explaining how and why a set of multilevel factors involving personal, interpersonal, and organizational variables affect the recognition of creative ideas. In a programmatic manner, my coauthors and I (Zhou, Wang, Song, & Wu, 2017) conducted four studies in which we found that perceivers who were high on promotion focus perceived greater creativity in ideas that were creative. Innovation culture led perceivers to recognize greater creativity in ideas that were highly creative. Contextual cues in terms of gain-framing helped perceivers who had prevention focus to recognize greater creativity in ideas that were highly creative. Zhou, Wang, Bavato, Tasselli, and Wu (2019) provide a multidisciplinary review of creativity receiving. Gong, Zhou, and Chang (2013) examined conditions under which core knowledge workers' creativity contributed to firm performance. Liu, Gong, Zhou, and Huang (2017) investigated effects of human resource management systems on employee creativity, and the impact of employee creativity on firm innovation in terms of the introduction of new products. Together, these conceptual and empirical works have broadened creativity research, moving from an exclusive focus on antecedents of creativity to introducing a new research stream—the receiving side of creativity.

In the next three sections, I will recount how each of these three aspects was developed, respectively. In each section, I will describe in detail a few representative studies, revealing how decisions were made at key decision points during the processes of conceptualizing, designing, and executing the studies.

Antecedents of Creativity: Understanding the Interplay between Actor and Context

I began building the research program by focusing on an understanding of antecedents of creativity. My professional area of specialty is managing behaviors in organizations. Hence, I am deeply interested in finding out what managers may do and what conditions organizations should create in order to promote, instead of restrict, employee creativity. On the other hand, my training in psychology lets me appreciate the fact that individual differences can shape how employees react to contextual conditions. This dual interest has led me to be fascinated by the interplay between the actor and the context, thereby subscribing to the interactional perspective for an understanding of the antecedents of creativity. A journey of a thousand miles begins with the first step. Let me recount how the first study of my research program happened.

How the First Study Came to Be

When I started doing research on creativity, I was not thinking about designing a research program that will be influential. Instead, I was mystified, and really wanted to solve a mystery. The mystery started in a pair of first-year PhD seminars at the University of Illinois at Urbana-Champaign (UIUC): Greg Oldham's seminar on research in organizational behavior and Huseyin Leblebici's seminar on research in organizational theory. Each week we had a long list of reading assignments, and during each class meeting we discussed those readings, and, of greater importance, we talked about new research ideas that stemmed from reading those books or articles. For the most part, I liked those readings. They were usually a nice mix of classic and contemporary works, and I enjoyed learning about the theories and empirical findings presented in those articles. When I read them alone, I was often intrigued by the clever research questions the authors posed and the smart ways in which they designed their studies to test those ideas. However, I dreaded the class segments when we discussed new research ideas, because all the other students always seemed to have interesting ideas whereas I was often the only person who did not have any. To say that I was frustrated is an understatement. Though I did not realize this until years later, the seeds were planted during those two seminars of my desire to solve the puzzle of how people come up with creative ideas.

The first piece of the puzzle I tried to solve became my dissertation work. The research question stemmed from my fascination at the time with the various kinds of feedback that my fellow PhD students and I received with regard to the coursework, term papers, and research work we did as part of our research assistantships or projects with faculty mentors. As an international student who had never had any experience with taking research seminar types of courses or working on a research assistantship, I paid a great deal of attention to the feedback I received from professors. Perhaps because this was the first time in my life that I was living in an entirely new environment as a nonnative English speaker, I also paid a great deal of attention to what my fellow students said about the feedback they received from their professors. It soon became apparent to me that feedback was really important for the students' subsequent efforts, and that the feedback received by different students was very different. No surprise there. What puzzled me was that after receiving feedback the students produced different results: some students came up with much better ideas after receiving feedback, whereas others did not show much improvement.

A straightforward interpretation of this phenomenon is that some students are just better suited for PhD studies than others. I was not satisfied with this conventional answer. Though during most PhD seminars I was pretty quiet because I was struggling with both English and the discussion-based learning format, my mind was working actively. After each class meeting, I would go to the library to read a lot of articles. This was in the mid-1990s, when people still physically checked out journals and books instead of what is typically done today—getting electronic copies of articles. In retrospect, physically checking out journals facilitated my reading and broadened my knowledge base, because after locating an article in an issue of a journal, I often found other articles published in the same issue interesting and read them as well. This worked out great, because to find a good research question one needs to be observant, so as to identify an important real-world phenomenon. For many researchers, such observation often involves their personal experiences. To extract a worthwhile research question from personal observation and experience, however, one needs to pair up the observation and personal experience with a broad knowledge base. This knowledge base helps one to identify the core narrative and isolate key constructs that are buried in the particularities of a specific event or experience. Though I started to develop dissertation ideas a couple of years later, the habit of tuning in to and interpreting other students' reactions to feedback and reading the literature broadly, which was formed in my first year in the PhD program, contributed to my finding the identity as a researcher and building a systematic program research.

Compared to my interest in the effects of feedback, my fascination with creative activities had gone on for much longer, initially not so much as an intellectual pursuit as in the pursuit of personal hobbies. Growing up in Beijing, I was immensely interested in the visual arts, particularly drawing and painting. It was an era in which students were encouraged to devote their time and energy to studying more "substantive" fields than the arts, such as math, physics, chemistry, and biology. From middle school to high school, students doing well in those science courses were looked up to. I did well in science courses, so I was on the science track in high school. The high school curriculum had zero offerings in the arts. I had to teach myself how to draw and paint by going to museums and learning from books how to draw and paint. I even drew a cartoon series and tried to turn those drawings into a homemade animated motion picture, which failed miserably. After I passed the national college entrance exam as a science student and got into Peking University, I had more freedom, and I was overjoyed to find out that there were extracurricular clubs on campus. I joined a club to learn how to play the guitar. I took a seminar series on how to interpret and appreciate classical music. I joined a club to learn film photography and spent a lot of time taking pictures and developing films in a darkroom. Though I did not realize it at the time when I was engaged in those artistic/creative activities, in retrospect, all those creative activities I had participated in years ago made me see the value, the joy, and the ups and downs in creative activities, and perhaps even developed some intuition about people and the process of creative idea generation. Thus, when I was developing dissertation ideas, though creativity was not yet an established topic in organizational behavior, my experiences in those earlier and formative years sensitized me to creative activities and sowed the seeds of intellectual curiosity about creativity, which blossomed during my PhD studies.

My fascination with creativity as an intellectual pursuit grew after my first year I in UIUC's PhD program. During the time that I was thinking about what topic I might work on for my dissertation, one day the two things just connected: I could study how feedback influences creativity—the generation of original and useful ideas. By then I had observed a consistent pattern from my own experiences and from those of my fellow PhD students: feedback that was positive in nature kept me and my fellow students going. But I also observed that quite a few students who received positive feedback didn't come up with creative ideas in their subsequent research work. So something else must be operating, not just positive feedback. I delved into the creativity literature, and in published articles and unpublished dissertations I could not find what this "something else" was. I sensed an opportunity for me to contribute, because feedback was used widely, yet its effect on creativity had received little research attention!

Before making a decision on whether it really was a good idea to focus my dissertation work on feedback and creativity, however, I thought about whether creativity would become a legitimate area within the broad field of organizational behavior, and concluded that it would. The reason that I considered this issue was that it would be exciting if a community of scholars conduct research in this area, exchanging ideas and drawing insights from each other's work. By then, I had already realized that I would enjoy developing a career in academia. I read all the studies published by the UIUC professors or former professors whom I admired: Greg Oldham, Barry Staw, Jeff Pfeffer, Jerry Salancik, Keith Murningham, Dave Whetten, Jerry Ferris, Harry Triandis, Bob Weir, Chuck Hulin, Fritz Drasgow, and Carol Kulik, to name but a few, and noticed that they all had built a systematic program of research. They focused on a specific behavior or phenomenon, aiming to achieve full understanding of it in all its breadth and depth. They did so by engaging in conceptual innovation and conducting multiple empirical studies to reveal mechanisms explaining the behavior or phenomenon, the factors that predicted it, or its consequences. Such a systematic way of conducting research appealed to me, as I saw it as the most promising path toward truly understanding a behavior or phenomenon, as opposed to the practice of trying to catch "hot topics" and to get as many publications as possible.

I wondered whether I could build a program of research by studying employee creativity. This was in the mid-1990s, few researchers in the field of organizational behavior specialized in creativity, few articles on employee creativity appeared in top management journals, and few fellow students showed much interest in researching creativity in the workplace. On the other hand my dissertation advisor, Greg Oldham, who had been a thought leader on job characteristics theory and the design of physical work environments, was starting to research employee creativity. Another student of Greg, Anne Cummings, was developing her dissertation on employee creativity. The Internet was poised to fundamentally change how businesses were conducted, and how people lived their lives. Yet at that point in time, it was difficult to predict exactly how things would change. So there was a great deal of excitement about the seemingly endless possibilities of creating new things, and creativity and innovation seemed to be key drivers for individuals and companies to adapt to and thrive in the dynamic environment. Though I did not fully envision at the outset that the employee creativity research area would become the booming area it is today, my earlier experiences in creative activities probably helped me to make sense of various pieces of information scattered in the intellectual environment at UIUC and to feel genuinely attracted by the emergent area of employee creativity research.

Having made a careful choice of a research area and increasingly feeling excited about this area, I carried out my dissertation work in earnest. My identification of phenomena concerning effects of feedback on creativity, in combination with a thorough study of the feedback and creativity literatures, led me to make a novel conceptual distinction between feedback valence (positive v. negative) and feedback style (informational v. controlling) (Zhou, 1998a). Theoretical analysis using cognitive evaluation theory led to the predictions that positive feedback delivered in an informational style would boost creativity via elevating intrinsic motivation, and that task autonomy would strengthen this interactive effect. To test the hypothesized relations that involved two novel constructs—feedback valence and feedback style—I ran a laboratory experiment to establish direction of causality. Empirical results supported the hypotheses. Using an interactional lens, I also hypothesized that achievement orientation, an individual difference variable, would interact with those contextual conditions such that individuals who had high levels of achievement orientation would react more positively to the joint contextual condition of positive feedback delivered in an informational style and high task autonomy. This hypothesis was not supported. After reflecting on the theoretical analysis and empirical execution of this study, I concluded this was not because the interactional lens was not valid but because I was hypothesizing a four-way interaction effect, which would be extremely difficult to detect. Having learned from this experience, I would not want to hypothesize a four-way interaction again!

In sum, the process of choosing a dissertation topic essentially started my systematic program of research into employee creativity and innovation. In choosing the dissertation topic, I was thinking longer term and wanting to find a really interesting, large, and complex puzzle that I could spend my academic career solving. To a degree, creating an influential research program is akin to the exploration of crude oil. In oil exploration, the goal is to find a field that is likely to have a large oil reserve, instead of drilling many wells that are dry or will dry up soon. To create an impactful research program, the goal is to identify a research area that is not just interesting for the researcher and important for practice but also presents the opportunity for creating a rich body of new knowledge. The message for PhD students is to use your dissertation as the opportunity to choose a research area first, and then a dissertation topic. In choosing a research area, the information embedded in your social and intellectual environments matters a great deal. However, it is your cumulative personal experiences that direct your attention to certain information and your interpretation of it. This combination of contextual influences and personal agency accounted for how the choosing of my dissertation topic was the first step of the journey of building a systematic program of research.

The dissertation work captured the phenomenon of using feedback as a tool to nurture creativity. Thanks to the high standards used by Greg Oldham and my committee members—Fritz Drasgow, Jerry Ferris, and Carol Kulik—the study (Zhou, 1998a) based on my dissertation went through the journal review process rather smoothly. It was accepted by the first journal to which I submitted it, after two rounds of review and revision. More important, it laid the foundation for a number of programmatic studies along the line of using feedback to nurture creativity. In a project aimed at identifying the conditions under which job dissatisfaction leads to employee creativity in the workplace, my coauthor and I included useful feedback from coworkers as one of the necessary conditions to turn job dissatisfaction into creativity (Zhou & George, 2001). In another field study, I showed that supervisory developmental feedback—the extent to which supervisors provide their employees with information that enables the employees to learn, develop, and make improvements on the job, in combination with the presence of creative coworkers, enhanced creativity in employees who had few creative personality attributes (Zhou, 2003).

The feedback and creativity research stream continues to advance. A particularly exciting development is that as organizations increasingly use teams to carry out work, research concerning feedback and creativity has expanded to team creativity. In the first study focusing on feedback and team creativity, and as one of three high-quality papers in her dissertation research, Hoever conducted a large-scale laboratory experiment to investigate effects of feedback on team creativity. She found differential effects of feedback valence: positive feedback promoted the creativity of teams that were informationally homogeneous, whereas negative feedback facilitated the creativity of teams that were informationally heterogeneous (Hoever, Zhou, & van Knippenberg, 2018).

Formulating Phenomenon-Driven Research Questions

To investigate the actor-context interplay as antecedents to creativity, I favor the practice of formulating a research question based on observations of a real-world phenomenon. I find such phenomenon-driven research questions to be meaningful and to have a greater chance of impacting management practices than research questions one attempts to come up with by just reading journal articles. A representative work in this regard is "When Job Dissatisfaction Leads to Creativity: Encouraging the Expression of Voice" (Zhou & George, 2001). Prior to coming up with the core idea of that study, I was wrestling with the question of whether having high levels of job satisfaction is good or bad for creativity. The trigger for this question was a conversation with an HR manager, who mentioned her company's annual employee survey. Among other things, the survey asked the employees to report their job satisfaction. A fundamental assumption was that employees' having high levels of job satisfaction was a good thing for the company. If in a given year a high percentage of employees reported being satisfied with their jobs, the HR manager would get praise from higher-ups for a job well done. This practice seemed to be consistent with decades of OB research: many journal articles included job satisfaction as a dependent variable, with the fundamental premise that having high levels of job satisfaction was desirable and led to high performance. At some point in my mind two things connected: I started to wonder whether job satisfaction would lead to creativity. The company's

HR practice and the OB literature seemed to suggest it would. Yet I felt something was not quite right, but I could not articulate what it was. This bothered me for quite some time.

During the time that this puzzle was bothering me, I went about my work and routine activities. In addition to research articles and books, I routinely read fiction and nonfiction works, and I enjoy a wide variety of genres. Probably due to this mix of observations, thinking, and readings, one day it suddenly struck me that a better question was whether job satisfaction or job dissatisfaction would lead to creativity. I felt excited and talked with my colleague Jennifer George, whose office was a couple of doors down the hall. I still remember how we sat in her office, discussing whether job satisfaction or dissatisfaction led to creativity, feeling more and more excited as our research ideas became more and more concrete. Initially, we could argue either way: job satisfaction would lead to creativity because when workers were satisfied with their jobs they would be likely to invest time and effort in coming up with creative ideas. Conversely, job dissatisfaction would lead to creativity because only when workers felt that some aspects of their jobs were unsatisfactory would they identify problems and initiate change—new and better ways of doing things, which are the essence of creativity. We felt that it was a challenge to predict which of the two would likely occur, if we just relied on personal intuition. We then realized that Hirschman's (1970) work provided a helpful conceptual lens.

Hirschman argued that workers had four alternative responses to feelings of dissatisfaction: exit, voice, loyalty, and neglect. Workers may choose to respond to their job dissatisfaction actively, either by quitting the organization (*exit*) or by remaining in the organization and trying to make things better (*voice*). Alternatively, they may respond to their job dissatisfaction passively by remaining in the organization but either accepting the status quo without expressing any objections (*loyalty*) or by exhibiting withdrawal types of behaviors (*neglect*). Our thinking became crystallized. Coming up with creative ideas, we theorized, was a form of responding to dissatisfaction via voice. Dissatisfaction was often caused by real problems in work processes. Feeling dissatisfied at work, the employees might take a proactive stance to identify the root causes of the problems, and generate new and useful ideas to eliminate the problems' root causes and improve the work processes. We further theorized that because employees had four options as responses to their job dissatisfaction, certain conditions needed to be in place for them to choose the voice option. We identified continuance commitment as a necessary condition, as choosing the voice option requires that the employee remains in the organization. Continuance commitment refers to employees' being committed to their organization because of necessity, instead of on the basis of affective attachment or identification with organizational values and goals. We integrated these insights from Hirschman's framework with the interactional perspective of creativity, theorizing that useful feedback from coworkers, coworkers' helping, and perceived organizational support for creativity were additional conditions that each worked jointly with continuance commitment to facilitate employees channeling their dissatisfactions into creativity.

We conducted an empirical investigation at a company that manufactured petroleum-drilling tools, and we published a study reporting this work (Zhou & George, 2001). Since its publication in the *Academy of Management Journal*, it has been cited 2,410 times (as of January 28, 2020, per Google Scholar). For an empirical study, this is a relatively high citation count, suggesting that readers find it interesting and useful. They may find it interesting because its central idea challenged existing assumptions. (I will explain this point in more detail in the next section.) They may find it useful because by identifying job dissatisfaction as a trigger for creativity, it indicates that the first and crucial step for creativity is to identify problems, and that factors associated with problem identification are important triggers for creativity. The study also argues that to channel job dissatisfaction into creativity, the organizational context needs to support employees' expression of voice. This perspective has stimulated later research to examine additional negative events or factors that may trigger creativity, and contextual factors that support the expression of voice. In addition to contributing to the creativity literature, the study also suggests there is a link between creativity and voice. Thus, the study is useful both conceptually and empirically.

I've mentioned that the interestingness and usefulness of the Zhou and George (2001) study may explain why it has been impactful, as indicated by its high citation count. Identifying an important behavior or phenomenon is an essential first step for starting an impactful research project. At some point in this process, thinking about theoretical perspectives will enable the researcher to find an interesting angle for understanding this phenomenon, and to crystallize a specific research question aiming at advancing knowledge about it. Though Hirschman's conceptual framework was not specifically developed for predicting whether job dissatisfaction triggers creativity, its identification of voice as an active response to job dissatisfaction helped my coauthor and me to develop our theoretical reasoning about conditions under which job dissatisfaction would lead to creativity. At the same time, if we had not identified it in the first place, we would not have gone on to capture a phenomenon that was interesting, poorly understood, and important. And without Hirschman's conceptual framework and the interactional perspective of creativity, we might have had a hard time capturing this phenomenon and formulating a specific research question to address it. Thus, though I am a big fun of phenomenon-driven research, I also appreciate the role that theories play in the research process.

Sometimes a phenomenon captured in a non-Western context faces push-back from journal reviewers, and authors need to be prepared to overcome more hurdles to get such work published than studies that describe phenomena originally observed in a Western context. From the authors' perspective, submitting such work to a special issue may increase the chance that reviewers find their work interesting, valid, and useful. From a journal editor's perspective, creating a special issue is a productive way of attracting phenomenon-driven research that focuses on a specific kind of phenomenon or in a specific type of context. A case in point is a study on introversion and creativity that my coauthors and I placed in *Organizational Behavior and Human Decision Processes* (Zhang, Zhou, & Kwon, 2017). We were fascinated by the phenomenon we had identified: the way the individual difference of introversion related to individuals' creativity. Upon close examination of the phenomenon and a careful analysis of relevant factors, we formulated our research question as whether introverted employees came up with more fresh ideas when they worked on more rather than less complex tasks while not being distracted by the demands of managing guanxi with their supervisors. Essentially, we considered task complexity and guanxi management as critical contextual conditions that influenced how the personal factor of introversion related to creativity.

Guanxi management, which was among the constructs we investigated, was originally identified by research in the Chinese context (Chen & Chen, 2004). It refers to employees' developing, managing, and maintaining informal and personal connections with their supervisors by engaging in work and non-work activities (Law, Wong, Wang, & Wang, 2000). Knowing some reviewers might not readily comprehend the full meaning of this construct, we worked diligently to make our arguments thorough and convincing. On the basis of our observation and our prior work on guanxi, we explained the concept of guanxi management, which emphasizes the dynamic nature of employees' relationships with their supervisors. It suggests that to build a positive and high-quality *guanxi* () with their supervisors, employees often invest much time and energy. Once a good guanxi is built, the employees still need to invest a great deal of time and energy to maintain it an ongoing basis. Guanxi management requires that the employees interact with their supervisors in an effort to build and maintain an excellent guanxi both in and outside the workplace. The interaction may involve both work and nonwork issues (Law et al., 2000). We highlight a distinctive feature of guanxi management: the activities that employees engage in for building and maintaining guanxi often deal with matters outside the workplace. They often involve employees providing favors to help their supervisors with matters related to their families and friends (Chen, Friedman, Yu, Fang, & Lu, 2009).

As I've suggested, making the connection between an identified phenomenon and previous theory and research related to it in order to develop constructs and predict relations among the constructs is essential for formulating phenomenon-driven research questions. Thoroughly reviewing and consulting previous theory and research is especially important when the phenomenon is originally identified in a non-Western context, because it gives the researchers confidence that the phenomenon they capture will interest a wide range of readers. In addition, our experience with this paper indicates that submitting the paper addressing a phenomenon captured in a non-Western context to a special issue may increase the chance that the paper will be more carefully considered by the review team. Being part of a special issue may also elevate the visibility and impact of the study over time.

On the other hand, there may be times when a phenomenon captured in a non-Western context resonates readily with reviewers and readers in the West, so authors should not be discouraged if there are no special issues available when they are ready to submit their work to a journal. For example, in Lin, Law, and Zhou (2017) we captured the phenomenon of underemployment relating to creativity via task crafting. Though the studies reported in this article were conducted in China, journal reviewers at the *Academy of Management Journal* seemed to be quite interested in the phenomenon and the study. So the study was accepted by the first journal to which we submitted it, and it was not part of a special issue. Interestingly, after the study was published in an academic journal, the popular press quickly picked up the story and reported the findings.

In sum, articulating phenomenon-based research questions and using the interactional perspective as the primary theoretical lens, the first aspect of my research program has systematically examined the interplay between an actor (an individual employee or a team) and the context. This programmatic research effort has contributed to a research stream concerning antecedents of employee creativity, and collectively, this research stream has accumulated an impressive body of work. On the basis of this body of work, Zhou and Hoever (2014) conceptualize a typology of actor-context interaction, describing nine types of actor-context interaction effects on employee creativity. In this section, I have selected a few representative studies and described the process of conceiving and conducting them in some detail to illustrate what I have learned as a researcher. In the final section of this chapter, I will pull key takeaways from each section and list them together.

Think Different, Break New Conceptual Grounds

In addition to subscribing to the principle that research should be phenomenon-based, another principle I use to guide the formulation of research questions is whether they challenge a widely held assumption or conventional wisdom. Research consumes financial and human resources. It requires researchers to spend time and money as well as mental and physical energy. Because researchers who study human behaviors at work need to collect data from employees and managers, research also requires participants to contribute their time and energy. Because there are tangible and intangible costs associated with each research project, I believe researchers should aim to address research questions that are highly meaningful, which usually involves challenging a commonly held assumption or conventional wisdom. This kind of research has the potential to substantially deepen our understanding of a phenomenon. This goal is consistent with the notion of "responsible research." (See the website of the virtual organization Responsible Research in Business and Management, https://rrbm.network/.) To accomplish this goal, the researchers need to adopt the mindset "think different," to borrow a famous Apple slogan, and dare to break new conceptual grounds. The second aspect of my research program reflects my pursuit of this goal.

The second aspect of my research program is a series of systematic investigations revealing how dissatisfaction or negative affect may benefit creativity (George & Zhou, 2002, 2007; Zhou & George, 2001). In the first of this series, Zhou and George (2001) formulated a voice account of creativity, theorizing conditions under which job dissatisfaction led to creativity. According to this account, under certain circumstances (e.g., continuance commitment and coworker useful feedback-helpful information provided by coworkers that enables an employee to make improvements on the job), *dis*satisfied employees may engage in creative activities as an expression of voice. This study broke new conceptual grounds not only because it was the first published study that theorized and tested a voice account concerning job dissatisfaction and creativity but also because it challenged, both theoretically and empirically, one of the fundamental assumptions in the field of organizational behavior: that job satisfaction is desirable and, conversely, job dissatisfaction is undesirable and detrimental for organizations. In the prior section,

I recounted the research process that eventually led to this study. At the core of the process was the aforementioned mindset "think different." This mindset propelled my coauthor and me to think critically and analyze deeply with the goal of breaking new conceptual grounds and advancing knowledge.

The Role of Negative Affect: Engaging in a Provocative Theoretical Discourse

Encouraged by the insights gained from our study on job dissatisfaction and creativity, my coauthor and I conducted more studies to systematically build on and extend our first study revealing the impact of dissatisfaction on creativity. Two additional projects are particularly noteworthy in this regard. Whereas job dissatisfaction may include an affective component and a cognitive component, these two additional studies focused on affect and creativity so as to contribute more broadly—to the burgeoning research into creativity and the literature on affect as well. I was fortunate to collaborate with Jennifer George, who is a leading scholar in the research area of affect, emotion, and mood, on those projects. Our complementary research interests and areas of expertise—her primary area is affect and mine is creativity—were crucial in the success of those projects.

In George and Zhou (2002), on the basis of the mood-as-input model in the affect literature (e.g., Martin & Stoner, 1996), we hypothesized that under certain conditions, negative moods might foster creativity and positive moods might inhibit it. This reasoning challenged the traditional view in research on divergent thinking and creativity, which suggested that positive moods were always beneficial for creativity. According to the mood-as-input model, individuals' mood states provide them with information (e.g., Schwarz & Clore, 2003), and the significance and consequences of the information depend on the context (Martin & Stoner, 1996). Adapting this model to creativity research, we argued that employees' work environments or contexts provide them with cues concerning their ongoing creative behaviors. These cues are valuable to them because when they are engaged in creative activities at work, they often have little objective information and have to decide for themselves when they have tried hard enough to come up with new and improved procedures, or put forth enough effort to come up with new and better ways of completing tasks. Consistent with our theoretical arguments, we found that negative moods were positively related to creativity when perceived recognition and rewards for creativity and clarity of feelings (a meta-mood process) were high. We also found that under the same conditions, positive moods were *negatively* related to creativity. This study contributed to the creativity literature by being the first to (1) demonstrate when negative moods fostered, and positive moods inhibited, creativity in an ongoing organization, and (2) examine the implications of meta-mood processes for creativity.

Toward a Dual-Tuning Theoretical Perspective

In George and Zhou (2007), we continued our quest to untangle the complex relations between mood states and creativity. We made even greater theoretical contributions by theorizing and testing a dual-tuning perspective concerning interactive effects of positive mood, negative mood, and supportive contexts on creativity.

More specifically, according to the mood-as-information theoretical framework, moods can exert tuning effects on cognitive processes. Thus, both positive and negative moods may be functional for creativity in the workplace. By signaling a satisfactory state of affairs, positive moods lead to more use of integrative top-down strategies, simplifying heuristics, and schemas and scripts (e.g., Fiedler, 1988; Kaufmann, 2003; Schwarz, 2002; Schwarz & Clore, 2003). They lead to less systematic and effortful information processing. By signaling a problematic state of affairs, negative moods push individuals to address and correct problems. They encourage a bottom-up, detail-oriented, analytic approach to understanding the situation, more focused on understanding the data at hand and less focused on preexisting schemas, scripts, and simplifying heuristics (Kaufmann, 2003; Schwarz & Clore, 2003). As such, both positive and negative moods can benefit creativity. Negative moods alert us to problems, cause us to focus on the current situation rather than our preexisting assumptions, and motivate us to exert high levels of effort to make improvements (George & Zhou, 2002; Kaufmann, 2003; Martin & Stoner, 1996; Schwarz, 2002). Positive moods allow us to be playful with ideas and willing to take risks and explore novel ways of doing things, and positive moods facilitate divergent thinking.

Importantly, and consistent with the person-context interactional perspective I've mentioned, the joint effects of positive and negative moods only manifest themselves in a supportive context provided by supervisors. That is, our dual-tuning perspective predicts that positive mood, negative mood, and a supportive context interact to affect creativity in such a way that when positive mood and a supportive context are both high, negative mood has the strongest positive relation with creativity. Our data have supported this prediction. By articulating and testing this dual-tuning perspective, we have contributed to the creativity literature by being the first to (1) theorize the interactive effects of positive mood, negative mood, and context on creativity, and (2) provide a reconciliation of the seemingly contradicting views concerning relations among positive mood, negative mood, and creativity.

In sum, the dual-tuning perspective broke new conceptual grounds in creativity research. The development of this perspective was made possible by our attempt to think different and our traveling along a programmatic research path. This path was started by our willingness to challenge the commonly held assumption that job satisfaction was a desirable employee outcome in the workplace and, following the same logic, that job dissatisfaction was undesirable and detrimental. We made significant advancement along this path when we engaged the field in a provocative conversation with regard to the role of negative affect in the creative idea generation process, and we ultimately integrated the differential effects of negative and positive affect on creativity into the dual-tuning perspective of creativity.

Opening a New Frontier: Creativity Receiving

The third aspect of my systematic research program focuses on the other side of the coin: creativity receiving. The process of discovering this topic was serendipitous. It started with a simple desire to have fun playing with radically new ideas. Let me recount the milestones, the turning points, and the thought process that formed this line of research.

Managers' Recognition of Employees' Creative Ideas

In 1998, when I was an assistant professor in the Management Department at Texas A&M University, a senior colleague, Dick Woodman, invited me to present at a conference on organizational change. Dick is a leading scholar in the field of organizational change. As far as I can remember, the conference grew out of his discussion with the faculty at University of Missouri in their process of building a center of excellence in the field of organizational change. Organizational change is related to my research field of creativity in the workplace, because new and useful ideas can bring forth meaningful change. Intrigued by the opportunity to engage in a dialogue with researchers in an adjacent field, I accepted the invitation. The next question was: what shall I present? During that time, I was working on several empirical studies focusing on the antecedents of creativity. I could choose any one of them to present at the conference. But I felt the urge to take a risk and have some fun by creating a new and different paper. I wanted to let my imagination run freely, instead of restricting myself to the calibration necessary for a top journal publication. As an assistant professor, I was doing a lot of the latter type of work already and wanted to find joy in creating a paper that was radically new and different.

I gave myself a week to figure out what this "radically new and different" paper would be. I worked at the office every night, ordering dinner from the only Chinese restaurant in College Station that had delivery service at that time. I ended up ordering MaPuo tofu every night, because nothing else on the menu brought out my appetite. I cannot remember after how many nights of having MaPuo tofu it was, but one evening, while eating MaPuo tofu, an idea came to me: the action of generating creative ideas does not necessarily bring about organizational change. Change is the *result* of *implementing* new ideas. Before idea implementation, however, managers need to *recognize* employees' creative ideas. The more I thought about this idea, the more I became excited. Ultimately, I developed a paper titled "Managers' Recognition of Employees' Creative Ideas: A Social-Cognitive Approach" and presented it at the conference (Zhou, 1998b). The paper theorized about managers' personal characteristics, the social context, and the cognitive mechanisms that predicted managers' recognition of their employees' creative ideas. The audience was very interested in the idea, and Dick suggested that I further develop the paper and submit it to the Academy of Management annual meeting. I did and invited Dick to be a coauthor. The paper was accepted and presented at the 1999 Academy of Management annual meeting (Zhou & Woodman, 1999). Later, Dick received an invitation to contribute a chapter to *The International Handbook on Innovation,* so we published the paper there (Zhou & Woodman, 2003). After completing this conceptual work, I changed jobs, started a family, served in a series of leadership positions in a professional organization, and worked as an associate editor of the *Journal of Applied Psychology.* From a paper-publishing standpoint, my work on this topic experienced a few quiet years. In retrospect, this quiet period was beneficial, because it incubated a number of unusual empirical papers, described here.

Is It True That "Employee Creativity Contributes to Firm Performance"?

Since the emergence of research into workplace creativity, the field has primarily focused on identifying antecedents of creativity. In order to justify examining creativity as the dependent variable, many papers state in the first paragraph that employee creativity contributes to firm innovation and performance. One day it struck me that this was a major assumption, and it needed to be examined. Yaping Gong, an expert in the field of human resource management systems, and I leveraged our complementary areas of expertise and designed a study on how firms' human resource management systems affect employee creativity. Serendipitously and fortunately, the first product of our collaborative effort was a study examining the impact of core knowledge workers' creativity on firm performance. Among other things, we found that the correlation between employee creativity and firm performance was −.03, highlighting the need to understand what happened after employees produced creative ideas (Gong et al., 2013).

In a more recent study, my coauthors and I found that the correlation between employee creativity and firm innovation, which was measured by the number of new products introduced, was .23 (Liu et al., 2017). Though this correlation was statistically significant, it was modest in magnitude. As such, while it indicated that employee creativity was positively related to firm innovation, it also implied that it was challenging to translate employee creativity into organizational innovation. This study's results, in combination with the results obtained by Gong et al. (2013), suggest a need to delve deeper at the individual level of analysis and reveal how individuals who are on the receiving side of creativity react to creative ideas when they encounter them. These two papers were turning points in this third aspect of my research program. I felt they validated not only the conceptual work I've mentioned (Zhou, 1998b; Zhou & Woodman, 1999, 2003) but also a multiyear effort aimed at understanding how individuals perceive creative ideas. I now turn to describe this multiyear effort.

Toward Programmatic Research on Creativity Receiving

To create a coherent body of knowledge, I have been doing both conceptual and empirical work with regard to creativity receiving. The aim was to create a systematic body of knowledge that would be both scientifically rigorous and practically useful. One example is an empirical paper that reported four studies that systematically examined the personal and contextual factors influencing individuals' perceptions of novelty and creativity. *Creativity* is defined as the generation of novel and useful ideas (Amabile, 1996). My coauthors and I argue that novelty recognition is the crucial starting point for extracting value from the ideas generated by others (Zhou et al., 2017).

Few theories have been developed in this nascent research area. So we first developed an associative evaluation account explaining how personal and contextual factors facilitated or inhibited individuals' perceiving novelty and creativity. We then conducted four studies to provide programmatic tests of the hypotheses we had formulated on the basis of this new theoretical account. Study 1 was a lab experiment. It found that perceivers' regulatory focus, as an experimentally induced state, affected novelty perception. Study 2 was a field study that used a sample of employees working in a manufacturing setting. It showed that perceivers' (the employees') promotion focus and prevention focus, measured as chronic traits, each interacted with normative level of novelty (or creativity): perceivers who scored higher on promotion focus perceived more novelty (or creativity) in novel (or creative) ideas than did those who scored lower, whereas perceivers who scored higher on prevention focus perceived less novelty (or creativity) in novel (or creative) ideas than those who scored lower. Study 3 was also a field study. It used a manager sample. Study 3 demonstrated that organizational culture affected managers' perception of novelty and creativity: innovative culture facilitated managers' perception of novelty and creativity. Study 4 was a lab experiment. It found three-way interaction effects of perceiver by idea by context: for perceivers with a prevention focus, the positive relation between normative level of novelty and novelty ratings was weakened in the loss-framing condition than in the gain-framing condition.

We started the collaboration in 2011, and the paper came out in 2017. Although it took my coauthors and me that many years to formulate the theory, conduct the four studies, develop the study, and to through the journal review process, I felt that such programmatic research design facilitates a deep understanding of the phenomena, enhances scientific rigor, and promotes the creation of a truly useful body of knowledge. Doing programmatic research is not without costs. The most obvious cost is that it is time consuming. This multiyear effort has resulted in only one empirical paper. Even so, it is my view that researchers should strive to do high-quality work that truly generates insights. Indeed, the insights we gathered through those four studies sketch out a road map for the field to grow, and we present this road map in a multidisciplinary review on the receiving side of creativity in Zhou, Wang, Bavato, Tasselli, and Wu (2019).

Concluding Remarks

Thus far, I have recounted my journey toward building a systematic program of research on employee creativity and innovation. I have primarily described three pillars, the three aspects of this systematic program, while focusing on telling the "back stories" of how the journey evolved and advanced. I am grateful that in the process of building this research program, I have received help from research participants, mentors, coauthors, colleagues, journal editors, and reviewers. I believe it is important to give back to the community. One way to give back to the community is via teaching. Indeed, I have developed courses to disseminate knowledge accumulated via systematic research. My students, especially executives, appreciate the systematic nature of this body of knowledge because it provides holistic insights and tools that enable them to build innovative organizations in which employees may achieve their full creative potential and customers, as well as the society at large, may benefit from these employees' creativity. Because this chapter is part of a book focusing on research, in the next two subsections I will summarize how I have given back to the research community by editing books and writing review articles, and I will share key takeaways.

Books and Review Articles

A unique way that I have been giving back to the community is to edit books, write review articles, and publish studies that point out future research directions. Though these outputs are usually not considered "top journal publications," they help fellow researchers and aspiring PhD students in terms of both saving them the time they otherwise would have to spend to gather papers and review literatures and providing them with intellectual stimulation , so as to accelerate knowledge creation and advance the creativity and innovation research field.

Even when editing books and writing review articles, I have tried to create a programmatic path. In particular, I have coedited two books (Shalley, Hitt, & Zhou, 2015; Zhou & Shalley, 2008b) in a programmatic fashion: the first book focuses on research into organizational creativity, and the second book connects research into creativity, innovation, and entrepreneurship.

My coauthor Chris Shalley and I have invested a great deal of time in systematically developing papers that review the creativity research area extensively and point out new research directions specifically. In Zhou and Shalley (2003) we provide detailed information on definitional issues, theories, research designs, and measurements. Newcomers to the creativity research field can become acquainted with the field quickly by reading this chapter. In Zhou and Shalley (2008a) we point out new directions for expanding the scope and impact of organizational creativity, calling for greater attention to multilevel and cross-level theorizing and research. This work has stimulated research into identifying multilevel or cross-level antecedents of creativity. In Zhou and Shalley (2011) we focus on the affective, cognitive, and motivational mechanisms of creativity, thereby building on and substantially extending Zhou and Shalley (2003, 2008b). By reviewing and analyzing affect, cognition, and motivation as three types of mechanisms, this work has stimulated research into the next frontier of developing a scientific understanding of creativity: revealing the different types of psychological mechanisms that explain why various antecedents exert impact on creativity. Zhou and Hoever (2014) present new typology for an understanding of the interplay between the actor and the context at different levels of analysis, thereby providing a comprehensive conceptual lens that integrates the interactional perspective of creativity with multilevel or cross-level theorizing. Liu, Jiang, Shalley, Keem, and Zhou (2016) conducted a metaanalytic review of motivational mechanisms for creativity. By focusing on three types of motivational drivers for creativity, this quantitative review deepens our understanding of various motivational drivers for creativity. Shifting creativity research to the receiving side of creativity, Zhou et al. (2019) provided a multidisciplinary review of research conducted in the arts, education, psychology, sociology, and marketing, in addition to a small number of existing studies in management. This review demonstrates the limited attention management researchers have paid to this topic and suggests ways that management research on creativity receiving might benefit from other disciplines.

Finally, my coauthors and I have also crafted review articles that have been published in the influential *Journal of Management* annual review issue: Shalley, Zhou, and Oldham (2004) focused on a review of creativity research and new research directions, while Anderson, Potocnik, and Zhou (2014) reviewed both creativity and innovation literatures and provided integration and 60 new research questions. Not only conducting a thorough review but also providing concrete ideas for new research directions demanded a great deal of time and energy. Because the review process for the *Journal of Management* annual review issues is rigorous, going through the revision process is also challenging and time-consuming. These significant investments by my coauthors and me have paid dividends—citation counts suggest that readers find these articles useful. As of January 28, 2020, Shalley et al. (2004) has garnered 2,599 citations, and Anderson et al. (2014) has been cited 1,655 times already (both citation counts per Google Scholar). It is very gratifying that both of these papers received the *Journal of Management* Best Paper Award, in 2009 and 2019, respectively.

Key Takeaways

Throughout this chapter, I have shared various principles and approaches that I have learned and used in the process of building a systematic program of research that advances our understanding of the antecedents and consequences of creativity and innovation. Here I pull them together and list the key takeaways.

- Create a systematic program of research (e.g., employee creativity and micro foundations of organizational innovation) that aim to produce a coherent body of knowledge about a type of behavior, topic, or phenomenon in a given field, instead of attempting to publish papers on different and scattered topics.
- Choosing a nascent research field (e.g., creativity and innovation) is the first and critical step toward building a systematic program of research.
- After choosing a research field, observe relevant human behaviors in their natural context and capture interesting phenomena for research in the chosen field (e.g., what do employees do after experiencing job dissatisfaction).
- Be deeply curious, observe, read, and reflect a lot before deciding on a research project and the specific research question to address (e.g., conditions under which job dissatisfaction leads to creativity).
- Read widely and diversely; let yourself wander into neighboring domains.
- Question commonly held assumptions and pursue research questions that challenge these assumptions (e.g., job dissatisfaction may be valuable for identifying problems).
- Be programmatic: identify how each project ties into the broader picture (e.g., what contextual and personal factors boost employee creativity? What contextual or personal factors undermine it? What are the psychological mechanisms? How is creativity recognized and received by others?)
- Seek advice and learn from those who have high standards and conduct responsible research.
- The ultimate goal is to advance our understanding, not to accumulate a large number of publications. Craft each paper to address an interesting question and demonstrate creative insights.

References

Amabile, T. M. (1996). *Creativity in context: Update to the social psychology of creativity.* Boulder, CO: Westview Press.

Anderson, N., Potocnik, K., & Zhou, J. (2014). Innovation and creativity in organizations: A state-of-the-science review, prospective commentary, and guiding framework. *Journal of Management, 40,* 1297–1333.

Chen, X-P., & Chen, C. C. (2004). On the intricacies of the Chinese guanxi: A process model of guanxi development. *Asia Pacific Journal of Management, 21,* 305–324.

Chen, Y., Friedman, R., Yu, E., Fang, W., & Lu, X. (2009). Supervisor-subordinate guanxi: Developing a three-dimensional model and scale. *Management and Organization Review, 5,* 375–399.

Costa, P. T., & McCrae, R. R. (1992). *Revised NEO Personality Inventory (NEO PI-R) and NEO Five-Factor Inventory (NEO-FFI) professional manual.* Odessa, FL: Psychological Assessment Resources.

Dong, Y., Liao, H., Chuang, A., Zhou, J., & Campbell-Bush, E. (2015). Fostering employee service creativity: Joint effects of customer empowering behaviors and supervisory empowering leadership. *Journal of Applied Psychology, 100,* 1364–1380.

Fiedler, K. (1988). Emotional mood, cognitive style, and behavior regulation. In K. Fiedler and J. Forgas (Eds.), *Affect, cognition and social behavior* (pp. 101–119). Toronto: J. Hogrefe.

George, J. M., & Zhou, J. (2001). When openness to experience and conscientiousness are related to creative behavior: An interactional approach. *Journal of Applied Psychology, 86,* 513–524.

George, J. M., & Zhou, J. (2002). Understanding when bad moods foster creativity and good ones don't: The role of context and clarity of feelings. *Journal of Applied Psychology, 87,* 687–697.

George, J. M., & Zhou, J. (2007). Dual tuning in a supportive context: Joint contributions of positive mood, negative mood, and supervisory behaviors to employee creativity. *Academy of Management Journal, 50,* 605–622.

Gong, Y., Zhou, J., & Chang, S. (2013). Core knowledge employee creativity and firm performance: The moderating role of riskiness orientation, firm size, and realized absorptive capacity. *Personnel Psychology, 66,* 443–482.

Gough, H. G. (1979). A creative personality scale for the Adjective Check List. *Journal of Personality and Social Psychology, 37,* 1398–1405.

Hirschman, A. O. 1970. *Exit, voice, and loyalty: Responses to decline in firms, organizations, and states.* Cambridge, MA: Harvard University Press.

Hirst, G., van Knippenberg, D., & Zhou, J. (2009). A cross-level perspective on employee creativity: Goal orientation, team learning behavior, and individual creativity. *Academy of Management Journal, 52,* 280–293.

Hirst, G., van Knippenberg, D., Zhou, J., Quintane, E., & Zhu, C. (2015). Heard it through the grapevine: Indirect networks and employee creativity. *Journal of Applied Psychology, 100,* 567–574.

Hoever, I. J., Zhou, J., & van Knippenberg, D. (2018). Different strokes for different teams: The contingent effects of positive and negative feedback on the creativity of informationally homogeneous and diverse teams. *Academy of Management Journal, 61,* 2159–2181.

Kaufmann, G. (2003). The effect of mood on creativity in the innovation process. In L. V. Shavinina (Ed.), *The international handbook on innovation* (pp. 191–203). Oxford, UK: Elsevier Science.

Law, K. S., Wong, C-S., Wang, D., & Wang. L. (2000). Effect of supervisor-subordinate guanxi on supervisory decisions in China: An empirical investigation. *The International Journal of Human Resource Management, 11,* 751–765.

Lin, B., Law, K., & Zhou, J. (2017). Why is underemployment related to creativity and OCB? A task crafting explanation of the curvilinear moderated relations. *Academy of Management Journal, 60,* 156–177.

Liu, D., Gong, Y., Zhou, J., & Huang, J. (2017). Human resource systems, employee creativity, and firm innovation: The moderating role of firm ownership. *Academy of Management Journal, 60,* 1164–1188.

Liu, D., Jiang, K., Shalley, C., Keem, S., & Zhou, J. (2016). The underlying motivational mechanisms for employee creativity: A meta-analytic examination and theoretical extension of the creativity literature. *Organizational Behavior and Human Decision Processes, 137,* 236–263.

Martin, L. L., & Stoner, P. (1996). Mood as input: What we think about how we feel determines how we think. In L. L. Martin & A. Tesser (Eds.), *Striving and feeling: Interactions among goals, affect, and self-regulation* (pp. 279–301). Mahwah, NJ: Lawrence Erlbaum.

Schwarz, N. (2002). Situated cognition and the wisdom of feelings: Cognitive tuning. In L. Feldman Barrett and P. Salovey (Eds.), *The wisdom in feelings* (pp. 144–166). New York: Guilford.

Schwarz, N., & Clore, G. L. (2003). Mood as information. *Psychological Inquiry, 14,* 296–303.

Shalley, C. E., Hitt, M. A., & Zhou, J. (Eds.). (2015). *The Oxford handbook of creativity, innovation, and entrepreneurship.* New York: Oxford University Press.

Shalley, C. E., Zhou, J., & Oldham, G. R. (2004). The effects of personal and contextual characteristics on creativity: Where should we go from here? *Journal of Management, 30,* 933–958.

Shin, S., & Zhou, J. (equal contribution). (2003). Transformational leadership, conservation, and creativity: Evidence from Korea. *Academy of Management Journal, 46,* 703–714.

Shin, S., & Zhou, J. (2007). When is educational specialization heterogeneity related to creativity in research and development teams? Transformational leadership as a moderator. *Journal of Applied Psychology, 92,* 1709–1721.

Zhang, X., & Zhou, J. (equal contribution). (2014). Empowering leadership, uncertainty avoidance, trust and employee creativity: Interaction effects and mediating processes. *Organizational Behavior and Human Decision Processes, 124,* 150–164.

Zhang, X., Zhou, J., & Kwon, H. K. (Zhang and Zhou contributed equally) (2017). Configuring challenge and hindrance contexts for introversion and creativity: Joint effects of task complexity and guanxi management. *Organizational Behavior and Human Decision Processes, 143,* 54–68.

Zhou, J. (1998a). Feedback valence, feedback style, task autonomy, and achievement orientation: Interactive effects on creative performance. *Journal of Applied Psychology, 83,* 261–276.

Zhou, J. (1998b, June 12–14). Managers' recognition of employee creative ideas: A social-cognitive approach. [Paper presentation]. The 21st Century Change Imperative: Evolving Organizations & Emerging Networks Conference, Center for the Study of Organizational Change, University of Missouri-Columbia, Columbia, MO, United States.

Zhou, J. (2003). When the presence of creative coworkers is related to creativity: Role of supervisor close monitoring, developmental feedback, and creative personality. *Journal of Applied Psychology, 88,* 413–422.

Zhou, J., & George, J. M. (2001). When job dissatisfaction leads to creativity: Encouraging the expression of voice. *Academy of Management Journal, 44,* 682–696.

Zhou, J., & George, J. M. (2003). Awakening employee creativity: The role of leader emotional intelligence. *Leadership Quarterly, 14,* 545–568.

Zhou, J., & Hoever, I. J. (equal contribution) (2014). Workplace creativity: A review and redirection. *Annual Review of Organizational Psychology and Organizational Behavior, 1,* 333–359.

Zhou, J., & Shalley, C. E. (2003). Research on employee creativity: A critical review and directions for future research. In J. J. Martocchio and G. R. Ferris (Eds.), *Research in personnel and human resource management* (Vol. 22, pp. 165–217). Oxford, UK: Elsevier Science.

Zhou, J., & Shalley, C. E. (2008a). Expanding the scope and impact of organizational creativity research. In J. Zhou and C. E. Shalley (Eds.), *Handbook of organizational creativity* (pp. 347–368). Hillsdale, NJ: Lawrence Erlbaum.

Zhou, J., & Shalley, C. E. (Eds.). (2008b). *Handbook of organizational creativity*. Hillsdale, NJ: Lawrence Erlbaum.

Zhou, J., & Shalley, C. E. (2011). Deepening our understanding of creativity in the workplace. In S. Zedeck et al. (Eds.), *APA handbook of industrial-organizational psychology* (Vol. 1, pp. 275–302). Washington, DC: American Psychological Association.

Zhou, J., Shin, S. J., Brass, D. J., Choi, J., & Zhang, Z. (2009). Social networks, personal values, and creativity: Evidence for curvilinear and interaction effects. *Journal of Applied Psychology, 94*, 1544–1552.

Zhou, J., Wang, X., Bavato, D., Tasselli, S., & Wu, J. (2019). Understanding the receiving side of creativity: A multidisciplinary review and implications for management research. *Journal of Management, 45*, 2570–2595.

Zhou, J., Wang, X., Song, J., & Wu, J. (2017). Is it new? Personal and contextual influences on perceptions of novelty and creativity. *Journal of Applied Psychology, 102*, 180–202.

Zhou, J., & Woodman, R. W. (1999, August 6–11). Managers' recognition of employee creative ideas: A social-cognitive approach. [Paper presentation]. Academy of Management Annual Meeting, Chicago, IL, United States.

Zhou, J., & Woodman, R. W. (2003). Managers' recognition of employees' creative ideas. In L. V. Shavinina (Ed.), *International handbook on innovation*. Hillsdale, NJ: Lawrence Erlbaum.

10

Fostering Enterprise

The Journey as the Destination

Rajshree Agarwal

> In times of change, learners inherit the earth, while the learned find themselves beautifully equipped to deal with a world that no longer exists.
> We are told that talent creates its own opportunities. But it sometimes seems that intense desire creates not only its own opportunities, but its own talents.
>
> **—Eric Hoffer**

My purpose in life is enabling upward mobility—in intellectual, psychological, and economic realms—so my journey is by its own right my destination. As engines of growth, innovation and enterprise have always fascinated me. In terms of content, my journey represents learning about dynamics unleashed by these twin engines, spanning all levels: individuals, teams, firms, industries, and economies. In terms of process, my journey represents a scholarly life enriched by meaningful relationships with mentors, coauthors, and students, all of whom represent strong alignment of values and high complementarity in capabilities.

I begin with acknowledging a debt I owe to Michael Gort. Michael was not just my advisor, he surrogated as father at my wedding. Steven Klepper, his coauthor on pioneering work on industry evolution (Gort & Klepper, 1982) noted in an interview how his own influential work had benefited from Michael Gort's legacy (Agarwal & Braguinsky, 2015). Their work, and the process I have emulated, represents deep dives into important and interesting real-world phenomena. The phenomena and the data inform theory development. This often requires not canned data sets but painstaking creation of databases from scratch, triangulating from multiple sources, to develop a

Rajshree Agarwal, *Fostering Enterprise* In: *A Journey toward Influential Scholarship*. Edited by: Xiao-Ping Chen and H. Kevin Steensma, Oxford University Press. © Oxford University Press 2021. DOI: 10.1093/oso/9780190070717.003.0010

comprehensive and complete "lay of the land." And underlying these theory and data development efforts is an intellectual curiosity spanning levels of analysis (and disciplines).

I have also benefited from paying this debt forward. My advisees—fine scholars making their own marks in the field—have been my teachers, as each has conducted his or her own empirical deep dive, and created new theoretical insights to inform my knowledge of evolutionary dynamics.

As an evolutionary scholar, I cannot help but use the same lens in this reflection of my intellectual journey. I discuss its content (summarized in table 10.1) and process (summarized in table 10.2) across four stages, spanning the period from my dissertation research to the present day.[1]

Stage 1 represents my study of industrial organization in an economics department, first at the State University of New York (SUNY) at Buffalo (my alma mater) and then at the University of Central Florida (UCF), where I started my career. Stage 2 corresponds to my transition to strategic management and my move to the University of Illinois. Stage 3 represents a gradual incorporation of strategic entrepreneurship, and yet another move—this time to the University of Maryland. Stage 4, my current stage, is reflected in my decision to become the founding director of the Ed Snider Center for Enterprise and Markets at Maryland—an interdisciplinary center that integrates research, teaching, and engagement in the study and dissemination of the causes and consequences of enterprising people and organizations creating value through trade.

Stage 1: Industrial Economics and the Study of Industry Evolution

> The competition from the new commodity, the new technology, the new source of supply, the new type of organization . . . [is] competition which strikes not at the margins of the profits and the outputs of the existing firms but at their foundations and their very lives. This kind of competition . . . in the long run expands output and brings down prices.
>
> — Joseph Schumpeter (1942: 84)

---

[1] As is true in industry evolution studies too (Gort & Klepper, 1982; Christensen, 1997), these stages are not sharp discontinuities in time; rather there are "in-between" years of coexistence of different foci and "incubation" years in the preceding stage when new research interests germinate.

Table 10.1. The journey as the destination: Content

	Stage 1: Industrial organization (1992–2002)	Stage 2: Strategic management (1999–2012)	Stage 3: Strategic entrepreneurship (2007–2017)	Stage 4: Enterprise and markets (2014–present)
Dominant lens	Structure-conduct-performance; evolutionary economics	Evolutionary theory of the firm	Lifecycle theories of human capital; knowledge contexts of entrepreneurship	Evolutionary views of individuals, firms, industries, and markets; psychological theories of motivation
Intellectual foundations	Caves & Porter (1977); Gort & Klepper (1982)	Penrose (1959); Nelson & Winter (1982); Teece (1986)	Mincer (1958); Schultz (1961); Becker (1962, 1972)	Chase & Simon (1973); Maslow (1954); Locke (1968); Rosenberg (1982); North (1990)
Unit(s) of analysis	Industry; firm	Firm	Individual; firm	Individual; firm; industry
Methodological toolkit	Large-n trend and survival analysis across multiple industries	Large-n trend and survival analysis in single industry contexts	Panel-data analysis of linked employee-employer data sets	Qualitative methods; historical methods; panel-data analysis of individual-firm "census" within industries
Key drivers	Life-cycle stages; firm characteristics (size; age; prior experience)	Life-cycle stages; firm characteristics and capabilities (tech; market; integrative)	Life-cycle stages; firm characteristics and capabilities; human capital (education; experience)	Experimentation; knowledge-sharing; human enterprise (human capital, motivations and preferences)
Key outcomes of interest	Entry, exit, and survival	Entrepreneurial entry; survival, renewal, and growth	Firm survival and growth, individual mobility, entrepreneurship, and earnings	Innovation (industry) emergence and diffusion; firm entry, survival, and growth; individual mobility, entrepreneurship, and earnings
Examples of research articles	Agarwal (1994, 1997, 1998); Agarwal & Gort (1996, 2002); Agarwal & Audretsch (2001); Agarwal & Bayus (2002)	Agarwal, Sarkar, & Echambadi (2002); Agarwal, Echambadi, Franco, & Sarkar (2004); Agarwal, Audretsch, & Sarkar (2007, 2010); Ganco & Agarwal (2009); Agarwal & Helfat (2009); Agarwal, Croson, & Mahoney (2010); Chen, Williams, & Agarwal (2012); Qian, Agarwal, & Hoetker (2012)	Campbell, Ganco, Franco, & Agarwal (2012); Carnahan, Agarwal, & Campbell (2012); Agarwal & Ohyama (2013); Agarwal & Braguinsky (2014); Agarwal & Shah (2014); Ganco, Ziedonis, & Agarwal (2015); Agarwal, Campbell, Franco, & Ganco (2016); Shapiro, Hom, Shen, & Agarwal (2016)	Mindruta, Moen, & Agarwal (2016); Moen & Agarwal (2017); Greenwood, Agarwal, Agarwal, & Gopal (2017, 2019); Byun, Frake, & Agarwal (2018); Shah, Agarwal, & Echambadi (2019); Agarwal, Braguinsky, & Ohyama (2019); Shah, Agarwal, & Sonka (2019); Wormald, Agarwal, Braguinsky, & Shah (2021a, 2021b); Kim, Agarwal, & Goldfarb (2021); Agarwal, Ganco, & Raffiee (2021)

Table 10.2. The journey as the destination: Process

	Stage 1: Industrial organization (1992–2002)	Stage 2: Strategic management (1999–2012)	Stage 3: Strategic entrepreneurship (2007–2017)	Stage 4: Enterprise and markets (2014–present)
Underlying premise	Industry life-cycle stage (structure) determines firm strategy (conduct) determines industry/firm dynamics (performance)	Industries don't make decisions, firms do	Industries and firms don't make decisions, individuals do	Industries and firms don't make decisions, individuals do, taking into account their operational context, and their abilities and aspirations
Aspirations/"unmet need"	Deep dives into dynamics of industrial change	Deep dives into (discretionary) differences in capabilities among firms to unlock the "black box" of firms	Deep dives into (discretionary) differences in capabilities among individuals to unlock the "black box" of strategic human capital markets	Deep dives into motivations and "embracing" of selection to examine interdependencies between individual abilities and aspirations, and interactions between enterprise and markets
Key influencers	Michael Gort	Raj Echambadi; MB Sarkar	Ben Campbell; Sonali Shah	Ed Snider; Steve Sonka
(New) complementors	David Audretsch; Barry Bayus	Janet Bercovitz; Rachel Croson; April Franco; Connie Helfat; Glenn Hoetker; Joe Mahoney; Charlie Williams; Rosemarie Ziedonis	Serguey Braguinsky; Debra Shapiro	Ritu Agarwal; Gilad Chen; Miriam Erez; Brent Goldfarb; Anand Gopal; Ella Miron-Spektor; Evan Starr
Student-teachers	Pao-Lien Chen; Denisa Mindruta; Martin Ganco; Lihong Qian; Kumar Sarangee	Seth Carnahan; Mahka Moeen; Atsushi Ohyama; Shweta Gaonkar		Heejung Byun; Joonkyu Choi; Justin Frake; Brad Greenwood; Seojin Kim; Moran Lazar; Najoung Lim; Dan Olson; Audra Wormald
Key learnings	Data-building investments in novel, rich data sets have high long-term payoffs.	Identify common interests and ensure goal alignment among colleagues who have complementary capabilities, and are willing to codevelop PhD students who match effort for effort.	Craft project teams through selection and training of PhD students for high resource complementarity, strong interpersonal attraction, and alignment of goals.	Steer project teams toward developing "historical" data sets and methods, where qualitative and quantitative analysis together identify deeper causal factors at play; be willing to challenge inferences made in earlier studies.

Mainstream economics PhD programs during the early 1990s largely utilized neoclassical equilibrium theory, characterized by steady state, marginal analysis. Microeconomics and industrial organization (IO) course texts (Carlton & Perloff, 1990; Varian, 1992) utilized the linear "structure-conduct-performance" (SCP) paradigm to distinguish market structures (e.g., perfect competition, monopoly), which then determined firm conduct (strategy), for performance implications in terms of both firm profitability and social welfare(Bain, 1951; Schamalensee, 1989). This is in spite of Schumpeter's research in the early twentieth century, as exemplified by the epigraph to this section. Moreover, game theory was the dominant lens—the study of innovation largely constituted an examination of "patent races" and win-lose portrayals of firm dynamics; for example, incumbents versus startups, large versus small firms (e.g., Reinganum, 1981). The study of entrepreneurship was largely absent, causing Baumol (1968: 68) to famously note: "the theoretical firm is entrepreneurless—the Prince of Denmark has been expunged from the discussion of Hamlet."[2]

Within this context, Michael Gort stood out in sharp refrain, and his IO course informed my choice of field of specialization of IO (studying innovation) over labor economics (studying human capital). He covered SCP theory for sure, but he also introduced theories of industrial dynamics. Empirically, he embraced *abduction*—the best explanation among alternatives based on data and facts—decades before mainstream econometricians highlighted its value (Heckman & Singer, 2017). And he cared deeply about practice—he routinely provided insights and advice to firms on regulation and antitrust issues. Processwise, Michael was effective and efficient. The images indelible in my mind are his purposeful strides down the hallway, clear and concise phone conversations on administrative issues, and long deliberations on intellectually thorny issues. He was very choosy among whom he picked as an advisee. The department administrator gave me sound advice as I prepared to approach him. "Michael matches effort for effort," she said; "if he sees you working hard, he will work hard with you. If you slack off, he will match that too."

Gort & Klepper (1982) documented "stylized facts" in industry evolution, tracking net firm entry rates, patents, major/minor innovations, and industry output and price from industry inception (Stage 1) through maturity (Stage 5). They abducted across five competing theoretical explanations

---

[2] Schumpeter (1945: 86) made a similar analogy when referring to the failure of economics failure to study the process of creative destruction: "a theoretical construction which neglects this essential element . . . even if correct in logic as well as fact, it is like Hamlet without the Danish Prince."

to highlight a new theoretical explanation—shifts from external to internal industry knowledge repositories—over theories that represented variations among the dominant neoclassical theories of the day. For my dissertation, I built off the Gort & Klepper (1982) industry-level analysis to examine underlying firm-level dynamics for both firm- and industry-level implications. This required recreating unbalanced panel data from scratch for 33 industries from 1883 to 1991 to identify which firm entered when, its salient characteristics (firm size, age, prior experience), and its performance outcomes in the focal industry in terms of survival and exit (Agarwal, 1994). It also required triangulation across multiple data sources (e.g., the Thomas Register, the Census of Manufactures, the Bureau of Labor Statistics, US patent data) for additional firm- and industry-level characteristics. Though these data collection efforts in a predigitized era of microfilms and hard copies took three years (and extended my graduation date by at least one year), they enabled 12 scholarly publications over the next decade.

A key process takeaway for me was the importance of such data-building investments; while several publications stemmed from the original intent and design, others arose from unanticipated insights due to an immersion in the context and follow-on collaboration opportunities with other scholars. For example, per intention, some studies hypothesized and tested the effect of industry characteristics (life-cycle stages, technological intensity, intermediate v. final goods sector) and firm characteristics (size, age, startup v. established firm) on firm entry and survival (Agarwal, 1996, 1997; Agarwal & Audretsch, 1999, 2001; Agarwal & Gort, 1996, 2002). Other studies, which also shaped my research focus and interest in *industry emergence* rather than later stages (e.g., shake-outs), surfaced from the data construction efforts. For instance, I realized an important fact when compiling data and conducting the analysis: the time to firm takeoff (end of stage 1), that is, the period of entrepreneurial "first-mover" entry, seemed to be systematically shrinking over chronological time. As a stark example, in the late nineteenth century, the Edison Phonograph Company enjoyed 33 years of monopoly status before competitive entry into the industry, compared to a mere three years in CD players, introduced a century later. Exploring the reasons behind this interesting observation, in Agarwal and Gort (2001), Michael and I ruled out "obvious" explanations such as industry capital intensity and demand characteristics and concluded that knowledge diffusion through individual mobility (which had risen sharply over time) was a more likely explanation.

The data also enabled fruitful collaborations with Barry Bayus, a marketing scholar. Within marketing, sales diffusion and pioneering firm (dis)-advantage were of enduring interest. In Agarwal & Bayus (2002), we built off my dissertation data to generate insights through the integration of the two disciplinary lenses about why firm take-off was a *necessary* precondition to sales take-off in an industry. [3] In highlighting the important role of demand-shifts through technological, infrastructural, and legitimacy enhancement investments enabled by firm take-off, we called into question the dominant explanation in marketing—we showed that the model of price declines inducing sales increases by firms with market power was simply not consistent with the empirical analysis.

These studies laid the foundation for the next stage in my research career through two critical realizations. One, even though I was an industrial organization scholar, my interests seemed to lie not in industries per se but in the firms who were the fountainhead of these industry dynamics. Put simply, I realized at this juncture: industries don't make decisions, firms do (as embodied in their strategic actions). Two, coupled with the aforementioned greater awareness of parallel work on first mover advantage in management (Lieberman & Montgomery, 1988) and in marketing (Kerin, Varadarajan, & Peterson, 1992; Robinson, Kalyanaram, & Urban, 1994) was the realization of how much I was enjoying hallway conversations with my colleagues in these areas. (The economics department was in the business school at UCF). Raj Echambadi and MB Sarkar, two fellow assistant professors, also became dear friends in the process. Given our common research interests, Raj, MB, and I had already embarked on two research projects based on my dissertation data (Agarwal, Sarkar, & Echambadi, 2002; Sarkar, Echambadi, Agarwal, & Sen, 2006). Raj quoted a phrase that has since stuck with me: "Ideas don't know what discipline they are in." Agarwal, Sarkar, and Echambadi (2002) integrated disparate research streams in economics, management, and sociology to investigate the effects of various organizational and environmental variables and firm survival. And MB encouraged me to write articles aimed at management journals and, later, to apply for positions in strategic management, which led to my move to the University of Illinois.

[3] As an interesting side note, Barry—already an established scholar and full professor at the time—"cold-called" me for access to my dissertation data. Given common research interests (and a high endorsement of Barry by Raj Echambadi, then an assistant professor at UCF's marketing department), I proposed we work together. Our collaboration was largely through phone, email, and regular mail—the first time Barry and I met physically was six years after the original email and a year after our first publication.

Stage 2: Strategic Management and Study of Industry and Firm Evolution

> Every piece of business strategy acquires its true significance only against the background of that process and within the situation created by it. It must be seen in its role in the perennial gale of creative destruction; it cannot be understood irrespective of it or, in fact, on the hypothesis that there is a perennial lull.
>
> —Joseph Schumpeter (1942: 83–84)

Given my interest in firms as *endogenous drivers of industry evolution*, the next stage of my research evolution led me to become a "diversifying entrant" into strategic management. Theoretically, my intellectual foundations expanded to firm growth (Penrose, 1959), firm evolution (Nelson & Winter, 1982), and profiting from innovation (Teece, 1986) frameworks.[4] Empirically, while I had paid some attention in Stage 1 to firm heterogeneity in examining firm and industry panel data, aggregating across industries necessarily restricted the studies to examining firm characteristics such as firm size, age, or dummies for prior experience. This is because industry-specific differences precluded the creation of richer capability or strategy measures. Accordingly, I needed to complement the multiindustry data sets with single industry deep dives to gain a better understanding of how "every piece of business strategy," as Schumpeter noted, was the cause or consequence of the process of creative destruction. These industry data sets (e.g., bioethanol, disk drives, personal computing, semiconductors, wireless telecommunications) also required compilation efforts through triangulation across multiple sources.

Processwise, a key takeaway was the shift away from working largely with senior scholars and learning to craft research projects with peers and PhD students. Glenn Hoetker and Charlie Williams were fellow assistant professors at Illinois with shared interests.[5] I will remain grateful to the collaborative

---

[4] Having received my PhD in a mainstream economics department in arts and sciences (and given estrangement between Michael Gort and Steven Klepper), I had been unaware until 2003 of the creation of the Consortium for Competitiveness and Cooperation (CCC) movement in the same year as my graduation (1994). The CCC was pioneered by a handful of evolutionary economists in business schools who collaboratively invested in talent development by bringing together their current PhD students in an annual conference.

[5] While I had received tenure and promotion at UCF in the economics department, I gave these up to start a fresh clock in business administration at the University of Illinois in 2001. Glenn joined at the same time, and Charlie a year later. I did not have to wait the entire six years though—mobility options enabled me to get tenure and promotion by 2003 and to endowed professor by 2007.

culture at Illinois, where senior faculty invested in the success of the junior faculty, and all were deeply committed to PhD students' development. When coupled with my Stage 1 experiences, this established a "routine" I have replicated multiple times: rather than do-it-alone, identify (and actively search for) scholars with common interests, aligned goals and complementary capabilities, and willingness to codevelop/learn from PhD students who match effort for effort. Three implications of this routine are of note. One, I made the conscious choice to shift focus to journal outlets in management alone, as this was my new home and consistent with goal alignment of my current coauthors. Two, in all equal coauthored studies,[6] the order of authorship was not alphabetical but was predicated on the career needs of junior team members. While both implications meant I was often not listed as first author, they were important in ensuring goodwill and win-wins and instrumental in reducing potential strife. Three, in order to fund the data collection efforts and support PhD students and fellow coauthors, I invested in writing grant proposals. I also learned how to reduce the "overhead" of such proposals by ensuring they were based on ideas I was planning on pursuing regardless of whether they were funded, and by using the proposal writing itself as a disciplining mechanism and an interim deadline for research projects to stay on track.[7]

Mapping firm and industry evolution upon each other led to several related research themes that resulted in multiple dissertations and coauthored studies. First, and building on the aforementioned industry evolution research, it allowed the distinction between entrepreneurial startups and diversifying firms among entrants to an industry and, similarly, between diversifying entrants and industry incumbents among established firms. Such distinctions, when examined within the richness of contextual data of single-industry data sets studies, enabled my coauthors and me to shed light on causes and consequences of firm entry into related industries. For example, Bayus & Agarwal (2007) documented that diversifying entrants in the personal computer industry had a survival advantage over entrepreneurial startups among early entrants, but the reverse was true among later entrants. Our explanation rested on variations in

---

[6] It is even difficult to determine "equal" contribution. As an example, I may have contributed say 90% of the hourly time investments in all coauthored studies with Michael. However, the *quality* and *impact* of his, say, 10% time investment made the value creation truly equal. And this does not even take into account the valuable learning spillovers into subsequent projects I embarked upon without him. Moreover, research projects represent "multiplicative" rather than "additive" production functions: complementarities in teams truly come to life when division of labor and comparative advantage are compounded with a "yes-and" problem-solving mindset in brainstorming sessions.

[7] I am enormously grateful for the early and generous support by the Kauffman Foundation—creating the multiproject, multiauthor proposal for data and PhD support helped cement this routine. Notable in this process are Paul Magelli—a champion of my research to Kauffman, and Bob Strom, the research director at Kauffman who also became a very dear friend over subsequent years.

firms' product technology strategies, given interaction effects with prior experience and entry timing. Intense conversations during walks around the Illinois campus with Charlie or Glenn resulted in coadvising relationships. Charlie and I served as dissertation co-chairs to Pao-Lien Chen, who invested in data development of the wireless telecommunications industry and theoretically integrated firm and industry evolution lenses. This resulted in Chen, Williams, & Agarwal (2012), where we linked diversifying firm advantage among early entrants to their ability to reconfigure capabilities as they transitioned into industry incumbency and confronted growth impediments arising from larger size, longer tenure in industry, and technological discontinuities. Lihong Qian developed the bioethanol industry data and integrated the transactions cost and capability lens under joint supervision with Glenn to examine vertical integration decisions of diversifying entrants and startups over industry lifecycle stages (Qian, Agarwal, & Hoetker, 2012). Separately, in Agarwal & Helfat (2009), Connie Helfat and I examined longevity of firms due to strategic renewal rather than relying on legacy-based advantages through a deep dive into a single firm, such as IBM, that had survived more than 100 years. In addition, in Franco, Sarkar, Echambadi, & Agarwal (2009), we studied firms' ability to stay abreast of new technologies and markets across five discontinuities within the disk-drive industry.

Second, several projects examined the strategic decisions of firms in and of themselves. Rather than a focus on "competitive advantage" per se, these parsed out value creation and capture through cooperative and competitive dynamics. Here, Glenn Hoetker and I encouraged our coadvisee Denisa Mindruta to explore her interests in the matching model theory (Becker, 1973) and methodology (Fox, 2007), as she examined value creation in firm-university scientist relationships (Mindruta, 2009). I learned a lot from Denisa in the process, and these learnings spilled over into later projects (Agarwal & Ohyama, 2013; Mindruta, Moeen, & Agarwal, 2016). Separately, hallway conversations with Joe Mahoney led to our use of a social dilemma game-theoretic lens and economic experiments to examine the role of incentive alignment and communication for ensuring that realized value creation in alliances lived up to the envisaged potential. In hindsight, it is remarkable how Agarwal, Croson, & Mahoney (2010) embodied the insights it generated. Amid efforts to educate myself on experimental research design, I reached out to an old acquaintance, Rachel Croson, who had built deep expertise and recognition in the field.[8] Realizing her ability to add significant value

---

[8] Serendipity played a huge role in the creation of this "network tie." Back in 1997, Rachel and I were randomly assigned as roommates when attending a workshop organized by the American Economic

(higher quality, lower time cost), I invited her to be a coauthor, and in turn, Rachel's goal-alignment stemmed from her interests in strategic management applications of experimental theory and methods. We were also very attentive to creating effective coordination and communication routines. These served us well in "future alliances" where we discussed applications of experimental methodology in strategy research (Croson, Anand, & Agarwal, 2007) and the role of formal and informal interaction in postacquisition integration (Agarwal, Anand, Bercovitz, & Croson, 2012).

Third, and deeply instrumental in defining the next stage of my research evolution, several research projects examined mechanisms of knowledge diffusion that shaped firm and industry evolution. While assisting in research for Bayus & Agarwal (2007), Martin Ganco identified an idea that drew upon his knowledge and interest in complexity theory. Ganco & Agarwal (2009) used simulations to show how later entrants draw upon industry-specific knowledge stocks built by earlier entrants, enabling entrepreneurial startups with strong learning mechanisms in particular to outperform diversifying entrants. Hoetker & Agarwal (2007) traced the diffusion pathways of knowledge created by innovative firms who become defunct, showing how and why access to "private" knowledge is a strong complement to public domain knowledge. Harking back to the insights from Agarwal & Gort (2001), a critical diffusion mechanism is employee mobility and entrepreneurship. Noteworthy here is Agarwal, Echambadi, Franco, and Sarkar (2004), which won the *Academy of Management Journal* Best Paper Award for the year. April Franco had gained access to the disk-drive industry data to examine the phenomena of spinouts—when employees of existing organizations engage in new venture creation in the same industry. Based on a conversation with me at an economics conference, she agreed to team up with Raj, MB, and me. We studied the role of existing organizations as key knowledge contexts for individuals to gain relevant technological and market pioneering capabilities; such knowledge "inheritance" enables them to found new ventures so as to attain performance advantages relative to other entrants in the industry. When I was presenting this study at University of Michigan, Rosemarie Ziedonis challenged an implicit assumption of this study—the view of incumbents as passive repositories of knowledge. Our resulting brainstorms led to joint work examining how firms can and do develop reputations for enforcing intellectual property so as to deter knowledge diffusion through employee mobility

---

Association's Committee for Status of Women in the Economics Profession. Our interactions then were social rather than intellectual, given widely different research interests.

(Agarwal, Ganco, and Ziedonis, 2009). Here, Martin started off as a research assistant compiling data on semiconductors and subsequently earned equal coauthor status due to his intellectual engagement. Finally, in Agarwal, Audretsch, & Sarkar (2007, 2010), we integrated the insights from employee entrepreneurship with insights from economic models of endogenous growth theory to link entrepreneurial action by the cocreators of knowledge to growth of industries and economies.

These deep dives into firm capabilities and strategies within single industry contexts created an almost seamless transition into the next stage through three critical realizations. One, although all the aforementioned studies were at the firm level of analysis, the drivers were often at the individual level. Put simply, the realization at this juncture was: industries and firms don't make decisions, individuals do. However, evolutionary studies both in economics and in strategy were silent about individuals. And even in my studies of employee entrepreneurship, I had abstracted away from the founders themselves. Two, Ben Campbell and I bonded during his recruiting visit at Illinois, and we realized the high potential of utilizing linked employee-employer data sets for questions core to strategy and entrepreneurship.[9] Three, Denisa's dissertation on university scientist–firm relationships, coupled with conversations with Sonali Shah (who was in the organizational behavior group at Illinois) where we compared insights on user and employee entrepreneurship, led to the realization of the need to examine how differences in knowledge contexts may shape individual capabilities and strategies for innovation and entrepreneurship. These realizations were also very instrumental in my career move to University of Maryland, where the Management and Organizations Department represented deep theoretical and empirical expertise across the different levels of analysis I was now interested in: industries, firms, teams, and individuals.

Stage 3: Strategic Entrepreneurship and Study of Industry, Firm, and Individual Evolution

The function of entrepreneurs is to reform or revolutionize the pattern of production.... To undertake such new things is difficult ... first, because they lie outside of the routine tasks which everyone understands

---

[9] Ben had a labor economics PhD and had served as a research assistant on the assimilation of the US Census Linked Employer Household Dynamics data set. One of his dissertation chapters examined the returns to entrepreneurship for individuals who chose to return to paid employment (Campbell, 2013).

and secondly, because the environment resists in many ways. . . . To
act with confidence beyond the range of familiar beacons and to overcome that resistance requires aptitudes . . . that define the entrepreneurial type as well as the entrepreneurial function.

—**Joseph Schumpeter (1942: 132)**

The budding interest in individuals as fountainheads of innovation
and enterprise rekindled my interest in (strategic) human capital. The
premise here was that innovation patterns displayed by industry dynamics are best understood through underlying individual-firm and
individual-level dynamics. This required expanding my intellectual
foundations to classic work in labor economics (Becker, 1962; Mincer,
1958; Schultz, 1961) and integrating them into our theories of strategic
management and entrepreneurship. Empirically, a focus on strategic entrepreneurship required data on individual career histories to map mobility and new venture creation. In addition to building such databases
(e.g., disk-drive data used to develop qualitative data through founder
interviews; triangulation across sources for semiconductors), such data
could also be accessed through secondary sources. Databases such as
the Linked Employer Household Dynamics database of the US Census
(LEHD) and Scientists and Engineers Statistical Data System of the
National Science Foundation (SESTAT) provided rich panel information
to do so, but required substantial investments in securing access and understanding their use.

Processwise, a key takeaway was learning how to build effective project
teams. The scope and size of the data compilation and analysis efforts required teams of industrious coauthors, each embodying the entrepreneurial
type Schumpeter described. Building on those established in preceding
stages, the routines here involved development of effective strategies for selection and training of doctoral students, who in turn trained other students
as they acquired seniority. Within the "LEHD team," for instance, Ben first
trained Martin, and together they trained Seth Carnahan; the three then
formed the bas for later cohorts that included Dan Olson, Justin Frake, and
Florence Honore (Martin's first doctoral student). Important elements of the
routine were also what Sonali, Raj, and I later observed in disk-drive team
formation (Shah, Agarwal, & Echambadi, 2019): the crafting of teams with
high "resource complementarity" among individuals who also experienced
strong "interpersonal attraction" and who ensured alignment of goals. While
a trial and error process, a collaborative atmosphere with a focus on developmental and candid feedback was a critical ingredient of success. The feedback

cut both ways, and I gratefully remember all the instances when my students courageously challenged my thoughts and actions.

In this stage, the examination of individual career decisions within strategic human capital markets occurred in interrelated themes. First, and incorporating an industry evolution lens, Sonali and I examined knowledge contexts that shaped new venture creation by individuals. In Agarwal & Shah (2014), we integrated across literature streams developed in silos on academic, employee, and user entrepreneurship. Our conceptual model depicts academics and users as sources of "outside" information in early industry stages—Gort & Klepper (1982) had noted the importance of outside information but not really identified where entrepreneurial entrants came from. As industries grow and mature, employees with "inside information" represent an increasing fraction of new ventures. We additionally linked the knowledge context of founders to their ability to engage in product/process innovation and their competitive/collaborative strategies with established firms, with novel implications for both firm and industry evolution.

A second theme consisted of a deep dive into high-performing individuals. As part of the "LEHD team" of scholars, Campbell, Ganco, Franco, & Agarwal (2012) theorized and provided evidence that high-performing individuals were much more likely to stay at established firms, but if they left, they were more likely to spinout than move to other firms and, in so doing create stronger competitive pressures for their "parent" firm. Carnahan, Agarwal, & Campbell (2012) examined the effect of firms' compensation structures on employee mobility and entrepreneurship—high-performing individuals gravitated toward pay-for-performance compensation and, somewhat surprisingly, were willing to bear declines in compensation to create spinouts. Agarwal, Campbell, Franco, & Ganco (2016) linked superior spinout performance to high-performing individuals' ability to create larger and more experienced teams of cofounders. Separately, Ganco, Ziedonis, & Agarwal (2015) developed and tested hypotheses, using hand-collected semiconductor data, that intellectual protection strategies of established firms deterred employee mobility on average but did not prevent departures by star inventors.

A third theme focused on career life-cycles, and a budding recognition of preferences and nonmonetary aspirations in this research paved the way for the next stage in my own research career. Atsushi Ohyama, Michael's last student before he passed away, had chosen to visit with me at Illinois as my postdoctoral student (completing the circle, if you will). In Agarwal & Ohyama (2013), we integrated insights from human capital life-cycle models with matching theory to examine sorting patterns of scientists into different careers (academia or industry, basic or applied research). The SESTAT panel data set is unusual, inasmuch as it provides rich quantitative information not only on human capital but also on monetary and nonmonetary preferences, so it enabled the creation of rich insights into reasons for initial career choices and resultant evolution of both human capital and earnings of individuals. Separately, Shapiro, Hom, Shen, & Agarwal (2016) utilized a micro organizational behavior lens to develop a relational perspective for explaining the likelihood of subordinates leaving after leader departure, taking into account attachments of the focal employee to the departing leader, team, and organization.

The important realization at this juncture can be simply stated as follows: Industries and firms don't make decisions, individuals do—taking into account their operational context and their abilities and aspirations. Two implications arose from this realization. One, operational contexts included not only the knowledge context, but participation in markets for commercialization, resources (including human capital and ideas), and corporate control. Moreover, my work thus far had focused on the United States as the country context of my empirical studies, and a critical assumption for interaction among entrepreneurial individuals and firms was the foundation of well-functioning institutions enabling trade. Around this time, Steven Sonka—my mentor harking back to when I was at Illinois—invited me to study a Rockefeller Foundation "Yieldwise" initiative to address post-harvest loss—an issue of major significance in many developing countries. The focus was not aid per se but aid directed specifically at market creation to enable trade and develop robust supply chains for industry growth well after aid efforts had run their course. Two, examining interdependencies between individual ability and aspiration required a move away from studying "treatment" effects alone in research designs that "controlled" for selection and toward embracing the study of selection (and sorting) in and of itself as a critical cause and consequence of individual- and firm-level strategy. In addition, quantitative analysis of secondary and archival data enabled a study of capabilities but not necessarily motivations, particularly those related to nonpecuniary reasons. Here, my own aspiration for integrating research, teaching, and engagement was deeply enabled by Ed Snider, a Maryland alumn and the founder of the Philadelphia Flyers. Ed embodied all the entrepreneurial qualities—high ability and aspiration, and strong values—that I not only studied but drew inspiration from personally. Our meeting (of mind, heart, and soul) resulted in his generous gift to create the Ed Snider Center for Enterprise and Markets, of which I became the founding director.

Stage 4: Enterprise and Markets and the Study of Entrepreneurial Systems and Processes

> There is the joy of creating, of getting things done, or simply of exercising one's energy and ingenuity. [The entrepreneurial] type seeks out difficulties, changes in order to change, delights in ventures.
>
> —Joseph Schumpeter (1934: 93–94)

> [Creative destruction is a] process of industrial mutation . . . that incessantly revolutionizes the economic structure from within, incessantly destroying the old one, incessantly creating a new one. This process of Creative Destruction is the essential fact about capitalism.
>
> —Joseph Schumpeter (1942: 83)

A "systems view" requires concurrent attention to enterprising individuals' abilities and aspirations and to the organizations, markets, and institutions within which they engage in exchange. My intellectual foundations accordingly expanded in both directions. I now also draw upon social/cognitive psychology and organizational behavior for a better understanding of psychological motives as Schumpeter expressed them in the epigraph to this section (Chase & Simon, 1973; Coleman, 1986; Locke, 1968; Maslow, 1954). And to truly understand how economic structures revolutionize from within (Schumpeter, 1942), I draw upon institutional economics and economic history (North, 1990; Rosenberg, 1982). Empirically, a focus on enterprise and markets requires rich micro level data on entrepreneurial individuals and/or firms, and data that capture relevant institutional and market-level factors. These databases simply don't exist, so they have to be compiled through triangulation across primary and secondary sources.

In terms of process, a key learning centered around involvement in project teams (and steering of PhD students) toward developing "historical" data sets and methods, where qualitative and quantitative analysis together identify deeper causal factors at play. A second takeaway was embracing the fact that such deep dives may often challenge inferences made in my own earlier studies. Both have become increasingly important in how I now conduct research—while I had all along relied on panel data sets to examine evolutionary phenomena, the depth and breadth of many of the research questions I am now interested in precludes use of just one type of analysis for credible answers. Accordingly, the "arsenal" of methodological tools have to include randomized control experiments or credibly exogenous shocks to infer causality, qualitative and inductive theorizing to generate novel explanations, and a meld of quantitative and qualitative analysis to examine endogeneity and selection factors at play in dynamic phenomena of interest. Concurrently, this has meant eschewing the "straitjacket" of hypothesis-deductive frameworks that we often impose upon the way we conduct or present research, in favor of "question-based" research and truly embracing abduction. Such triangulation may also span multiple studies written at different points in time, hence the need to revisit inferences made from macro levels of analysis using a more micro lens.

Several themes emerge as pieces of a puzzle. The first relates to my conceptualization of human enterprise. As I write in Agarwal (2019), while human capital theory centers on monetary returns to past investments in capability *stocks* (typically acquired through education and experience), human enterprise encompasses monetary and nonmonetary drivers of current and future investments (*flows*) of activity that may potentially result in human capital and/or capitalize on it. Thus, while human capital focuses on *what* capabilities are embodied in an individual and their potential economic benefits, human enterprise focuses on *why* individuals pursue different activities and *how* this both shapes and benefits from human capabilities. This conceptualization draws upon two recent articles. In Shah, Agarwal, & Echambadi (2019), we revisited inferences made in Agarwal et al. (2004) and other spinout studies that entrepreneurial ideas or innovation projects form the basis of employee teams venturing out, either because they optimize economic returns or because they capitalize on knowledge spillovers (see review in Kaul, Ganco, & Raffiee, 2018). Thanks to Sonali's superb qualitative methodology skills, interviews with disk-drive founders uncovered a different process. Our inductive study revealed that ringleaders who decided to venture out are drawn by the desire to create in the presence of fertile opportunities and are pushed by either interpersonal/ethical frictions with managers, strategic disagreements, or bureaucratic hurdles. Moreover, the more successful spinouts represented ringleaders purposefully engaging in an endogenous team-building process for "workplace instrumentality"—creating workplaces through deliberate selection of cofounders who have complementary functional knowledge but are similar in their superior problem-solving abilities, best-in-class talent, and common workplace values. Thus, this research highlighted for me the importance of mechanisms embodied in two pithy quotes from Ed Snider: "money is the reward, not the reason," and "hire good people and let them do their job." Separately, an integrative review of economics, psychology, and sociology disciplinary perspectives on entrepreneurial team formation revealed the process and performance benefits that accrue when founders simultaneously employ "interpersonal similarity-attraction" and "resource seeking" strategies within small world networks to ensure smooth coordination routines within functionally diverse teams (Lazar, Miron-Spektor, Agarwal, Erez, Goldfarb, and Chen; 2020).

The second theme highlights the role of individuals and teams as micro foundations of firm, industry, and economic evolution. As firms evolve, so do their top management teams (TMT). Williams, Chen, & Agarwal (2017) examined how firm strategic renewal in the wireless telecommunications industry is shaped by additions to TMTs that may vary in their firm-specific or industry-specific knowledge, as well as prior experience as TMT members. We hypothesized and showed that "outside rookies"—TMT additions new to both TMT level and to the firm—are associated with higher firm growth than other types of executives, and seasoned outsiders—those with prior TMT experience outside the focal industry—contributed to growth only when the existing TMT had long tenure and thus higher relational capital among themselves. Here, our quantitative analysis used the best available methods to establish credibility in the results, including a battery of tests in the spirit of abduction to rule out plausible alternative explanations and concerns of reverse causality. In a separate study—spearheaded by two doctoral advisees, Heejung Byun and Justin Frake,[10] we delved deeper into the role of generalized versus specialized knowledge in affecting returns to relational capital (Byun, Frake, & Agarwal, 2018) acquired by lobbyists through prior experience working with congresspeople. Heejung had compiled a comprehensive data set on the lobbying industry, and the study used an exogenous shock to lobbyists' relational capital to make causal inferences. Notable also is the process through which Justin and I integrated insights from economics and sociology to develop the conceptual framework, earning the study the "Best Interdisciplinary Paper Award" study in 2016 from the Strategic Human Capital Interest Group at the Strategic Management Society. Similarly, an integration between cognitive psychology and economics framing enabled insights regarding diffusion of innovation and organizational practices in medical stenting due to different types of expertise, and based on differences in organizational mission and incentives (Greenwood, Agarwal, Agarwal, & Gopal, 2017, 2019). In Agarwal, Braguinsky, & Ohyama (2020), we tied together multiple levels of analysis by examining stable shared TMT leadership at play in the Japanese cotton spinning industry, for the growth of firms, the international success of

[10] While many of my coauthors and doctoral students have subsequently published with each other without me, I note with pride Heejung and Justin's "ringleading" a project and inviting me to coauthor.

the industry, and the ascension of Japan as the only developed country in the East in the early twentieth century. This study utilized a massive data collection effort spearheaded by Serguey Braguinsky,[11] which yielded rich quantitative firm-level data and detailed business histories to integrate econometric and historical methods. The data informed our conceptual model linking a focus on value creation and promotion of talent in defiance of prevailing cultural "glass ceilings" to a scant few entrepreneurial firms achieving stable shared leadership so they could engage in long-term expansion and emerge as "centers of gravity" for output and talent in the industry.

A third theme lies at the interface of firm and industry evolution through the leverage of markets. Notable here is what Mahka Moeen taught me. When engaging in her dissertation deep dive of the agricultural biotechnology industry, Mahka uncovered key facts about an industry's incubation period—the period of precommercialization entirely missing in the Gort & Klepper (1982) industry life-cycle model. While Barry and I had noted this period could last several decades in Agarwal & Bayus (2002), we and other scholars were largely silent regarding industry incubation. Moreover, the fact that industry pioneers often entered with integrated capabilities led Gort & Klepper (1982: 632) to say that "peculiar properties of markets for information . . . may leave the innovator with no option but to enter the market if he wishes to realize the full value of his informational capital." This begged the question of how pioneers integrated necessary capabilities. Moeen & Agarwal (2017) showed that contrary to the incubation period being fallow ground, enterprising academic scientists, diversifying entrants, and incumbent seed firms engaged in significant experimentation and leveraged vibrant markets for technology (through alliances) and corporate control (through acquisitions). Agarwal, Moeen, & Shah (2017) highlighted how industries may incubate in response to distinct triggers: unmet user needs, academic discoveries, or mission-oriented challenges. Moeen, Agarwal, & Shah (2020) linked underlying processes of experimentation and knowledge exchange among entrepreneurial actors to the building of industry knowledge and thus the reduction of uncertainty across technological, market, ecosystem, and institutional dimensions. Seojin Kim,[12] a current doctoral student, is examining incubation and nascent industry stages in the bionic prosthetic limb industry

---

[11] Reflective of simultaneous use of interpersonal-attraction and resource-seeking strategies within small-world networks, I first met Serguey at a conference I had coorganized in Michael's honor in 2007 when Serguey was Michael's colleague at SUNY Buffalo and co-advisor to Atsushi . Subsequently, Serguey moved to Carnegie Mellon to work with Steve Klepper. Numerous interactions later, and upon Steve's passing, Serguey agreed to join Maryland in response to my active recruiting efforts based on funding for a faculty hire at the Ed Snider Center.

[12] In an unfortunate and heartbreaking twist of fate, MB Sarkar passed away unexpectedly due to an accident. Seojin was his graduate student during that time. Reflective of their benevolence, the faculty at

in her dissertation through primary and secondary data compilation. In Kim, Agarwal, & Goldfarb (2021) we map the capabilities of incumbents, diversifying entrants, and startups (users, academic, and employees) to the technological convergence required for this industry's creation.

A final theme examines the role of institutions for market creation and facilitation of trade in both product and resource markets. This has involved expanding focus to developing regions of the world. In Shah, Agarwal, & Sonka (2019), we used qualitative case comparison methodology to shed light on how nonprofit organizations may help address institutional voids as they encounter them when creating markets and facilitating industry inception, rather than in and of themselves. These efforts could include either the seeding of entrepreneurial firms, as in the case of metal silos in Latin American countries to reduce postharvest loss, or leveraging an existing telecommunication firm through matching grants to create the mobile money industry in Kenya. Building on the latter, Audra Wormald, another current doctoral student, is amassing a rich data set on the worldwide mobile money industry. Wormald, Agarwal, Braguinsky, & Shah (2021a, b) utilize historical methods and triangulation of quantitative and qualitative data to examine how entrepreneurial startups and diversifying entrants alike address technological, market, ecosystem, and institutional uncertainty when pioneering platforms, and when diffusing these platforms to other (largely developing) countries. Here, we also see pioneers leveraging resource markets to acquire complementary capabilities, through both alliances and acquisitions. Finally, institutional constraints also shape human capital markets in the United States. Evan Starr, who is currently assistant professor at Maryland, conducted a unique and groundbreaking survey of the incidence and use of noncompete agreements across multiple industries and regions in the United States. Evan invited Justin and me to examine externality effects of noncompete agreements on unconstrained individuals, that is, those who *do not sign noncompetes*. Starr, Frake, & Agarwal (2019) hypothesized and provided evidence that in regions with higher incidences of enforceable noncompetes, even the unconstrained received fewer job offers, were less likely to move, and received lower wages. Another institutional constraint, and a subject of heated debate today, relates to immigration restrictions on work. In Agarwal, Ganco, & Raffiee (forthcoming), we used SESTAT data on scientists and engineers graduating from US universities to show how immigration-related institutional constraints limit early career entrepreneurship and deflect individuals into

Temple University, where Seojin was enrolled, and at Maryland, were unhesitant in their support of her move across the schools midprogram. This is a poignant example of the manner in which our hearts and our minds intertwine as we pursue our scholarly purpose.

jobs closely matched to their education in their initial organizational affiliation. When released from these constraints, immigrants—who represent positive selection in terms of entrepreneurial motivations—can leverage their higher job-education match to found incorporated new ventures with larger employment size at entry.

A Concluding Realization

I recall vividly a time during my third year of graduate school after I had advanced to candidacy, when I was experiencing the "valley of the lost"—floundering in my ability to hone in on a topic for my dissertation. A not-so-nice faculty member remarked to another, deliberately within my earshot: "I don't understand these doctoral students and their inability to figure out what they want to do—off the top of my head, I can identify at least four or five dissertation topics." And I remember thinking in desperate longing, filled with insecurity, "One! one is all I really need."

Fast forward a few years later, I too could identify multiple dissertation topics off the top of my head. But, were I to go back in time, I would say to myself what Sir Anthony Leggett, Nobel laureate in physics, said more kindly to a group of middle school kids learning entrepreneurial discovery in an Illinois camp I codirected: "The more we know, the more we know what we don't know." For me, this profound statement is not about the "unknowability" of the universe. Rather, given that the mind is the most important tool for our survival, it is about human enterprise targeted towards a continuous building of knowledge to achieve greater heights. Moreover, as I often now say to my students as they advance to candidacy, "any topic I identify, no matter how worthwhile, may not be the right one for you—let's figure out what you are passionate about among all the topics you read and that will be a good place to start."

So the journey is truly the destination—for it is the journey of a scholar from apprenticeship as a PhD student to a lifelong learner. For each of us, then, this journey is where we are armed by our prior knowledge, propelled by our intellectual curiosity, and bolstered by a collaborative and constructive team of like-minded fellow travelers.

Acknowledgments

The following enterprising individuals have fueled my academic journey, and I am grateful for their enrichment of my life: Ritu Agarwal, John Allison,

Anand Anandalingam, David Audretsch, Jay Barney, Barry Bayus, Serguey Braguinsky, Heejung Byun, Ben Campbell, Seth Carnahan, Gilad Chen, Paolien Chen, Joonkyu Choi, Prithwiraj Choudhury, Rachel Croson, Marilee Dahl, Ed Day, Raj Echambadi, Christina Elson, Justin Frake, April Franco, Martin Ganco, Shweta Gaonkar, Avijit Ghosh, Brent Goldfarb, Michael Gort, Brad Greenwood, Connie Helfat, Glenn Hoetker, Richard Hofler, Steven Klepper, Seojin Kim, Rudy Lamone, Moran Lazar, Najoung Lim, Joseph Mahoney, Paul Magelli, Jacqueline Manger, Raveesh Mayya, Denisa Mindruta, Ella Miron-Spektor, Mahka Moeen, Atsushi Ohyama, Dan Olson, Lihong Qian, Joseph Raffiee, Brian Rungeling, MB Sarkar, Henry Sauermann, Sonali Shah, Debra Shapiro, Steve Sonka, Ed Snider, Evan Starr, Robert Strom, Paul Tesluk, Charlie Williams, Sarah Wolek, Audra Wormald and Rosemarie Ziedonis. And through it all, my husband and best friend Robert Tronetti is the wind beneath my wings.

References

Agarwal, R. (1994). *The evolution of product markets* [Unpublished doctoral dissertation]. State University of New York at Buffalo.

Agarwal, R. (1996). Technological activity and survival of firms. *Economics Letters, 52*(1), 101–108.

Agarwal, R. (1997). Survival of firms over the product life cycle. *Southern Economic Journal, 63*(3): 571–584.

Agarwal, R. (2019). Human enterprise. In A. Nyberg & T. Moliterno (Eds.), *Handbook of Research on Strategic Human Capital Resources*. Edward Elgar, . Ch. 30, p 482-501

Agarwal, R., Anand, J., Bercovitz, J., & Croson, R. (2012). Spillovers across organizational architectures: The role of prior resource allocation and communication in post-acquisition coordination outcomes. *Strategic Management Journal, 33*(6), 710–733.

Agarwal, R., & Audretsch, D. B. (1999). The two views of small firms in industry dynamics: A reconciliation. *Economics Letters, 62*(2), 245–251.

Agarwal, R., & Audretsch, D. B. (2001). Does entry size matter? The impact of the life cycle and technology on firm survival. *The Journal of Industrial Economics, 49*(1), 21–43.

Agarwal, R., Audretsch, D., & Sarkar, M. B. (2007). The process of creative construction: Knowledge spillovers, entrepreneurship, and economic growth. *Strategic Entrepreneurship Journal, 1*(3-4), 263–286.

Agarwal, R., Audretsch, D., & Sarkar, M. B. (2010). Knowledge spillovers and strategic entrepreneurship. *Strategic Entrepreneurship Journal, 4*(4), 271–283.

Agarwal, R., & Bayus, B. (2002). The market evolution and take-off of new product innovations. *Management Science 48*(8), 1024–1041.

Agarwal, R., & Braguinsky, S. (2015). Industry evolution and entrepreneurship: Steven Klepper's contributions to industrial organization, strategy, and technological change. *Strategic Entrepreneurship Journal, 9*(4), 380–397.

Agarwal, R., Braguinsky, S., & Ohyama, A. (2020). Centers of gravity: The effect of shared leadership and stability in top management teams on firm growth and industry evolution. *Strategic Management Journal 2020, 41*(3): 467-498.

Agarwal, R., Campbell, B. A., Franco, A. M., & Ganco, M. (2016). What do I take with me? The mediating effect of spin-out team size and tenure on the founder–firm performance relationship. *Academy of Management Journal, 59*(3), 1060–1087.

Agarwal, R., Croson, R., & Mahoney, J. T. (2010). The role of incentives and communication in strategic alliances: An experimental investigation. *Strategic Management Journal, 31*(4), 413–437.

Agarwal, R., Echambadi, R., Franco, A. M., & Sarkar, M. B. (2004). Knowledge transfer through inheritance: Spin-out generation, development, and survival. *Academy of Management journal, 47*(4), 501–522.

Agarwal, R., & Gort, M. (1996). The evolution of markets and entry, exit and survival of firms. *Review of Economics and Statistics 78*(3), 489–498.

Agarwal, R., & Gort, M. (2001). First mover advantage and the speed of competitive entry: 1887–1986. *Journal of Law and Economics 44*(1), 161–178.

Agarwal, R., & Gort, M. (2002). Products and firm life cycles and firm survival. *American Economic Review 92*(2), 184–190.

Agarwal, R., Ganco, M., Raffiee, J. (forthcoming). *Immigrant entrepreneurship: The effect of early career immigration constraints and job-education match on science and engineering workforce.* Organization Science

Agarwal, R., Ganco, M., & Ziedonis, R. H. (2009). Reputations for toughness in patent enforcement: Implications for knowledge spillovers via inventor mobility. *Strategic Management Journal, 30*(13), 1349–1374.

Agarwal, R., & Helfat, C. E. (2009). Strategic renewal of organizations. *Organization Science, 20*(2), 281–293.

Agarwal, R., Moeen, M., & Shah, S. K. (2017). Athena's birth: Triggers, actors, and actions preceding industry inception. *Strategic Entrepreneurship Journal, 11*(3), 287–305.

Agarwal, R., & Ohyama, A. (2013). Industry or academia, basic or applied? Career choices and earnings trajectories of scientists. *Management Science, 59*(4), 950–970.

Agarwal, R, Sarkar, M. B., Echambadi, R. (2002). The conditioning effect of time on firm survival: An industry life cycle approach. *Academy of Management Journal 45*(5), 971–994.

Agarwal, R., & Shah, S. K. (2014). Knowledge sources of entrepreneurship: Firm formation by academic, user and employee innovators. *Research Policy, 43*(7), 1109–1133.

Bain, J. S. (1951). Relation of profit rate to industry concentration: American manufacturing, 1936–1940. *The Quarterly Journal of Economics, 65*(3), 293–324.

Baumol, W. J. (1968). Entrepreneurship in economic theory. *The American economic review, 58*(2), 64–71.

Bayus, B. L., & Agarwal, R. (2007). The role of pre-entry experience, entry timing, and product technology strategies in explaining firm survival. *Management Science, 53*(12), 1887–1902.

Becker, G. S. (1962). Investment in human capital: A theoretical analysis. *Journal of political economy, 70*(5, Part 2), 9–49.

Becker, G. S. (1973). A theory of marriage: Part I. *Journal of Political economy, 81*(4), 813–846.

Byun, H., Frake, J., & Agarwal, R. (2018). Leveraging who you know by what you know: Specialization and returns to relational capital. *Strategic Management Journal, 39*(7), 1803–1833.

Campbell, B. A., Ganco, M., Franco, A. M., & Agarwal, R. (2012). Who leaves, where to, and why worry? Employee mobility, entrepreneurship and effects on source firm performance. *Strategic Management Journal, 33*(1), 65–87.

Carlton, D. W., & Perloff, J. M. (1990). *Modern industrial organization.* Scott, Foresman.

Carnahan, S., Agarwal, R., & Campbell, B. A. (2012). Heterogeneity in turnover: The effect of relative compensation dispersion of firms on the mobility and entrepreneurship of extreme performers. *Strategic Management Journal, 33*(12), 1411–1430.

Chase, W. G., & Simon, H. A. (1973). Perception in chess. *Cognitive psychology, 4*(1), 55–81.

Chen, P. L., Williams, C., & Agarwal, R. (2012). Growing pains: Pre-entry experience and the challenge of transition to incumbency. *Strategic Management Journal*, *33*(3), 252–276.

Coleman, J. S. (1986). Social theory, social research, and a theory of action. *American journal of Sociology*, *91*(6), 1309–1335.

Croson, R., Anand, J., & Agarwal, R. (2007). Using experiments in corporate strategy research. *European Management Review*, *4*(3), 173–181.

Fox, J. T. (2007). Semiparametric estimation of multinomial discrete-choice models using a subset of choices. *The RAND Journal of Economics*, *38*(4), 1002–1019.

Franco, A. M., Sarkar, M. B., Agarwal, R., & Echambadi, R. (2009). Swift and smart: The moderating effects of technological capabilities on the market pioneering–firm survival relationship. *Management Science*, *55*(11), 1842–1860.

Ganco, M., & Agarwal, R. (2009). Performance differentials between diversifying entrants and entrepreneurial start-ups: A complexity approach. *Academy of Management Review*, *34*(2), 228–252.

Ganco, M., Ziedonis, R. H., & Agarwal, R. (2015). More stars stay, but the brightest ones still leave: Job hopping in the shadow of patent enforcement. *Strategic Management Journal*, *36*(5), 659–685.

Gort, M., & Klepper, S. (1982). Time paths in the diffusion of product innovations. *The Economic Journal*, *92*(367), 630–653.

Greenwood, B. N., Agarwal, R., Agarwal, R., & Gopal, A. (2016). The when and why of abandonment: The role of organizational differences in medical technology life cycles. *Management Science*, *63*(9), 2948–2966.

Greenwood, B. N., Agarwal, R., Agarwal, R., & Gopal, A. (2019). The role of individual and organizational expertise in the adoption of new practices. *Organization Science*, *30*(1), 191–213.

Heckman, J. J., & Singer, B. (2017). Abducting economics. *American Economic Review*, *107*(5), 298–302.

Hoetker, G., & Agarwal, R. (2007). Death hurts, but it isn't fatal: The postexit diffusion of knowledge created by innovative companies. *Academy of Management Journal*, *50*(2), 446–467.

Kerin, R. A., Varadarajan, P. R., and Peterson, R. A. (1992). First-mover advantage: A synthesis, conceptual framework, and research propositions. *Journal of Marketing 56*, 33–52.

Kaul, A., Ganco, M., & Raffiee, J. (2018). *A general theory of employee entrepreneurship: A knowledge-based view. University of Wisconsin working paper*, Presented at Academy of Management meetings, August 10–14, 2018. https://mackinstitute.wharton.upenn.edu/wp-content/uploads/2018/03/Ganco-Martin-Kaul-Aseem-and-Raffiee-Joseph_A-General-Theory-of-Employee-Entrepreneurship.-A-Knowledge-Based-View.pdf

Kim, S., Agarwal R., & Goldfarb, B. (2021). *Mapping (radical) technology evolution onto firm capabilities*. (Management and Organizations Working Paper). University of Maryland.

Lieberman, M. B., & Montgomery, D. B. (1988). First-mover advantages. *Strategic Management Journal*, *9*(S1), 41–58.

Locke, E. A. (1968). Toward a theory of task motivation and incentives. *Organizational Behavior and Human Performance*, *3*(2), 157–189.

Maslow, A. (1954). *Motivation and personality*. Harper & Row.

Mincer, J., (1958). Investment in human capital and personal income distribution. *Journal of Political Economy*, *66*(4), 281–302.

Mindruta, C. D. (2009). *Markets for research: A matching approach to university-industry research collaborations* [Unpublished doctoral dissertation]. University of Illinois at Urbana-Champaign.

Mindruta, D., Moeen, M., & Agarwal, R. (2016). A two-sided matching approach for partner selection and assessing complementarities in partners' attributes in inter-firm alliances. *Strategic Management Journal, 37*(1), 206–231.

Moeen, M., & Agarwal, R. (2017). Incubation of an industry: Heterogeneous knowledge bases and modes of value capture. *Strategic Management Journal, 38*(3), 566–587.

Moeen, M., Agarwal, R., & Shah, S. K. (2020). *Building industries by building knowledge: Uncertainty reduction through experimentation, knowledge release and knowledge acquisition* Strategy Science, 5(3):147-291

Nelson, R. R., & Winter, S. G. (1982). *An evolutionary theory of economic change.* Harvard University Press.

North, D. C. (1990). *The path of institutional change.*

North, D. C. (1990). *Institutions, institutional change and economic performance.* Cambridge: Cambridge University Press.

Penrose, E. (1959). *The theory of the growth of the firm.* Wiley.

Lazar, M., Miron-Spektor, E., Agarwal, R., Erez, M., Goldfarb, B., & Chen, G. (2020). *Entrepreneurial Team Formation Academy of Management Annals* 14(1): 29–59 .

Qian, L., Agarwal, R., & Hoetker, G. (2012). Configuration of value chain activities: The effect of pre-entry capabilities, transaction hazards, and industry evolution on decisions to internalize. *Organization Science, 23*(5), 1330–1349.

Reinganum, J. F. (1981). On the diffusion of new technology: A game theoretic approach. *The Review of Economic Studies, 48*(3), 395–405.

Robinson, W. T., Kalyanaram, G., & Urban, G. L. (1994). First mover advantages from pioneering new markets: A survey of empirical evidence. *Review of Industrial Organization 9*, 1–23.

Rosenberg, N. (1982). *Inside the black box: Technology and economics.* Cambridge University Press.

Sarkar, M. B., Echambadi, R., Agarwal, R., & Sen, B. (2006). The effect of the innovative environment on exit of entrepreneurial firms. *Strategic Management Journal, 27*(6), 519–539.

Schmalensee, R. (1989). Inter-industry studies of structure and performance. *Handbook of Industrial Organization, 2*, 951–1009.

Schultz, T. W. (1961). Investment in human capital. *The American Economic Review, 51*(1), 1–17.

Schumpeter, J. A. (1934). *The theory of economic development.* Harvard University Press. First published in German in 1911.

Schumpeter, J. A. (1942). *Capitalism, socialism and democracy.* Allen & Unwin.

Shah, S. Agarwal, R., & Echambadi, R. (2019). Jewels in the crown: Motivations and team building processes of employee entrepreneurs. *Strategic Management Journal, 40*(9): 1331–1514.

Shah, S., Agarwal, R., & Sonka, S. (2017). *A time and a place: Non-profit engagement in market creation and industry emergence.* SSRN 2959714.

Shapiro, D., Hom, P., Shen W., & Agarwal, R. (2016). How do leader departures affect subordinates' organizational attachment? *A 360-degree Relational Perspective Academy of Management Review 41*(3), 479–502.

Starr, E., Frake, J., & Agarwal, R. (2019). Mobility constraint externalities. *Organization Science, 30*(5):869–1123.

Teece, D. J. (1986). Profiting from technological innovation: Implications for integration, collaboration, licensing and public policy. *Research Policy, 15*(6), 285–305.

Varian, H. R. (1992). *Microeconomic analysis* (3rd ed.). New York: Norton.

Williams, C., Chen, P. L., & Agarwal, R. (2017). Rookies and seasoned recruits: How experience in different levels, firms, and industries shapes strategic renewal in top management. *Strategic Management Journal, 38*(7), 1391–1415.

Wormald, A., Agarwal, R., Braguinsky, S., & Shah, S. (forthcoming). David Overshadows Goliath: Specializing in Generality for Internationalization in the Global Mobile Money Industry *Strategic Management Journal*

Wormald, A., Agarwal, R., Braguinsky, S., & Shah, S. (2021). *Pioneering multi-sided digital platforms: The effect of firm characteristics and platform strategies on pioneer outcomes.* (Working Paper). University of Maryland.

11

Tales from a Late Bloomer

Ten Principles for Influential Scholarship

Sandra Lynn Robinson

So here I sit putting words to paper about my academic journey. It will soon be exactly 31 years since I sat down at my assigned cubicle as a new PhD student. In some ways, it feels exactly like yesterday because of vivid memories and part of me believing I am still 24. In other ways, it feels a bit like those movie scenes where numbers fly off the day planner to represent a massive passage of time with so much that has happened, most of which was very unpredictable.

I was honored and excited to be invited to write this chapter. I immediately accepted the invitation because I believed this would be both an enjoyable and a rewarding task, the two criteria I use for all my work decisions nowadays. Although I am still glad to have this opportunity, it has also been much more difficult than I had anticipated. It turns out to be much harder to write about myself, especially my success, than it is to write academic articles. I have never written anything autobiographical, and I am a bit uncomfortable sharing myself in a way that is necessary to be useful. Another difficulty I have encountered is with regard to how to structure my story. I originally intended to tell a chronologically organized tale in the same order in which my career unfolded. I came to realize however that my journey has been more akin to a spiral. I think I have been moving forward, but I also know I have often revisited similar experiences, successes, and challenges over time. As such, if I want the story of my journey to be useful to others, it made more sense for me to frame it around things I have learned along the way, attaching personal stories to illustrate them.

So without further ado, here is my story. I will begin with a brief overview of my career, so as to put my insights into context. Then the remainder of this chapter will focus on ten interrelated principles that I believe were crucial to my influence as a scholar. For each of these principles, I have sought to provide exemplar stories from across my career, although it is important note that,

Sandra Lynn Robinson, *Tales from a Late Bloomer* In: *A Journey toward Influential Scholarship*. Edited by: Xiao-Ping Chen and H. Kevin Steensma, Oxford University Press. © Oxford University Press 2021. DOI: 10.1093/oso/9780190070717.003.0011

because I was on such a steep learning curve earlier on, many of the most pivotal moments or epiphanies come disproportionately from my earlier years.

My Career in a Nutshell

I was the only person in my family of six to graduate from high school, let alone attend university. Thanks to the Canadian public education system, I was able to get several degrees on my own dime at the University of British Columbia (UBC). I worked my way through school, and those jobs impacted my career choices. Interesting jobs as a research assistant uncovered my affinity for behavioral research, and various bad summer jobs encouraged me to stay in school. Toward the end of one summer job with many student coworkers, we had a party at the house of two twins who were part of our crew. They had a cool dad who played guitar at our party in the rec room. His name was Larry Moore, and he was a professor in OB at UBC. He introduced me to the field, and he encouraged me to apply to UBC's master's program in OB.

I pursued that degree working with Larry, and then, with the incredible guidance of Craig Pinder, I applied to PhD programs. In the spring of 1988, I chose Northwestern University because Craig had said "it's a powerhouse!" and because I had liked the people I met there when they flew me in. I was not particularly strategic in my decision making, but I believed that so long as I followed my interests and had more education than my parents, I would have a better life.

At Northwestern, my cosupervisors were Denise Rousseau and Jeanne Brett, along with Dawn Iacobucci from the Marketing Department. I was told it would raise eyebrows to have only women on my committee, so Paul Hirsch agreed to join as a token male. Although Northwestern's culture was dominated by experimental research on negotiations and conflict resolution, my research interests were unrelated and best pursued with field survey research.

We were told to graduate in four years, which I did. We were also told on our first day of class to have 1.5 publications ready for the job market when we graduated, which I did not. Nevertheless, I landed a job as assistant professor at New York University in 1992. I had fruitful years there, and I made it to associate professor, but I left in 1998 to return to Vancouver and UBC. Getting to come home had been a major life goal, but I was able to fulfill it much sooner than I had anticipated. A position opened up at UBC because of a retirement. Who had retired? Larry Moore, who had introduced me to the field of OB 13 years earlier. I have remained at UBC for several decades now, where I am currently a full professor, hold a Distinguished Scholar Designation, and have served as PhD director for the university's business school.

My research has always been phenomena based. I have almost exclusively studied relatively new phenomena in the realm of the "dark side": expressly deviant, dysfunctional, and harmful workplace behaviors. In graduate school, I began my research program focused on psychological contracts, and I was the first to study psychological contract breach and violation and continued to do so for about a decade. I believe my initial studies (Morrison & Robinson, 1997; Robinson, 1996; Robinson & Rousseau, 1994), especially because they made it into *AMJ*, *AMR*, and *ASQ*, helped legitimize the study of psychological contracts and thus pave the way for the decades of studies that have followed in this domain. Moreover, as firsts, they provided empirical, theoretical, and conceptual clarity for some key constructs, such as how breach and violation are distinct, what causes them to occur, how broken psychological contracts are much more than merely unmet expectations, and the central role that trust plays in the recognition of, and reaction to, psychological contract breach.

A few years into my career, in 1995, along with my coauthor Rebecca Bennett, I developed the broad construct of workplace deviance (Robinson & Bennett, 1995; Bennett & Robinson, 2000). Our goal was to say: "Hello field, you've been preoccupied with positive constructs such as commitment, motivation, and citizenship behavior but what about considering dysfunctional and harmful workplace behaviors?" We developed a conceptual definition of workplace deviance, a typology that would make disparate types of deviance hang meaningfully together, as well as several measurement scales. Our initial article was the first to identify and highlight what was to become an extremely popular area of study, which is focused on negative behaviors in the workplace. Our construct of workplace deviance set the stage for subsequent articles that introduced similarly negative constructs, such as counterproductive work behavior, incivility, social undermining, and abusive supervision. I like to imagine that our initial articles on workplace deviance may have brought "negative behavior" to the field's attention and opened up a wide area of our field by inspiring the study of these other negative constructs, as well as subsequent studies on positive deviance. At the same time, it is a bit ironic that while our initial typology had sought to integrate a myriad of different deviant behaviors, this area of study instead splintered into a dozen different subareas.

Later, with my graduate student Graham Brown, I introduced and developed initial studies on territorial behavior, adapting the work on physical territoriality from environmental psychology. I really believed and hoped that these articles, especially our *AMR* article introducing the construct of territoriality (Brown, Lawrence, & Robinson, 2005), would spawn a large area of study as my earlier work on contracts and deviance had, but thus far these articles have only garnered about 850 citations. More recently, my focus has been on examining ostracism in the workplace. It is too early to tell what kind of influence these studies might have, but the study of workplace ostracism seems to be starting to grow.

My research interests have typically been sparked by observing phenomena out in the world, which I have then sought to study in an organizational context. My studies have often involved defining, conceptualizing, and operationalizing a new construct, and answering early, fundamental questions about it. Much of my research has taken a field survey approach, in part because I have always been interested in work experiences from the perspective of employees—such as their psychological contracts or how they have been treated at work—so surveys get the closest to that for me. Like most scholars, however, I have also used other methods when they have been more suitable, whether multidimensional scaling to develop a typology, an experiment to garner stronger confidence about cause-and-effect relationships, or content analysis when seeking to initially understand a new phenomenon.

I like to think or hope that my work will have an enduring impact given that has been the whole point of it all along. There are, of course, different ways to have influence and different ways to measure it as well. For me, two sets of metrics have been important when it comes to thinking about my potential influence. One set focuses on the number and kinds of research awards I have won, or how my work has been useful to others' work. At the risk of sounding boastful, my current citations are around 35,000, and that includes nine articles with over 1,000 citations and five with over 3,000. I have also received a wide range of research awards, sometimes for specific articles and other times career-related, for example the Cummings Award from the Organizational Behavior Division of the Academy of Management or the JMI Distinguished Scholar Award from Western Academy of Management. The other set of metrics reflects how my work has resonated with the general population through the media, typically starting with press releases about my studies. It has been incredibly fulfilling to discover that my findings are interesting and meaningful to nonacademics. Whether through article comments or people reaching out to me, it has been very heartening to be thanked for validating someone's workplace experience or for addressing issues they believe are important.

Ten Principles

In looking back on my successes, along with my mistakes and memorable turning points, I have identified 10 things that I believe were important for my career. Before elaborating on each, there are a few caveats worth noting. First, these come from post hoc sense making around my career. Sadly, since I could not do experiments with myself to determine cause and effect, it is anyone's guess if these are the right 10, or the number should be 3 or 17. Moreover, there are likely other ingredients I have overlooked, including a ton of good luck and plenty of interaction effects. In addition, of course, who knows if these are generalizable to different contexts, scholars, or time periods. So even if I am correct in capturing what worked for me, it is just one way, and by far not the only way, to be influential. Finally, I am not going to suggest that anyone else follow the path I followed, such as studying the "dark side" or seeking to introduce new phenomena. Instead, I hope some others might find it useful to consider some of the more basic underlying principles that I think worked for me.

You Do You: Chase Your Interests and Be Programmatic

The hardest part of my development as a scholar was figuring out who I was and who I wanted to be in the field. Learning the literature and the research skills was straightforward, but uncovering my real interests and talents and then learning to be guided by them was a slower and more complex process. This was not something I even knew I needed to do, but with retrospection, it is clear that it was critical to my success. Guided by my interests, I was able to produce more and better work and develop an identity as a scholar.

Chase Your Interests

This has been so fundamental throughout my career that if I were to choose just one thing I did right, it was trusting my gut feelings and allowing myself to be guided by what interested me most. That has been a consistent force in deciding the topics I study, the questions I seek to answer, and the roles I have taken on. My interests have also equally guided my decisions to pass on opportunities that have come my way or to stop working in certain areas.

Following my research interests has meant not only choosing topics that excite me but also the research questions and the facets of the research process that I enjoy the most. For some in our field, their strongest guiding interests are with regard to theory, or finding and solving conflicts, or certain methodological approaches. For me, my interests have evolved around uncovering and introducing a new behavioral phenomenon to the field that addresses the dark side of organizational behavior. I have also gravitated to understudied phenomena, which allows me to pursue my favorite research tasks. I absolutely love the hunt, seeking disparate studies or streams of research of unrelated work and integrating them into a single research domain. I also love the conceptual theorizing that goes into a new area of study.

The value of chasing interests. Chasing my intrinsic interests has been hugely advantageous to me. The primary advantage is that it nicely substitutes for self-discipline. I'm not particularly self-disciplined, but if I'm doing something I enjoy, it doesn't require nearly as much effort. This has been especially important when running into barriers and negative feedback, which is inherent in the work we do. In general, I find doing good research is mentally challenging and requires sustained effort. To the extent I am enjoying it, however, I do not mind the effort and the outcomes of my labor are superior.

Chasing my interests has also enabled my work to be programmatic. By following what I want to do, invariably my research studies share a lot of similarities, even if I do not know what those similarities are. As I will explain a little later, its hugely valuable to be doing programmatic work.

I believe this principle is so important that I have always encouraged my PhD students to study what excites them, not what excites me. For example, my last student to graduate, Kira Schabram, who is now at the University of Washington, studied the opposite of my interests: she focused on very positive topics, including callings, courage, and compassion. Though my students have to become the experts of their focus, I can still effectively and enjoyably guide them along. It is just very important to find the people and places that will let us study what we feel we are called to study.

Uncovering my own interests. My interests as a scholar, at least with hindsight, have been with me since childhood. As a kid, I loved to build forts and make up clubs for them. One summer I emptied and scrubbed our very old unused wood garage. I swept up the dirt floor and covered it with a carpet, and it became the home of our macramé club. I helped a friend build a treehouse-type fort on a large empty lot, but we couldn't get kids to join because it was too far away. And across two summers, with neighbors, we built a fort of wood slats placed between two garages on adjacent lots, and we had a list of things you had to learn before you could belong. The role I have gravitated to as a researcher, introducing new phenomena to the field, has involved the building of similar forts and clubs. Looking for some niches, cleaning them up, creating a structure, deciding on some ground rules, and inviting people to join.

Since childhood I have also been drawn to social dynamics and especially people who do bad things. For example, I did a seventh-grade book report and presentation on a technique the author called "photo-analysis" with which one could analyze relationships by examining photographs. This technique, by the way, never took off as a legitimate area of study, but I was enthralled by it. I also recall the librarian at the public library raising concerns about me taking out an adult book titled *Orrible Murders: Victorian Crime and Passion,* replete with sketches and crime stories taken from Victorian news sources.

Despite all of this, I remember in graduate school feeling very anxious because I did not know what I wanted to do. I did not understand what my genuine interests were or what my niche as a scholar might be. I recall that in my first semester OB seminar, as we worked through topics each week, from motivation to leadership to job design, nothing was grabbing me. Perhaps I had an advantage over my classmates who struggled with liking too many topics, but we both faced the same problem: how to recognize our true interests and discover who we wanted to be in the field.

In the last week of that seminar, the theme was "emerging topics in OB," and one of the articles we read was on psychological contracts. My interest was piqued—I wanted to read more—and I felt a sense of relief that I might enjoy studying this topic. It was not love at first sight, and I did not yet have feelings of excitement; it was simply more interesting to me than all the other topics we were learning about. It was only with experience that I fell for this area. Denise Rousseau, my advisor, had developed the concept of psychological contracts. I was in search of a Summer Paper idea involving psychological contracts, and she let me look at surveys she had collected. The last question, an open-ended one, asked respondents about whether and how their employers had failed to fulfill their psychological contracts. I proceeded to write out each answer on index cards, and it was readily apparent that this was an extremely common experience and one that was very emotionally impactful for those writing about it. This was where I found my first research love: the experience of psychological contract violation. This also led to my first meaningful publication: Robinson and Rousseau, 1994.

Around this time, I also followed advice given to me to keep a journal of "interesting things." Every time something popped into my head that interested me while I was reading an article or watching a presentation or just thinking wildly, I wrote it down. Every encounter with an article I found very interesting to read, in any field, I made note of in my journal. It took me time and some false starts to uncover the fundamental interest I had always had: the "dark side" of human behavior. And whereas I used to worry that I would not have enough interesting things to study, my biggest challenge in my career has been the opposite: I have too many things I would like to study and not enough time to study them all.

After graduate school, my approach to pursuing my interests shifted away from articles I was reading and toward events in the world around me. This was a great approach that helped me to discover interesting things to study, because I was always most interested in phenomena. For example, my interest in workplace deviance came about from very frequent headlines in the 1990s about workplace shootings and employees "going postal." (In those days there was frequent news about postal workers shooting coworkers.) Becky and I really wanted to study this "sexy" topic. After reviewing the existing literature, we realized that no one was studying workplace aggression, and more broadly or abstractly, no one was systematically examining negative workplace behaviors, except for occasional isolated studies, such as Ashforth's work on petty tyranny or Greenberg's study of theft in response to injustice. So we developed a construct we called "workplace deviance." In Robinson and Bennett (1995) we used multidimensional scaling to integrate disparate behaviors reflecting workplace deviance into a typology that varied along two dimensions. Then in Bennett and Robinson (2000) we developed a survey instrument so that we could empirically assess workplace deviance.

I believe the search for interests to pursue can be aptly described with a dating analogy. It may be love at first sight, as it was with my excitement about workplace deviance. In such cases, run with it and see how it unfolds, and do not worry too much at the outset about practical concerns. Alternatively, we do not always have to wait for Mr. or Mrs. Right to show up and knock us off our feet. What we may later be excited to study may not immediately jump out at us and grab our attraction on first encounters. We might just have to spend time with a topical area, get to know it very well, and then discover that the attraction blossoms into long-term love. This is what happened with my interest in psychological contracts.

It has taken mistakes to learn how to listen to my gut and follow what I am truly interested in. Though I still do not always get it right, I have gradually learned what not to do. I believe my career success has been as much about what I have said no to as what I have said yes to. On occasion, though, I still make the mistake of joining projects that do not excite me enough and that I agree to join because they are convenient, or easy, or have great data, or involve people I want to work with. None of these are good reasons *alone* to join a project. If I am not intrinsically excited about an area of study or a given study—if I am not excited to see what we might find—I do not usually enjoy the process or experience the best outcomes.

Caveats of following interests. Before I end this section, I want to add a few caveats about following one's interests. First, I do not think that following one's interests should be confused with the "follow your passion" mantra because I think passion is way too high a bar for many. If we wait for passion, we may never uncover what to study. I really enjoy what I do, but I would not describe myself as passionate about it. I recall a colleague of mine sharing a story of how she had read the latest issue of *JAP* under the blankets with a flashlight so as not to wake up her husband. She couldn't wait until the next day to read it. This story left me in awe and with envy . . . that someone could actually love it *this* much. But I am just not that person, and I do not think we need to be.

Second, following my interests also does not mean that all the research I do is always interesting. Every project has its ups and downs. Even the most initially exciting projects involve periods of drudgery, such as when we have to revise an article based on 15 pages of criticism. Does anyone find that fun? As I will discuss later on, another principle to follow is to persevere in the face of adversity.

And finally, as a junior scholar, I had to be much more pragmatic about publications than I do now. Back then, I did not have the luxury of saying no to most of the opportunities that came my way. Only over time did I have the increasing freedom to focus solely on what interested me. But all things being equal and given a choice, I believe we should work only on what we are truly interested in or excited about.

Be Programmatic

I believe being programmatic has also been critical to my achievement as a scholar. By *programmatic* I mean that my research hangs together as a collection in a meaningful way. There is an overarching theme to the nature of my work. To someone reading my articles, it would be apparent "what I'm about" or might be "known for" and what kind of influence I have been able to have. In my case, as someone doing phenomenon-based work, I have developed a reputation as someone studying the "dark side," especially with regard to my work on psychological contracts violations and workplace deviance.

Benefits of being programmatic. Being programmatic has helped me in a lot of different ways. One benefit is that it naturally led me to a community of scholars focused on the same issues as me. As I will elaborate on later, finding your people and belonging to a community of like-minded others has been very valuable.

Second, being programmatic has facilitated my ability to conduct and publish research by giving me economies of scale, such that expertise and resources I gain from one study can be transferred to others. For example, when working in the area of workplace deviance, I knew the literature inside out and did not have to start from scratch with writing front ends of articles. With the topics of territoriality or ostracism, I knew which were the most accepted measures and definitions. On occasions when I have worked on articles in entirely unfamiliar domains, it has been readily apparent from the reviewers' feedback how important it is to have fluency in the nuances of a domain. Each area has its shared norms about how things should be studied and expectations about which articles should be cited and what pitfalls to avoid. I have found it challenging to get through the review process without that fluency.

Finally, being programmatic has helped me to communicate to the field, and my school what kind of scholar I am; that is, someone who is doing research with a purpose and a larger goal to make a difference in the field, rather than a scholar who is collecting publications in an instrumental or opportunistic way.

How to be programmatic. I do not have an easy answer for this, because I believe I became programmatic inadvertently because I followed my interests. Because I followed what I wanted to study rather than what I thought I *should* study, most of my research naturally shared some commonalities.

It is worth nothing that when I was working on my articles I did not see the commonalities across them; their commonalities were revealed to me retrospectively. I recall having great difficulty attempting to write my research statement for promotion, as I could not see how my work on psychological contracts was related to my work on workplace deviance. I believe I was so into the trees—that is, my articles—that I was not able to see the forest. At some point I had an aha moment and I realized that my work as a collection was about dysfunctional workplace behavior, on the part of the employer (psychological contract violation) and the employee (workplace deviance). This seems incredibly obvious now, but it honestly was not at the time. Later on, again with more articles in other areas and a higher level or bird's-eye view of a larger collection of my work, I came to realize that my work was not just about dysfunctional behavior but about negative discrepancies: the discrepancy between what should be (norms, laws, contractual obligations, social expectations) and what was (deviant behavior, unfulfilled obligations, social invisibility). I did not set out to study the exact same topic, but rather gravitated to phenomena that excited me: contract violation, trust betrayal, workplace deviance, territoriality, aggression, ostracism. Although different phenomena, they all reflect my underlying interest: dysfunctional behavior that can be understood as a negative discrepancy between perceived behavior and an existing standard.

I believe it is not a critical concern in the early stages of our careers, when we are still finding our interests and may have to jump on any opportunities for publication. But as we gain the opportunity to pick and choose where we spend our research energy, and hone in on our genuine interests, I believe being programmatic at some level of abstraction is important.

Ask Good and Timely Research Questions

Finding my areas of research interest went hand in hand with identifying and pursuing the good research questions within those areas.

Find and Ask Good Questions

My best articles have in every case begun with, and been developed from, what I've believed to be a really good research question. From a good research question, everything else follows: the relevant theory, the hypotheses, the research design and analysis. The top journals that give our work the most exposure are looking for good research questions that are tested with rigorous methods. As a reviewer and editor, I have noticed that many of the submissions that get rejected are those that seem to have been developed from data or findings, rather than developed from a strong research question. They are written as if the authors found some results and then worked backwards to jury-rig a research question around them. This is not a path to being influential and not a good use of our scarce resources.

What is a good research question? A good research question, for me, is one that is straightforward and clear, has real-world relevance and importance, and whose answer is not very close to what we already know from prior studies. My good research questions have been ones whose answers changed or helped shape our current knowledge base and motivated and provided the basis for other future studies. In other words, they helped push the field forward.

I believe that important questions are necessary questions, but not necessarily ones that are counterintuitive or surprising, even though we might want them to be. This may be especially true with phenomenologically focused studies. Although some of my more impactful studies have yielded unsurprising outcomes, they have opened a door or provided a necessary and important building block for future research. To me the goal is not to be surprising per se, but to get people to view things or study things differently from the way they would have before my study.

How I have found my good research questions. I believe my good research questions have come from a necessary combination of immersion in the literature and exposure to outside forces. By immersion, I mean a deep knowledge of literatures of interest to me so I could be attuned to what would be considered an interesting, important, and novel research question at a given point in time. Immersion ensures that you already know what your field knows so that you can recognize a good and novel research question that needs to be answered next. However, at least for me, the questions themselves are not found in the literature. As a graduate student I thought I could read "future directions" in research articles to find my next research project, but that never seemed to bear fruit. I also never found my future studies by looking at building on or improving an existing study, such as by adding moderators, or mediators, or considering a better measure or context in which to study the topic. For me at least, the questions are not found in the literature, they are found in real world observation. So immersion in the literature is the backdrop, a necessary but not sufficient condition, for finding good research questions.

Exposure has meant, for me at least, being out in the world. I study phenomena, so I have a habit of routinely observing my environment and seeing potential research questions. These observations might include experiences told by my family, something I have read in the news, an odd finding in my data, or mental wanderings while standing in line and observing peoples' behavior. My research questions start as curiosities that emerge as I see or read or hear something, and I might start to look for or see patterns. Lots of my questions are not even related to organizational behavior, but I am just constantly asking myself "I wonder why . . . " or "I wonder if . . ." Some of those questions will feel in my gut like good questions, and I immediately start to think of how I might study them.

I will illustrate the foregoing with a few examples of how I came upon a few of my specific research questions. A number of years ago I was consoling my mother-in-law via email during our workdays. She was working in Pennsylvania for a small government agency, and she absolutely hated her job. Her current problem, and why she was reaching out to me, was that the other two women in the office were giving her the cold shoulder. They seemed to treat her as if she was invisible, and whenever she entered the space where they were chatting, they would immediately stop talking, and she would email me for emotional support to lessen the pain of it. These women were not doing anything *to* her, such as calling her names or criticizing her. Yet she was so clearly very hurt from being ignored. She was always a tough and strong person, so I was surprised by her pain, especially given that she did not even like these coworkers. Around the same time, I had been reviewing the literature on bullying for a book chapter I was writing, so I knew that area well. And I felt confident that no one had studied the research question this experience of my mother-in-law brought to mind: could being ignored or invisible be as painful as being the target of more obvious or overt forms of bullying at work? This was a good research question to me because I felt that my writing about it could potentially change how both researchers and the general public viewed something as seemingly innocuous as ignoring someone. Moreover, if I were to show it was harmful, or more harmful, than more obvious forms of mistreatment, it might be a valuable motivator for scholars, policy makers and practicing managers to seek to reduce its occurrence. This research question led to a publication in *Organizational Science* (O'Reilly, Robinson, Berdahl, & Banki, 2015).

Another, more recent example: I developed a research question from reading Canada's national news, where I encountered stories about Canadian telecom employees who were whistleblowing on unethical sales tactics they were being pressured to use. It was noted that these employees were often in entry-level positions. I already felt sufficiently familiar with the research on employees' unethical behavior, so this story brought to my awareness, in an "aha" kind of way, a potentially novel and practically relevant research question: how does being pressured to engage in unethical behavior early in one's career impact one's subsequent moral compass at work? I then turned back to the literature to see whether and how much this would indeed be a novel question and where it would fit or add to a conversation in organizational ethics. To me, this was important because I believe that such pressure is likely a common work experience and one that is likely to have a strong impact. If teaching ethics is important, so too is understanding the forces that may more powerfully shape the ethics of our business school students after they head into the work world. This one is still a work in progress.

Confirming that I have good research questions. I routinely ask myself questions such as these: Why would someone cite my study? How would it be useful to someone working on a study in the future? Would this be a newsworthy study and what would the headline be? What is the point of my study for the field?

Because my research questions come from observation rather than the literature, and I am most interested in understanding relevant organizational phenomena, I have found it useful to confirm the value of my research questions to those outside academia. If I find myself at a cocktail party or family get-together, or with strangers in the dog park, my good questions are ones that, first, I can easily explain to nonresearchers, and second, their eyes light up with recognition when I tell them about it. It is an especially good sign when they respond with "Oh, you oughta come study my workplace!" and then give me examples. I should add here that it seems that most if not all people seem to think their own workplaces are unique in being dysfunctional when really they are not.

Timing Matters: Being in Synch with the Field

I have come to realize that good questions also have to have good timing. Our questions have to align with what the field is looking for or needs or finds exciting at the time, whether that is a topical area or a specific research question within it. Good questions can be ahead of their time or seen as "too old." There is a sense of order as to what makes sense for the next question, given our current state of understanding. What may be truly interesting to one scholar and even important to the field will not get the attention it deserves if the editors and reviewers do not recognize it as such. Here are some examples of this timing from my own early experiences.

Too new. It is possible to have a great idea that is perceived by the field as being before its time. Denise Rousseau was just starting to study psychological contracts when I joined her. She had had success in the journal *Employment Rights and Responsibilities* but felt that the field was not yet accepting this idea of psychological contracts. Her idea was exciting and important, but she was just a bit early. By the time of our first publication, however, in 1994, the field was ready.

Just right. With Anne O'Leary Kelly, I published a study on the social influence of coworkers on employees' deviant behavior and factors that would moderate this influence (Robinson & O'Leary-Kelly, 1998). We titled it "Monkey See, Monkey Do." We did this entire study in 12 months, start to finish, and entirely by email. (We had only met in person once before.) Aside from the important advantage of having a fantastic coauthor, this study was so well received because it came at the right time. Research was already coming out on workplace deviance, and this study felt like it fit into the perfect groove of the "next question to be answered." It was in a growing domain of study, and though much had been said about the more "rational" factors influencing deviance, the role of social context had not yet been addressed. It was the first of many future articles looking at the impact of coworkers on employees' harmful behavior.

Too late. As an example of "too old," my dissertation fits well. I decided to examine the research question of why employees respond the ways they do to job dissatisfaction. Although my main interest was in the responses themselves (some of which are dysfunctional behaviors that I later focused on), my dissertation was perceived as being about job satisfaction. The title, the abstract, and the literature my study sought to extend was on job satisfaction. Though my research question was novel, it was viewed by the field as boring because job satisfaction was "so yesterday." It was considered an older and "already done" research area at the time, so neither schools that were hiring nor journal reviewers were excited about my dissertation. I never published it (though I did use some of the data I collected for the study with Anne O'Leary Kelly I've mentioned). I had no idea at the time that it was important to study a topic the field was currently excited about.

How to time well. Timing, for me, was not a conscious process or one I knew how to manage. And surely a good part of good timing for me has been sheer luck. But I improved my timing with experience. Maybe it is a process that is similar to osmosis—by being fully immersed in the field, we develop an intuitive sense of where the field has been and, more important, where it is going. Through this deep immersion, we are more likely to naturally develop interests and research questions that align with what the field will find interesting too.

A fashion analogy might be useful here. If you rarely shop for clothes or follow fashion through magazines, advertisements, and people-watching, quite likely your taste in clothes will be entirely out of synch with what others find attractive. In contrast, if you frequent malls, subscribe to *Vogue*, take an interest in fashion, quite likely your current fashion sense will be more aligned with the world of fashion. This would explain why young authors often do well in this regard, just as do new fashion designers coming out of Central Saint Martins. Because of young authors' deep immersion, by way of their PhD training, studying for comprehensive examinations, and seeking their places, they are often far more attuned to where the field is at and is going than we older folks who may be more wedded to particular areas of study.

Aside from ideal timing, however, I do believe we can nudge the field along as well. One big way to have impact is to *convince* the field that it needs something that otherwise it might not realize it does. As such, the onus is on us as authors to convince readers that what we are studying is interesting and important. We cannot simply say "Here is a novel question" or "Wouldn't it be interesting to see if A causes B?" We must say instead, "Here is a novel question that is interesting and important for the following particular reasons." For example, when I and my coauthors published the first study on territoriality (Brown, Lawrence, & Robinson, 2005), we told the reviewers of *AMR* why the study of territoriality should matter to our field and the kinds of research this study might spawn. The more novel your work, the more this justification is needed. But one study in print can spark interest and encourage others to follow, which adds legitimacy to the area and fosters more ready acceptance of subsequent related studies. I have no doubt that my first study, with Denise Rousseau, on psychological contracts (Robinson & Rousseau, 1994) helped to pave the way for our subsequent ability to publish articles on this topic for many years. Once a few of these articles became known, the field seemed eager for more.

Do Not Take Short Cuts!

I have definitely had good luck and bad luck, but there is no free lunch. I have felt that the process goes a bit like this. We have to invest a lot of time and energy on high-quality work just to qualify for the coin flip that decides how the publication process will go. By coin flip, I mean the factors that are out of our hands, such as who our editors or reviewers happen to be. At least, if I've wanted to have impact as a scholar, I've had to take some risks and do the difficult things. Now maybe others have found effective shortcuts, but I am not qualified to speak to that.

Study the Exciting and Hard, Not the Safe and Easy

I have studied relatively new phenomena, but I am not advocating for others to do that too. In fact, I think it is increasingly difficult to do so. Our field has so many overlapping constructs at this point, and possibly consolidation will be what we need next. Having said this, the same principles apply even if one is not tackling new unstudied topics per se; that is, to have influence, it is imperative to avoid the safe and easy.

My big mistake. I feel strongly about this after learning a hard lesson from failure. My most difficult year as an academic was the one that came after course work ended and before finding what to study for my dissertation. In the face of the uncertainty, the pressure to find that ultimate, all-important dissertation idea, which felt paralyzing, I was miserable. I erroneously believed at the time that my choice of dissertation topic would either make or break my entire career, and would be the only launchpad for what I would do for the next decade or so. While that might be an ideal goal if one can achieve it, as I will demonstrate later with my sample of one, a successful career can emerge even with a weak dissertation.

Although I had discovered an interest in psychological contract violations, I quickly dismissed doing my dissertation on it because I felt it was too risky. There were too many unknowns about it: no one had studied it yet, and I did not know how to measure it. Using my journal of "interesting things" as inspiration, I went through lots of different ideas, but every time I uncovered the difficulties of a particular research question, I abandoned it. It was as though difficulties meant risk, and I could not take any. Ultimately, I opted for an extremely safe research topic that seemed to pose few barriers or problems to overcome: reactions to job dissatisfaction. It was interesting enough to me, but more important, it felt safe and easy. Unfortunately, few found my dissertation interesting. Despite graduating from a great school, I had few job interviews and basically an unpublishable dissertation. I attribute these outcomes to the fact that my dissertation elicited yawns. It would have been far better for me to do an exciting dissertation with more problems than a tidy one that was ho-hum.

But there is more to this story. While working on my safe yet boring dissertation, I also collected some fun data as a side hobby on psychological contract violation. This was easy because I had very little riding on it, and maybe because I felt secure having my safe dissertation on its way. I used our graduate alumni office to follow recent MBA graduates' experiences with their employers over time. I was interested in whether and how much their perceived obligations to their employers at the time they got hired would later be fulfilled or broken by their employers, and the impact that would have. To me it was critical to conduct a longitudinal study if I was ever to accurately assess psychological contract violations, even though that meant that the final article would be far in the future. So I surveyed graduating MBAs when they accepted jobs and then followed up with them several times over the next two years. (They willingly agreed to keep participating, as I was providing them with benchmark salary and promotion data about their peers, which I also collected on the surveys.) And here is the kicker or the moral of the story: unlike my boring dissertation, which did not see the light of day, my risky but exciting "side hobby" data collection on psychological contract violation became a single-authored ASQ study (Robinson, 1996) and has been my most cited study to date with almost 5,000 citations.

If our goal is to have influence, I believe we benefit from going bold. This perhaps means: high risk, high impact. This is of course not the only way to be a successful academic, but it is the best way to be one who is influential.

Ideas on being bold. There is no one action or piece of advice I can share to easily address this. I can, however, share a bit of the thought process that led me astray and how my thought process changed with experience and confidence. The main factor, for me, was learning not to get discouraged by barriers. I made this mistake many times and probably still do. I would start on a research question that seemed very interesting and important, but invariably when I dug deeper, I would encounter what seemed like a big wall or something too challenging, and I would shy away. It felt too hard and looked insurmountable. How could I study psychological contracts if I did not know how they could be measured? In actual fact, as I learned over time, doing good research is *hard*. At least for me it is, and it has stayed hard because the standards of the field keep going up. But if it was easy and risk free, it would have likely been published by someone else already. All the low-hanging fruit on the trees in our field has already been picked, so we all have to climb higher.

Experience has allowed me to appreciate that our research is inherently flawed, and that the point of doing good work is to work through the hurdles the best way we know how at the time. Challenges are inevitable, but they're a sign that we are going down the right path for adding value. Though our solutions to problems will be imperfect today, it will be the job of future scholars to improve on them. To continue with an earlier example, in earlier studies (Robinson & Rousseau, 1994; Robinson & Morrison, 1995; Robinson, 1996) I and my coauthors addressed the problem of how to measure psychological contract breach by initially reverse scoring self-reported fulfillment scores, and later by taking the difference between what employers promised to employees and what they reported they received from their employers. Years later, method gurus Jeff Edwards and colleagues (Lambert, Edwards, & Cable, 2006) provided a much more sophisticated and insightful approach to measuring contract breach, which invariably highlighted the limitations of the approach we had taken. It makes me cringe a bit now to think about what I did back then, but I have to remind myself that I gave it my best shot at the time and the reviewers agreed with me. And what I did was so much better than not tackling the topic at all. Do not avoid a research question because the solutions to obstacles are not obvious or ideal; instead, pursue it with the best solution you can find.

Quality over Quantity

Doing both high-quality studies and a high quantity of them is an obvious ideal, but if one has to choose, I say go for quality over quantity. I have fewer publications than many of my peers, but most of my articles have a high citation count. Some scholars are motivated and talented enough to do both—high quality and high quantity—but given that I had to decide between the two, I gravitated to the former. I am not suggesting that all my work is high quality by any means, but I do not *knowingly* produce poor-quality work or cut corners. I've even sometimes abandoned articles and ideas when I've felt unable to bring them up to a level of quality I can be proud of.

I have not been able to do both high-quality studies and a high quantity of them for a few reasons. First, in the first two decades of my career, I had neither the ability nor the desire to find more work hours in the week, because I was the primary and often sole parent at home. Second, it has always taken me a long time and a ton of concentration to do my best work, and when I've felt pulled between projects it's been difficult for me to focus deeply enough on any one of them, and the quality has suffered. So, given the circumstances and how I've worked best, I've chosen to work on fewer projects.

I strongly believe that it is a point of integrity to do the best quality of work one is capable of. My primary goal has been to move the field forward, not collect lines on my CV. I learned from my mentors that cutting corners and knowingly producing poor-quality research when one is capable of better is not responsible research. The last thing I want to do is add noise rather than value. So, for example, I have sought to avoid practices such as slicing up a data set into many studies, repeating existing studies with slightly different variables, or crafting articles around observed relationships rather than developing them a priori. There are tons of ways to knowingly produce weak research and gather publications if that's your goal, but these are not conducive to your work being useful or helpful to the field moving forward.

This issue is increasingly challenging given the expectations put on faculty to produce high quantities of work and some schools' valuation of numbers over content. As I've said, of course it is ideal to do a lot of high-quality work, but if one cannot do that, then choose fewer high-quality studies over a lot of low-quality studies. And look to work in environments that will support and reward this approach because they share with you the values that justify it.

Related to quality, I was taught to aim for top-tier journals. Although many of my studies end up being published elsewhere, I try to develop each study with a particular high-quality journal in mind. Although the status of journals varies somewhat with time and across institutions and areas of expertise, for me the potential A journals for my work have always included *AMJ, AMR, ASQ, OBHDP, OS, JAP, PP, JOM,* and *ROB.* These outlets maximize my chances for exposure and influence. This has been especially important for my approach to research, which has often involved developing a new line of inquiry or stream of work for which I've needed to establish legitimacy and gain exposure to the maximum number of other scholars.

With a particular journal in mind, I try to design and write up my study in a way that aligns well with the journal. Over the years, I've always found it very helpful to look at exemplars in the journal to see how to approach it and what constitutes good-quality research in the area of my topic. For example, when I wrote up Robinson (1996), my psychological contract study, with *ASQ* as my goal, I recall holing up with five *ASQ* micro-OB articles on my bed. I studied them, underlined them, and made notes in an attempt to crack the code for what they were looking for. I had noticed at the time that the micro-OB articles in *ASQ* tended to pit one theory against another, and this led me to change my article in ways that not only altered its presentation but greatly improved its contribution.

Along with the journals I've mentioned, I want to call out two other great places for publishing. First, as an associate editor of *Academy of Management Discoveries,* I can say that it is a journal that greatly values research focused on phenomena. Second, I want to bring attention to book chapters. Some of my most cited works have been book chapters. The right book with the right editors has been a godsend when I've needed a platform to share my thoughts. Book chapters have given me the latitude and flexibility to say what I want to say, along with providing a community where I could have a voice.

Persevere

Closely related to doing the riskier, harder, high-quality work is developing the ability to persevere. This means moving forward despite negative feedback and failures. I have had a lot of both, so I am happy to put these experiences to use here.

Persistence in the Face of Negativity

I am convinced that a necessary attribute for success as an academic is to be able to persist despite a great deal of negative feedback. Not a lot of occupations centrally involve receiving a lot of negative anonymous feedback from multiple sources over and over again. I have found it worth remembering that even the most influential publications usually started with pages of negative feedback from reviewers. At least mine have. In fact, I'm fairly certain that almost all my publications had at the outset at least one reviewer who was not convinced that my study should get published in the first place.

I am not alone in having vivid memories of negative feedback and feeling the sting of failure. Because I think it can be very valuable to realize how common feelings of failure can be, I will share a few stories of my own. In graduate school, I sent three articles in to two conferences (one of which I later learned accepted almost every submission). I recall sitting on the orange sofa below our mailboxes, opening my decision letters. (This was before email.) By the time I got to the third rejection letter, I'd started to tear up, and for the next while, I seriously thought that maybe I should quit academia. At the time, I thought it should have been much easier to write a conference paper and that, given my obvious lack of talent, maybe I should consider a different career. The truth was, however, I just had much more to learn and improve on. Of course, this painful rejection experience had zero predictive information about my future career. Thankfully I did not quit.

I also blew one of my comprehensive exam questions. In our program, we had two 48-hour exams. One question was in OT, the other in OB. And I think of the five of us writing, I was the only one to fail my OB question! So here is proof that failing your exams is not necessarily indicative of one's future as an academic.

I also felt a sense of failure on the job market. At Northwestern, I was blessed with classmates from whom I learned a great deal and with whom I am still close today. But the downside of these incredible peers was sharing the job market with them! Few schools invite two, let alone three, from the same school, and with five of us on the market together, and my boring dissertation and lack of publications, initially I was not faring so well. It was incredibly discouraging to have almost no job interviews when some of my peers had 10 or more. I did ultimately get a fabulous job at the eleventh hour, in late March, after a tumultuous experience. I was called for an interview and then it was canceled, and then they changed their mind again. During my job talk, as the questions flew and I fumbled, I thought silently to myself (as I continued to speak): "Just hang in there, you can always go back on the market next year, just don't start crying . . . just finish your talk." And then, to my great surprise, the department chair made me an offer before my visit was over. Thankfully a senior colleague told me something true: "Don't worry, institutions have short memories." New York University took a chance on me, and it turned out to be an extremely supportive and wonderful place to start my career, as I was able to publish a lot during my time with them.

I felt negative forces pushing against my goals also when I decided to embark on a study of workplace deviance. I was told it would be too difficult to study because these were rare behaviors that no one would admit to. And some even suggested that only cynical or unethical people would study such a topic. It turns out that negative workplace behavior is common and people are more than willing to anonymously admit to their own or their coworkers' counternormative behaviors. And I would argue today that those of us who are drawn to study negative behavior find it intriguing and perplexing because it is alien to us.

Setbacks get easier with tenure because less is at stake, and with experience because we know we get over our setbacks. But I think the sting of rejection can still impact even the most seasoned academic. I have found a few things that have helped me. One is having a coauthor or set of coauthors to share the experience with. I have also found it helpful to wait for the negative feelings to subside somewhat before tackling the feedback itself. I think that doing so improves my ability to understand and learn from the feedback, as well as to formulate what should happen to the study next. I know some scholars send articles off again to journals without incorporating feedback from revisions, but I think this is a mistake. There is a lot to gain from improving your article with the aim of success at another journal by heeding the general insights the first reviews gave you. Finally, I am a big fan of perspective. A bad work day or disappointing outcome is a reminder to focus on my relationships, my students, my hobbies, or that which I am good at, value, or identify with. In the big scheme of things, it's a job with many facets beyond research; and my intelligence, worth as a human, or contribution to the world are not dependent on nor changing on the basis of what, I can assure myself, "some random anonymous (and obviously unqualified!) reviewers think of one of my studies." Moreover, this particular outcome does not predict my lifelong happiness or success.

These stories highlight one of the very best pieces of advice I ever received, which was from Frances Milliken, when she was my colleague at New York University. I was telling her about some set of things going wrong, and she said something to the effect of "our careers and productivity are not linear." What she explained to me was that what looks like defeat or failure *now* has no predictive validity about one's trajectory and future success. This is absolutely true! Especially when we are young scholars. All of us have low points or losing streaks, but they are just temporary blips along our career paths. We have to go with the ebbs and flows; just because some days, weeks, or semesters can feel like a low point doesn't mean we will stay down there. Accept the bad news, and disappointments, but do not engage in forecasting with them. Learn from mistakes, but keep putting one foot in front of the other.

Rocking the Revisions

A key activity that needs perseverance is doing revisions. Since I started my career and even today, I still at some level hold this crazy belief in the back of my mind that my article is done when I submit it to a journal. Of course, that belief is very far from reality. The reality is that I often put more work into my revisions than the initial submission.

No revision is too hard to try, and few review processes from start to finish have been fast and easy for me. And sometimes the revision process is a strange journey. One article got to fourth revision and then was rejected. (The journal's name will go unmentioned here.) Another article, I believe it was Morrison & Robinson (1997), had five reviewers and a very involved editor offering her own feedback, and we went through three revisions over a very long period of time before it was accepted. I have also experienced reviewers being replaced partway through the process. One article was rejected by an editor who later called me, out of the blue, to ask if I agreed with the rejection. On another occasion, an editor rejected an article and then called later to discuss it with me. He had changed his mind and was accepting it for a special issue.

No matter the negativity, the daunting feedback, or the high goals the reviewers set, I believe it is easier to work with the editor and reviewers I know than to start over again. For this reason, I invest a huge amount of time and attention in my revisions. And so my revisions often required more data collection. Indeed, the editor of a current revise and resubmit on my desk wrote: "you will have to develop a new theory, collect more data, and conduct another content analysis of your new data, but I believe your paper has promise." But I will go to the Arctic and back if it means another kick at the can with the same review team. My response document is always as detailed, precise, and logical as I can make it. I also attempt to make it as easy as possible for the reviewers (1) to know that I greatly respect the feedback they have given me—by putting it to good use in my improvements—and (2) to understand all the changes I've made and why.

Almost every point the reviewers raise can be used to improve your article. Even when I believe a reviewer's comment is entirely wrong, I can find a way to change the article in response. My rule is to always give the reviewer something in return, because even when a reviewer may be inaccurate on a specific point, it's on me as an author to make sure the issue in question is clear to readers in all subsequent versions.

Find Your People

My last set of principles focuses on the support of other people. I know I have not gone through my career alone. My success as an academic has been dependent on my own motivation and talent, but as much credit goes to those who I have learned from, worked with, and been supported by, as well as those I've been able to support. Two key areas worth noting here are the importance of finding a supportive community of scholars and of finding good coauthors.

Find Community

If you are immersed in your field and in synch with it, you will very likely find out that you are not the only one excited about the same research questions or areas of study. The same forces that drew us in are also drawing in others, invisibly. It reminds me of what happened when I named my daughter, and what happens to many new parents. I thought I had found a relatively original name for my daughter, but when she got to preschool there were three such children with variations on the same name. And in my research, I have faced this exact same experience many times. When Rebecca Bennett and I decided to study workplace deviance it felt very original, as the field had mostly been focused on positive topics, and we felt the area of "negative behavior" had been overlooked. Yet shortly after we published our conceptual model in *AMJ* in 1995 (Robinson & Bennett, 1995), Vardi and Wiener (1996) developed a conceptual model of organizational misbehavior that came out in *OS*. And after we published our measure of workplace deviance in *JAP* in 2000 (Bennett & Robinson, 2000), Fox, Spector, and Miles (2001) introduced their very similar counterproductive work behavior measure in the *Journal of Vocational Behavior*. This is always a good sign because it suggests we are onto something that matters in the field. And when others share your interests, even under somewhat different names or from somewhat different perspectives, it means that you have a community to belong to that is critically important. When we join or build a community of scholars focused on similar interests, there is synergy to be had. Those with the same research interest can give us feedback, coauthor with us, join us in conferences and symposia, and be useful reviewers too.

How to find community. I am not a networking kind of person. I have much preferred to develop a new friendship from randomly being seated next to someone at a dinner or during the course of serving on a committee together, rather than through shaking hands at Academy of Management Meeting (AOM) social hours. When it comes to meeting those who share my research interests, I have found it much more useful to connect at presentations. When I have developed an interest in a new area, I have also found it helpful to create a community by organizing a caucus at AOM and seeing who comes to the table or, better yet, organizing a symposium on the topic and asking colleagues to suggest contributors. Nowadays I still reach out to scholars who I believe share my interests. When I started studying workplace ostracism a few years ago, for example, I contacted Kipling Williams because he had written so much on the subject in psychology. I am certain that he did not know anything about me, but he was very kind and helpful in providing excellent advice to me, and our connection led to several book chapter invitations, several symposia collaborations, and joining a miniconference in Switzerland on social exclusion.

Find Good Coauthors

Good coauthors are another ingredient that has been central to my achievements as a scholar. They have shared my workload, allowing me to be much more productive. More important, they have also complemented my weak spots and taught me a great deal. And the greatest benefit of having good coauthors has been making the process fun and social. For me, the best coauthors have been those whose company I enjoy and who share my research values and work ethic but who are also differently talented and/or interested in working on different aspects of a project.

Sources of coauthors. My coauthors have come from all kinds of places and often through serendipity. It is one reason we should be out and about in the world, making random connections to others with similar interests. I've met some of my coauthors through a common network, as when Rob Folger asked me to join a project involving a really cool data set from the US Postal Service, which led to a publication on workplace aggression (Dietz, Robinson, Folger, Baron, & Schulz, 2003). Other collaborations came about at presentations and conferences. My study with Anne O'Leary Kelly (Robinson & O'Leary-Kelly, 1998) came about after I approached her to say that I had data from my dissertation that we might repurpose to test the theory she had just presented at an AOM session. Similarly, Jennifer Berdahl saw me present at her school, and suggested that we join forces because she had ostracism data that could twin my own. This connection turned into our study comparing the effects of workplace ostracism to those of harassment (O'Reilly et al., 2014). Some of my coauthors were people I worked with before I came to know them personally and who later became friends, such as Joerg Dietz and Jacqui Coyle-Shapiro. Some fantastic and repeat coauthors were my friends first, in graduate school, such as Rebecca Bennett and Elizabeth Morrison.

Earlier in my career I coauthored more with senior faculty and peers, but over time more of my coauthors have been my wonderful graduate students. The best part of my career has been mentoring them, getting to publish with them, and enjoying their development. They have not only provided me with fulfillment but also helped me become a better scholar. For example, my former student Graham Brown introduced me to the construct and literature on territoriality from environmental psychology, and my last graduating student, Kira Schabram, was and still is my go-to person for all things methodological. I also have to give credit to my former graduate students for helping me to write this chapter, as it contains many of the stories and experiences I have shared with them over the years.

Conclusion

So this is my academic journey, or at least a sampling of some of its highlights, along with advice, that will hopefully be useful to others on the same path. It is only one journey, told with a lot of retrospective and likely biased sense-making. Nevertheless, with a whole lot of other authors in this book also providing their sense-making accounts of their careers, I am certain some common themes will emerge.

The theme of my journey has been this: to be an influential scholar is to move the field forward. This means focusing primarily on adding to our base of knowledge with high-quality, challenging research rather than only collecting a lot of lower-quality, easy publications. As scholars, one way to be influential on our field is to stay true to our interests while identifying novel, important, and timely research questions that we then answer with a lot of effort, investment, and perseverance. And this whole endeavor is ideally done with the joy and support of others.

Acknowledgments

I would like to thank my colleagues Michael Daniels and Sima Sajjadiani, my former student Kira Schabram, and my current student Rui Zhu for feedback and insights on an earlier draft of this article.

References

Bennett, R., & Robinson, S. L. (2000). The development of a measure of workplace deviance. *Journal of Applied Psychology, 85*(3), 349–360.

Brown, G., Lawrence, T., & Robinson, S. L. (2005). Territoriality in organizations. *Academy of Management Review, 30,* 577–594.

Dietz, J., Robinson, S. L., Folger, R., Baron, R, & Schulz, M. (2003). The impact of community violence and an organization's procedural justice climate on workplace aggression. *Academy of Management Journal, 46*(3), 317–326.

Fox, S., Spector, P. E., & Miles, D. (2001). Counterproductive work behavior (CWB) in response to job stressors and organizational justice: Some mediator and moderator tests for autonomy and emotions. *Journal of Vocational Behavior, 59*(3), 291–309.

Lambert, L., Edwards, J., & Cable, D. (2006). Breach and fulfillment of the psychological contract: A comparison of traditional and expanded views. *Personnel Psychology, 56,* 895–934.

Morrison, E., & Robinson, S. L. (1997). When employees feel betrayed: A model of how psychological contract violation develops. *Academy of Management Review, 22,* 226–256.

O'Reilly, J., Robinson, S. L., Banki, S., & Berdahl, J. (2014). Is negative attention better than no attention? The comparative effects of ostracism and harassment at work. *Organizational Science, 26*(3), 774–793.

Robinson, S. L. (1996). Trust and breach of the psychological contract. *Administrative Science Quarterly, 41,* 574–599.

Robinson, S. L., & Bennett, R. (1995). A typology of deviant workforce behaviors: A multidimensional scaling study. *Academy of Management Journal, 38,* 555–572.

Robinson, S. L., Kraatz, M., & Rousseau, D. (1994). Changing obligations and the psychological contract: A longitudinal study. *Academy of Management Journal, 37,* 137–152.

Robinson, S. L., & Morrison, E. (1995). Psychological contracts and OCB: The effects of unfulfilled obligations. *Journal of Organizational Behavior, 16,* 289–298.

Robinson, S. L., & O'Leary-Kelly, A. (1998). Monkey see, monkey do: The influence of work groups on the antisocial behavior of employees. *Academy of Management Journal, 41,* 658–672.

Robinson, S. L., & Rousseau, D. (1994). Violating the psychological contract: Not the exception but the norm. *Journal of Organizational Behavior, 15,* 245–259.

Vardi, Y., & Wiener, Y. (1996). Misbehavior in Organizations: A motivation framework. *Organization Science, 7,* 151–165.

12
Messages to My Younger Self

Anita M. McGahan

Introduction

There's an old adage that runs along the following lines. Once you are asked how you achieved success, you should retire. You are done. So it is with trepidation and relief that I write here what has occurred over the course of my career that led me to the place that I am today. The truth is that I failed as often as I succeeded. The things for which I am known are not the things for which I aspired to be known. My failures are mainly traceable to mistakes that I should have known even at the time not to make. My successes all arose from a mix of luck, persistence, and the generosity of many people, including especially my collaborators, students, family, and mentors. I happened to have been born at a moment in history and on a continent and to parents all from which I benefited as an educator and a scholar. I have been extremely fortunate.

My research today is on private entrepreneurship in the public interest. This topic is fundamentally about the effective governance of organizations to address the world's most pressing problems. I see organizations as tools for getting things done, and the most important problems of our time—such as climate change, global health, immigration, and poverty alleviation—as public issues at their core. By "private," I mean nongovernmental enterprises, including corporations of all types and nongovernmental agencies. The reason that I focus on private organizations is because I believe that scaled, timely solutions to big problems must engage the private interests of large numbers of people working together. To do this, private organizations have to work within frameworks established by governments, and often in partnerships with public-sector agencies. By "entrepreneurship," I mean innovative, nontraditional approaches to solutions. This is important because the institutional structures that dominate organizational life today are systematically exacerbating most big problems, such as unsustainable climate impact and persistent inequality. By "public interest," I mean the subset of shared interests in communities of people that can only be pursued collectively.

Anita M. McGahan, *Messages to My Younger Self* In: *A Journey toward Influential Scholarship*. Edited by: Xiao-Ping Chen and H. Kevin Steensma, Oxford University Press. © Oxford University Press 2021. DOI: 10.1093/oso/9780190070717.003.0012

I hope that previous paragraph wasn't boring. The reason that I worry that it was is because, fundamentally, I find the theoretical, construct-oriented rhetoric of our field largely incoherent and unpersuasive. I am sorry about this, and believe that at least 50% of the problem is my own deficiency. This makes what I write as theory often uninspired (hence my apology). What truly motivates me—and gives life to what I study and, hopefully, what I write—are humanistic, humane approaches to social problems such as the grand challenges I have mentioned. This means that I am an empiricist who seeks to raise questions for theory and public policy based on what is happening in important domains of public interest, such as healthcare, firefighting, prisons, policing, military, and immigration.

I am also a structuralist in the sense that I believe that if someone in a role or job or position takes action that is aligned with that person's understanding of the organization's purpose, but something goes wrong, then the structure of the organization needs to change. In other words, I believe that people mainly try to do what they think they are supposed to do, and that perverse organizational outcomes are doomed to recur if structural problems are not addressed. I also seek to be integrated across domains of my life, which means that I do not have boundaries between my professional and private beliefs. I try to write only what I believe is true although I am also aware that, like anyone, a large part of what I write will not be entirely correct or robust because of deficiencies in understanding, data, methods, theory, research design, and analysis. As one of my professors once said: "half of what I say is wrong, and if I knew which half, I wouldn't say it." But at least the flaws in my work do not arise from known gaps between what I discern as a researcher and what I think is true. I push myself in a structured way to identify what I once thought was true but have now learned is untrue. Through this process, I try to make sure that my private beliefs are as aligned as possible with what I have learned.

I believe that what I am mainly known for in the field is my call to action for research on grand challenges (Amis, Munir, Lawrence, Hirsch, & McGahan, 2018; Devinney, McGahan, & Zollo, 2013; George, McGahan, & Prabhu, 2012; Mahoney & McGahan, 2007; McGahan, 2007, 2018, 2019a, 2020; McGahan & Keusch, 2010; McGahan, Zelner, & Barney, 2013; Yang, McGahan, & Farmer, 2010). My early contributions on industry structure and industry change (McGahan, 2000, 2004a, 2004b; McGahan & Porter, 1997, 2003; McGahan & Silverman, 2001). which reflected my beliefs about the primacy of structural problems, have primarily had impact through the case studies I wrote (McGahan, 1992, 1994a, 1994b; McGahan & Coxe, 1996; McGahan, Coxe, Keller, & McGuire, 1997; McGahan & Keller, 1995; McGahan, McGuire, & Kou, 1996; McGahan & Verter, 1997) and courses I designed when I was at

Harvard Business School (HBS) and Boston University early in my career. What I published during this period also has had some impact, especially my papers coauthored with Professor Michael E. Porter, but primarily because they showed what most people in our field already sensed was true. I agree with my friend Professor Kathy Eisenhardt who once told me that I became a lot more interesting after I left HBS. (She meant it kindly and supportively, and she was right.) This is because once I was awarded tenure, I took a hard intellectual turn toward working on the structural problems in the private sector that were complicit in grand challenges, and I started working on them by broadening my activities to include much more fieldwork, especially in healthcare. After arriving at the University of Toronto in 2007, my research on grand challenges became more systematic, organized, and—surprisingly to me, anyway—theoretical (Cabral, Mahoney, McGahan & Potoski, 2019; Dutt, Hawn, Vidal, Chatterji, McGahan, & Mitchell, 2016; Klein, Mahoney, McGahan, & Pitelis, 2010, 2012, 2013, 2019; Mahoney & McGahan, 2007; Mahoney, McGahan, & Pitelis, 2009; McGahan, 2007, 2019b; Rezaie, McGahan, Daar, & Singer, 2012; Vakili & McGahan, 2016). Much of my intellectual growth since I joined the University of Toronto has arisen from collaborations with scholars across the university and elsewhere, for which I am intensely grateful. One thing I'm sure of is that I would be nowhere without my academic friends.

The rest of this essay is some messages that I wish I could go back in time to offer to my younger self.

Keep a Journal, and Pursue Continuity of Ideas

Please keep track of your ideas, especially those that are not contemporaneously integrated into research projects. This is because what is interesting tends to stay interesting, and it is useful to have ideas written down for reference in moments of confusion, discouragement, and lost inspiration. The continuity in my interests swamps the discontinuity. For example, the kernels of my late-career interests are evident in my early choices of undergraduate concentrations in humanities, political science, and mathematics. I've gotten off track when I've deviated from ideas that engaged me.

Turning back to your interests as an undergraduate for insights into your core passions is worthwhile for yet another reason: as undergraduates, most of us want to change the world. The beliefs that inspire you tend to shape your choices. My experience is that you will have the greatest impact if you work on issues that are important to you. Often the genesis of your ideas about what you want to do is evident in your early commitments. (I should note that some scholars are not able to follow their interests as undergraduates for many reasons, such as lack of resources, social and familial constraints, and lack of opportunity. The broad point here is to look into your past for inspiration.)

I also suggest that you keep a journal of your ideas, both so that you can clear your head of distractions without worry that you will lose track of what you find interesting and so that you find threads over time that unify the conceptual framework that you bring to your research and teaching. I think of myself as painting a broad picture of ideas about the remediation of global health inequality, for example. Each research project is only a small piece of the picture—like a puzzle piece. This is because, to publish in our journals, a study must delve deeply into a specific topic. All of my projects, as well as those of others in my subfield, constitute pieces that together accumulate into a broader picture of how public and business policies work. Ultimately, I am interested in improving these policies to improve human health and, generally, fairness, especially for the poor. A journal helps keep track of the pieces as well as the big picture.

Work on What You Think Is Important, and Always in Consultation with Practitioners

I am quite fortunate in that I worked at Morgan Stanley and McKinsey for several years early in my career—both before and after I was an MBA candidate at HBS. I saw how talented people competed for opportunities and resources often by currying favor in various ways with decision makers, and then building the capabilities to deliver after they beat the competition. Upon arriving at HBS for the MBA program back in the mid-1980s, I realized that (1) economic theories of free-market capitalism that emphasized the efficient allocation of resources were not fully aligned with what happens in investment banking and corporate finance, and (2) talented, trained people in finance met at places like HBS, developed strong relationships, and then relied on these relationships to accomplish things that were important. In other words, the theory was seriously incomplete regarding what really happens in finance. This led me into some difficulty from time to time, especially when, as a doctoral student, I was asked why market inefficiencies arose, but I soon learned that there was opportunity to develop theory grounded not on inaccurate foundational principles but on solid phenomenological and empirical realities.

Because theory is often incomplete and/or grounded in principles that are either imperfectly understood or wrong, it can lead you in directions that are not aligned with reality. As a result, talking with practitioners saves you a great deal of time and can lead you to important insights. This is especially important when studying grand challenges, such as climate change, survival-driven immigration, and the escalating costs of healthcare. The reason is that established systems justified by outdated but established theory, such as neoclassical economic logic, are complicit in creating the grand challenges. Practitioners expose these paradoxes because they do their work within them. They know that some of the most entrenched theories in our field justify a system that gives rise to grand challenges. In other words, they understand that the theory is fundamentally inadequate for revealing essential truths about how to remediate those challenges. Here's an example. Neoclassical economic theory suggests that private ownership of prisons is a comparative-governance problem that can be understood as an efficiency issue. Because this theory does not consider the prejudicial, behavioral, social-psychological, or historical underpinnings of imprisonment, it does not sufficiently explain how the privatization of prisons can lead to the brutalization of prisoners. It also does not consider comprehensively the purposes of imprisonment. Thus, it is insufficient for understanding why and how private prisons operate. For me, the best way to understand such a phenomenon is to talk with practitioners involved in each of these processes. This approach also has the benefit of accelerating revision of the theory.

I have learned that many scholars do not talk with practitioners because they feel that it will be time-consuming and distracting. The elegance and simplicity and parsimony of theoretical modeling is more attractive to them. Many theorists also feel that theory is harder than empirical work and thus shun talking with practitioners because they feel it is not relevant to their purpose. My experience is that theoretical work is indeed difficult, but not because modeling is difficult; rather, because theory is often a house of cards built on a fragile foundation that cannot withstand scrutiny. Remediating this problem is daunting because so much is at stake for so many people, including other theorists, who have accumulated various insights and approaches that rest on the fragile foundation. For me, talking with practitioners saves a lot of time, because it leads directly to insights about the elements of established theory that are problematic, as well as to the elements that may be useful. Practitioners also point to problems that theory does not address at all. Perhaps most important, practitioners also generally express clearly how the entire apparatus of various systems built on received theories is complicit in generating the grand challenges that may put the systems at risk of failing. As a result, talking with practitioners leads to insights about what is important. Always do it.

Learn the Methods That Are Relevant, and Accept That They Are Imperfect

The methods that are relevant are, a priori, almost always imperfect just by virtue of their relevance. This is because anything that is novel, and therefore interesting and research-worthy, has idiosyncrasies that make it difficult to understand using conventional methods. In the first place, quantitatively analyzable data are not well developed for truly novel phenomena because the time series on them is not established, and the phenomena therefore cannot be well instrumented. This is why qualitative methods are so useful and important in such situations. Of course, qualitative analysis of various types also commonly raises many questions, many of which can only be addressed through complementary techniques, including quantitative analysis. Multiple methods are therefore often most effective in situations of true novelty, especially when the issues are grand challenges. This requires flexibility and a willingness to learn new approaches. Great phenomenologists, I have learned, are not wedded to specific methods.

I also have learned that the puzzle-piece-picture problem makes the writing of books an important vehicle for addressing grand challenges. There are many different models for writing books, and various types of publishers. Your goals as a scholar for reaching a practitioner audience may not emerge until you become senior. Yet books can also be an important vehicle for reaching an academic audience. Edited books are an important opportunity to pull together the unencumbered perspectives of others writing on a topic in a way that supports cumulative insights about an important phenomenon. For me, what makes academic books on grand challenges interesting is the drawing together of insights from different pieces of scholarly research into a picture that is compelling, important, and informative.

Be Resilient and Persistent with the Journals

You have to work awfully hard to succeed in this profession. This is true no matter what you are doing. You are an entrepreneur trying to build a franchise of ideas, educational achievements, and impact on other scholars and in practice. There is a lot of hazing, especially among reviewers, and senior scholars may genuinely experience your ideas and approaches as concerning if you demonstrate that widely held beliefs are not robust. It is not easy to be proven wrong, and it also not easy to prove someone else wrong. These facets of our profession create extraordinary stress and pressure, especially for junior scholars.

You must love the work enough to persist through these challenges. It is important to know why you are doing what you are doing. Be motivated by a desire to have an impact on something that you feel is important. Try to be motivated primarily by the importance of the phenomenon you are studying. Try to learn from failure, especially in the journals.

I was fortunate when I was young to receive the advice that the framing of a study is as important as the analysis. I still believe this is true. Most academics—including editors and reviewers—are unable to sustain interest in a study that does not know its purpose and explain its contribution up front. You cannot spend too much time on the abstract and the introduction.

Try to persist in submitting to the journals. Keep revising and going back. Work on the thing that is closest to publication, and try to keep your work under review at a journal for at least as much prepublication time as it is on your desk.

Be Coachable, But Not Too Coachable

Every doctoral symposium that I've ever been to includes a session on mentoring. We teach our students to seek mentors and to network. This is important, but I don't think it's enough. It's also important to learn how to be coachable, but not too coachable.

Early in my career, I benefited greatly from the great mentorship not only of my parents but also of Professor Jane J. Mansbridge, then of Northwestern University and now at Harvard, and of Professor Richard E. Caves at Harvard University. Professor Mansbridge was my undergraduate thesis advisor, and Professor Caves was my graduate thesis advisor. They both encouraged, taught, and supported me. They also helped me to make good decisions and to avoid black holes both intellectually and academically. In other words, they coached me, but mainly to prevent me from making rookie mistakes. They did not direct me away from my core interests. I trusted them, and they were trustworthy. As a result, I took much of their advice even when I didn't like it. (As I think back, I believe that I had this skill drilled into me by parents, who were also great teachers.) There is no question in my mind that I can trace whatever success that I have achieved in this profession directly to choices that I made under the supervision of Professors Mansbridge and Caves, and to their care and tutelage.

It's critical to be coachable in this profession.

Once I graduated and became an assistant professor, I tried too hard to do what I thought was necessary to get tenure. I wrote lots of HBS case studies, some of which I enjoyed and some of which I did dutifully. I took on collaborations with a few senior faculty who cared about me but were not as engaged by my interests as I was by theirs. I did too much diffuse, unorganized service to HBS and Harvard University that did not accumulate to real impact. I also relied too much on the advice of a dean who was not aligned with the senior faculty. In other words, I acted as though I was in a conventional job in which career progress would progress in a structured, linear way. I was too coachable.

What does it mean not to be too coachable? Some of the adverse and troubling experiences I have had over my career arose because I set aside my responsibilities as a scholar to follow paths that well-meaning colleagues suggested for me but turned out to be distractions and dead ends. It's not their fault, of course. There was no failure of intentions by anyone on these paths. It's just that some of the suggestions you get are not truly mentorship or coaching but are problem-solving by senior people who view you as a resource that can be deployed to accomplish something required for the institution.

So here's my hard-won advice. Please think hard about how, why, and what you are being advised to do. Please make sure that you don't follow anyone's advice automatically. Try to figure out what you are being coached *not* to do. Seek depth and coherence in your commitments, including to the people on whom you rely for mentorship, and give back as much as you can to people you care about, and who care about you.

Worry Less about Career Success

My college roommate is now also a professor, although in a different field from management. When we get together, we regularly reflect that, if we had known as undergraduates that our lives would have turned out this way, we would have been so much happier then, but not for reasons that we then thought were important.

Every promotion I have been awarded—every honor—has been gratifying yet pales in comparison to the satisfaction that arises from a student's success, or from the response by a practitioner to something I've written or said, or from the implementation of a public policy that reflects something I've been involved with.

Promotion and recognition are duties. I will never forget the amount of committee work I was assigned in the days subsequent to my promotion to the rank of full professor (which is why I often advise tenured associate professors to stick with their rank for as long as possible). Now please don't get me wrong: committee work is important. But the amount of energy and worry in our field associated with career success is greatly out of proportion to the lived experience of seniority. The truth is that we are all—right from the newest student through the most senior emeritus professor—enormously privileged to be in this profession. The challenge is to enjoy it. My advice would be to focus less on the specific decision of tenure and more on having a backup plan that is attractive enough to make you as indifferent as possible to the tenure outcome. You can do this by engaging with practitioners, and by working on something you feel is important regardless of whether it is academically impactful in the short run.

What I also have noticed is that real commitment to the generation of important ideas, coupled with treating colleagues decently, tends to lead you to longevity in the profession over time, regardless of inevitable career setbacks. Many of the world's greatest scholars had difficulty in academic career progress (Albert Einstein, Carl Sagan, Martha Nussbaum, and Robert Axelrod, to name a few). In the field of management, many scholars switch schools, and some leave academics. (More and more frequently, I notice that tenured faculty are leaving because they do not like either the work or the job.)

Please do not allow an entire decade of your life to be defined by a bid to achieve tenure, when the decision regarding whether to award it to you may have as much to do with unforeseeable idiosyncrasies at the institution on the day your case is considered as with what you have accomplished. It's not worth it.

Go to Conferences and Review for the Journals

Going to conferences is time-consuming and can be daunting and arduous. Yet you can learn an enormous amount, make great friendships, and get priceless feedback on your work. Your standing in the field depends on awareness among other scholars of you, your ideas, the tenor of your engagement, and your generosity in providing feedback to others. There is no more efficient or effective way to establish yourself than by going to conferences.

At first, it takes some persistence to meet people and become involved. The best way is to attend doctoral and junior faculty symposia, to submit your research for consideration on the program, and to participate in predevelopment workshops and paper sessions. I also suggest that you pick one or two divisions or interest groups that are most related to your interests, and then spend most of your time in sessions related to those interests. Go to these groups' business meetings and learn what volunteer opportunities are available. After a few years, start volunteering. Try not to do too much, but do something: reviewing, chairing sessions, acting as discussant, and helping with logistics are all good options. Try to meet people and be friendly.

I also think it's worthwhile to get involved in divisional leadership and to run conferences if you believe that the field would benefit from focusing effort in a domain you feel is important. In 2010, I did a TEDx talk in which I claimed that management education was complicit in the grand challenges around us, such as climate change and global health inequity. I thought I was going to get slammed by my colleagues. Instead I got elected into Academy leadership, which I took as a signal that others were also worried about our complicity in the world's most pressing problems.

Reviewing for the journals is a balancing act. Do too much, and you don't have time for your research. Don't do enough, and you do not learn about research in your domain. Perhaps most important, by reviewing, you have an opportunity to contribute to a synthetic and coherent conversation among scholars on issues of importance. You can shape trajectories of research as a reviewer. It's important to participate if you want to achieve impact in our field.

Be a Great Collaborator and Friend, but Put the Oxygen Mask on Yourself before Helping Others

What does it mean to be a great collaborator and friend? There are some basics, such as letting others who depend on you know if you are going to miss a deadline, and doing what you say you are going to do. Most of my regrettable mistakes in the field of management as a collaborator and friend have arisen from underestimating the importance of my commitments to others.

The more difficult thing for me has been to be a great collaborator and friend in the sense of not succumbing to the interests and pressures that infiltrate a research collaboration to make it untenable. For example, I was once involved in a research project about which a senior colleague was genuinely excited. His excitement was infectious. I trusted him and his ideas. I wanted to collaborate with him. But as the project progressed, I felt that the research design was flawed, in the sense that we would not be able to deliver insight on the research question. To make matters more difficult, I also struggled to understand behavior of this senior colleague outside our collaboration, particularly as it related to some of his professional decisions regarding the promotion of junior colleagues. I tried to get through it. I pushed myself. I tried to talk with him about what worried me. I spent years working on the project but could not get past these concerns. We were unable to achieve a publication from what was a wholehearted effort on both sides. The way the project unfolded—and the impact it had on our friendship—is one of my great regrets.

What went wrong, fundamentally, was that I did not do a good enough job of explaining exactly what was bothering me about the research design. As we poured more and more effort into the project, it became harder and harder to deal with the foundational challenges. This kind of problem is especially prevalent in grand challenges research where theory is fragile, identification is difficult, and confounding implications are the norm. Usually the stakes are also high because the phenomenon is important. I think I failed as a friend, primarily because I could not get straight in my head how to work with someone whose unrelated behavior was so concerning to me. I could not find the boundary. I should have worked on this harder, communicated better, and found energy in those things that had caused me to commit to the collaboration initially.

In the announcements that are routinely made at the inception of airplane flights, you are told to put the oxygen mask on yourself before assisting others. In the situation of this research project, I failed to do this, and thus the collaboration and even the friendship failed. Putting on my oxygen mask would have required doing a better job of understanding how the project fit into my overall program of activities. I did not think hard enough about the structural problems in the project. I also did not think hard enough about my collaborator's decisions regarding promotions. Had I done those things, I would have been able to work out a path forward deliberately and carefully instead of pushing myself to make something work when I did not believe in it anymore.

Develop a Service Strategy for Consolidating Your Contributions to Achieve Impact

Grand challenges are overwhelming. In writing a series of recent studies on immigration, I have learned about truly unconscionable circumstances at the southern border of the United States that are so concerning that I find it difficult to sleep at night. I know of a judge who has sentenced people to imprisonment in a privately owned prison that had illegally paid the judge for the business. My work in global health has taken me to places where death by starvation and unimaginable cruelties are daily occurrences.

The emotional toll of the work itself is compounded in our profession by several structural challenges, including the problems of theory, competition, hazing, and rejection that I have briefly discussed in this essay. It is essential to find a way to stay balanced and resilient. Everyone does this in their own way, of course. Maintaining strong personal relationships and owning an identity separate from the field are critical.

I have also learned that it is very difficult to participate responsibly in committee work at a university after having lost sleep over the issues that I've listed in the last two paragraphs. It's hard to care about administrative concerns especially when the institution doesn't provide you with job security.

Please allow me to offer my resolution on this front in the hope that it might be helpful: I try to contribute to the university in ways that are aligned with my research interests. Specifically, I do a lot of volunteer teaching around the university, including for faculties to which I was not initially appointed, such as global affairs, medicine, and public health. (I'm now appointed onto these faculties, largely as a result of this volunteer teaching.) I tutor students from all corners of the university who are working on issues that are related to mine. I also serve on university committees that are related, for example on a committee that shapes collaborations with other scholarly institutions in Africa.

The irony is that it's important to contribute in some way when you are junior to demonstrate your commitment and capability. When you are senior, it is important to contribute because the institution depends on it. I try to resolve this irony by achieving some degree of alignment between how I contribute to the university and what I am interested in phenomenologically. In general, I would suggest picking a specific area of focus for service activities, and then apologizing politely when asked to do service that is outside that area of focus. Of course, the other side of that deal is to say yes to things that are aligned.

A Few Final Reflections

This essay has been written as advice to my younger self. I have sought to reach back through time to say things that I wish I had known back when I started. I hope that these ideas will be useful in some way to you.

As I conclude, please allow me to offer a few thoughts about responsible research in our century. These thoughts are motivated by truths with which I am currently grappling, and again I hope that you find them useful in some way.

The first is that I believe that you are doing responsible research as long as you are not acting instrumentally to conduct research and publish findings primarily for perverse personal gain of some kind. As long as you are motivated to seek the truth, and as long as you embody academic values of integrity and purpose, then your research is responsible as far as I'm concerned. Just because I think our theory is too fragile for me to build on its foundations does not mean that you cannot do that. One of the most important of academic values is pluralism. What works for you may not work for me. The fact that you may be different from me in your approaches and ideas does not mean that you are irresponsible. Go for it.

The second thing is that it is undeniably clear to me that there is unconscionable inequality in suffering in the world around us, and that these unacceptable conditions that plague so many living beings on this planet are due at least in part to the systems that have been cultivated over the last century in business schools. I know that, in every generation, and in every country, and in almost every decade over the past century, leaders have said that their societies were at turning points. The thing is that I agree with all of them who have said this: for the past hundred years, we have been at one huge turning point. Industrialization and digitization and globalization have yielded unbelievable prosperity in many corners of the globe. At the same time, they have also yielded the grand challenges that are at the center of my work as well as that of many of the other scholars writing for this book and in the field more broadly. In human terms, the suffering that these systems has cultivated is not tolerable, sustainable, or even bearable.

Third, the climate crisis is upon us, and there has been no successful implementation of management and organizational principles at any level of governmental, corporate, or nongovernmental life to address these at a scale commensurate with the problem. The world desperately needs governance innovation and leadership to address this challenge. This problem is our problem as management scholars.

Fourth, we are attracting more talented young people into our classrooms than ever. In North America, for example, about 20% of undergraduates study business, and about 25% of graduate students are in management programs of various types. Yet in many schools, the curriculum does not reflect the most important problems these students will face over the course of their lives: climate, environmental pollution, healthcare costs, immigration, health inequality, job loss, job insecurity, and the sociopsychological dislocation that accompanies these problems. We're not doing enough to teach our students what we know about these issues so that they can stand on our shoulders rather than replicate our mistakes.

Fifth, the promise of technological improvements such as digitization, including artificial intelligence, 5G, and advanced analytics, is extraordinary and well worth pursuing. Better communication, infrastructure, distribution systems, and mutual understanding are critical elements of solutions to the world's most pressing problems. At the same time, digitization of these types creates basic trade-offs that may threaten prosperity if they are not managed and organized in ways that reflect core principles of mutual governance. These include privacy, representation, voice, and procedural justice. Somehow, we have to figure out how to accrue benefits from digitization without putting ourselves under digital microscopes and computer-driven algorithmic governance.

Sixth, we also need governance innovation for another reason, which is that more and more of the solutions to the world's most pressing problems require rapid coordination and careful management of shared resources. In short, the simple math of sustainable consumption will require that humanity does more with less. I am encouraged by our students on this front, as it seems to me abundantly clear that the generations of young leaders who will come of age in our century are not interested in consuming so much stuff, or eating unhealthy food, or inflicting suffering on others. Governance innovation over common resources is front and center in their interests.

Seventh, the failure of Globalization 1.0 in the second decade of the twenty-first century has led to basic questions about the macroeconomic framework of international business. Nationalism, job loss, and illegal treatment of immigrants and refugees are all failing as well. New approaches for understanding, organizing, managing, and governing relationships across international boundaries between productive organizations is the central agenda of government policy in our era. Management and organizations scholarship is essential to progress on this front.

Finally, a reconceptualization of what constitutes prosperity is under way in our communities, corporations, governmental agencies, educational institutions, and other places of association. Management and organization scholarship has not caught up. The shareholder supremacy argumentation of the twentieth century continues to dominate much of our curriculum despite the fact that most of humanity is not interested in the enrichment of corporate shareholders, and that the shareholder supremacy argument itself is theoretically flawed in the first place. The very purpose of management and organization is not effectively understood in our field.

The implications of these eight observations about the relationships between grand challenges and our field are compelling and profound, particularly because our scholarship and educational activities have been part of the systems that have given rise to the grand challenges of this century. We are not just studying the problems around us, we have been one of the reasons that these problems exist.

These days, I consider the essence of responsible research to be taking account of the ways that I am—however unintentionally—part of the problem. Advocacy and analysis are each thin for me these days if they are only about how other people should change. Structural problems require structural solutions. For me, responsible research must be designed to reflect my best ideas and my hardest-won understanding of what may be true about these systems, informed by practitioner interviews and thoughtful interrogation of the foundational principles of theory. The methods are tools. The organizations themselves are transient. The system in which organizations are embedded is the focus. Because the grand challenges of our time are so extraordinary in scale, I am interested in leadership and governance of these systems. I seek inspiration from people who are making a difference in changing them. I try to read more of what others are writing on these topics. My goal and hope is to conduct research with compassion, integrity, and attentiveness toward my collaborators. Students give me hope for the future, and so I try to spend as much time with them as I can. I try never to "mail it in" to a classroom. My university invites improvement, which creates an avenue through which I can test ideas about educational change, and through which I am trying to do more. I'm sure that I am failing on many of these fronts, but these are my aspirations. As I step toward the end of my career, what I am finding is that I am seeking to be more like the undergraduate I was decades ago: inspired, driven, and striving to learn. In the end, for me, the heart of responsible research is in conveying my best stuff—as imperfect an offering as it is—to the next generation.

References

Amis, J. M., K. A. Munir, T. B. Lawrence, P. Hirsch, & A. M. McGahan. (2018). Inequality, institutions, and organizations. *Organization Studies, 39*(9), 1131–1152.

Cabral, S., J. T. Mahoney, A. M. McGahan, & M. Potoski. (2019). Value creation and value appropriation in public and non-profit organizations. *Strategic Management Journal, 40*(4) (April), 465–475.

Devinney, T., A. M. McGahan, & M. Zollo. (2013). A research agenda for global stakeholder strategy. *Global Strategy Journal, 3*(4) (November), 325–337.

Dutt, N., O. V. Hawn, E. Vidal, A. Chatterji, A. M. McGahan, & W. Mitchell. (2016). How do firms and markets co-develop? Exploring the role of incubators in emerging market economics. *Academy of Management Journal, 59*, 766–790.

George, G., A. M. McGahan, & J. Prabhu. (2012). Innovation for inclusive growth: Towards a theoretical framework and a research agenda. *Journal of Management Studies, 49*(4) (June), 661–683.

Klein, P., J. T. Mahoney, A. M. McGahan, & C. Pitelis. (2010). Toward a theory of public entrepreneurship. *European Management Review, 7*(1) (Spring), 1–15.

Klein, P., J. T. Mahoney, A. M. McGahan, & C. Pitelis. (2012). A property rights approach for a stakeholder theory of the firm. *Strategic Organization, 10*(3), 304–315.

Klein, P., J. T. Mahoney, A. M. McGahan, & C. Pitelis. (2013). Capabilities and strategic entrepreneurship in public organizations. *Strategic Entrepreneurship Journal, 7* (March), 70–91.

Klein, P., J. T. Mahoney, A. M. McGahan, & C. Pitelis. (2019). Organizational governance adaptation: Who is in, who is out, and who gets what. *Academy of Management Review, 44*(1). (January), 6–27.

Mahoney, J. T., & A. M. McGahan. (2007). The field of strategic management within the evolving science of strategic organization. *Strategic Organization, 5*(1), 79–99.

Mahoney, J. T., A. M. McGahan, & C. Pitelis. (2009). The interdependence of private and public interests. *Organization Science, 20*(6) (November-December), 1034–1052.

McGahan, A. M. (1992). Philips' compact disc introduction (A). *Harvard Business School Publishing* 9-792-035.

McGahan, A. M. (1994a). Lotus Development Corporation in 1994. *Harvard Business School Publishing* 9-794-114.

McGahan, A. M. (1994b). Sunrise Medical, Inc.'s wheelchair products. *Harvard Business School Publishing* 9-794-069.

McGahan, A. M. (2000). How industries evolve. *Business Strategy Review, 3* (Autumn), 1–16.

McGahan, A. M. (2004a). How industries change. *Harvard Business Review* (October), 98–106.

McGahan, A. M. (2004b). *How industries evolve: Principles for achieving and sustaining superior performance*. Boston, MA: Harvard Business School Press.

McGahan, A. M. (2007). Academic research that matters to managers: On zebras, dogs, lemmings, hammers & turnips. *Academy of Management Journal, 50* (August), 754–761.

McGahan, A. M. (2018). Freedom in scholarship: Lessons from Atlanta. *Academy of Management Review, 43*(2), 173–178.

McGahan, A. M. (2019a). My presidency of the Academy of Management: Moral responsibility, leadership, governance, organizational change, and strategy. *Journal of Management Inquiry, 28*(3) (July), 251–267.

McGahan, A. M. (2019b). Where does an organization's responsibility end? Identifying the boundaries on stakeholder claims. *Academy of Management Discoveries* (December). https://journals.aom.org/doi/10.5465/amd.2018.0218.

McGahan, A. M. (2020). Immigration and impassioned management scholarship. *Journal of Management Inquiry, 29*(1), 111–114.

McGahan, A. M., D. O. Coxe. (1996). African Communications Group. *Harvard Business School Publishing* 9-796-128.

McGahan, A. M., D. O. Coxe, I. M. Ganot, & G. Keller. (1996). Passion for learning. *Harvard Business School Publishing* 9-796-057.

McGahan, A. M., D. O. Coxe, G. Keller, & J. F. McGuire. (1996). The pharmaceutical industry in the 1990s. *Harvard Business School Publishing* 9-796-058.

McGahan, A. M., & G. Keller. (1995). Saturn: A different kind of car company. *Harvard Business School Publishing* 9-795-010.

McGahan, A. M., & G. Keusch. (2010). Economic valuations in global health. *Global Public Health, 5*(2) (March), 136–142.

McGahan, A. M., J. F. McGuire, & J. Kou. (1996). The baseball strike. *Harvard Business School Publishing* 9-796-059.

McGahan, A. M., & M. E. Porter. (1997). How much does industry matter, really? *.Strategic Management Journal, 18*(S1), 15–30.

McGahan, A. M., & M. E. Porter. (2003). The emergence and sustainability of abnormal profits. *Strategic Organization, 1*(1) (February), 79–108.

McGahan, A. M., & B. S. Silverman. (2001). How does innovative activity change as industries mature? *International Journal of Industrial Organization, 19*(7) (July), 1141–1160.

McGahan, A. M., & G. Verter. (1997). Coming soon: A theater near you. *Harvard Business School Publishing* 9-797-011.

McGahan, A. M., B. A. Zelner, & J. B. Barney. (2013). Entrepreneurship in the public interest: Introduction to the special issue. *Strategic Entrepreneurship Journal, 7* (March), 1–5.

Rezaie, R., A. M. McGahan, A. Daar, & P. Singer. (2012). Globalization of health innovation. *Nature Biotechnology, 30*(10) (October), 923–925.

Vakili, K., & A. M. McGahan. (2016). Healthcare's grand challenge: Basic science on diseases that primarily afflict the poor. *Academy of Management Journal, 59*(6), 1917–1939.

Yang, A., A. M. McGahan, & P. E. Farmer. (2010). Sustainability in global health. *Global Public Health, 5*(2) (March), 129–135.

Concluding Remarks

Toward a Process Model for Influential Scholarship: A Synopsis and Integration of Our Contributors' Stories

H. Kevin Steensma and Xiao-Ping Chen

We set out to uncover common themes and, perhaps, some disparities in the career stories from exemplar scholars in the field of organizational studies. Along with Robinson and Sorenson, we caution readers to be mindful of the inherent limitations of post hoc sense making. All of our contributors have reflected on their own paths toward success through their own biased lenses. Moreover, we have sampled on the dependent variable and have not considered the paths of those whose efforts have led to more modest success. Nonetheless, for rising scholars and those considering academic careers in organizational studies, consistencies across these individuals may provide some points to ponder. While none of the factors described by the exemplars profiled in this book is likely sufficient to achieve their level of success, one can speculate on the necessity of these factors.

Although it would be convenient to present our analysis in a deterministic fashion, a theme that is consistent across many of our contributors is the role that *random events* played in their career paths. Ashforth's chance reading of Zimbardo's prison study in high school sparked a curiosity that guided his academic pursuits and career choice. Robinson points to a fortuitous meeting with the father of a coworker who happened to be a scholar of organizational behavior. A fateful interaction with an undergraduate professor spurred Colquitt's career. Unplanned events not only steered our contributors to enter the field but also opened doors once their careers had launched. Several reflect on how their careers benefited from seemingly random encounters at professional meetings that led to impromptu discussions and collaborative opportunities that changed the direction of their scholarly inquiries. Both Rao and Westphal describe multiple chance encounters and suggest that their successes have been a function of a series of random events. We do not believe that our contributors are simply the recipients of good fortune. Rather, we

H. Kevin Steensma and Xiao-Ping Chen, *Concluding Remarks* In: *A Journey toward Influential Scholarship*.
Edited by: Xiao-Ping Chen and H. Kevin Steensma, Oxford University Press. © Oxford University Press 2021.
DOI: 10.1093/oso/9780190070717.003.0013

suspect that they are particularly receptive to chance events and have an innate ability to avail themselves of opportunities.

Upon reflection, Barsade emphasizes the need to put oneself out there, saying yes to professional engagements that, on the surface, may not appear to be directly beneficial to one's career. Being overly strategic and calculative in one's career can possibly lead to lost opportunities. For sure, attending conferences, performing academic service, or investing in junior talent development entail substantial opportunity costs in terms of time away from the office and writing papers. However, Agarwal notes many instances of conversations that started in conference encounters, rookie recruiting, or PhD advising and subsequently shaped her research trajectory. Perhaps such engagements can be viewed similarly to investments in early-stage ventures. Although the majority are unlikely to be net positive, it takes only a couple of fortuitous encounters to alter the course of one's career.

To further assess common themes across our contributors in this book, we took our cue from Colquitt and relied on Spreitzer's (1995) theory of psychological empowerment. According to her model, psychological empowerment is a function of self-determination, competence, meaning, and impact. We apply this theory in the analyses of our contributors' success stories.

Self-Determination in the Face of Adversity

All exemplar scholars in this book conveyed a strong sense of *autonomy* and *independence* in their career paths. As opposed to building on the work of mentors or advisors, they struck out on their own to develop their unique research identities. Robinson relied on her gut feelings and allowed herself to be guided first and foremost by her interest in the dark side of human behavior in organizations. In doing so, she had to let go of a completed dissertation that she was not passionate about and, as a result, was never published. For some, self-determination and intrinsic motivation may emerge later in their careers. On reflection, McGahan found her true passions to ultimately align with her undergraduate studies. These interests, however, were overshadowed early in her career by the pursuit of research questions that she had been convinced were critical to her career success. She suggests that there is a fine line between being coachable by mentors and maintaining one's own identity and cautions against conducting research for purely instrumental reasons, devoid of passion. Ashforth points to the need to ask questions that matter and are worthwhile. The worthiness of such questions, however, is likely endogenous and depends on scholars believing the questions they ask to be truly worthy.

In recounting her own initial struggles with finding a worthwhile question, Agarwal now counsels students to identify what they are passionate about among the topics they read to determine which one is right for them, rather than relying on their advisor to identify it for them. Without scholar *passion*, research questions are unlikely to receive the careful attention and tireless effort they deserve in the face of negative feedback and setbacks and will not likely be viewed as credible by their targeted audiences. Indeed, following one's passion may ultimately be strategic, as it will more likely lead to successful outcomes. These exemplar scholars now preach what they practiced and encourage their own doctoral students to follow their interests and not merely become replicas of their mentors.

Being independent and following one's passion is not without hazard, however. Many of these exemplar scholars embraced considerable risk by studying new phenomena for which extensive theoretical grounding was lacking. Yet it is easy to look at the success of our contributors and to surmise that their paths to distinction were without setbacks. This is clearly not the case. Sorenson's first attempt at research resulted in a dependent variable devoid of variance! Many of them struggled with self-doubt early on due to job market challenges (e.g., Robinson) or failure to get positive feedback on their work (e.g., Westphal). As described by McGahan, it is the passion for one's scholarly pursuits that gives one the fortitude to endure the inevitable "hazing" by reviewers and senior scholars whose work one may be questioning.

Indeed, persistence and patience are evident in all of these stories. These qualities allowed Agarwal to painstakingly collect dissertation data that delayed her graduation and quick gratification but ultimately set the stage for longer-term success. Barsade credits her persistence in maintaining work-life balance with giving her the necessary perspective to carry on in the face of adversity. In sum, these exemplar scholars had the self-determination early on to pursue research questions they were passionate about. Such passion provided the fortitude to withstand the challenges and setbacks that are typical in our field.

Individual and Collaborative Competence

Self-determination and passion bear fruit only when matched with competency. To say that each of the exemplars who contributed to this book is a highly skilled and competent individual would be an understatement. Their competencies span both individual and collaborative skills. Of their own accord, all undoubtedly would be able to establish themselves as reputable *independent* scholars, albeit not of the stature they have ultimately achieved. The notion of academic life as being one of solitude, however, has not been adhered to by these exemplar scholars. In the words of one, "It takes a village." Such attitudes may be ubiquitous among scholars who study managerial issues based on human interactions. It stands to reason that those who gravitate to the study of these questions will likely recognize the value of collaboration. Nonetheless, some are better at collaboration than others, and, based on the number and variety of their coauthors, the contributors to this book stand out in this regard.

One distinctive feature of these individuals is that they are aware of their relative strengths and weaknesses. The notion of comparative advantage seems applicable here. For example, Ashforth readily acknowledges that statistical analyses are not what he is best at. One could surmise that, if he were to put his mind to it, he could likely excel at statistics, possibly surpassing the expertise of his collaborators. Yet taking time away from what he does best (theory development) is neither efficient nor in the collective best interests of his collaborators or audience. "Do what you do best and collaborate for the rest" may be an applicable catchphrase.

Although all of our contributors are highly successful collaborators, their success in this regard is rooted in their individual competence and the result of a virtuous cycle: by exhibiting individual competence early on in their careers, our exemplars became attractive collaborative targets of others who wanted to tap into their competence. By having the luxury to choose among high-potential collaborative opportunities and converting them into successful outcomes, the collaborative stock of these exemplars was boosted further, generating additional collaborative opportunities. In essence, the individual competence of these individuals initiates a Matthew effect, whereby high-potential collaborative opportunities spawn additional high-potential collaborative opportunities. Strong collaborators also can expose one to new perspectives from different disciplines or subdisciplines.

Many of the contributors to this book followed a natural progression by initially building their collaborator portfolios with senior mentors, followed by peers, and finally supplementing them with doctoral students. Few are better at systematizing a collaboration ecosystem than Agarwal. She has developed a cadre of collaborators that spans multiple generations, including mentors, peers, graduate students, and even the graduate students of her graduate students. Such an ecosystem allows productive data collection efforts and complements Agarwal's distinctive competence in asking interesting questions that only rigorous data analyses can answer.

All the emphasis the contributors place on collaboration does not suggest that it comes easy. Indeed, their competencies in navigating collaborative pitfalls are what set them apart. Several offer sage advice on managing coauthors and expectations. As noted by one, effective collaboration should not be viewed as merely additive but as multiplicative; an effective and attractive collaborator makes the contributions of others better than they would have been otherwise. We encourage our readers to tap into the savvy our contributors have attained over their years of collaboration.

Despite the benefits of collaboration, our contributors provide some caution. Both Barsade and Greve highlight the value of working independently for both scholarly credit and control, particularly early in one's career or at the start of a new research stream. When there are multiple authors on a scholarly article, one needs to be concerned about who receives attribution for the article's ideas. Relying extensively on the collaboration of senior scholars and mentors, particularly early in one's career, can water down one's contribution as perceived by the marketplace. Similarly, Greve emphasizes the benefits of control that only solo authorship provides, particularly when beginning a new research stream. Having absolute autonomy over data collection, analysis, and crafting provides the scholar with the discretion to craft the sentences he or she feels best convey the key arguments. Once the work has been shown to have an impact on the field, potential collaborators will enthusiastically emerge.

Meaning and Impact

It goes without saying that all of the exemplar scholars represented in this book believe that the work that they do has meaning and is impactful. Impact entails at least two aspects: scholarship and practice. Impactful research contributes to new theoretical perspectives that not only demonstrate and explain important organizational phenomena but also influence managers' thinking and organizational practices.

How do these scholars achieve impact? Although recipes for impact may vary, a consistent theme that emerges from many of these contributors is the value of simple stories that are easily understood and broadly applicable. Even those who focus on intricate theory building (e.g., Ashforth) have an eye toward how their theories can improve organizations. There are abundant examples of published work in which theory and empirics have been tortured to the point of their yielding a withering narrative. In contrast, our contributors are highly effective in getting their ideas across in ways that do not tax their audiences. As they describe it, simple stories resonate with nonacademics and can be shared at cocktail parties without invoking eye-rolls. Westphal typically formulates one-minute elevator pitches to communicate the essence of his work. Doing so refines his message.

Paradoxically, crafting simple stories that make the forest distinct from the trees is often more difficult than laying out those that are more complex, and writing and attention to detail is critical in this process. Ashforth exemplifies attention to detail when he suggests that he notices a mere change in the placement of a comma by a coauthor or editor. Although our contributors are undoubtedly always open to improvements in their work, such attentiveness suggests that every sentence, phrase, and word is deliberate and used only after considering how each will be interpreted by the intended audience. Sorenson points out that writing is often an afterthought in graduate training. Indeed, we suspect that many contributions are not published because editors and reviewers are reluctant to struggle through poorly written studies. Sorenson, for one, proactively improved his craft by mimicking studies he found to be well written and abundantly clear.

There is, however, a fine line between a simple story and one that is obvious and mundane. Our contributors emphasize the need to find that sweet spot, to pursue questions that are neither incremental nor so novel as to be unfathomable. Ideas that are too contrary to dominant beliefs may face an uphill battle toward publication. How did these exemplars make judgment and frame their research questions in that sweet spot? Where did they derive the inspiration for their research questions? Were they driven by theory or phenomenon? What is notable is where many of them did *not* derive inspiration. Unsurprisingly, few gave any consideration to future research questions highlighted in the discussion sections of recently published top-tier articles. Neither did they find inspiration sitting in a library!

Often, these scholars have derived research questions by simply being active participants in the world and observing real-world phenomena. For example, Barsade's curiosity regarding emotional contagion in the workplace was piqued at a job prior to graduate school. A short but influential consulting career prior to academia provided the inspiration and insights needed to propel Westphal's career. Such examples point to the value of having a professional life prior to one's academic pursuits. Perhaps aspiring scholars can compensate for a lack of such experience by engaging indirectly with the workplace. For example, Ang and McGahan, throughout their careers, have relied on ongoing interaction with practitioners not only to refine and simplify their message but also to identify potentially impactful research that might call into question existing theory built on fragile assumptions. Alternatively, Agarwal dived deep into archival data to understand phenomena by triangulating across multiple qualitative and quantitative sources in painstaking efforts to create a complete understanding of the "lay of the land."

Our exemplars have combined their curiosities regarding real-world phenomena with their immersion in the academic literature so as to understand the limitations of existing theory in describing the real-world phenomena of interest. In essence, there is a feedback relationship between immersing oneself in existing literature and one's curiosity about the world. Each provides perspective on the other. As Ang notes, old ideas can constrain new ideas. Although all of these preeminent scholars are experts in their respective literatures, they have not allowed the existing literature to inhibit their creativity. As highlighted by Greve, the emergence of new perspectives and questions also can revive previously used data that can be repurposed to gain insight on these questions.

Sorenson cautions against a practice that is becoming increasingly common, particularly among macro scholars, that is, choosing questions primarily because the context and data provide a strong internally valid design. Although concerns regarding endogeneity and identification are well founded, overemphasizing these threats to validity can lead to the pursuit of rather mundane questions. Both Sorenson and Agarwal have used creative means and processes of abduction to address issues of endogeneity and to support the inferences they make from their data regarding the relevant and thought-provoking questions they are addressing. In a similar vein, micro scholars caution against incremental research such as studying another moderator or mediator of an established phenomenon. Barsade has studied the role of emotions in the workplace, but every study has explored a new phenomenon rather than added a new moderating variable. Robinson's research focuses on the dark side of organizational behavior, but she has kept uncovering different kinds of dark behaviors (e.g., counterproductive behavior, workplace deviance, ostracism) rather than devoting her attention to only one.

Many of our exemplars have pursued influential scholarship by drawing on and integrating *multiple disciplines*. As Agarwal suggests, disciplines do not own ideas. Although appreciating economic theory and methodologies, several of our contributors have recognized their limitations and supplemented them with perspectives from other disciplines. Westphal is particularly notable for his ability to weave together multilevel theoretical stories rooted in psychology, sociology, and economics. As he describes it, doing so creates challenges in terms of finding the right voice and framing for a potentially broad audience. Nonetheless, integrating multiple disciplines has the potential to have more impact than staying in a narrower lane.

Toward a Process Model of Influential Scholarship

While the constructs *self-determination, competence, meaning,* and *impact* capture the cross-sectional characteristics of our exemplar scholars, a longitudinal process model can also be derived from their success stories. The model involves five stages for a new research stream to take shape, to be recognized in the field, and to become mainstream.

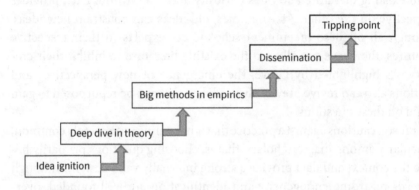

Idea ignition. Research ideas come from many sources that take different shapes and forms. For Rao, historical events inspired him to discover patterns and look for explanations. For Robinson, current events reported in the news triggered her interest to investigate why disastrously negative responses occur in the workplace. For Westphal, the extra information he gleaned from tedious financial analyses enlightened his perspective on corporate governance. For Barsade, the absence of a bad-tempered coworker, which relieved her colleagues' tension, induced her interest in studying emotions in the workplace. For Ashforth, reading Zimbardo's prison experiment inspired him to pursue an academic career and to later become a keen observer and deep thinker in regard to many prominent organizational phenomena. For Zhou, negative feedback on a term paper from her professor motivated her to look for creative ideas for conducting research and to eventually pick creativity as her lifetime research interest. For Agarwal, the more she knew about a phenomenon from a particular theoretical lens or level of analysis, the more she realized what she did not know from a different lens or level of analysis. For Greve, a theory on firm performance feedback resonated with him so strongly that it pushed him to look for perfect data to demonstrate its predictive validity. For Sorenson, the entrepreneur embeddedness phenomenon that he observed over and over intrigued him to find explanations beyond efficiency. For Colquitt, the immediate attraction to the social justice construct sustained his interest in expanding and advancing this literature. For Ang, her international experience and constant interactions with expatriate managers provided her with unique insights into cultural intelligence research. For McGahan, her calling to address the grand challenges, such as global warming, poverty, and inequality, that humans face today keeps her passionate about studying private entrepreneurship in the public interest. It is clear that inspiration can come from different sources and directions, but what is important is that only when the idea strikes a chord or when you feel a special connection with the idea will you be able to develop unique insights to enrich the idea and to sustain interest in developing a research program to study the topic.

Deep dive into theory.   Once the research idea or theme is identified, our exemplar scholars all took a deep dive into the related literature to inform their theoretical perspectives, which were distinct yet connected to existing theories. In general, micro scholars tend to delve into theories in social psychology, whereas macro scholars are most likely to apply theories in sociology or economics to establish their theoretical bases. For example, Barsade immersed herself in the theories on affect, mood, and emotion in social psychology (Hatfield, Cacioppo, & Rapson, 1992, 1994; Lazarus, 1991) and articulated how emotion would influence interpersonal interactions in the workplace at the individual, team, and firm levels. Ang took a deep dive into the multifoci intelligence literature (e.g., Sternberg, 1986) to conceptualize the cultural intelligence construct and then develop a valid measurement for it. Greve had a deep understanding and appreciation of theory on how low performance leads to organizational change and identified a data set in the radio broadcasting industry that could best show its validity. Sorenson immersed himself in the literatures on social embeddedness and entrepreneurship. As mentioned earlier, a few have also adopted a multidisciplinary approach and integrated theories in psychology, sociology, and economics to inform their theory development (e.g., Agarwal, Westphal, McGahan). This entails particularly extensive effort to find coherence at the intersection of multiple disciplines in relation to the phenomenon being explored.

In addition to a deep dive into the literature, our scholars also conducted interviews with relevant parties, including workers, managers, top management teams, CEOs, and venture founders, to verify their ideas' relevance in real organizations. They also sought their colleagues' feedback via corridor conversations, informal seminars, or structured meetings. This step of checking with practitioners as well as fellow scholars provides additional information regarding the meaningfulness and potential impact of the research idea/question.

Big methods in empirics.   Although theoretical studies can exert great influence and inspire empirical inquiry by other scholars, as Ashforth did with his influential studies on organizational identification, dirty work, emotional labor, and organizational anthropomorphism, the majority of influential management scholars are empiricists. Empirical demonstration of a newly discovered phenomenon or newly construed theory often plays a very important role in establishing a new research stream. On this front, rigor is the key means to demonstrate competence in conducting scientific research; in Barsade's words, "big method" is what her research is aiming for.

Big method refers to the use of multiple methods to test theoretical underpinnings and to ensure the stability, replicability, and generalizability of the findings reported in a study. Methods in management research include two overarching categories: qualitative and quantitative. Qualitative methods, such as interview, observation, case study, and archival search, are often used in research that is exploratory in nature or for the purpose of theory building. Quantitative methods, such as survey, secondary data, and experiment, are used mainly for theory testing purposes. To start groundbreaking research often requires both qualitative and quantitative methods. For example, to develop the workplace deviance behavior construct and measurement, Bennet and Robinson (2000) conducted two studies, each of which involved multiple samples and methods (qualitative and quantitative). To examine the influence of positive affect on creativity in innovation teams over time, Barsade and colleagues (Amabile, Barsade, Mueller, & Staw, 2005) engaged questionnaire surveys, and then the coding of 11,471 open-ended diaries, using both quantitative and qualitative analyses. As every method has its own strengths and weaknesses, using multiple methods to study the focal phenomenon can help to triangulate the findings. What is remarkable about our scholars is that many started with one methodology but over time incorporated more and more methods in their toolkits, with a focus on matching methods to questions. Agarwal, Rao, and Greve are exemplars in terms of combining rich qualitative analyses with rigorous empirical analyses, both within and across individual studies.

In addition to methods in research design, big method also implies adopting the most appropriate analytical tools for data analyses, that is, knowing when to use ANOVA, ANCOVA, regression, logistic regression, HLM, SEM, path analyses, or time-series analyses; how to ensure internal validity; how to address endogeneity problems; and so forth. Big method also involves knowing which tools to use to conduct content analysis, social network analyses, panel data analyses, and so forth. The contributors to this book were not bound to a narrow set of analytical tools; rather, they have either trained themselves to use tools appropriate for the data or found collaborators with such skills.

Having a rigorous methodology is essential to establishing the credibility of research findings, especially when exploring a new phenomenon, providing a novel perspective, or starting a new research paradigm. This is what the majority of our exemplary scholars have done in their academic careers and is one of the main reasons that their research has become influential.

Disseminating and sustaining a research stream. Publishing your paper in peer-reviewed top-tier journals is by far the most important means to disseminate research discoveries. As such, the question is "Where to publish?" Although we all would like to publish in *Administrative Science Quarterly* and the Academy journals (e.g., *AMJ, AMR, AMD, Annals*), not every study fits their mission. As many micro scholars have doctoral training in psychology, and many macro scholars have doctoral training in sociology or economics, some studies may fit the disciplinary journals and will be better received by scholars in these fields. It is the scholar's responsibility to judge where he or she would like his or her research to have the most influence before writing a paper to fit a certain journal and the target audience. For example, Colquitt, Robinson, and Zhou published studies in the *Journal of Applied Psychology* or *OBHDP*, and Rao, Greve, and Agarwal published papers in *American Sociological Review, American Journal of Sociology, American Economic Review,* and *Economic Letters.* Which audience is most receptive to the topic and method of your study, and with whom you want to engage in dialogue, enables the identification of the most appropriate journal in which to publish your work.

To start a new research stream, one study is often not enough. A series of studies on the same topic with broader exploration or deeper theoretical insight will facilitate its process. Every scholar included in this book has done this. (They would not be here if they had not.) Some, like Agarwal, have even challenged inferences they made in an earlier study in follow-on work. Such revisiting of insights enables a richer understanding of nuances and stronger theory building. We encourage you to study their CVs for more detailed information.

Taking a long-term view of the research stream and putting down your thoughts, concerns, and future predictions in a book is another way of informing the research community about the current status of the research stream, but a more important consideration is what questions to ask to advance the research that can inspire more scholars to become interested. Greve did this to promote his research on firm performance feedback (Greve, 2003); Ang wrote three books to promote cultural intelligence research and development (Ang & Van Dyne, 2008; Earley & Ang, 2003; Earley, Ang, & Tan, 2006); Zhou has edited several books to encourage more studies on creativity and innovation (e.g., Shalley, Hitt, & Zhou, 2015; Zhou & Shalley, 2008); and McGahan has written books for both managers and practitioners on sustainability—including books on how firms can fight against human trafficking and for global health (Ahn, Burke, & McGahan, 2015; Bhattacharyya, McGahan, Mitchell, & Mossman, 2019; McGahan, 2004).

Working with doctoral students is another effective way to sustain a research stream and make it influential. In psychological and engineering research, it is often the norm that a professor starts a research stream and works with several generations of doctoral students on it (e.g., group decision making), and the students become professors and establish their own labs and work with their doctoral students to continue that stream of research. In management, it is not as common for scholars to continue with one research topic for their entire careers, but we have seen scholars who have adopted this model become very influential. Kathy Eisenhardt, a professor at Stanford Engineering School who has been studying entrepreneurship for decades, is such an exemplar scholar. As we have noted here, Agarwal has developed an elaborate network of doctoral student collaborators.

Of course, there are many more conventional approaches to expand the influence of your research. For example, presenting your findings at academic conferences or department research seminars or posting your study on social media platforms can increase awareness and visibility of your research. Organizing Academy of Management symposia or workshops can also be effective in gauging other scholars' interest in participating in your stream of research, and doing it over a number of years will keep the interest energized and fresh. Presenting a study at other universities or over the Zoom platform that provides free access for all scholars in the field is also a good means of exerting influence.

In addition to academic influence, practical influence is an important dimension for our work to have real impact. On this front, writing articles that use nonacademic language for managers is probably the most viable way to exert influence. Outlets such as *Harvard Business Review*, *Sloan Management Review*, and *Management Insights* are good choices. Blog posts on popular websites such as the *Huffington Post* are also helpful.

Reaching a tipping point. After you have gone through the four stages we've described, it is likely that your research stream will gain momentum and inspire scholars outside your immediate circle to join forces. When more studies are conducted, more new findings emerge, and a tipping point is reached in which the previously "small" research stream becomes mainstream and gains a life of its own.

This process model appears to capture the journey that all of the scholars in this book have gone through. It is evident that this process often takes 20 or more years to complete. We hope that our contributors' stories shed light on this long, sometimes dark and lonely, and ultimately highly rewarding journey to influential scholarship. We are confident that, with self-empowerment characterized by passion, patience, and persistence, you will get there!

References

Ahn, R., Burke, T. F., & McGahan, A. M. (Eds.). (2015). *Innovations, urbanization and global health.* New York: Springer.

Amabile, T. M., Barsade, S. G., Mueller, J. S., & Staw, B. M. (2005). Affect and creativity at work. *Administrative Science Quarterly, 50,* 367403.

Ang, S., & Van Dyne, L. (2008). *Handbook on cultural intelligence.* New York: M. E. Sharpe.

Bennett, R., &Robinson, S. L. (2000). The development of a measure of workplace deviance. *Journal of Applied Psychology, 85*(3), 349–360.

Bhattacharyya, O., McGahan, A. M., Mitchell, W., & Mossman, K. (Eds.). (2019). *Private sector entrepreneurship in global health innovation, scale and sustainability.* Toronto: University of Toronto Press.

Cyert, R. M., & March, J. G. (1963). *A behavioral theory of the firm.* Englewood Cliffs, NJ: Prentice-Hall.

Earley, P. C., & Ang, S. (2003). *Cultural intelligence.* Stanford, CA: Stanford University Press.

Earley, P. C., Ang, S., & Tan, J. S. (2006). CQ: *Developing cultural intelligence at work.* CA: Stanford University Press.

Greve, H. R. (2003). *Organizational learning from performance feedback: A behavioral perspective on innovation and change.* Cambridge, UK: Cambridge University Press.

Hatfield, E., Cacioppo, J., & Rapson, R. L. (1992). Primitive Emotional Contagion. In M. S. Clark (ed.), *Review of personality and social psychology: Emotion and social behavior* (Vol. 14, pp. 151–177). Newbury Park, CA: Sage.

Hatfield, E., Caciopoo, J., & Rapson, R. L. (1994). *Emotional contagion.* New York: Cambridge University Press.

Lazarus, R. S. (1991). *Emotion and adaptation.* New York: Oxford University Press.

McGahan, A. M. (2004). *How industries evolve: Principles for achieving and sustaining superior performance.* Cambridge, MA: Harvard Business School Press.

Shalley, C. E., Hitt, M. A., & Zhou, J. (Eds.). (2015). *The Oxford handbook of creativity, innovation, and entrepreneurship.* New York: Oxford University Press.

Spreitzer, G. M. (1995). Psychological empowerment in the workplace: Dimensions, measurement, and validation. *Academy of Management Journal, 38,* 1442–1465.

Sternberg, R. J. (1986). A framework for understanding conceptions of intelligence. In R. J. Sternberg, & D. K. Detterman (Eds.), *What is intelligence? Contemporary viewpoints on its nature and definition* (pp. 3–15). Norwood, NJ: Ablex.

Zhou, J., & Shalley, C. E. (Eds.). (2008). *Handbook of organizational creativity.* Hillsdale, NJ: Erlbaum.

Index